Law for the Elephant, Law for the Beaver

Essays in the Legal History of the North American West

ENLARGING EXPEDITION ALONG THE COASTS OF VANCOUVER'S ISLAND AND BRITISH COLUMBIA.—H.M.S. PLUMPER IN PORT HARVEY, JOHNSTON'S STRAIT.   START OF THE SURVEYING-BOATS.   AT STEVEN-POINT.

Frontispiece: "Exploring expedition along the coasts of Vancouver's Island and British Columbia — H.M.S. Plumper in Port Harvey, Johnston's Strait: Start of the Surveying-Boats." Reproduced courtesy of the Province of British Columbia, Ministry of Provincial Secretary, British Columbia Archives and Records Service, Visual Records Unit, Catalogue No. PDP257.

Law for the Elephant, Law for the Beaver

Essays in the Legal History of the North American West

Edited by John McLaren, Hamar Foster
and Chet Orloff

Canadian Plains Research Center
University of Regina
Regina, Saskatchewan

Ninth Judicial Circuit Historical Society
Pasadena, California
1992

Canadian Cataloguing in Publication Data

Main entry under title:

Law for the elephant, law for the beaver: essays in the legal history of the North American West

(Canadian plains proceedings, ISSN 0317-6401 ; 23)
Proceedings of a conference held at the University of Victoria, Feb. 22-24, 1991.

ISBN 0-88977-072-7

1. Law - West (U.S.) - History and criticism - Congresses. 2. Law - Northwest, Canadian - History and criticism - Congresses. I. McLaren, John, 1940- II. University of Regina. Canadian Plains Research Center. III. Ninth Judicial Circuit Historical Society. IV. Series.

KE394.A66 1991   349.712   C92-098124-0

Cover design by Mark Brusman, Portland, Oregon.

Cover illustration reproduced courtesy of the Province of British Columbia, Ministry of Provincial Secretary, British Columbia Archives and Records Service, Visual Records Unit.

Printed and bound in the United States of America by: McNaughton & Gunn, Inc., Saline, Michigan.

Contents

Preface

John McLaren

This book of essays draws upon eleven of the papers presented at "Law for the Elephant, Law for the Beaver: A Transboundary Conference on the Legal History of the West and Northwest of North America," held at the Faculty of Law, University of Victoria, 22-24 February 1991. The conference was, it is believed, the first Canada-United States initiative on the comparative legal history of territory shared by both countries. Some 130 researchers, judges, practitioners and students from both sides of the border were in attendance. A variety of disciplines were represented, including not only law and history, but also political science, sociology, women's studies, aboriginal studies, criminology, geography, economics and public administration. Among the topics explored were frontier justice, aboriginal rights, police and policing, women and the law, the legal profession, racism and the law, child and family law, the law and economic development, and researching western legal history.

Events of this nature do not spring out of thin air. The germ of the idea for the conference emerged from the meeting of the Western Chapter of the American Association of Law Libraries held in Coeur d'Alene, Idaho in November 1989. An invitation to present a paper on the "Legal History of Western Canada" brought me into contact with a small but able and enthusiastic group of American western legal history scholars who were also sharing their research. Both the themes and substance of their papers set me to thinking about similarities and differences in the legal experience of the United States and Canada as European settlement spread inexorably to the West and Northwest and the new population began filling up the open spaces and disrupting or dislodging the indigenous inhabitants. The socioeconomic impulses behind European migration to the plains, western mountain ranges and the tundra were similar, it seemed to me, wherever it took place. The question which needed to be explored was the extent to which ideas about law and legal institutions in two separate and competing geopolitical units may have produced commonalities and divergences in legal responses to the challenges and tensions of life in the West and Northwest.

Happily, my enthusiasm for exploring in an international conference the relationship between legal culture and the history of law in a broader

North American context was shared by others. A group of American legal historians — Chet Orloff, then executive director of the Ninth Judicial Circuit Historical Society; Gordon Bakken of the Department of History, California State University at Fullerton; Christian Fritz of the School of Law, University of New Mexico; and Dale Goble of the School of Law, University of Idaho — agreed to act in an advisory capacity in the planning of a conference. Their help, especially that of Chet Orloff, was invaluable in identifying topics, scholarly contacts and potential funding sources.

On the Canadian side of the border there was also warmth to the idea of such a conference. As a consequence I was able to draw upon the talents and energy of a number of colleagues in British Columbia — my good friend and colleague, Hamar Foster of the Faculty of Law, University of Victoria; Patricia Roy, Ken Coates and Jim Hendrickson of the Department of History, University of Victoria; and De Lloyd Guth of the Faculty of Law, University of British Columbia. Fiona Hyslop of the University of Victoria Conference Office provided invaluable assistance with the administration and logistics of the conference. Helpful suggestions on funding were supplied by Fred Bennett of the Research Grants Office.

Although the notion that this was an idea whose time had come was well accepted by legal historians, it was not immediately evident to the world outside the academy, and in particular funders. However, after a number of false starts, the conference was able to tap into a number of funding sources. The Social Sciences and Humanities Research Council in Ottawa went almost to its conventional limits for conference funding in providing support. On the Canadian side the conference also drew generous support from the Vancouver law firms of Ladner, Downs and Blake, Cassels, from the University of Victoria President's Fund and from the Faculty of Law. John Reid's keynote lecture was supported by the Hugh Alan Maclean Fund, generously donated annually by the Maclean family. In the United States, through the offices of Chet Orloff, we were able to secure a very generous grant from the William F. Donner Foundation. In combination this funding enabled us to put on a very successful conference and to provide part of the money for publication of this book. The remainder of the funds for publication have come from the joint publishers: the Ninth Judicial Circuit Historical Society, through its journal, *Western Legal History*, and the Canadian Plains Research Center (CPRC) of the University of Regina. Thanks are due on that account to Chet Orloff, Brad Williams, Chet's successor as executive director of the

Ninth Judicial Circuit Historical Society, and to Brian Mlazgar, the coordinator of publications of the CPRC.

The "Law for the Elephant, Law for the Beaver" conference was also notable for its expansive treatment of the history of aboriginal rights. In addition to the sessions dealing with this issue, a very special and significant ceremony, organized by Hamar Foster, took place. On the final day of the conference, Philip Paul formally presented a map of the traditional territories of the Saanich people to Dr. David Strong, president of the University of Victoria. Among other things, the map shows the fishing locations, village sites and burial grounds of the Tsartlip, Tsawout, Tseycum and Pauquachin bands, with place names in the Sencoten language. Those taking part in the ceremony included John Elliott and Earl Claxton, Jr., and elders Gabe Bartleman and Earl Claxton, Sr. The original idea for the map was that of the late Dave Elliott, Sr., and we were therefore especially pleased that his widow, Beatrice Elliott, also attended the presentation. The map, which is used at the Lau Welnew tribal school and in the Indian Title course here, now hangs in the Diana Priestley Law Library, where it serves to remind us all of the history of the ground upon which we live our lives.

This book is respectfully dedicated to the elders and other band members, living and dead, who took part in the production of the map and the generous decision to make the c'ela'nen of the Saanich people a part of our conference.

John McLaren
University of Victoria

Law for the Elephant, Law for the Beaver: Tracking the Beasts

Hamar Foster
John McLaren

Given the novelty of comparative North American legal history, all that is possible in this book is to expose a series of snapshots of the historical record, and what it may tell us of the nature and impact of the spread of European conceptions of law to the North American West. The project of opening up transboundary legal history is a daunting one. The present venture is confined to the modest objectives of raising questions about the legitimacy of the enterprise; of charting some, but only some, of the substantive issues that seem to warrant exploration; of pointing to the methodological challenges which lie ahead; and of providing examples of the first tentative steps towards considering the coexistence and interaction of legal cultures in North America.

The criteria which were used in selecting papers for inclusion in this book were two. Did a paper take an avowedly comparative, that is American-Canadian, approach to the topic or area investigated, *or* could a paper by one scholar be paired with that of another to provide the basis for examining a common theme from both an American and a Canadian perspective? With one exception, we believe that the eleven essays fit those criteria. John Reid's prodigious historiographic lead essay, and the essays of David Percy on western water law and John McLaren on the courts and anti-Chinese legislation, are consciously comparative in nature. Eight of the essays fit into four sets of complementary pairings: both Richard Maxwell Brown and Rod Macleod investigate the culture and ideology of frontier justice; the common theme of the essays of Stephen Haycox and Paul Tennant is the treatment of aboriginal rights in two jurisdictions to which conventional land policy did not extend; Hamar Foster and the team of Ken Coates and Bill Morrison explore problems of overlapping jurisdiction in the Northwest, albeit at very different points in time; and the essays of John Wunder and John McLaren consider the cultural and legal implications of anti-Chinese discrimination.

The one exception to the criteria is Chris Fritz's study of constitution making in the American West. Apart from its evident quality, it seemed to us the sort of piece to which scholars on both sides of the border, but especially in Canada, should be exposed, because of its treatment of the important issue of mediating pervasive political and legal values and local constitutional and legal priorities in the western context.

The lead essay by John Reid, "The Layers of Western Legal History," is designed both to warn and encourage those bent on exploring "western legal history." The dangers, he argues, lie both in the field being so broadly defined as to defy an honest characterization as "western," yet so narrowly drawn that it represents a quaint, "High Noon" caricature of reality. Drawing on an extensive knowledge of the literature of both Canadian and American legal history, he suggests that the appropriate way to approach the legal history of the western half of North America is not as a body of experience and practices which are uniquely western. Instead, he advocates unpeeling a series of layers which demonstrate that law and law-mindedness worked themselves out in ways, at levels and in geographical contexts reflecting both continuity and discontinuity with developments elsewhere. Reid points out that in constructing regional legal history we are in danger of ignoring commonalities and pervasive elements in North American legal culture.

The association of western legal history with "the frontier" is, as Reid argues, problematic. Although the main patterns of European settlement in North America ran westwards, the frontier at any particular time was the next mountain range, water basin or even valley, whether in western Massachusetts or Montana. Indeed, in one special case, British Columbia, where white settlement occurred first on Vancouver Island and the lower mainland, the frontier was to the east and north. At least that is how it must have seemed from the drawing rooms of Victoria and New Westminster.[1]

Reid cautions us against assuming that there was a uniquely "western" judge or lawyer. As he has shown in his book, *Law for the Elephant: Property and Social Behavior on the Overland Trail*, Europeans who moved westwards across the plains and mountains, whether legally trained or not, took well-formed notions of law and law-mindedness with them.[2] In the particular context of the common law, he suggests, one is unlikely to find fundamental differences in judicial ideology or approach whether the judge was sitting in Massachusetts or California. A similar claim might be made in Canada, although there is some evidence that as formalism was taking hold in more settled parts of the country in the latter decades of the nineteenth and early twentieth centuries, most notably in Ontario, western judges such as Matthew Baillie Begbie in British Columbia and later Nicholas Beck and Charles Stuart in Alberta, did endeavor to mold the common law to fit local conditions and realities.[3] In other words "settledness" and "unsettledness" may well have affected judicial ideology. It is difficult to make the claim for a pervasive and consistent North American common law embracing both Canada and the United States. However, regional connections or problems peculiar to a region were capable of producing a degree of transboundary identification. In the West, as David Percy and John McLaren demonstrate in their essays, the problems of what to do about scarce water resources and Chinese immigration drew similar responses and a discernible movement of legal ideas from south to north.

Despite the problems with defining western legal history as the "history of *the* frontier," the story of law on the western frontier had some unique qualities to it. One which John Reid identifies is the clash of European legal cultures — American and Mexican — on the southwestern frontier, explored most recently by David Langum and Morris Arnold.[4] At first blush there may seem to be no western Canadian analogue to this story. Although there was an equivalent clash in Canada between English and French law and legal culture, this has been seen largely as an eastern phenomenon, played out in Quebec City and Montreal and manifest in the separation of Upper and Lower Canada. However, a moment's reflection suggests that the tension between English and French conceptions of law did cast a very definite shadow on the Prairies and for a season produced conflict. This was resolved in much the same way as in California. As the Canadian government began to assert and extend its political and legal control, and as settlers from Ontario began to fill up the plains, the concepts of law which they brought with them were allowed to stifle preexisting systems of law and custom. The often scandalous tale of the victory of dominion land policies and notions of land holding over the law and custom of the Métis (which in terms of land holding reflected their French heritage) has recently been chronicled by D.N. Sprague.[5] Unlike the situation in California, the vestiges of the traditional system were erased only by armed conflict, in the suppression of the North-west Rebellion of 1885.

The roots of that conflict reach back of course to the Selkirk Settlement at Red River and the massacre at Seven Oaks in 1816. This episode was also a contest between different legal cultures, although they cannot be described as purely English and French without risking distortion. On the one side was Lord Selkirk, claiming governmental powers by virtue of the Hudson's Bay Company (HBC) charter of 1670, and claiming title because the Company, relying upon its charter, had granted him Assiniboia. In short, he saw himself as enjoying all the legal authority that the proprietor of a chartered colony traditionally possessed; unable to enforce the law of trespass against his opponents in the courts at Westminster, he sought to establish his own courts at Red River.[6] Bitterly opposed to this view were the agents and wintering partners of the North West Company, whose claim was based on a right of prior possession and extensive exploration and discovery. They traced their predecessors back to the French traders who first penetrated and exploited the region, and a number of them held commissions as justices of the peace for the Indian territories as well.[7] Two other factors further complicated this confrontation between a Scots lord and a resuscitated charter on the one hand, and Highland traders well connected to the governmental power elites in Montreal on the other. Each side claimed the support of the aboriginal peoples, and the Nor'Westers allied themselves with the Métis of Red River. Out of the latter came the concept of a "new nation," with its own legal culture and its own unique claim to the land.

If the "frontier" was the first layer, the second, Reid suggests, comprised those situations in which the legal issues in the West were unique and found either no or inapposite answers in the experience of jurisdictions further east. Several of the topics have transboundary significance. Although Mormon settlement in Canada was not surrounded by the constitutional controversy evident in the mountain states of the union, it was a reality, especially in southern Alberta. Arriving, as they did, with something of a negative halo, there were attempts to discriminate against the Mormon population. Parliament reacted by including polygamy as a criminal offense with the Mormons specifically in mind.[8] However, their capacity for hard work, successful colonization of a notoriously arid area of the Canadian Prairies, and willingness to commune at certain levels with the broader community ultimately persuaded the dominant society that they were in many respects ideal immigrants.[9] As David Percy makes clear in his essay, they were also to play an important role in the campaign for an orderly and fair system of irrigation in southern Alberta. To date, Canadian legal historians have shown little or no interest in Mormon immigration and its legal implications. Had the Colonial Office given the nod in 1848 to a rather inchoate Mormon plan to colonize Vancouver Island instead of the HBC, this situation might have been different.[10]

Percy's essay picks up on another of John Reid's uniquely western themes — the reconstruction of water law and rights to accommodate the topographical and climatic realities of the West. Here both countries were faced with the same challenge of how to allocate scarce or hotly contested resources. Given the earlier pattern of settlement in the American West, it is not surprising that borrowing took place, with Canadian policy makers and legislators relying on American legal theory and doctrine for inspiration. It remains to be seen whether something similar will happen when pressure on water resources begins to collide with aboriginal rights in Canada, as it has in the United States.[11]

A further example of a distinctively western legal culture cited by Reid is the regime of mining law. Mining law existed on both sides of the border, and illustrates the phenomenon of the power of law-mindedness in circumstances where neither a coercive state nor a business monopoly exercised immediate control. Because of the rather different history of the relationship between the customs of the mining camps and embryonic government in the Sierras and British Columbia, the comparative method can be particularly revealing in testing the extent to which law-mindedness was felt or imposed. John Reid argues that mining law is a particularly helpful area for investigating the claims of Canadian historians that mining communities in British Columbia were relatively peaceful as compared with their American counterparts, a phenomenon which some attribute to the efficient application of British conceptions of law and order by the representatives of colonial government.[12] Reid suggests that the record may show other factors were just as important, notably the miners' experience of violence in the California and Australia goldfields, and their attempts to replace it with communal regulations.[13]

Reid's third layer reflects methodological as opposed to substantive considerations. His contention is that an especially compelling aspect of researching western legal history is the richness and volume of the materials available as compared with other regions at earlier periods. The fact that in exploring western legal history the researcher is faced with a society where, as Reid puts it, "the trappings of the coercive state ... are not fully in place" makes the exercise particularly instructive,[14] because it is possible to see the extent to which individuals and groups felt that they carried their law and conceptions of legality with them. Reid's own work on the phenomenon of law-mindedness on the overland trail, informed as it is by the availability of diaries and journals, and David Langum's detailed examination of the tenacity with which the Americans who settled in California held to Anglo-American legal rules and processes in their new home, provide obvious examples.[15] There is, of course, much more to be done on the relationship between law and the culture of this enormous region, not least in the context of European settlement patterns in western Canada, where relatively little work has been forthcoming.

What conceptions of law and legitimacy did European settlers in British Columbia and the Prairies bring with them? Were they affected by the sense of law-mindedness or legal nationalism of which Reid and Langum speak? To what extent was it a view of law which reflected British or British North American political and social ideology? At a comparative level there is the tantalizing question of whether, and the extent to which, differing attitudes towards democracy and governmental authority resulted in divergent experiences and conceptions of the relationship between law, order and authority on each side of the 49th parallel. Certainly, Chris Fritz's work suggests that western Americans had and felt that they had some leeway in choosing and working out the elements of their basic law. The impression about Canada is that the process of legal and constitutional development was much more constrained by tradition, by colonial thinking and the intermediate status of the country somewhere between colony and sovereign nation. The picture is in need of sharpened detail, and Red River may be an excellent place to start.[16]

The final layer identified by Reid is genuine transboundary law which travelled with people wherever they went in this immense territory, whether they belonged to an aboriginal nation or one of the fur companies. He makes a particular plea for historians to know better the law of the Indian nations which, as he points out, was "a law of all categories."[17] This is a field of research where anthropologists and ethno-historians have much to offer legal historians in the way of insight. It is also an area of study which will benefit from reliance on oral sources, as first nations' groups seek to reestablish their identity and search for their traditional law-ways.[18]

Reid's essay represents a significant challenge and much food for thought for western legal historians. What follows is a series of essays which picks up on several of the more specific themes of transboundary legal history which he outlines, and which sets about the immense task of peeling back the layers of the western Canadian and American legal experience which he has identified.

The essays by Richard Maxwell Brown and Rod Macleod, both of whom are prominent historians of law and order in the North American West, were presented at one of the plenary sessions of the conference. Brown's paper, "Law and Order on the American Frontier," takes Trachtenberg's notion that economic forces were "incorporating" America in the late nineteenth century and applies it to two specific groups: the "glorified" and "grassroots" gunfighters of the Trans-Mississippi West.[19] Brown refers to this phenomenon as the "Western

Civil War of Incorporation," in which gunfighters from both groups fought on each side, engaging in such well-known clashes as the one at Mussel Slough in California.[20] Men like Wyatt Earp and Wild Bill Hickock, who were in the pay of industrialists, land speculators and the like, are classified as conservative, "incorporation" gunfighters. On the other side were the dissident, "resister" gunfighters such as Billy the Kid, some of whom have been described by E.J. Hobsbawm as "social bandits."[21] According to Brown, this civil war was not confined to the gunfighters and their corporate or settler employers. Incorporating jurists such as Justices Stephen J. Field, Lorenzo Sawyer and Matthew P. Deady were also implicated, as was an apparently much smaller number of resister lawyers and judges, one of whom, David S. Terry, was shot and killed by Field's bodyguard in 1889.[22] This phenomenon, perhaps more than any other, ought to provide a suggestive source of comparison for historians of the Canadian and American frontiers.

Given that the incorporators were acting on behalf of the transformative forces of industrial capitalism, one might quarrel with the decision to call them "conservative." As Canadian philosopher George Grant has repeatedly argued, the real conservatives were and are those who oppose such forces, and seek to conserve and protect communitarian values against the disintegrating influence of unrestrained corporate "progress."[23] Nonetheless, the idea is a provocative one, and towards the end of his essay Brown speculates as to whether it may be useful in analyzing developments in Mexico — where conflict between similar groups led to fighting in the North and eventually to the Mexican Revolution — and Canada. "Was Louis Riel's rebellion of 1885," he asks, "an episode in a Western Canadian Civil War of Incorporation?"[24] The implication is that it may have been.

In "Law and Order on the Western-Canadian Frontier" Macleod takes a somewhat different tack. He expresses some polite skepticism about the "grand theoretical approaches" of such historians as Trachtenberg and Frederick Jackson Turner (whose "frontier" thesis has never been accorded in Canada the explanatory power that it once enjoyed in the United States).[25] Instead, Macleod stresses that more attention should be paid to local and regional variations in "ambient" levels of violence that may not be a product of economic or class conflict, especially in the years before settlement began. According to this view, a certain level of violence exists in every society, involving factors — family dynamics, the different cultures of the Indian nations, the institutional structures imported by Europeans — that often operate independently of wealth and class. When such variations are isolated and examined, he says, they may reveal a difference between the two countries, or at least between their historians. The contrast between town and gold camp law enforcement that Thomas Stone documented in the Klondike indicates to Macleod that the role of the state is critical, and that the coincidence of violence and a "new form of economic or legal structure suggests a causal relationship but does not prove it."[26]

Still, although Macleod rejects this equation and draws attention to at least six unique regional combinations of factors, he concludes that in nineteenth-century western Canada differences were not great. The HBC and the North West Mounted Police saw to that, more through the image they cultivated and the judgment they brought to bear than by regularly resorting to a force which they often did not have. However, drawing on a thoughtful article published a number of years ago by Robin Fisher, Macleod does suggest that the frontier may not have been as peaceful west of the Rockies as it was to the east.[27] Others will no doubt want to make similar cases for other regions, especially as researchers increasingly resort to archives and open up new information for analysis.

The debate over the extent to which wealth and class shape the state's role in law enforcement will therefore go on, as will the equally determined argument about whether Canadian frontier policy really left certain groups — notably aboriginal people — any better off than their counterparts in the more "lawless" South. Certainly the latter proposition is far more controversial now than it was a generation ago.[28] As Canadians realize the need to look to their past in order to help define who they are — as English, French, aboriginal and other Canadians — these investigations seem increasingly important.

Mention of Canada's aboriginal peoples leads naturally to the next pair of essays. Both Brown and Macleod briefly discuss their role in frontier law enforcement, but Paul Tennant's "Aboriginal Rights and the Canadian Legal System: The West Coast Anomaly" and Stephen Haycox's "Tee-Hit-Ton and Alaska Native Rights" bring them to center stage. These essays deal with aboriginal rights in British Columbia and Alaska, each of which — to use the apt term employed by Tennant in the title of his essay — is indeed something of an anomaly. Until quite recently, neither jurisdiction conformed to the regime of aboriginal land title or rights that governed most of North America. Thus, although aboriginal people in British Columbia came to be just as subject to the federal Indian Act as other aboriginals (except for the Inuit), from about 1860 onwards successive colonial and provincial governments refused to recognize Indian title. As a result, they neither extinguished it by treaty nor compensated aboriginal owners when the Crown transferred land to non-aboriginals or dealt with it in other ways that interfered with traditional rights. A further consequence of this attitude was that British Columbia blocked attempts by Ottawa both to resolve the title issue and to impose dominion reserve lands policy west of the Rockies. As Tennant points out, the few treaties that were made in British Columbia are, in this light, an anomaly within an anomaly.

Although an agreement was reached with respect to reserves in 1938, British Columbia's intransigence on title proper did not begin to change until 1990. In this respect one is reminded of what the United States Court of Claims said in a case dealing with the aboriginal policy of Texas prior to its joining the United States. Responding to an argument not unlike the position advanced by British Columbia, the court noted legal recognition of Indian title in Spanish, Mexican, American and other legal systems, and concluded that only a "convincing demonstration could show that the Republic of Texas uniquely departed from the consensus of the whole western world."[29] The question of whether British Columbia's "unique" departure was sufficiently explicit to be legally effective is currently before the courts.

In a sense, Alaska is even more exceptional. The failure to address the native title issue there flowed, at least in part, from the fact that the courts declared very early on that, unlike the states south of the 49th parallel, Alaska was not "Indian Country."[30] It was therefore not subject to the regime of aboriginal rights and title that was first articulated by the Marshall Court in the years between 1823 and 1835. The fact that Alaska natives, like those in British Columbia, were organized in villages rather than tribes was also important, because it hindered the application of the Indian Reorganization Act, the New Deal's belated reassertion of some of the Marshall Court principles.[31] What Alaska does have in common with other jurisdictions, however, is that the title issue was ultimately addressed when government and business realized that, in order to develop the region's resources, land claims had to be settled and compensation paid. The result, in 1971, was the Alaska Native Claims Settlement Act, which may be regarded as the legislative embodiment of the first of the post-World War II land treaties. *Tee-Hit-Ton Indians v. United States*,[32] the case that provides the vehicle for Haycox's examination of the law and politics of aboriginal title in Alaska, was a critical part of that evolution.

Tennant and Haycox both focus upon the legal process, especially the roles of lawyers and courts. But Haycox looks at a single case and the role in it of one man, William Paul, from one organization, the Alaska Native Brotherhood (ANB). Tennant, on the other hand, engages in a historical survey of over one hundred years of protest and, ultimately, litigation. Together, they provide both a particular and a general view of what seems, for all its many variations, to be a strikingly similar process. As Tennant has pointed out elsewhere, native organizations also played a central role in what, since 1875, has been known as the "Indian land question."[33] More research needs to be done, but there should be little doubt that there was a great deal of contact between the two jurisdictions, and that the strategies employed by Alaska natives were studied and adapted further south. Certainly the careers of Andy Paull, Peter Kelly and Frank Calder of the Allied Tribes and the Nisga'a Land Committee (tribal council) in British Columbia deserve the sort of scrutiny that Haycox has accorded William Paul and the ANB.[34] Perhaps a case could even be made that Calder and the Nisga'a were just as "renegade" in the British Columbia land claims movement as William Paul in Alaska, although not of course in the same way.

However that may be, it seems likely that transboundary influences will soon operate in both directions, and that the British Columbia aboriginal rights cases charted by Tennant towards the end of his essay may come to affect events to the north. Ever since the publication in 1974 of *The Fourth World* by George Manuel and Michael Posluns, the international nature of the aboriginal rights movement has become more and more pronounced, reemphasizing that the national borders agreed to by the colonizing powers in North America are as artificial as those they imposed in Africa, Asia and elsewhere.[35] It is true that there are important differences in the constitutions of Canada and the United States, especially now that the Supreme Court of Canada has ruled that section 35 of the Constitution Act of 1982 protects aboriginal rights from legislative extinguishment; but transboundary influences need not be total nor even direct to be significant.[36]

The transition from Tennant and Haycox to the essays by Foster and by Coates and Morrison is an easy one, since their studies are also set in the northwest corner of the continent. But here the focus shifts from aboriginal issues to an explicitly transboundary one: how does an occupying power, be it the HBC or the American armed forces, adjust to the legal regime of a territory in which it temporarily finds itself? Foster looks at a single case from southeastern Alaska which played itself out between the years 1842 and 1846. Coates and Morrison examine a complex set of issues in adjacent Canadian territory, exactly a century later. But both essays are about major commercial or industrial undertakings (the northern fur trade in the one, and the construction of the Alaska Highway, the Canol Pipeline, and associated projects in the other); both describe law enforcement in and by military or (in the case of the HBC) paramilitary organizations; and both focus, to varying degrees, upon practical questions concerning the diplomatic and political context of jurisdictional disputes.

In "Killing Mr. John: Law and Jurisdiction at Fort Stikine, 1842-1846," Foster deals with the alleged murder of a HBC man in a British fort on land leased from the Russians in Tlingit territory. He argues that problems with the HBC's hiring and discipline policies exacerbated relations in what was already a tense and remote environment. As a result, the conditions of labor on the northwest coast, and at Fort Stikine in particular, gave rise to social pressures that made conflict and legal intervention of some kind inevitable. However, the various overlapping jurisdictions, coupled with the distance and expense involved in trying the case where there were courts supposedly empowered to do so, were a formula for inaction.

In theory, the HBC brought its law with it, but lacked effective institutional means of enforcing the law in serious cases. Although it had leased Fort Stikine and its environs from the Russians, the HBC was really there at the sufferance of the southern Tlingits. It also depended on the Tlingit people for trade, for many of its provisions, and for other important, but less material, social needs. To a certain extent the Company was subject to local law as well: conditions of trade and the means for settling what the HBC regarded as minor disputes were largely dictated by the Tlingits. Offenses involving life and limb, however, were another matter.

Thus when John McLoughlin was killed by his men, trial in the courts of faraway Russia, Britain or Lower Canada were the only options that were considered. For a number of reasons each of these proved impossible or impractical. The Russians had no real interest in trying the case, so the secretary of the HBC was probably correct in describing their jurisdictional concerns as mere "fudge alleged to get rid of the business."[37] Nor were the Tlingits, to whose authority the Company would never have submitted the case in any event, interested in interfering with what was essentially a white man's problem. This left only the options of sending the case to London or Montreal, and no one in the HBC — including, eventually, even the dead man's father — was prepared to go to the expense of doing that. So, armed with a dubious legal opinion denying the jurisdiction of Canada's courts and even raising doubts about that of England's, the case was dropped and was treated instead as an internal, disciplinary matter. This lack of authoritative action, not to mention the relatively brief duration of the HBC's stay in Alaska, helped to ensure that it made no lasting impression on the geopolitics of the region.[38] Indeed, by the time the HBC departed Alaska when Russia sold the territory to the United States in 1867, it had done virtually nothing to affect either Tlingit sovereignty or Russian claims to supercede it.

In "Controlling the Army of Occupation: Law Enforcement and the Northwest Defense Projects, 1942-1946," Coates and Morrison write about events associated with the defense of Alaska during World War II, and therefore must give an account of an occupying power much grander than the HBC. Unlike the "Honourable Company," the United States and its armed forces had the military, economic and political clout to bring their legal institutions with them, and to oblige a reluctant Canada to cede them wide and ultimately exclusive administrative and judicial authority. Here the problem was not coping with the reluctance of the major players to enforce the law, but reconciling their competing desires to do so. After a period in which the two nations shared jurisdiction, much as Rupert's Land and Canada were supposed to have done under the Canada Jurisdiction Act of 1803, Ottawa yielded to American pressure and more or less withdrew from the field. Although this may seem to involve a serious abdication of responsibility, the authors conclude that this episode (like the HBC's rather longer sojourn in Alaska) in fact left Canada's sovereignty "essentially" intact.

The bulk of the essay, however, concerns the practical impact of the Americans and their law upon the host country. Where the HBC may have had, perhaps, forty or fifty men at their posts at Stikine and Taku, the United States sent tens of thousands of soldiers and civilians into Canada. This not only caused discomfort at the governmental level, where officials were concerned both about due process *and* strict enforcement, but down on the ground, where Canadians going about their business regularly found themselves being stopped and unwillingly subjected to the authority of the American military police. The latter, it seems, were not especially loved by their countrymen either. In a passage that will delight those enamored of the traditional view of the difference between the Canadian and American frontiers, the authors report the following questionnaire response from a Louisiana man, nearly fifty years after the fact. The United States military police were, he said, "horse's butts," but the Royal Canadian Mounted Police were "fine professional people."[39]

Coates and Morrison conclude that, for all the friction, the "legal occupation" of a large chunk of Canada was accomplished with "surprisingly little strife and considerable good will." They ascribe this to the fact that the system was an integral part of "the overall management structure in the northwest, serving as a means to keep the workers dedicated to the task at hand."[40] Something similar might be said about the HBC a century earlier. Although Fort Stikine was never a happy place, McLoughlin's death was the only major incident; and although the internal, "club" law that the Company's officers used to deal with most other transgressions was even less a model of due process than the methods of the American military police, it was tolerated — although not exactly with "considerable good will." Above all, the HBC's approach to discipline was central to its management structure, and was equally dedicated to keeping the workers in hand. If it was less successful, this appears to have been largely due to economics. On a purely cost-benefit basis, the Russians and the Company calculated that formal enforcement was not worth the trouble, and agreed to do nothing. It is hardly surprising that, in the very different circumstances of World War II, the Canadian and American governments came, just as amicably, to a quite different conclusion.

A shared element of the western experience in both the United States and Canada not canvassed by John Reid was the tension created by oriental immigration. The Chinese were the first sizeable group of non-white immigrants to arrive in the western regions of North America. Of all the populations of Asian immigrants, they have received the most attention from political, social and economic historians.[41] Explanations of the widespread contempt and fear in which they were held have ranged from the materialist to the cultural. Although the Chinese and other Asian peoples did not settle exclusively in the West or Northwest, geographic and demographic realities ensured that the majority located in the mountain and west coast states of the union and in the province of British Columbia.

John Wunder, in "Anti-Chinese Violence in the American West, 1850-1910," argues that the extent and intensity of violence against Chinese residents and workers in the West has been largely glossed over by historians.[42] The result is that we have a limited conception of its duration and frequency. Although the 1880s were the most violent decade, the phenomenon began in the 1850s and continued until 1910. Moreover, he suggests, the geographical reach of Sinophobia was larger than is generally recognized; California has attracted the "lion's share" of attention, but the phenomenon extended to all the mountain, west coast and desert states. Indeed, Wunder notes that while California led the pack in terms of violent outbreaks and the resulting dislocation of the immigrants, Oregon by virtue of the 1887 Snake River Massacre, and Wyoming through the 1885 Rock Springs Massacre, matched it in terms of Chinese deaths.

The major focus of the essay is not so much the law as an instrument of the oppression of the Chinese, as it is the law's callous unconcern for and complicity in their victimization by extralegal and illegal conduct. Despite the fact that, in the period and jurisdictions examined, the ideology and agencies of the "rule of law" were firmly in place, the view was widespread in the white population that it was legitimate to treat the Chinese as "outlaws" or "outcasts" who lacked any rights and could be abused at will. Not only the settler community, but also its political and legal representatives, especially at the local level, were imbued with this Sinophobia. As a consequence the legal system and its officers often failed the Chinese. The latter were faced with the choice between flight and other forms of self-protection on the one hand, and serious injury or death on the other. Only where state or territorial authorities were willing to intervene with armed force was protection, albeit belated, afforded to the immigrants. Using three case studies of Chinese who were the victims of random group violence in Los Angeles, Denver and Tonopah, Nevada, Wunder graphically shows the cruel and devastating effect of these outrages on the immigrants and the disillusionment which it caused to those who survived. With calculated irony, he concludes by demonstrating that the term "hoodlum," which was derived from a Cantonese word meaning "devil," was used increasingly both in China and in Chinese immigrant communities during the nineteenth century to describe whites who persecuted and did violence to them.

It would be tempting to claim smugly that this egregious pattern of physical violence was absent north of the 49th parallel. Historical interpretations which stress the dominance of a rule of law ideology in the Canadian West, the early emergence of official policing and the orderliness of settlement tend in that direction.[43] As the riots in Vancouver in 1887 and 1907 show, however, the reality is that the potential for violent manifestations of the frustration felt by many white workers and settlers at the Chinese presence were never far from the surface in British Columbia.[44] Furthermore, while there is even less published material on other outbursts of anti-Chinese violence in Canada than John Wunder has found in the United States, various fragments of evidence suggest that, especially in the more remote quarters of the province, individuals and groups of Chinese were abused, violated and even killed.[45] The virus was in truth North American in character, reflecting not, as some Canadian propagandists liked to claim, the sinister work of American agitators, but the combination of racism, capitalist exploitation of cheap labor and fear of economic competition which afflicted the settler societies in both countries.[46] Wunder has opened a vein which should challenge further speculation on the phenomenon of Sinophobic violence, and its motivations throughout this vast region.

There are, of course, limits to the human capacity for violence, even in racially sensitive frontier conditions. There was life to be led, work to be done and recreation to be had on all sides. The daily existence of Chinese immigrants was not invariably or even frequently a "Hobbesian twilight" in which life was predictably "nasty, brutish and short." But there were more subtle "legal" ways in which the dominant population and its political representatives were to make life difficult for this visible minority. The law was invoked on both sides of the border by state and municipal governments to exclude, ghettoize and harass the Chinese. It is this use of law which provides the focus of the McLaren essay on "The Early British Columbia Judges, the Rule of Law and the 'Chinese Question': The California and Oregon Connection."

What this study reveals is that in both Canada and the United States a dialectic existed on the "Chinese question." On the one hand there were those who wished to invoke the law to oppress the Chinese and, to quote Justice Henry Pellew Crease of the British Columbia Supreme Court, "make this country too hot for them to live in."[47] On the other stood the self-styled guardians of the rule of law, the superior court judges, who challenged those attempts with appeals to what they perceived to be basic constitutional values. On both sides there was open articulation of the political, social and economic reasons arguing in favor of legal discrimination or resistance to it. What is particularly intriguing is the fact that significant borrowing took place within and among the jurisdictions around the Pacific in which white settlers had established themselves. In the context of racist legislation, Canada was an importer of ideas, drawing its inspiration from both the United States and Australia.[48]

For their part the judges of the superior courts of British Columbia acknowledged a very clear debt to the decisions of the federal courts in both California and Oregon. John Reid's argument that in many areas of the law similarities in judicial ideology and doctrine in particular time frames preserved doctrinal consistency, has clear transboundary resonances in the litigation of anti-Chinese legislation. This is one point at which it may be said there is some evidence of the conscious acceptance of a North American legal culture and values which transcended geo-political divisions. The fact that, as McLaren has discovered, there was contact and correspondence between some of these Canadian and American judges raises the possibility that extensive cross-fertilization of legal ideas at a personal level may have existed in North America. It is also apparent that, whatever skepticism there may be about consigning major issues of social policy to determination by appointed judges, as opposed to democratically elected legislatures, in the context of treatment of the Chinese the former provided about the only refuge of sanity and civilized thought in a political wilderness of crude and cruel racism.

Like the legal treatment of the "Chinese question," the evolution of a legal regime of water rights in the Canadian West also reveals the influence of transboundary fertilization. In his essay, "Water Law of the Canadian West: Influences from the Western States," David Percy shows how the harsh and water-starved topographical features of the eastern slopes of the western mountain ranges, and the plains and desert beyond them, created environmental conditions in which the traditional rules of English water law were found wanting. In the United States, as a result of bold judicial innovation, the law of riparian rights, which assumed abundant supplies of running water, was replaced by the doctrine of prior appropriation with dominant rights going to the first exploiter of the available and often scarce water resources. Civil servants and legislators in both Victoria and Ottawa looked to the experience of the western states and adopted variants of the doctrine of prior appropriation in crafting water-law enactments for British Columbia and the North-West Territories. In British Columbia, where from earliest days the operational imperatives of gold miners and the "laws" some of them brought with them from California spoke in favor of the adoption of prior appropriation, it was only by a relatively slow process that riparian-rights doctrine was exorcised.[49] However, by the mid-1890s an allocative regime which depended on preemption was firmly in place. It was at that time that Ottawa was formulating water legislation for the North-West Territories with particular concern for ensuring adequate water supply in order to attract settlers to the arid Palliser Triangle. Perhaps as a reflection of the colonial idiosyncracies and geographic and political isolation which marked the evolution of Canada's regions, the water legislation of British Columbia appears to have had no impact on the law applicable to the Prairies. The latter drew its inspiration instead from both American and Australian legal experiments.

Although shared geographic and climatic conditions spoke in favor of looking for new doctrinal answers south of the border, the law which was devised reflected political and economic considerations that were distinctively Canadian. Inspired by legislative initiatives which had already taken place in Australia, Canadian control of the resource was placed firmly in the hands of the Crown in which the property in rivers, streams and lakes was vested. Moreover, the process of allocating rights and administering the system was reposed not in the courts as in the United States, but in administrative mechanisms. In Canada, unlike the United States, it had long been a well-accepted principle of public policy (if not an article of faith) that economic development was necessarily a partnership between the state and private enterprise, and that state initiative was often necessary to create the stable conditions in which private investment and initiative might prove attractive and so be encouraged.[50]

In a conclusion reminiscent of Patricia Limerick's view that western history can and should be seen in terms of continuity and recurring themes,[51] Percy argues that there is a contemporary lesson for Canadians to be drawn from its emulation of western United States water-law theory. His point is that although to date the Canadian half of the West has had access to sufficient water supply, there is evidence that it may be in jeopardy in some areas, especially the Prairies. The experience in the United States, where pressures on shrinking water resources are now extreme, has been that the doctrine of prior appropriation with its emphasis on initiative and acquisitiveness is no longer adequate to the task of organizing and managing those resources. Percy warns that in the same way that Canadian jurisdictions looked south for inspiration in establishing legal regimes for the allocation of water rights, so they should look south again and take note of the serious physical, social and economic problems which adherence to the prior appropriation doctrine has wrought. They need, he suggests, to act now with imagination and creativity to systems which avoid these problems and ensure an orderly and equitable program of both conservation and allocation.

The evolution of politico-legal culture in the American West is the focus of Chris Fritz's essay, "Constitution Making in the Nineteenth-Century American West." Drawing upon rich sources of documentary material prepared for and generated by the constitutional conventions of several of the trans-Mississippi western states, he examines the extent to which the constitution makers of the new America blended traditional legal and constitutional verities with propositions which reflected the more complex world in which they were operating, and regional and local issues which were unique or novel. Despite the fact that constitutional experts such as Thomas Cooley counselled the desirability of having pithy constitutions and the need to resist the temptation to legislate through constitutions, those of the western states were longer and more complex than their predecessors. Fritz believes that an examination of the process and ideology of state constitution making is essential to a clear understanding of how constitutionalism developed in the United States.

In embarking on the enterprise of constructing state constitutions it is clear that delegates viewed the mission as a progressive one. Although they naturally looked back to and borrowed copiously from the framers of the United States Constitution and early state constitutions, they were also concerned to learn from the mistakes that had been made in shaping those documents. Close attention was paid to the most recent constitutional conventions elsewhere which had also been faced with the challenges of balancing venerability and modernity, especially the conventions of other western states. In this way it was felt that they would build on the latest improvements. Fritz suggests that the borrowing which clearly took place was not mindless, but prompted by the value of accepting a tested formulation along with the interpretative jurisprudence that went with it. The conventions were assisted by a remarkable outpouring of publications which contained compilations of state constitutions.

The discussions in the constitutional conventions on whether or not they represented a *sui generis* manifestation of popular sovereignty or were subject to preexisting fundamental law demonstrates, in Fritz's view, the tension between revolutionary sentiment and the desire for stability in American political culture. The already well-established conception that a state constitution was "a constitution of restrictions" was played through in the discussion over whether "constitutional legislation" was a legitimate function of the conventions. In an era when the distrust of legislatures was growing the answer was a resounding "yes" in most western states. The result was that a range of contemporaneous experiments (for example, free schools in Oregon), as well as solutions to particular irritants (such as lotteries in California and the activities of railways almost everywhere), found their way into state constitutions. At least some constitutional conventions provided a forum in which the "anti-incorporation" forces mentioned by Richard Maxwell Brown had their day.[52]

Despite the differences in politico-legal culture and constitutional ideology between Canada and the United States, Fritz's work points to the value of similar comparative research on the process of constitution building in the Canadian West. Much is made today of a tradition of western alienation in Canada. We know that the roots of that sentiment reach back to the period when the shift from colonial or territorial status to provincehood was occurring, and we know something of the political tensions which made the process uncertain and fitful.[53] What is less clear is our appreciation of what all this tells about constitutionalism in the Canadian context and the stake, or lack of it, which the populations of the western provinces felt they had in the process and product of nation building. Was the commitment to a significant degree of central authority and an ideology of lawful and orderly development secured at the price of a weak sense of attachment to a national identity and constitutional values?

As we stated at the beginning of this introductory essay we have done no more in this book than scratch the surface of transboundary history in western and northwestern North America. There are glaring gaps in the topics covered — women's issues, the work of bench and bar, and policing are but three omissions which come to mind. These were in fact issues addressed in papers at the conference, but they did not meet the criteria which we set, were being published elsewhere, or represented work in progress. We have found it particularly troubling that all the contributors to this book are men. On reflection we recognize that we perhaps should have been more vigorous in our attempts to persuade female scholars to participate in the conference. However, rather than engage in undue self-flagellation, we prefer to see this as a challenge for the future — one which has already been taken up on the Canadian side of the border by the Faculty of Law at the University of Manitoba with its recent and successful symposium on "Conversations Across Disciplines: Women, Law and Prairie History." At a more general level we hope that we have created a spark which will not die but produce flame. The prospect of a second transboundary conference in the United States, which was briefly discussed in Victoria, is one which we look forward to.

NOTES

1. Hamar Foster, "The Kamloops Outlaws and Commissions of Assize in Nineteenth-Century British Columbia," in David Flaherty, ed., *Essays in the History of Canadian Law*, vol. 2 (Toronto: Osgoode Society, 1983), 323.

2. J. Reid, *Law for the Elephant: Property and Social Behavior on the Overland Trail* (San Marino, CA: Huntington Library, 1980).

3. Compare R. Risk, "Sir William Meredith C.J.O.: The Search for Authority," *Dalhousie Law Journal* 7 (1982-83): 713, with D. Williams, *The Man for a New Country: Sir Matthew Baillie Begbie* (Victoria, B.C.: Sono Nis, 1977), 224-58. On western Canadian justice generally see L. Knafla, "From Oral to Written Memory: The Common Law Tradition in Western Canada," in Knafla, ed., *Law and Justice in a New Land: Essays in Western Canadian Legal History* (Calgary: Carswell Ltd., 1986), 31-77. Although Justices Beck and Stuart have yet to receive serious biographical treatment, a reading of several of the

cases on which they sat and rendered judgment gives the impression of judges who viewed the common law as a vital force which was capable of growth and change to accommodate new circumstances and challenges. Two examples are *Makowecki v. Yachimyc* (1917), 10 Alta. L.R. 366 (Alta S.C.) (rights and obligations relating to surface water drainage), and *R. v. Cyr* (1917), 29 Can. C.C. 77 (Alta S.C.) (right of women to hold public office as magistrates).

4.   D. Langum, *Law and Community on the Mexican California Frontier: Anglo-American Expatriates and the Clash of Legal Traditions, 1821-1846* (Norman: University of Oklahoma Press, 1987); M. Arnold, *Unequal Laws Unto a Savage Race: European Legal Traditions in Arkansas, 1686-1836* (Fayetteville: University of Arkansas Press, 1985).

5.   D. Sprague, *Canada and the Métis, 1869-1885* (Waterloo: Wilfred Laurier University Press, 1988). For a somewhat different view, see the work of Thomas Flanagan, for example, his "Comment on Ken Hatt, 'The North-West Rebellion Scrip Commissions, 1885-1889'," in F. Laurie Barron and James B. Waldram, eds., *1885 And After: Native Society in Transition* (Regina: Canadian Plains Research Center, 1986).

6.   There are a number of copies of the legal opinions Selkirk obtained from eminent British counsel. For that dealing with bringing suit for trespass, see the Hudson's Bay Company Archives, A.39/1, at 117-120d and A.38/3 at 72-77d.

7.   Pursuant to the Canada Jurisdiction Act, 43 Geo. III (1803), c. 138 (U.K.).

8.   Act Further to amend the Criminal Law, S.C. 1890, c. 232, s. 11.

9.   For passing reference to the legal ramifications of the "Mormon problem," see R. Macleod, *The NWMP and Law Enforcement 1873-1905* (Toronto: University of Toronto Press, 1976), 155-56; C. Betke, "Pioneers and Police in the Canadian Prairies, 1885-1914," *Canadian Historical Association Papers* 9 (1980): 15-16.

10.   See J.B. Munro, "Mormon Colonization Scheme for Vancouver Island," *Washington Historical Quarterly* (1934): 278.

11.   See the jurisprudence and scholarly literature that has grown up around *Winters v. United States*, 207 U.S. 564 (1908).

12.   See for example, B. Gough, "Keeping British Columbia British: The Law and Order Question on the Gold Mining Frontier," *Huntington Library Quarterly* 38 (1975): 269.

13.   An example of this sort of regulation that was promulgated at Hill's Bar, B.C. in May of 1858 is reproduced in Walter N. Sage, *Sir James Douglas and British Columbia* (Toronto: University of Toronto Press, 1930), 223.

14.   See Reid, "The Layers of Western Legal History," in this book.

15.   Ibid., note 1; Langum, *Law and Community*, note 3.

16.   See notes 6 and 7 above, and accompanying text.

17.   See Reid, "The Layers of Western Legal History," in this book.

18.   As was demonstrated at the Conference, when elders of the Saanich nation presented a map of their traditional territories to the Faculty of Law. The map is based upon the oral traditions of the Coast Salish people of Juan de Fuca and Georgia Straits. Coast Salish (Tsartlip, Tsawout) and Nuu-chah-Nulth (Ahousat) elders have also contributed to legal histories currently being researched at the University of Victoria Faculty of Law.

19.   See Brown, "Law and Order on the American Frontier," in this book.

20.   Depicted in Frank Norris's novel, *The Octopus* (1901; Garden City, NY: Doubleday, 1941).

21.   See E.J. Hobsbawm, *Primitive Rebels: Studies in Archaic Forms of Social Movement in the 19th and 20th Centuries* (Manchester: Manchester University Press, 1971).

22. Thirty years before Terry had resigned his chief-justiceship in California to fight a duel with Senator David C. Broderick, whom he shot and killed. Field, who was also no stranger to duels, had replaced Terry as chief justice.

23. See especially George P. Grant, *Lament for a Nation: The Defeat of Canadian Nationalism* (Toronto: McClelland and Stewart, 1965) and Grant, *English-Speaking Justice* (Toronto: Anansi, 1985).

24. See Brown, "Law and Order on the American Frontier," in this book.

25. See Alan Trachtenberg, *The Incorporation of America: Culture and Society in the Gilded Age* (New York: Hill and Wang, 1982) and Frederick Jackson Turner, "The Significance of the Frontier in American History," excerpted in Michael S. Cross, ed., *The Frontier Thesis and the Canadas: The Debate on the Impact of the Canadian Environment* (Toronto: Copp Clark, 1970), 12-22.

26. See Macleod, "Law and Order on the Western-Canadian Frontier," in this book.

27. See Robin Fisher, "Indian Warfare and Two Frontiers: A Comparison of British Columbia and Washington Territory During the Early Years of Settlement," *Pacific Historical Review* 50 (1981): 31.

28. See, for example, John L. Tobias, "Canada's Subjugation of the Plains Cree, 1879-1885," *Canadian Historical Review* 66 (1983): 64.

29. *Lipan Apache v. United States*, 180 Ct. Cl. 487 (1967), at 493.

30. *United States v. Seveloff*, 27 F.Cas 1021 (D. Ore 1872).

31. Also known as the Wheeler-Howard Act: 25 U.S.C.A. 461.

32. 348 US 272 (1955).

33. See Paul Tennant, *Aboriginal People and Politics: The Indian Land Question in British Columbia, 1849-1989* (Vancouver: University of British Columbia Press, 1990).

34. To date, only Peter Kelly's career has received book-length treatment: see Alan Morley, *The Roar of the Breakers: A Biography of Peter Kelly* (Toronto: Ryerson Press, 1967).

35. George Manuel and Michael Posluns, *The Fourth World: An Indian Reality* (Don Mills: Collier Macmillan, 1974). See also the references to Canadian aboriginal title law in *Mabo v. Queensland* (1992, not yet reported), a decision of the Australian High Court.

36. See *R. v. Sparrow* (1990), 70 DLR (4th) 427 (SCC).

37. Archibald Barclay to George Simpson, 18 November 1843 (private), quoted by W. Kaye Lamb, "Introduction," in E.E. Rich, ed., *The Letters of John McLoughlin from Fort Vancouver to the Governor and Committee: Second Series, 1839-44*, vol. 6 (London: Hudson's Bay Records Society, 1943), xlv.

38. Nor provided much in the way of ammunition for the legal dispute over ownership of the Panhandle at the turn of the century. For a discussion of this dispute and the role of the man who was to become British Columbia's first member of the Supreme Court of Canada, see David Ricardo Williams, *Duff: A Life in the Law* (Vancouver: University of British Columbia Press, 1984), 44-51.

39. See Coates and Morrison, "Controlling the Army of Occupation: Law Enforcement and the Northwest Defense Projects, 1942-1946," in this book.

40. Ibid.

41. See for example, S. Miller, *The Unwelcome Immigrant: The American Image of the Chinese, 1785-1882* (Berkeley: University of California Press, 1969); A. Saxton, *The Indispensible Enemy: Labour and the Anti-Chinese Movement in California* (Berkeley: University of California Press, 1971); R. Daniels, *Asian America: Chinese and Japanese in the United States Since 1850* (Seattle: University of Washington Press, 1988); S. Tsai, *The Chinese*

Experience in America (Bloomington: Indiana University Press, 1986); S. Chan, *This Bittersweet Soil: The Chinese in California Agriculture, 1860-1890* (Berkeley: University of California Press, 1986); W. Ward, *White Canada Forever: Popular Attitudes and Public Policy Towards Orientals in British Columbia*, 2nd ed. (Montreal and Kingston: McGill-Queen's University Press, 1990); P. Roy, *A White Man's Province: British Columbia Politicians and Chinese and Japanese Immigrants, 1858-1914* (Vancouver: University of British Columbia Press, 1989); K. Anderson, *Vancouver's Chinatown: Racial Discourse in Canada, 1875-1980* (Montreal and Kingston: McGill-Queen's University Press, 1991).

42. Notable exceptions, according to Wunder, are: Tsai, *Chinese Experience in America*, 68; S. Chan, "Introduction," in J. Gillenkirk and J. Motlow, eds., *Bitter Melon: Stories from the Last Rural Chinese Town in America* (Seattle: University of Washington Press, 1987), 25.

43. See for example, Williams, *Duff*, note 38.

44. For details on these riots, their causes and outcomes, see Roy, *White Man's Province*, 72-73, 193-96; P. Roy, "The Preservation of the Peace in Vancouver: The Aftermath of the Anti-Chinese Riot of 1887," *B.C. Studies* 31 (1976): 44. There were no deaths in either of these riots, although there was both physical injury and property damage in the Chinese community.

45. Ward, *White Canada Forever*, 24-25, 37, 49, 63-64; Roy, *White Man's Province*, 18-20, 149-50, 176-77.

46. North American bodies, most notably labor unions which had their origins in the United States (for example, the Knights of Labor) and were anti-Chinese, were active in Canada as well as in the United States. Moreover, the emulation of organized violence against Chinese south of the 49th parallel as reported in the press and union newspapers should not be underestimated. All that this proves is that British Columbia was already fertile soil for Sinophobic activism. Roy in particular dispels the widespread belief that the 1907 Vancouver riot was the work of American *agents provocateur* — Roy, *White Man's Province*, 196.

47. *R. v. Wing Chong* (1885), 1 B.C.R. (Pt. II) 150 (S.C.), 162.

48. J. McLaren, "The Burdens of Empire and the Legalization of White Supremacy in Canada," in W. Gordon and T. Fergus, *Legal History in the Making: Proceedings of the Ninth British Legal History Conference, Glasgow 1989* (London: Hambledon Press, 1991), 187.

49. It seems that some elements of the doctrine still exist in relation to water quality — see D. Percy, "Water Rights in Alberta," *Alberta Law Review* 15 (1977): 142, 161-62.

50. See H. Nelles, *The Politics of Development: Forests, Mines and Hydro-Electric Power in Ontario, 1849-1941* (Toronto: Macmillan, 1974); R. Gillis and T. Roach, *Lost Initiatives: Canada's Forest Policy and Forest Conservation* (New York: Greenwood Press, 1986).

51. P. Limerick, *The Legacy of Conquest: The Unbroken Past of the American West* (New York: Norton, 1987), 134-75. Limerick employs as one example of the continuity theme the challenges presented by water use in the arid states.

52. G. Bakken, *Rocky Mountain Constitution Making 1850-1912* (New York: Greenwood Press, 1987).

53. See W. Morton, *The Critical Years: The Union of British North America 1857-1874* (Toronto: McClelland and Stewart, 1964), 232-50; P. Waite, *Canada 1874-1896: Arduous Destiny* (Toronto: McClelland and Stewart, 1971), 149-74, 214-17, 245-250, 255-77; R. Brown and R. Cook, *Canada, 1896-1921: A Nation Transformed* (Toronto: McClelland and Stewart, 1974), 12-17, 75-79.

The Layers of Western Legal History

John Phillip Reid

INTRODUCTION

In the vast unresearched reaches of North American legal history, there may be no area more neglected than what some people have started to call western legal history. We cannot be certain, of course, for so little has been written of the legal history of the American and Canadian West that we may only be guessing when we speak of relative neglect and when we say that there is a western legal history to be researched and written. We may, in fact, not appreciate how little we know and how much we have to guess. Legal historians of the generation working after Willard Hurst occasionally boast of the "explosion" that, during our years, has occurred in legal historical scholarship.[1] We seldom notice, however, how much of that activity has been on the substance of legal history and how much on debates about style. True, there has been a remarkable increase in the quantity of scholarship, but a significant proportion of it has been devoted to defining how we should write legal history, of applauding a shift from what Barry Wright has called the "traditional emphasis on doctrine and institutional description," reflecting the perceived autonomous legal system little influenced by politics, economics, or social change,[2] to what has been termed the writing of legal history "from a genuine historical perspective."[3] Perhaps discussions about methodology have distracted us from the narrative component of legal history. When we realize that there is not available one instance of the legal history of a state, a province, or an Indian nation,[4] it must be evident that we lack some of the basic scholarship needed for making judgments not just about whether western legal history has been neglected by American or Canadian legal historians, but whether there is, in fact, a western legal history for us to pursue.

If some of us doubt that there is a separate area of study to be labeled western legal history, or question whether western legal history can be developed as a distinct discipline, we nonetheless must be amazed at how swiftly the notion that western legal history in fact exists has gained not only acceptance but identity. Just a few years ago, to have heard "western legal history" mentioned would have raised thoughts of praetorian justice and of the worldwide legacy of the Roman legal system. The very idea that there could be a scholarly discipline concerned

with the history of the North American West has had an even more
serious image problem to overcome. We may suspect that mainstream
legal historians like the general historians of North America have thought
western legal history "intellectually barren and cluttered with trivia"[5] —
dealing with outlaws, cowboys, and beaver trappers. Although it is still
somewhat of a lonely figure, sharing the stage only with another shadow
called "southern legal history"[6] — we do not hear of New England legal
history or maritime legal history — western legal history or, at least,
American western legal history, has already experienced its rites of
passage. It has, since 1987, been visited at least twice, maybe thrice, by
that most wretched of all historiological exercises, the survey of current
literature.[7] These are surveys of itself, of course, not surveys of American
legal history in general, so perhaps we should not be impressed. The
surveys that we have of Canadian legal history are distinctive in one
sense: in two out of three cases they give attention to the West.[8] American
legal historians, by contrast, still believe they can adequately survey the
"historiography of the American legal system" without considering or
even mentioning developments or literature concerning law west of the
Mississippi.[9]

There is something to be said for eastern regional chauvinism. A
theory that remains to be disproved is whether common-law legal
history, at least — torts, contracts, property — and, perhaps, the bulk of
the legal history of our states or provinces, can fully be told by recounting
just the legal history of Massachusetts, New York, and Pennsylvania[10] or,
an American would suppose, the legal history of Ontario. Writing of torts
during the post-Civil War decades, Gary T. Schwartz has shown that
Chief Justice Charles Doe could as easily have been sitting on the
California Supreme Court as on New Hampshire's, and that Chief Justice
William Henry Beatty could as easily have been sitting on the New
Hampshire Supreme Court as on California's.[11] Applications of doctrine,
such as the meaning of the concept "vice-principal," would have differed,
but not the questions asked. Both judges started from the same
fellow-servant doctrine, for both were the intellectual heirs of Chief
Justice Lemuel Shaw of Massachusetts. Indeed, R.C.B. Risk has carried
the eastern chauvinism argument even further — just about as far as it
can be taken. "By the mid-nineteenth century," he claims, "the
organization and structure of law and most of the terms of doctrine were
substantially the same in Ontario and the United States, and a lawyer
from one jurisdiction would have little difficulty understanding and
coping with the differences."[12]

Surely general historians of the North American West cannot

complain if legal historians have scorned their region. They have neglected law in the history of the West even more than the legal historians have neglected the West in the history of law. Certainly American western historians have ignored it more than their colleagues in southern history, who have occasionally located law at the center of southern development.[13] Consider a set of studies whose focus is not western in a regional sense, but which center on a topic that in North America is often thought western since the settlement of the continent started on the Atlantic side. "Histories of the American Frontier Series" has ranged widely over the geographical and intellectual concept of the frontier, commissioning works on such topics as the transportation frontier,[14] the women's frontier,[15] and the Canadian frontier up to the fall of New France.[16] It did not contemplate a legal history of the frontier until about a decade ago. More to the point have been the western historians who have thought of law, and have decided that they say all that need be said of law if they link it with the word "order" and tell tales about violence.[17] This approach even used to characterize studies of judges in western territories. We would be told of the geographical limits of jurisdiction, of the provisions of criminal legislation applicable to the case at bar, and of the sentence, but explanations of rules and considerations of process seldom intruded on the telling of stories.[18]

Perhaps there is something inherent to western legal history explaining why, until very recently, biographies of western judges degenerated into accounts of episodes rather than discussions of principles. It may be a warning that the "western" component in western legal history is a hidden or unconscious tantalization capable of diminishing the substance of the legal-history component of western legal history. Except for his decisions on mining, water, and land law, the jurisprudential premises of Chief Justice Beatty's judicial biography could well be interchangeable with the jurisprudential assumptions of the judicial biography of Chief Justice Doe. Except for resolving some peculiarly regional issues such as those pertaining to Chinese immigrants or the public domain, could not Matthew Deady or Ogden Hoffman have been sitting on any federal court in any part of the nation during the postbellum decades of nineteenth-century America?[19]

It would be premature to dwell on the dangers awaiting western legal history whenever the "western" tail wags the "legal history" dog. Whether that is always inevitable depends on how western legal history can be shaped. To explore the potentials — to vaticinate the whats and the whys of western legal history yet to be written — we should discard conventional historical categories such as biography, or familiar areas of law like torts. Better to think of western legal history by its layers — not layers of historical knowledge but layers of "western" specificity. Some of us, after all, may wonder what is western about western legal history. Is it anything more than the history of developments in law that occurred somewhere west of somewhere else?

LAYERS OF SPECIFICITY

The first layer of western legal history probably should be omitted. It is not really western at all — at least not regionally — but so many nonwestern historians think of it as western that it requires some mention. It is, of course, "frontier legal history." Here is a problem of identification that has plagued western history in general, one that western legal history will surely share. "Many historians," Michael P. Malone has warned, "still confuse the West as a defunct frontier process with the West as a geographical region..., and this garbled terminology serves to hinder serious study of the region's modern past and to nudge western history toward antiquarianism."[20] Even without taking a poll, we may be certain that in the minds of most conventional legal historians as well, the words "frontier" and "western" are related if not synonymous.[21] "Western legal history," Lawrence M. Friedman has observed, "is 'frontier' history basically, that is, not the history of a fixed region, but rather of a borderland, and a moving borderland at that."[22] We may wonder if that conclusion would have any validity even if we were to look only from the Atlantic westward, and did not think of the West as a permanent geographical place. After all, the two best American studies that employ the concept of the frontier to measure the sophistication of legal systems administered at outposts of settlement, are histories of what was once called western Massachusetts,[23] and of the Mississippi Territory during the first decade of the nineteenth century.[24] Perhaps if we stretched a point about what makes a frontier, and another point about how legal history should be written, we would include studies of law in the Michigan Territory.[25]

There is, however, one aspect of the frontier in American history that tells us something of the impact of legal history on general western history. It is that special legal frontier where two laws met — English law and French law, American law and Spanish law, common law and civil law. This topic has attracted a few law professors willing to dabble in legal history, and a good deal of competent work has been completed,[26] but generally it has reflected an older school of legal history, lawyers asking how problems of peculiar interest to lawyers were solved. Our lesson is that general western historians — even when writing on law and knowing that their topic was legal — have tended to ignore this literature, not citing a single historical article published by law reviews, perhaps not even reading one.[27] Of course, the material can be technical and the issues that had to be resolved on these western legal frontiers may tend to push the legal-history researcher toward discussions of problems of practice, failure of process, and shortcomings of conflict resolution, but the focus need not be so narrow. As the recent works of Morris S. Arnold and David L. Langum demonstrate, law on the southwest borderlands may yield some of the most unique research in North American legal history,[28] providing clues perhaps found nowhere else on the continent to such questions as the resilience of legal doctrine, the conflict between legal tradition and legal design,[29] and the strength of law's cultural determinism.[30]

If "frontier" legal history is not western legal history properly so-called, then our first layer of transboundary western legal history is that category of scholarship concerned with the developments of law during the westward expansion that belong part and parcel to general American and Canadian legal history. This layer is potentially the broadest despite the fact that very little work has been done in it. Here, in this category, are books and articles dealing with western judiciaries by John D. Guice,[31] John R. Wunder,[32] and W.F. Bowker,[33] biographies of western judges by David R. Williams,[34] Christian G. Fritz,[35] or Ralph James Mooney,[36] and, of course, the studies of law within one or several jurisdictions by Gordon Morris Bakken,[37] and of the administration of criminal justice by several scholars including Hamar Foster and Lawrence M. Friedman.[38]

The positioning of this layer may be misunderstood. To say that certain developments in a western territory, state, or province pertaining to such matters as torts, bar practice, court procedures, or judicial behavior are not substantially different from developments in mainstream American or Canadian legal history, is not the same as saying that the law of the East was the law of the West. It is, rather, a further development of the point that was made about interchanging Chief Justice Charles Doe with Chief Justice William Henry Beatty. No one would suggest that had Sir John Beverley Robinson been sent to New Caledonia he would have acted as Sir Matthew Baillie Begbie acted. Individuals make a difference. In conference Doe and Robinson would have urged some decisions on the other California and British Columbia judges different than those urged by Beatty and Begbie, but geography alone does not fix an adjective on the law. When we read a discussion of *Farwell v. the Railroad*[39] we may think of Chief Justice Lemuel Shaw's famous decision as Massachusetts law, or railroad law, or common law. We do not think of it as eastern law. Even to attach the description "frontier" to a judge as has been done with Chief Justice Begbie,[40] or "pioneer" to the early years of one of our state or provincial bars,[41] tells us more about physical conditions or the quality of local law libraries than about the substance of the law or the primitiveness of law practice. One may reasonably suspect that the practice of the "frontier"[42] California lawyers was closer in nature and specialization to the practice of Charles O'Conor, perhaps New York City's last renowned single practitioner, than to the law practice of young Daniel Webster in Boscawen or young Andrew Jackson in Tennessee. We must remain on our vernacular guard and not forget that the adjective "western" in western legal history is geographic, not normative.

To make the point that every legal-history event set in the West is not western legal history does not mean geography played no role. Of course it did, and in ways we have not yet thought about as, for example, the railroads and law practice. When we think of the impact of the coming of the railroad upon law practice, we quite likely think of physical change — of taking circuit-riding lawyers off the backs of horses and law libraries out of saddle bags — not of social change or of the location of law offices. It may be that the prestige of law practice, at least as measured by its visibility, was effected by altered patterns of town settlement. As Americans moved westward down the Ohio and Tennessee rivers, and from the Georgia backcountry across the Mississippi, many of their important centers for commercial, social and economic life grew up around courthouses. The courthouse square was often the center of town or county, stores and trade shops located about it, and often the better residences were in the vicinity. That model was more or less abandoned when the line of settlement reached Nebraska, a state in which many of the towns were named by and for railroad officials. There are in Nebraska today no communities exceeding 250 inhabitants that are not now or once formerly were located on a railroad.[43] Planning may have taken into account the noise of train whistles and crossings, for in shire town after shire town the courthouse was built some distance from the railroad tracks and, consequently, away from the business district which grew up across from the depot, the freight platform, and the grain-storage facility.[44] Without study, it would be speculation to guess what difference it made to law practice for the court house, jail, and probate office to be on the edge of town. It could have been nothing more than the inconvenience of not having the office next to the registry of deeds. Then again, it could have meant that

Nebraska lawyers were more out of touch with civil affairs and business gossip than were their counterparts in county seats back east.

The second layer of western legal history is the one we might expect to have at least a few monographs but it has attracted little attention. It is that category of legal-history topics peculiar to the North American West; those areas of potential investigation that should set western legal history off from nonwestern legal history; the subjects that accent the adjective "western" in western legal history. Research undoubtedly will uncover many of these in the future, but even at the current stage of scholarship at least six can be identified. The first is the law of the Indian Territory, not the law of Indian-white contacts or the law of what was once called "Indian Country," but that special jurisdiction within the Indian Country set aside for the law of the Five Civilized Nations. It was here that the legislatures, elected chiefs, courts, sheriffs, juries, and process servers of the Cherokee, Choctaw, Creek, Chickasaw, and Seminole nations functioned in semi-independence.[45] For American legal history at least, in the old Indian Territory there can be found the only law of status based on nationality or blood, a criminal law in which jurisdiction might be determined not only by the citizenship of the victim or the accused, but by the status of fathers and grandfathers of the victim or the accused.[46] It was not an economically backward jurisdiction but one in which law was given a most unusual task: of retarding what is generally considered commercial progress. For example, telephone companies were located there, and railroads had rolling stock, employees, and stations in the Indian Territory, yet they could not enforce a contract nor could they be sued for tort in local courts.[47] Law played a role it would play in no other North American jurisdiction, at least no other that was active in the economic life of the continent.

Second, a subject that is generally peculiar to western legal history in the United States, although it may belong to eastern Canadian legal history, is the law of the borderlands. It is a new field of research for legal historians but not, of course, for law. There have been a few related articles in law reviews dealing with the concerns of lawyers — for example, the conversion from Spanish Louisiana law or Spanish Mexican law to American common law.[48] Of greater interest to historians in general, although not to lawyers, are questions of social attitudes and of the barriers of culture — of the experiences of ordinary people encountering an alien law not only after the common law becomes dominant in their homelands,[49] but also before, when Americans, British, Irish, and Canadians experienced a sense of apprehension living under civil law.[50]

A third section of this layer consists of what may be the most neglected of western legal-history topics, the law of the cattle drives and the open range. No one can guess what law lies hidden here, but surely, if nothing had been written on any western subject, and we were making a decision about what should be researched first, the law of the cowboy would seem more promising than the law of the elephant. A great deal has been learned of the social history of the cattle towns[51] and, even though we now know they were nowhere near as violent as once claimed by popularizers of history, Abilene, Ellsworth, Wichita, and Dodge City were the termini of long, hard drives, where men who had been governed for weeks by some yet unknown law of the trail conducted themselves with more or less conformity to the familiar law of the state. The dimensions of this scholarship will not be set by studies of the Lincoln County or Wyoming cattle wars. It will, rather, be determined by the unrestricted spread of barbed wire and the ambiguity and inherent conflicting interests implied by the concept of an open range.

Fourth is the law of the Mormons. No North American group of people who are not Indians more demands a legal historian than the Mormons — and not just on the topic of polygamy.[52] There was a time when American history survey courses told students that early Massachusetts Bay had been a theocracy. Massachusetts Bay was no theocracy but Deseret was. The Mormons are a much more challenging legal story than were the Puritans, a legal story that not only was surprisingly autocratic for the nineteenth century, but impossibly late, coming two generations after Madison and Jefferson set the standard of separation in Virginia, and a half century after the enactment of the First Amendment. There are problems with this topic, very serious problems, serious enough, it would seem, not only to explain why we have no acceptable Mormon legal history,[53] but why we may never get one.[54]

Fifth, there is the law of the great fur companies, the North West Company and Hudson's Bay Company (HBC). Aside from governments and government agencies, the HBC must be the most thoroughly documented institution in the history of the North American West. The governance, organization, and collective legal behavior of the gentlemen and servants of the HBC begot a jurisdictional hybrid that commercially was at home in competitive North America, but legally and constitutionally was an ocean and several centuries out of place. In part the privileges of a medieval liberty — can Rupert's Land be analogized to a county palatine? — and in part the autonomy of a nineteenth-century business corporation, it has been explained by Hamar Foster as "a sort of imperialism on the cheap, a way to maintain order and sovereignty without laying out cash."[55]

In truth, the HBC was less an agent of London than a law unto itself or, at least, the generator of an autonomous system of customary law.[56] One need only read the official letters of leading players such as Sir George Simpson and Dr. John McLoughlin,[57] and even the private correspondence of lesser figures such as Francis Ermatinger,[58] or the expedition journals of Alexander Ross, Peter Skene Ogden, William Kittson, and John Work[59] to realize that an innate legalism governed the conduct of HBC officers. Of course, there were external checks — the displeasure of the British government which always could have meant revocation of autonomy, awareness of the growing dislike of monopolies in London,[60] and international law, especially with regard to the United States and the Russian Empire.[61] But, basically, the conduct of HBC employees was internally controlled by a combination of corporate interest and norms of customary procedure, producing a social and even legal behaviorism that, although geared to company policy,[62] followed standards derived from practice and rules predictable from experience.

There are at least two side topics to be developed from studies of companies' law. The first is jurisdictional. Scholars who might think of undertaking a legal history of the joint occupation of the old Oregon Territory by Great Britain and the United States — a unique event in the development of North American law — should not be deterred by fears of insufficient evidence. The records of the companies — certainly of the HBC — reveal more than one would expect of daily affairs in the Columbia River region and of contacts with the native people. The second is comparative. It might be assumed that there are not many opportunities for comparative law in western legal history. But what of the contrast between the legal culture that in the Snake Country guided fur brigades of the North West or Hudson's Bay companies and the legal culture guiding the American mountain men who came up from St. Louis or over the continental divide from the headwaters of the Missouri to meet and compete with those brigades?[63] Canadian legal historians may doubt if much law-mindedness traveled up from the South, but even though the "Honourable Company" made a decided difference in the North, it may not have been the difference we too easily assume. If it was in kind, it was a kind the Blackfoot and Crows could not recognize.

Sixth is the most challenging topic in western legal history — mining law, notably the law of the placer diggings of early California. It is no exaggeration to suggest that the law of the mining camps of the Sierras and the Rockies may prove to be the most rewarding research that can be undertaken in the history of American jurisprudence. The customs of the mining districts and their enforcement in the miners' courts — plus the occasional enforcement of that enforcement in state and federal courts — provide legal historians with a very, very rare opportunity to ask not only what is law, but what is the source of law and the authority for law.[64] Such questions can be taken even further. Once it is agreed why the local rules voted by the first miners in what they called a "mining district" were in fact "law" and had the authority of law, there is the opportunity to investigate the legal attitudes — the law-mindedness as well as the understanding of law — of average nineteenth-century North Americans, in a social environment where there was no coercive state to impose and enforce norms of behavior. Or, to go still further, there is the same question to be asked once the state does begin to operate, but adds little or nothing to the definitions of property rights. "The right in a mining claim vests by the taking in accordance with local rules," the Supreme Court of California explained in 1859, leaving the law where it had been before the territory received an American government.[65] "Mining claims are held by possession, but that possession is regulated and defined by usage and local and conventional rules," it added the next year.[66] "The taking up of mineral land in pursuance of the mining regulation of the vicinage," the court said in another case, "gives a possessory title to the claims, just as an entry in the land office, or the following of the prescribed rule given by statute, gives a possessory title to public or agricultural land."[67] If we think a mere possessory right rather tenuous security in a new, undeveloped, frontier society, the California Supreme Court was not worried about social instability or self-help violence. "Having received the sanction of the Legislature," it said of the practice code directing the courts to uphold local mining rules, "they have become as much a part of the law of the land as the common law itself, which was not adopted in a more solemn form."[68]

Considering the uncertainty of the California Supreme Court as to the basis of title to a mining claim, we should marvel at the stability of the law of the folkmoots of the Sierras. There was even a case in which the court admitted it was not certain, referring to a claimant as "the *bona fide* possessor," and concluding that "the owner of a mining-claim has, in *practical effect*, a good vested title to the property, and should be so treated, until his title is divested, by the exercise of the higher right of the superior proprietor."[69] Whether the superior proprietor was the United States or some other agent of government did not have to be determined. Even as late as 1864 the California Supreme Court had no incentive to alter either the substance or the theoretical basis of the mining law that had been formulated during the years before American California had a formal government. It did not even think it necessary to determine against whom a claimant held his "possessory right" — the federal government, the state of California, or the other miners working claims in the diggings.[70]

The topic is too detailed to be even hinted at in this paper. It cannot be summed up as merely the law of local regulations adopted by miners when establishing a district. The California Supreme Court went that source of custom one better, applying a law of "general usage" in situations where there was no local regulation at the time a mining claim was made,[71] or where the local regulation had fallen into disuse.[72] In each of these cases the court assumed the authority of custom and never discussed the question that has so intrigued jurisprudents — why custom is authority — not even in the case where general usage was authority for divesting a party of a claim that, but for general usage, would have been upheld as a vested right.[73]

Mining law is the western legal-history topic that appears to have everything. Even more than the legal behaviorism of the fur trappers, it begs for comparative study. The common law, with its perpendicular side and end lines, ruled on the Fraser River, not custom as in California. With public recording, licensing, gold commissioners, and mining boards, the law in New Caledonia was both tidier and more certain than it was in New Eldorado. But how much did tidiness depend on the eye of the beholder? One would like to see evidence that miners' dissatisfaction with common law was caused by the fact that it was unfamiliar rather than a belief that miners' law, the law that had been made in 1848 through 1852 or so in California, was preferred as it divorced ownership of the metal from ownership of the real estate and — because labor and discovery were favored by the customs of the California camps — ensured a much greater equality of opportunity for those who worked their claims.[74] The dominant principle of California placer mining law, according to a leading practitioner of that law, was "the equality of every man and his right to an equal share with his fellows; on the one hand securing him his possession and the fruits of his labor, but on the other hand offering to each of his fellows the same privilege, if he failed to make use of them."[75] Comparative western legal history should also be made to prove that British Columbia law served the interests of ordinary miners by providing greater security of title than did California law, at least until American mining law broke down with lode mining — brought to grief, perhaps, by legislation freezing the custom of extralateral rights before the customs of those rights had been fully developed.

Lawful and unlawful violence in the diggings is another topic for comparative study. As Rodman Paul once noted, British, Australian, and Canadian writers boast of a "superior degree of law and order [that was] maintained in the gold fields of the British Empire as compared with those of the United States."[76] The point has been asserted so often it must be true and can be taken as a given.[77] Still, there is reason to ask whether it was a historical fact based on evidence, or, at best, an obvious assumption that follows from the good fortune of being British. Hamar Foster has expressed reluctance to believe that a legal historian was serious when, writing of the California mining camps, he referred to the "relatively colorless history of Canada."[78] Perhaps it would have been better to stress not the relatively colorless history of Canada, but relatively colorless history written by Canadian historians. The search for a national superiority by Canadian historians has produced a historical theme that western Canadian legal historians may not be able to sustain. Exercising the prerogatives of an immigrant, Peter C. Newman has called native Canadians to task for the way they have depicted their past. "I try to reveal the character of the country to itself," he explained. "This country is traditionally reluctant to do that. We like to think we're uninteresting. But our history, past and present, has fascinating characters who are just as heroic and just as villainous as the characters that Americans simply take for granted."[79]

It is not necessary for an American to explain the historical theme that Newman criticizes. There are Canadians who can explain it better. "Too frequently," Graham Parker has written,

> the Canadian preoccupation with law and order is not so much a symbol of legal culture as a smug, self-righteous criticism of the dynamic, violent and lawless republic to the south. When they rise above anti-American attitudes, they still take great pride in the lack of a Wild West in Canada and point to the tough but fair behaviour of the dignified Judge Begbie, and the calm control maintained by the red-coated North-West Mounted, a thinly disguised army called a police force.[80]

According to Louis A. Knafla, "historians of Western Canada have been fascinated with the question of lawlessness, and have sought to explain why the Canadian West did not have the violence and lawlessness which was seen to characterize the early American West." But the answers once assumed, he believes, are beginning to change as legal historians start to rephrase the questions. "[R]ecently some Canadian authors have revealed that the Canadian West was not without its elements of violence, while American authors have explained that most settlers and communities were notable in their demand for seeking legal instead of extra-legal means in the resolution of contracts, land titles and personal disputes."[81] It is in the stories told of law in the Fraser River mines that we one day may be able to trace a shift from the theme of Canadian law and order to the theme of a relatively common legal tradition in the North American West.

The old story — one still told in large part — is that the mining camps on the Fraser were orderly because the British Columbia government was strong, and one reason that it was strong was "to limit the potential for 'lawless misrule' and the violence that had characterized the 1849 California rush."[82] The price British Columbia paid for law and order has been counted small, just the usual cost of having a government: "petty tyranny" preventing "parties from having justice done them";[83] magistrates "ignorant of the law" who had "unbounded ideas of the dignity of their offices and themselves";[84] a justice of the peace who "overstepped his authority and acted with quite illegal severity";[85] and official corruption.[86] Altogether this was little cost when weighed against the success — Californians moved north in large numbers but California violence stayed at home.

This paper is not the vehicle for rekindling the debate as to whether violence was common in early American California or whether, when the San Francisco vigilantes took action against British criminal elements from Australia, they were enforcing "law," not breaking it. There are so many perspectives from which to view the evidence we may never arrive at a shared interpretation. Just consider a perspective that occurred to Judge Matthew Begbie: "party" organization. The Californians on the Fraser River, he suggested in a report to Governor James Douglas, were "deeply imbued with party spirit; and, like all United States citizens, very fond of political excitement and meetings, particularly when they conceive that some legal right has been infringed."[87] Once convinced there was effective governmental law, he believed, they no longer organized for self-help.[88]

A perspective more interesting for comparative legal history is whether law in New Caledonia can be explained as imposed from the top, while in California, for a few years at least, law had to be imposed from below.[89] It is a supposition that holds many attractions for legal-history investigation, but it may be that it has been disproven even before it can be developed. The initial historical perspective was first articulated by British officials apprehensive of the flood of California miners into New Caledonia. "The fact is," one of those officials wrote Governor Douglas in 1858, "there are a set of men on the [Fraser] River who are doing their utmost to treat the Authority with contempt, and establish the same system as in California. I am happy to say that their [sic] are many exceptions and the general mass of miners are well disposed."[90] The official said two things. The second, that the Americans were well disposed to law enforcement, was generally missed by early writers on western Canadian history, while the first, that some Californians treated authority with contempt, provided the scenario for the more familiar of the stories that have been told. They are stories that will bring western legal history into conflict with popular western history.

Legal historians, David Ricardo Williams has suggested, should look at legal behavior and law-mindedness rather than at the fearful apprehensions of government officials. It should be understood, he tells us, that the American gold miners, who made up almost the entire population of early British Columbia, "had had experience in the California gold rush with various forms of self-government, both in respect of mining regulations and criminal justice."[91] That experience, which they brought with them to the Fraser River, Williams adds, was one in which "self-government was the norm, and making money was dependent upon stable and just self-regulation by the miners."[92] True, the experience of some of the California miners who went up to the Fraser had been on the receiving end, and not just on the enforcing end of the so-called "American-style frontier" law. But there is much evidence that although some of the individuals upon whom the so-called "American-style frontier" law was applied in California did go up to the Fraser River, they were accompanied by many more individuals who, in California, had been the people imposing "American-style frontier" law from below. A question that a comparative study might answer is what legal values these people took north. Did Californians behave differently in British Columbia than they had down south because they felt something new: the threat of government? We may find, instead, that most acted as they had back in California, that is, they were part of the threat of government. We know that Begbie relied on American jurymen,[93] and perhaps there is evidence of what he expected and whether he was satisfied with the result. Indeed, there are good indications that he was not only satisfied with their law-mindedness, he permitted them to bring California substantive law and California legal methodology into British Columbia. "These men brought their experience and knowledge of mining camp regulations into British Columbia," Professor Williams has pointed out. "Because mining formed the principal commercial activity of the colony, because mining disputes formed by far the largest part of litigation during the colonial period, and because the Gold Fields Act of 1859 adopted many features of informal camp regulations inherited from California, an examination of the latter is instructive since their influence pervaded colonial laws for years."[94] It may even be that Begbie and his colleagues borrowed a page or two of California's jurisprudence of mining custom. "British Columbia judges had no hesitation in allowing miners to establish their own particular customs and laws, and the judges used them in resolving disputes," Professor Knafla has concluded.[95] "The mining camps, most of which were law-abiding, were left to supervise their own affairs in spite of the existence of Gold Commissioners so long as order was maintained."[96]

It would seem that these judges, including Chief Justice Begbie, realized that, in a new settlement where government was not as yet fully established, the administration of civil justice might require active as well as passive support by ordinary people. Being British, however, they were not capable of carrying this understanding over to the criminal side of the docket. Making the natural British assumption that criminal law in the California mining camps had been mere "lynch law,"[97] they did not appreciate the significance of the "compliant" way Americans obeyed British Columbia courts.[98] Even after the far west came under Canadian rule, and British officials were replaced by North Americans, the belief persisted that law imposed from the bottom meant a society that was not law-minded. After Americans flooded into the mining camps of the Yukon, Canadian officials, on "[t]he presumption that the police would be faced with the task of imposing order on a chaotic and crime-ridden society," hesitated to introduce the North West Mounted Police. Their apprehension, Thomas Stone has documented, proved to be "patently false":[99]

> Given the initial concerns of the police and authorities in Ottawa when the Mounties had first come into the Yukon in 1894 and 1895, not only the absence of crime, but even more, the apparent reaction of the miners to the police themselves was surprising. In spite of the sharply contrasting American and Canadian styles of frontier control, coupled with the fact that "to all intents and purposes, the Canadian Yukon was part of the American frontier, inhibited by American (or Americanized) miners...," the authority and control of the Mounties appears to have been accepted with relative ease. The miners appeared, in a sense, ready and willing to quickly abandon their American-style frontier "anarchy" for Canadian-style frontier "law."[100]

It may be indicative of the richness of the potential of mining legal history that Hamar Foster has suggested yet another, quite different historical model for comparing American rule from below with British rule from the top. Pointing out that Governor Douglas occasionally decided that the government had to depart from the rule of law, Foster proposed an alternative dichotomy. The distinction, he said, is between American insistence on law and British insistence on order. "An older mining population, stricter gun control, fewer rogues, and a host of other factors all contributed to Britain's relative success in keeping the peace on its mining frontiers. But so, in the beginning, did a willingness to go beyond the law to maintain order rather than wait for the population to do so." It was a difference explained in part by the American political system, the British class system, and differing emphasis on the rule of law. "[T]he appointed and autocratic British official was able to take this sort of stand without being subject to the electoral whirlwinds that always threatened his more democratic counterparts to the south."[101]

There is another component to this second layer of western legal history. It consists of those legal-history topics that are common to all jurisdictions and regions but contain significant elements peculiar to the West.[102] There are many examples,[103] but for the United States water law is the best known. The arid West gave the law new problems to solve but just how much the West changed the law of water is a question that has caused endless dispute and only recently may have found a definitive historian.[104] Another is the legal history of matters concerning the Indian nations or Indian people. Whether they involve claims to rights under treaties[105] or crimes committed by or against an Indian,[106] there is much more material from the West for study that there is in the East.[107]

The potential may not reach far but it could reach deep and provide richer depths to legal history than we have before known. That there is sometimes more evidence for western legal history than for the legal history of an earlier period provides the third layer of western legal history. It is not alone a matter of knowing more or knowing better, but of being able to know — of being able to ask questions and then to answer them. Although the topics of this layer are not peculiar to the West, some of the histories to be written about these topics will be based entirely on western research.

Our lesson can be illustrated by comparing two of the very best books of the 1980s, William Cronon's *Changes in the Land*,[108] and Arthur F. McEvoy's *The Fisherman's Problem*.[109] Cronon deals with the ecology of colonial New England. McEvoy's account of California's ecology starts in

1850. There is a world of difference between the time periods covered by the two books. Cronon has the theme of Indians in his title, but tells us little of rules and regulations governing land use by the natives of New England or how property rights were created in animals or in fisheries.[110] McEvoy has much more data and many more sources from which to work. He is even able to explain how different nations living along the same river possessed and asserted predictable rights in the fish of that river. Both historians consider change in the early years of native-white contacts. McEvoy, the western historian, is more specific and more confident when discussing rules, claims, duties and rights.[111]

THE RESOURCES OF WESTERN LEGAL HISTORY

This edge of recorded evidence that characterizes the nineteenth century when compared to the seventeenth century may provide the most compelling reason why western legal history has a role to play in general American and Canadian legal history. It is no accident that two of the very few American books written on western legal history have tested the question whether — and to what extent — a legal culture determines the personal behavior and social conduct of ordinary people not trained in law. Investigation of a legal culture can be focused on a diverse set of circumstances, but few situations seem better suited to answer our questions than a new or frontier settlement, sparsely populated, where the trappings of the coercive state — courts, police, lawyers — are not fully in place, and for which there is a sufficient amount of evidence — diaries, letters, newspapers — concerning the private and public thoughts of average people.

Although David Grayson Allen does not seem to have been looking for evidence of a legal culture, his study of the transferal of English local law and custom to Massachusetts Bay in the seventeenth century showed that much could be proven even with the relatively meager materials of the original settlements.[112] First, he paid closer attention than any previous study to rules of law and legal customs. Second, he traced back the law-ways and legal choices of five Massachusetts towns to their origins in the English communities from which the settlers of those towns came.[113] As some of those towns had been settled almost exclusively by people from a single English locality, Allen was able to trace specific transferal of rules and law-ways from the old to the new world. The evidence led him to three general conclusions that should be of use to legal historians of the westward movement and life in the nineteenth-century West. First, that average people could understand seventeenth-century local English law. Second, that consciously or unconsciously the first settlers of Massachusetts Bay carried with them to the New World as part of their cultural values a remarkable amount of local law. And third, once settled on the shores of Massachusetts Bay, they continued to behave according to the norms of English law-ways.

Allen established his thesis primarily through evidence drawn from public documents. He has very little private material such as comments or diary entries revealing personal attitudes or reactions to English or colonial legal folkways. Of course, he may not have been interested in carrying his investigation further than he did, but it must be suspected that the search for the legal culture of the first decades of settlement from the words of ordinary and average people would not be very rewarding. It is precisely on this question that western legal history may have special resources.

That relatively more diaries of the westward movement have survived than have those written by early immigrants to the eastern seaboard, is one reason why demonstration of a North American legal culture may depend on research in western legal history.[114] A few pieces of the evidence have already been examined and it has been demonstrated, for example, that a great deal can be learned from the journals written by the men and women who went west on the Oregon and California trails.[115] Considering the popular mythology of violence in the westward movement, much of the individual findings were surprising, and some even puzzling. We have to explain, for example, the legal behavior of two starving men left behind on Lassen's Cutoff in 1849. They were in desperate straits when a third man passed by their camp driving three oxen found in the mountains. He said he was keeping two and gave them the third — which "we might kill and eat." The men desperately needed food, but doubts that the animal belonged to the grantor produced some unexpected legalism. Thinking "it might not be his," they "desired him to shoot him himself, which he done." They then took the beef and survived on it.[116] Their behavior, refusing to receive from someone who might not have the "right" to give, was certainly legally as much as morally motivated, but was it too legal? Surely the two men knew there was no possibility that the animal "belonged" to anyone within three hundred miles of the transfer. Yet their insistence that the other man kill it, that the act of conversion had to be his, not theirs, is typical of behavior on the overland trail. Even if we cannot agree on just what it means, it is evident that it tells us something about legal behavior and law-mindedness in the nineteenth century. Indeed, a fact usually overlooked about legal behavior on the overland trail is that it tells us at least as much about law-mindedness in the communities from which the immigrants came as it does about what life was like out on the trail.

There is more to learn than legal historians ever suspected. The most perilous year on the overland trail was 1850, "the year of starvation," especially along the Humboldt River when thousands found themselves out of food, although in the midst of wagon trains stocked with a surplus of provisions.[117] One sufferer was a physician named Mendall Jewett. Consider the following excerpts of four entries in his daily journal, starting with his ninth day on the Humboldt and concluding with his arrival at the "meadows," where stock was rested and grass was cut for the dreaded passage across the Forty Mile Desert:

> 2 July 1850: We are verry short of provisions have to live on short allowance and have been for some time. Our teams are so much worn down that we must leave one of our waggons & I could easily load a team with the horse gear abandoned among these mountains. Provision[s] are very scarce with all some are altogether out. We this morning gave a man his breakfast that he had nothing to eat.

> 3 July 1850: So hot as to blister my feet by walking in the sand. P.M. passed where a horse [had] been regularly slaughtered for food by some emigrants a few days since. Enquiries are constantly made for food. We have been so lucky to day to find a man that had a supply of side meat. Bot 40 at 50¢ per lb dog cheap.

> 4 July 1850: How we are to fare God only knows. We are better off than thousands of our fellows who are out of provisions and teams worn down completely. Yesterday a man told me he gave 5$ per lb for 5 lbs of hard bread.

> 7 July 1850: Have here purchased 20 lbs of Beef such as it is called Beef any way at 57¢ per lb and a few messes of us have paid them 100$ for a cow this from the same Co.[118]

Again the word "typical" fits. What Dr. Jewett says is typical of all the other surviving diaries from the Humboldt of 1850. The evidence is in the emphasis and tone as much as the specific words. The law-mindedness is found not so much in the fact that the diarists never tell us of violence over food but that they seldom consider that violence is likely. The legal culture determined that none of the many diaries that have survived from the perilous trip of 1850 contend that the right to avoid starvation might be a higher right than the right of property. It was not common law, of course, but the law of a law-minded laity that permitted the "owner" of property to exercise total dominion no matter how morally objectionable that dominion might be. Moral obligation was a concept rigidly separated from right to property. Expectations were based on ownership, and to be able to purchase, even at exorbitant prices, was a stroke of good fortune for which to be thankful, not extortion to be resisted. This was legalism turning on technically narrow perceptions of rights to property and taking no account of humanity, Christianity, or lawyers' equity. Rights flowed from ownership and there was no demand right to survive.

The proof of how much can be made of the legal-culture theme is in David J. Langum's *Law and Community on the Mexican California Frontier*. It is, along with McEvoy's *Fisherman's Problem*, one of the two best western-legal-history books. Examining American, English, Irish and Scottish distaste for Spanish-Mexican legal ways, Langum not only explores the meaning of nineteenth-century common-law culture, but he measures some of its depths and strengths. Social expectations, as well as definitions of right institutional behavior and wrong institutional behavior, were shaped by past experiences in common-law jurisdictions. The evidence is as remarkable as it is revealing of the North American past. "The expatriates," Langum concludes of men and women from common-law countries residing in Mexican California, "drew on the local law only to the extent absolutely necessary. Instead, they did their best to order their present circumstances in a manner harmonious with the remembered law of the eastern and midwestern states from which they came."[119] What is striking is not that Anglo-Americans disliked Mexican law, but why they disliked it. North Americans, we learn, were set in their law-ways and committed to their received law-values. They did not object to the Mexican system on grounds of partiality. They were fairly treated in court.[120] They objected to imprecision, discretion, and the lack of certain institutions (for example, trial by jury) with which they associated the protection of personal and commercial rights. The practice of *hombres buenos* and the Spanish jurisprudence of conciliation, produced a cultural reaction that would be difficult to credit if Langum did not force us to the evidence.

Historians untrained in law may see merit in a legal system that judged by equity and social harmony, and which arbitrated conflicts rather than decreed solutions to conform to rigid rules, but Anglo-American expatriates on the frontier of Mexican California (also not trained in law) apparently concluded that the despised legalisms of lawyers are the individual's protection against arbitrariness. They wanted judgment not reconciliation, damages not flexible installments, and the certainty and predictability of "law" rather than "justice" upon which to premise their commercial decisions.[121] "In this Anglo-American legal expectation there was every demand for settled substantive law firmly applied, and no room at all for a quixotic judge varying the rules to achieve justice in a particular case. The [Mexican] California practices of installment judgments and modification deeply offended that principle."[122] Nineteenth-century Anglo-Americans, it seems, were imbued with a legal culture making them more comfortable with a system producing winners and losers than with a system under which risks were less and costs were shared.[123]

Legal historians of the West must give attention to Langum's jurisprudence. We must determine if there was in fact a legal culture in nineteenth-century North America, its strengths and its limitations, if not for scholarship alone or for having history serve legal theory, then to test some of the studies coming at us from the Left that, for whatever purpose, use the past to postulate an economic origin for rights in property. An instance is *A Theory of Property Rights* by John R. Umbeck. The cost of violence, he says, was the measure leading people to recognize each others' rights in property.[124] Because his case can be demonstrated only by conditions analogous to a state of nature, he looked to the West and to the mining camps of very early American California. At the beginning of American rule, "[a]ll nonprivately owned land and this included all of the gold-mining areas," was the property of the United States which, at the time, "had no law regulating the acquisition of privately owned mining rights" on the public domain.[125] "[F]rom 1848 to 1850 California was without any mining law, Mexican or American," he believes.[126] As a result, "[w]ith no law or law enforcing agency to regulate the use of mining property, anarchy prevailed."[127]

There is no way to overstate Umbeck's thesis; it leaves no room for exaggeration. The "ability" of those early California miners "to use violence," he says, "was the basis for all property rights."[128] Interestingly, unlike his Canadian counterparts, Umbeck found "very little reported violence" for the years that California mining law was taking shape. No matter, however, for a theory of violence can be proven by nonviolence. "Where information is available concerning each miner's ability to use violence, the threat of violence may be sufficient to maintain exclusive rights. I suspect that the sight of a six-shooter strapped to the hip of each miner made this type of information relatively inexpensive, and so reduced the incidence of actual violence."[129] It was a matter of economics, not social peace. Miners formed mining districts and promulgated mining customs, not only to avoid physical violence but to adjust the costs of violence. Mining districts were viable only if each claim was at least as large as the amount of surface that a miner could obtain by using personal or hired violence.[130]

We should marvel at more than the economic determinism.[131] Here is Austinianism writing the legal history of the West. What else can be made of the argument that all was anarchy when there was no federal or state "law" in the mining camps of California? All law is the command of the sovereign. No niche is left for the legal culture of David Langum's common-law expatriates in an even earlier California or for the law-mindedness of the immigrants who went west on the overland trail. Those emigrants are not irrelevant to Umbeck's claim that there was no law in the mining camps during 1849 and 1850. Most of those miners who supposedly selected between anarchy and "violence costs" were overland immigrants and the law they brought onto the trail was not abandoned on the eastern slopes of the Sierra Nevadas. "Seeking to decipher emigrant definitions of property and property rights, the test must not be how much the notions of travelers on the overland trail matched those of lawyers. More relevant is how consistently they applied uniform concepts when dealing among themselves."[132]

It would be easy to be led astray — to ask questions too narrow and to settle on answers too professionally erudite — by thinking only of sovereign, command, judgments, and the state. Once overland immigrants reached the California mining districts they needed neither state coercion nor studies on the costs of violence to respect the claim of an "owner" of property's right to the exclusive enjoyment of its fruits. Perhaps they did need experience in the diggings to learn how extralateral rights were owned and how rights to surface placer differed from rights to the mineral in quartz. They did not, however, need experience to understand and respect rights of discovery, rights of possession, and rights of tenure based on seasonable labor. It was a knowledge and behaviorism that had been part of the cultural baggage they had carried across the Rockies and over the Sierras.

The final layer of western legal history might easily be overlooked if this conference had not been organized. It is transboundary law, the law of personal behaviorism not only that people followed but which followed people, no matter what mountain they climbed and what flag they saw. We must pass over the most obvious instance of this law for it will probably remain forever a law that we do not know: the law of the Sioux and the Blackfoot, of the Chippewa and the Ottawa, of the Nez Perce and the Assiniboine. It is a law we should try to know for the challenge of the knowing. It was, after all, a law of all categories: public law, private law, property law, family law, international law, martial law and, most of all, an itinerant or transboundary law. It was truly transboundary for it knew no bounds, as much nonterritorial personal law as the European laws of the post-Roman Empire, a law that accompanied the native warrior to wherever there were horses to be converted and went with the hunter to wherever the buffalo ranged.

There are other, less obvious topics belonging to this layer that will be uncovered when more research is completed in western legal history, but for the moment only one comes readily to mind. It is the legal behavior of the fur-trapping expeditions sent out from Fort Vancouver on the Columbia and from St. Louis, and which met and interacted on the headwaters of the Missouri River, in the Snake Country, and on the streams that fell into the Great Salt Lake. This was the law-mindedness of William L. Sublette and Alexander Ross, of William H. Ashley and Sir George Simpson, and of the greatest of the fur men who explored the far West, Jedediah Strong Smith and Peter Skene Ogden. The stories of their courage, adventures and discoveries have been told. There is a story to tell about their legal behavior and how they respected and understood another person's rights.

LAW FOR THE BEAVER

Here, again, the records of the HBC enrich the possibilities. The leaders of its expeditions, and occasionally the clerk when one went along, were instructed to keep journals with daily entries. As the brigades stayed out in the field for nine to eleven months, the extant journals are often extensive documents. Since they were intended to be "used as guides for others who might follow," they tell of the climate, topography, and vegetation of the country, often being seen for the first time by a literate observer. But also, they discuss "methods of trade, [and] the conduct and character of subordinates,"[133] as well as problems of insubordination and measures of discipline.

We have been told what we will find even before anyone has looked for law. It has been said that HBC documents — letters, instructions, reports, accounts and field journals — will provide us with evidence of behavioral contrast, when comparing the company's officers and servants with the more individualistic entrepreneurs who made up the bulk of American mountain men. After all, the British fur trappers were just that, company employees, subject to superiors and answerable to a policy laid down at York Factory, if not in London. They were directed to conform and they did, if they wished to remain in the company. Yet when their own words are read, in the journals that they kept for their superiors, their attitudes and conduct do not appear significantly different from the attitudes and conduct of American mountain men such as Jedediah Smith, William Sublette, or Robert Campbell. Certainly the evidence from the journals does not give much support to the familiar black-and-white picture of a law-and-order northern frontier, peaceful and policed, compared to the lawless violence on the frontier to the South.[134]

The argument should not be misunderstood. The HBC did cramp the individuality of its field leaders, but not in all respects and not always with the emphasis usually assumed. Orders from York Factory were more concerned with economics than with behavior. Discretion for leaders from the Columbia was often as wide as for the leaders from the South. Certainly in the crucial matter of disciplining Indians, or taking vengeance against them, the supposedly bridled company people acted much as did the American free-lance trappers who, also supposedly, were loose in the mountains without restraints. There were incidents where the HBC officers were remarkably violent — to the surprise, even the wonder, of Americans.[135]

There is much that is familiar and much that is new here. The law of the beaver does more than merely repeat the behaviorism of the elephant's law. Much was legal behaviorism, true enough, yet large elements of the law following the fur brigades up and down the Snake Country was law of the type lawyers know — rules and procedure, contract and obligations. There was even a private criminal law, dealt with by the HBC, sometimes harshly, sometimes gently, as a company matter, administered wherever necessary, at headquarters, at the isolated fur posts, and out on field expeditions along the Bear, the Boise, and the Sacramento, places where the Crown's writ would never run. Visiting a post in New Caledonia during 1828, Governor George Simpson presided over the trial of a man accused of assaulting another resident of Rupert's Land whom he suspected of "tampering" with his wife. Simpson rendered a Scots' verdict — "not proven" — adding "a powerful recommendation to the accused not to try that sort of thing again."[136] On his 1826 expedition to the Snake Country, Peter Skene Ogden conducted at least three inquests. The first involved the homicide of a slave, and Ogden's account of the incident is worth considering in full not only for how Ogden saw his duties or the law, and for the standards of proof that he applied, but also as an example of evidence found in HBC field journals:

> Joseph Despard and deceased were employed taking the goods to the top of the hill when words took place between them, but no blows. Despard loaded himself to ascend and when nearly at the top of the bank, the deceased came up to him and struck him on the back. D—— then threw down his load and a battle took place, continuing for about 5

minutes, when deceased went to his camp. During the night he threw up blood, and this day at 2 P.M., expired, prior to death suffering greatly. On examining the body, I could not observe any marks of violence or blows, except a hard swelling of the abdomen. A report having circulated that D—— kicked the deceased, I made enquiry, but found it incorrect. I had a grave made and the body interred. It is not in my power to send D—— to Vancouver. I have allowed the affair for the present to remain quiet until we return to headquarters. The poor man is miserable and unhappy.[137]

Later the expedition experienced a long period when hunters found no game, and the men, many accompanied by wives and children, had nothing to eat except the few beaver they were trapping for pelts. "So many are starving in camp," Ogden wrote in his journal, "that they start before day to steal beaver out of their neighbors' traps if they find nothing in their own." He does not say so, but evidently there was an investigation. "Altho strong suspicions against the men," Ogden concluded, "we could not prove them guilty," and the matter was dropped.[138] Less than a month later a culprit was caught in the act. "One of the men detected this day stealing a beaver out of another man's trap; as starvation was the cause of this, he was pardoned on condition of promising not to do it again."[139]

We should be impressed with Ogden's respect for procedural values. In the first two cases he did not rush to judgment even though he thought he knew the perpetrators. In the third, he drew a distinction between stealing for gain, that is to get the fur, and stealing for survival, to obtain the meat. Of course, the thief could have ended up with both the pelt and the food, while the owner of the trap had nothing, or there could have been continual stealing with trappers getting angrier and more suspicious of one another every day. It had to be stopped or there could have been trouble no matter the causes of the conversion. Where Ogden lets us down is in giving no hint if his decisions reflected the collective judgment of the camp.

Another instance of law familiar to lawyers was probate. The mortality rate was high in the western mountains and the assets of the deceased often had to be administered on the spot. In September 1830, for example, three members of an HBC expedition were attacked by Blackfoot raiders and two trappers were killed. Two days later the leader, John Work, "Sold the property of the late P. L'Etang by auction."[140] The best guess is that no money changed hands. Work simply shifted the debts L'Etang owed the company from his account to the account of the buyer. If there was a surplus owed to L'Etang's widow, she most likely was with the expedition and could be made a party to the transaction. If she was back at Fort Nez Perce, Work made a note of what she was owed.

Perhaps the most exciting slice of probate law occurred at the American rendezvous of 1832. Robert Campbell was writing a letter to his brother when word came that the Blackfoot were fighting a party of trappers a few miles away. Campbell and his friend, William L. Sublette, dashed off with perhaps a hundred other mountain men to what became the most famous Indian fight of the American fur-trapping era, the Battle of Pierre's Hole. Sublette assumed command and Campbell carried him to safety when he was wounded. Next day, Campbell resumed the letter, telling his brother he had realized the danger: "Mr. S. and I without being aware of the cause or the nature of the approaching contest, felt convinced we were about entering on a perilous engagement, in which one, or both of us might fall. [They] therefore briefly directed each other as to the disposition of our property; — or in other words, made our wills, appointing each other sole executor." Campbell then added what may have been the first legal opinion written in what became the state of Wyoming. "So far as I have known, (and I have known too many instances,) the utmost respect is paid to the disposal of property in this manner, amongst the hunters; — and I question whether the dying wishes of your fellow citizens, — guarded as they are, by salutary laws, — are better, or more correctly fulfilled, than amongst our mountain traders."[141]

There was even custom that looks like a throwback to another age and another continent. Undoubtedly it is using too strong a term to speak of "the law of the regale," but it is no exaggeration to speak of "the custom of the regale." It was a drinking bout that the HBC put on for the men before each expedition. Generally held a comfortable distance from the trading post,[142] the affair entailed a great deal of rum and some very heavy drinking, as Alexander Roderick McLeod testified in 1828. "Gave the Men their Regale," he noted in his journal on 8 September, as he prepared to leave for the Umpqua River and avenge the attack on Jedediah Smith:

> 9 September: "[T]he Men, such as were not too much effected with liquor, employed making Saddles."
>
> 10 September: "[T]he Men employed as yesterday, many unable to do any job, from the effects of Liquor."
>
> 11 September: "Preparations to Start going forward, and nearly complete, horses attended to as usual. — the Men Still enjoying

themselves, but I am glad to observe that little Liquor now remains in their possession."[143]

The regale was something the men were said to "receive"[144] by what historians have termed "long established custom."[145] The strength of this custom can be measured not only by the fact that it was a fixed way of life, taken for granted even by British critical of Canadians and their folkways,[146] but it may have spread south among the American mountain men where it was said by a contemporary to be held "according to immemorial usage."[147] The practice was for St. Louis fur trapping expeditions to travel several weeks to the banks of the river where Fort Laramie would one day be built, a place well beyond the last settlement, and, whether or not there were Canadians in the brigade, give the men "a day of indulgence,"[148] or what also was described as "a big drunken spree."[149]

We cannot yet be certain, for a great deal of research remains to be done, but it seems likely that the freemen and the engaged servants of the fur companies did not think the regale a mere courtesy that they might or might not receive. They regarded it as an entitlement to which they had a claim right.

Holiday celebrations were a similar instance of cultural diffusion spreading south from Rupert's Land into the republic. At a North West Company trading post in 1801, the factor noted that New Year's Day was spent according to the "Canadian custom, which is to get drunk if possible."[150] Thirty-two years later, Warren Angus Ferris, an American trapper with an American company isolated somewhere in the American mountains east of the continental divide, spent New Year's Day "in feasting, drinking, and dancing, agreeable to the Canadian custom."[151] Even under the worst of conditions, when surrounded by Indians and trying to pass undiscovered,[152] or when trapped by snow and starving,[153] fur brigades both north and south celebrated the day with, at the very least, dog meat or horse flesh.[154] Other holidays were kept in the same way, Christmas,[155] for example, and Easter,[156] Independence Day for Americans, and All Saints Day for "Canadians."[157] Always the companies did the treating, and no matter the circumstances, they seem to have been expected to treat with liquor. Factors of both the North West and Hudson's Bay companies spoke of the celebration as a custom. "This being Christmas day, agreeably to the custom of the country, I gave our people a dram, and a pint of spirits each," the factor of Swan River Fort recorded.[158] "This day according to custom I gave the best rations I had in store with each one pint of rum after getting a few drams and cakes in my sitting room," the officer in charge of Nisqually House wrote thirty-four years later.[159] It was a custom brought to the Snake Country by the fur expeditions — 1825: the men "were treated to rum and cake, each a pint of rum and a half pound of tobacco";[160] 1826: "gave all hands a Dram";[161] 1827: "I gave them a dram and 1 foot Tobacco and my best wishes";[162] 1831: "Each man was treated with a dram and some cakes in the morning";[163] 1832: "The men and some of the principal Indians were treated with a dram and some cakes in the morning, and a small quantity of rum had been brought from the fort for the occasion";[164] 1833: "Did not raise camp. The men according to custom were treated with a dram of rum and some cakes each."[165] It is not necessary to contemplate an enforceable right to suspect that the ordinary trappers, especially those working for the North West and Hudson's Bay companies, thought of these drams and pints as property to which they were in some way entitled and which the companies were expected, if not obliged, to provide.

There is more waiting to be uncovered by legal historians. Along with the rules of law such as probate, or customary expectations such as the regale, there was in the western mountains a legal vocabulary, a vernacular or professional jargon that expressed both legal rights and legal obligations. At least two words leap out from the pages of fur expedition journals and from the writings of mountain men on both sides of the boundary — "freemen" and "desertion."

There were many efforts at defining "freemen," although none may prove satisfactory for the needs of historians. Alexander Ross sounded like a lawyer when he wrote, "They are in this country styled Freemen, because they are no longer hired servants of the Company."[166] He was distinguishing them from the servants or engaged employees who worked for a salary. Generally, freemen were paid for each beaver skin they trapped.[167] A Canadian lawyer said the name was "applied to men who have left the Company's service ... some distinctive appellation was necessary to distinguish those in the country [Rupert's Land] in the service of the Company, from those who were not, and hence the name."[168] In the American West, where the term had a somewhat different meaning than in Rupert's Land, a New York lawyer defined "free trappers" as "men on their own hook."[169]

A key question for legal history is how free the freemen were. For those in HBC territory at least, it may be that due to a combination of isolation, custom and debt, they were more in servitude than the name implies.[170] In the class-ridden world of the HBC they ranked near the bottom of the pecking order, perhaps above Indians but not by much,[171] a status made more oppressive by the contempt in which they were held by officers of the company.[172] True, the officers often mentioned a sense of responsibility for their welfare,[173] but generally that meant enforcing strict discipline, necessary because the freemen were too shiftless and irresponsible to take care of themselves.[174]

Another bit of vocabulary shaping and controlling life in the western mountains was "desertion," or, as a verb, "to desert." It will have to be defined before we can get very far with a transboundary legal history of the fur trade. The concept of desertion furnished HBC officers in the field with grounds for threatening freemen with force. One clue of the importance of desertion is that it was covered by one of the few agreements between the North West and Hudson's Bay companies.[175]

At first glance, the concept of desertion appears peculiarly British. Few normative terms were used more often in the records of the HBC and few other concepts played a larger role in the internal policing of the company. In fact, however, by the time St. Louis fur traders first moved up the Missouri, desertion was almost as active a legal principle among American mountain men as it was in Rupert's Land.[176] Lawyers used the term[177] and, although one would think they lacked the authority of their counterparts in the British companies, some American fur traders acted much as if they worked for the HBC. They employed force to keep men from deserting,[178] sent men in pursuit of those who did desert,[179] and, if the deserters were caught, used force to return them to service.[180]

This is not the place to develop the concept of desertion as it was applied to the freemen of the HBC. The topic is only one of many waiting to be pursued by the legal historians of the transboundary North American West. There remains, however, one area of law that looms so large in transboundary western legal history that we should note some of its implications even if there is space in this paper only to hint at them. It is a very special aspect of native Indian law, not the law of the Indian nations mentioned before, the domestic and international law of the Sioux or the Cree, but Indian law in a cross-cultural situation interacting with common law. Remarkably, this was one area of law that caught the curiosity of some fur men, especially officers of the North West and Hudson's Bay companies. At least they realized that the Indians had law and sometimes tried to learn about it,[181] which is more than can be said for the British colonial officials of the eighteenth century, who generally acted on the premise that Indians had no law — even when applying Indian legal principles and employing Indian legal vocabulary.

Interest, of course, did not mean understanding. Often fur men stated a legal action correctly but were not sure of the mechanics. Jean Baptiste Trudeau, for instance, did not realize that he was describing one of the Arikaras' legal sanctions when he noted that they had no physical sanctions. "[T]hey have no quarrels or feuds caused by theft, slander or cheating," Trudeau wrote in his journal. "If any one among them is discovered to have been guilty of such conduct they content themselves with telling him that he has no sense, or that he has a wicked heart, and usually in a case of theft, they say that the thief must have been in sore need, and do not carry the matter further."[182] Trudeau meant that they did not inflict what he thought of as "punishment," but they had inflicted a different kind of punishment. They had not carried the matter further because they had applied the sanctions that were, in their legal culture, likely to be effective — ridicule, satire and, perhaps, gossip — sanctions which could prove unbearable in a small, face-to-face society such as the Arikara villages, at least to bring about individual and collective conformity.

Shame, a sanction somewhat related to ridicule, was frequently encountered by fur trappers. Alexander Ross must have experienced it fairly often for he was discussing the Indians of the Columbia in general when he wrote:

> If a native flies into a passion with a white man, which is seldom the case, his passion or anger ought to be allowed to evaporate; and if you can muster patience enough to keep your temper till his rage is past, you can then do with him just what you please; for nothing subdues and reforms a savage more than patience and silence on your part while he is giving way to anger.[183]

Ross thought he was counseling patience. He would have been more correct to have advised silence. It was silence, signifying not disapproval but hurt feelings, that made the Indian more amenable by triggering in that Indian a sense of shame. It was quite out of character for an Indian of a culture such as Ross was describing to use angry words and shame, not guilt, was the reaction sought.

In the cross-cultural divisions separating the Indian from the European, Ross, a Scot, could accurately describe the expectations of Indian sanctions even if he did not understand them or realize their legal implications. He knew how an Indian would respond if greeted with silence and he probably used that knowledge in his dealings with the natives. When the process was reversed, however, and an Indian attempted to shame a Briton or an American into better conduct, Indian law generally failed. Just before arriving amongst the Arikaras in 1812, Manuel Lisa was greeted by La Gauche, chief of one of the villages, who presented him with some corn. In return, Lisa apparently gave La Gauche presents. Later, when he called a meeting of the chiefs of the villages, an observer noted, "the 2 other Chiefs did not come to the Council and Jealousy reigned among them." Becoming alarmed when the village grew silent, Lisa "went with 10 armed Men and sent for the Chiefs to explain their Conduct." Among other things, they told him they were unhappy with the announced location of his proposed trading post and that La Gauche had received presents. The observer said that "jealousy" had kept them from the first meeting, but that may not be the better explanation. If they thought Lisa was determined to build where he wished without taking their desires into account, they could have stayed away to avoid a quarrel. Responding to their own legal culture and not understanding Lisa's, they would have expected him to realize they had "withdrawn," a withdrawal caused not by disapproval of his plans but by his uncompromising attitude. Finding them not at the meeting, he should have sensed shame, realized it was he who was forcing the quarrel, and have made a gesture of reconciliation. Instead, he acted as his culture taught him. He confronted them and demanded that they see his side of the issue. It was the conduct of an American businessman but most un-Indianlike, perhaps making all the Arikaras uncomfortable. As the observer saw it, "Mr. M.L., came to an absolute Resolution and they gave up, they were satisfied to have a Fort built at the third point above their Village."[184]

The two chiefs also did not attend the first meeting because of La Gauche's presents. For the fur men, presents given to Indians were gifts or tokens. To the chiefs they were marks of respect and prestige. When the chiefs "withdrew" by not attending, Lisa was being told that he had behaved badly and was expected to experience a keen sense of shame, enough in Arikara society, we may suppose, that he could be expected to remedy the insult. Instead of shame, he probably felt the Arikara chiefs were "childlike" and greedy. We can be reasonably certain that the sanction of withdrawal was never effective when cross-culturally applied to any of the British or American fur trappers. It is doubtful if they understood that the ultimate form of withdrawal — suicide — had any legal meaning at all.[185]

Even more likely to cause cross-cultural conflict was for the officers of the HBC to misunderstand Indian law or to ignore it. Leading an expedition south from the Columbia in 1827, Alexander Roderick McLeod hired some members of the Cahouse nation to ferry the brigade's equipment across the Umpqua River. While performing the task, an Indian "was shot by the accidental going off of a gun, lying in the bow of a canoe, as the Indian was in the act of hauling the craft, on the beach, in the usual way, having hold of the bow or stern, the gun went off, and he fell lifeless on the beach." For the British — aside from questions of the deceased's contributory carelessness — the affair was nothing more than an accident. For the Indians of the nation, clan, or possibly the family of the victim, it was homicide. We cannot be certain of the law involved as we do not know the law of the Cahouse, but for many Indian nations the law of homicide was not concerned with guilt, intent, or malice aforethought. It was concerned with liability and causation. The gun was the cause and the owners of the gun, the British, were collectively liable. With most nations the law required "satisfaction," which could be obtained by the life of one member of the expedition. And that was what the Cahouse sought. They killed one of McLeod's men and only one. We may safely assume that the vengeance was both required by their law and that, once obtained, settled the matter in all respects. For McLeod, of course, the one crime committed was not the Indian's death but satisfaction exacted against his man. He was not interested in Indian law or Indian legal duty. He told members of a neighboring nation that he would return and "settle with the Cahouse." He meant to kill at least one — applying an Indian legal principle, although he did not realize it. To compound the misunderstanding further, he would have sought to kill only the "guilty," a European, Christian concept that probably had no meaning on the Umpqua.[186]

In the cross-cultural dimension of transboundary western legal history, our problem may be to know what questions to ask even if we do not know where to find the answers. To illustrate what is meant, consider something that Sylvia Van Kirk wrote. No American legal historian would criticize her discussion of Canadian law in her definitive work, *Many Tender Ties*. She appreciated that case law could be as important as legislation and gave due weight to both, as well as to the custom of the country. There were occasions, too, when she discussed Indian law as, for example, when asking the benefits white fur trappers obtained when marrying Indian women. Men in the fur trade had good political and business reasons to marry native women — to assure themselves a supply of skins,[187] to have an interpreter,[188] or a cultural liaison,[189] and for personal safety.[190] To these reasons, Van Kirk adds that "[a] marital alliance served to integrate the trader (i.e., stranger) into the Indians' kinship network."[191] But how was the trader integrated into the kinship system? Can we know unless we know the law of the nations of the women? Certainly the men who married those women were not very helpful. When they wrote of relationships they invariably put them in the context of European kinship patterns.[192]

If a mountain man married a woman of the Crow nation, let us say, how was he integrated into either the Crow kinship network or into her kinship network? He could not become a member of her kinship group if that matrilineal system did not allow marriages with "sisters."[193] We may safely suppose that to be allowed to marry a particular woman, the man would have been adopted by a clan that was not the clan of the woman or the clan of her father. If so, then adoption, not marriage, would be the legal relationship integrating the mountain man into the kinship network. It might be a technicality if the man would not have been adopted except to make it possible for him to marry, still it is the law of the nation that interests us and we are not understanding what happened if we think that marriage gave the mountain man a kinship system and that that kinship system was his wife's clan. Also, consider the "safe" supposition that the man would be adopted into a suitable clan. Are we certain that every single Indian nation had a law of adoption? It is conceivable that there was a western nation that left a nontribal member who married a tribal member to dangle in a legal limbo.[194]

Perhaps this is an area of transboundary legal history that can never be told. We do not know the law of most Indian nations and probably we never shall. Our problem, therefore, may be to realize there are questions we cannot answer, yet not assume the obvious, such as that in Cahouse law accident was not a defense, or that marriage meant integration into the "family" of the bride. These problems, however, do not give us an excuse to ignore the law. True there may be too much that is speculative about the cross-cultural aspect of Indian law for us ever to make it a viable part of western legal history. Still, we must try to peel the layer.

NOTES

1. Observers on both sides of the border have traced the "explosion" to 1960. For Canada, "On the whole, the number of pages written on or about our legal history before 1960, is quite impressive. However, the inventory of what may be considered 'fundamental' is surprisingly low. Apart from very few books and a small number of articles, the legal historian of the 1960s almost had to start anew." André Morel, "Canadian Legal History — Retrospect and Prospect," *Osgoode Hall Law Journal* 21 (1983): 159, 161. For the United States, William E. Nelson found that the overwhelming work in legal history, measured in quantity as well as by standards of scholarship, has occurred after 1960. William E. Nelson, "Legal History Before the 1960s," in William E. Nelson and John Phillip Reid, *The Literature of American Legal History* (New York: Oceana Publications, 1985), 1-32.

2. Barry Wright, "Towards a New Canadian Legal History," *Osgoode Hall Law Journal* 22

(1984): 349, 354. For a defense of the old theory of legal-history scholarship see, Roscoe Pound, "New Possibilities of Old Materials of American Legal History," *West Virginia Law Quarterly* 40 (1934): 205-11. It is not accurate to think of this period of legal-history literature as history written by lawyers for lawyers. Even legal history written by nonlawyers was locked into a presentist, professional orientation. Notably see, Francis R. Aumann, *The Changing American Legal System: Some Selected Phases* (Columbus: Ohio State University Press, 1940).

3.   Nelson, "Legal History," *supra* note 1, at 28. For an interesting, if very questionable, explanation for the development of Canadian "progressive legal history" see, Wright, "Towards a New Canadian," *supra* note 2, at 354-58.

4.   A potential area of research that must not be confused with the "history" or survey of a state or province's judiciary. For example, Charles H. Sheldon, *A Century of Judging: A Political History of the Washington Supreme Court* (Seattle: University of Washington Press, 1988).

5.   "[M]ost of us who labor in western studies still bear the onus, as heavy as it was twenty-five years ago, of working in a field that is deemed by many to be intellectually barren and cluttered with trivia." Michael P. Malone, "Beyond the Last Frontier: Toward a New Approach to Western American History," *Western Historical Quarterly* 20 (1989): 409.

6.   Paul Finkleman, "Exploring Southern Legal History," *North Carolina Law Review* 64 (1985): 77; Lawrence M. Friedman, "The Law Between the States: Some Thoughts on Southern Legal History," in David J. Bodenhamer and James W. Ely, Jr., eds., *Ambivalent Legacy: A Legal History of the South* (Jackson: University Press of Mississippi, 1984), 30-46; James W. Ely, Jr., and David J. Bodenhamer, "Regionalism and the Legal History of the South," ibid., 3-29.

7.   Kermit L. Hall, "The 'Magic Mirror' and the Promise of Western Legal History at the Bicentennial of the Constitution," *Western Historical Quarterly* 18 (1987): 429-35; Charles F. Wilkinson, "Law and the American West: The Search for an Ethnic of Place," *University of Colorado Law Review* 59 (1988): 401-25; Charles F. Wilkinson, "The Law of the American West: A Critical Bibliography of the Nonlegal Sources," *Michigan Law Review* 85 (1987): 953-1011.

8.   For the exception see David H. Flaherty, "Writing Canadian Legal History: An Introduction," in David H. Flaherty, ed., *Essays in the History of Canadian Law*, 2 vols. (Toronto: University of Toronto Press, 1981), 1: 3-42.

9.   Stephen B. Presser, "Historiography of the American Legal System," in Robert J. Janosik, ed., *The Encyclopedia of the American Judiciary*, 3 vols. (New York: Macmillan, 1987), vol. 1, 1335. The fact that the West has been less neglected in surveys of Canadian legal history may only reflect the fact that there is much less to survey:

> [T]aken as a whole, the published work to date shows a relatively even geographical and regional distribution of scholarly interest. Until perhaps as late as 1986 this could not be said. However, so meagre are the publications to date on Canadian legal history that the appearance of a single book in Western Canada and a single book in Atlantic Canada is sufficient to redress the balance. At the same time, it is important to state that the preponderance of legal history being done is about nineteenth-century Ontario with particular emphasis on Toronto. However, the lively attitudes toward legal history and recent published output at the Universities of Calgary and Victoria ... would suggest that the geographical distribution of publication

in the future will be more evenly balanced across Canada. However, to date, little work has been done with regard to Manitoba.

M.H. Ogilvie, "Recent Developments in Canadian Law: Legal History," *Ottawa Law Review/Revue de droit d'Ottawa* 19 (1987): 225, 230.

10. A perspective that may be less annoying to western legal historians than to southern legal historians. At least one complains "of skewing of data and consequent generalizations that has characterized much northern United States legal historiography — wherein Massachusetts and New York statutes and cases are blithely assumed to typify northern legal development as a whole." review of Arthur F. Howington, *What Saveth the Law: The Treatment of Slaves and Free Blacks in the State and Local Courts of Tennessee*, by A.E. Keir Nash, *American Journal of Legal History* 34 (1990): 79.

11. Gary T. Schwartz, "Tort Law and the Economy in Nineteenth-Century America: A Reinterpretation," *Yale Law Journal* 90 (1981): 1717-75.

12. R.C.B. Risk, "The Law and the Economy in Mid-Nineteenth-Century Ontario: A Perspective," in Flaherty, ed., *Essays in the History of Canadian Law, supra* note 8, at 1: 120; R.C.B. Risk, "Law and the Economy in Mid-Nineteenth Century Ontario: A Perspective," *University of Toronto Law Journal* 27 (1977): 403, 433.

13. For example, C. Vann Woodward, *The Strange Career of Jim Crow* (1955; New York: Oxford University Press, 1974).

14. Oscar Osburn Winther, *The Transportation Frontier: Trans-Mississippi West 1865-1890* (New York: Holt, Rinehart and Winston, 1964).

15. Sandra L. Myres, *Westering Woman and the Frontier Experience 1800-1915* (Albuquerque: University of New Mexico Press, 1982).

16. W.J. Eccles, *The Canadian Frontier 1534-1760* (Albuquerque: University of New Mexico, Press, 1969).

17. For example, William R. Hunt, *Distant Justice: Policing the Alaskan Frontier* (Norman: University of Oklahoma Press, 1987); Philip D. Jordan, *Frontier Law and Order: Ten Essays* (Lincoln: University of Nebraska Press, 1970); Sir Cecil E. Denny, *The Law Marches West* (London: J. M. Dent and Sons, 1939).

18. For example, Glenn Shirley, *Law West of Fort Smith: A History of Frontier Justice in the Indian Territory, 1834-1896* (New York: Collier Books, 1968); Aurora Hunt, *Kirby Benedict, Frontier Federal Judge; an Account of Legal and Judicial Development in the Southwest, 1853-1874* (Glendale, CA: A.H. Clark Co., 1961); Sidney G. Pettit, "Judge Begbie in Action: The Establishment of Law and Preservation of Order in British Columbia," *British Columbia Historical Quarterly* 11 (1947): 113-48.

19. Ralph James Mooney, "Matthew Deady and the Federal Judicial Response to Racism in the Early West," *Oregon Law Review* 63 (1984): 561; Christian G. Fritz, *Federal Justice in California: The Court of Ogden Hoffman, 1851-1891* (Lincoln: University of Nebraska Press, 1991).

20. Malone, "Beyond Last Frontier," *supra* note 5, at 409.

21. For example, the Library of Congress bibliography of legal-history books and articles entitled *Frontier Justice*, is actually a bibliography of western legal history, not the frontier. Works such as those cited in notes 23 and 24 are not mentioned. Larry M. Boyer, comp., *Frontier Justice* (Washington, DC: Library of Congress Law Library, 1979).

22. Friedman, "Law Between the States," *supra* note 6, at 30.

23. Joseph H. Smith, ed., *Colonial Justice in Western Massachusetts (1639-1702): The Pynchon*

Court Record — An Original Judge's Diary of the Administration of Justice in the Springfield Courts in the Massachusetts Bay Colony (Cambridge, MA: Harvard University Press, 1961). A book that is not concerned with the frontier, but which contains material that could have been used to develop a frontier thesis is, David Thomas Konig, *Law and Society in Puritan Massachusetts: Essex County, 1629-1692* (Chapel Hill: University of North Carolina Press, 1979). Similarly, it should be noted that one of the most thorough studies of native Americans and the legal system is also set in early Massachusetts Bay. See Yasuhide Kawashima, *Puritan Justice and the Indian: White's Man Law in Massachusetts, 1630-1763* (Middletown, CT: Wesleyan University Press, 1986).

24. William Baskerville Hamilton, *Anglo-American Law on the Frontier: Thomas Rodney and His Territorial Cases* (Durham, NC: Duke University Press, 1953).

25. William Wirt Blume, "Civil Procedure on the American Frontier," *Michigan Law Review* 56 (1957): 161-224; William Wirt Blume, "Criminal Procedure on the American Frontier," *Michigan Law Review* 57 (1958): 195-256; William Wirt Blume, "Probate and Administration on the American Frontier," *Michigan Law Review* 58 (1959): 209-46; William Wirt Blume, "Chancery Practice on the American Frontier," *Michigan Law Review* 59 (1960): 49-96; William Wirt Blume, "Legislation on the American Frontier," *Michigan Law Review* 60 (1962): 317-72.

26. For example, Hans W. Baade, "The Historical Background of Texas Water Law," *St. Mary's Law Review* 18 (1986): 1-98; Edwin W. Young, "The Adoption of the Common Law in California," *American Journal of Legal History* 4 (1960): 355-63; Joseph W. McKnight, "The Spanish Legacy to Texas Law," *American Journal of Legal History* 3 (1959): 222-41; Noel C. Stevenson, "Glorious Uncertainty of the Law, 1846-1851," *California State Bar Journal* 28 (1953): 374-80; George C. Butte, "Early Development of Law and Equity in Texas," *Yale Law Journal* 26 (1917): 699-709.

27. For example, a historian keenly aware of the role played by law, Paul W. Gates, "California's Embattled Settlers," *California Historical Quarterly* 41 (1962): 99-130; Paul W. Gates, "Adjudication of Spanish-Mexican Land Claims in California," *Huntington Library Quarterly* 21 (1958): 213-36. See also, Daniel Tyler, *The Mythical Pueblo Rights Doctrine: Water Administration in Hispanic New Mexico* (El Paso, TX: Texas Western Press, 1990) (a historical article from a law review was quoted in the introduction by Iris H. Engstrand).

28. Morris S. Arnold, *Unequal Laws Unto a Savage Race: European Legal Traditions In Arkansas, 1686-1836* (Fayetteville: University of Arkansas Press, 1985); David J. Langum, *Law and Community on the Mexican California Frontier: Anglo-American Expatriates and the Clash of Legal Traditions, 1821-1846* (Norman: University of Oklahoma Press, 1987).

29. A theme that Professor Haskins developed for a different kind of frontier. George Lee Haskins, *Law and Authority in Early Massachusetts: A Study in Tradition and Design* (New York: Macmillan, 1960). It is probably no accident that both Judge Arnold and Professor Langum also stress the concept of "tradition" in their titles.

30. John Phillip Reid, "Some Lessons of Western Legal History," *Western Legal History* 1 (1988): 3-21. See *post*, pp. 39-44. It may be that borderlands "frontier" legal history holds the greatest potential for future scholarship, at least in the discipline of historical jurisprudence. After all, if we think of it, the Americanization of Hawaiian law may be a more challenging and deeper subject of study than the more obvious — and surely more likely to be pursued — Americanization of the common law.

31. John D. Guice, *The Rocky Mountain Bench: The Territorial Supreme Courts of Colorado, Montana, and Wyoming, 1861-1890* (New Haven, CT: Yale University Press, 1972).

32. John R. Wunder, *Inferior Courts, Superior Justice: A History of the Justices of the Peace on the Northwest Frontier, 1853-1889* (Westport, CT: Greenwood Press, 1979).

33. W.F. Bowker, "Stipendiary Magistrates and Supreme Court of the North-West Territories, 1876-1907," *Alberta Law Review* 26 (1988): 245-86.

34. David R. Williams, *The Man for a New Country: Sir Matthew Baillie Begbie* (Sidney, B. C.: Gray Publishing, 1977). For an earlier biography see, Selwyn Banwell, *A Frontier Judge: British Justice in the Earliest Days of the Farthest West* (Toronto: Rous and Mann, 1938).

35. Fritz, *Federal Justice, supra* note 19; Christian G. Fritz, "Judge Ogden Hoffman and the Northern District of California," *Western Legal History* 1 (1988): 99-110.

36. Ralph James Mooney and David E. Moser, "Government and Enterprise in Early Oregon," *Oregon Law Review* 70 (1991): 257-332; Ralph James Mooney, "Formalism and Fairness: Matthew Deady and Federal Public Land Law in the Early West," *Washington Law Review* 63 (1988): 317-70; Mooney, "Federal Response," *supra* note 19.

37. Gordon Morris Bakken, *Rocky Mountain Constitution Making, 1850-1912* (New York: Greenwood Press, 1987); Gordon Morris Bakken, *The Development of Law in Frontier California: Civil Law and Society 1850-1890* (Westport, CT: Greenwood Press, 1985); Gordon Morris Bakken, *The Development of Law in the Rocky Mountain Society, 1850-1912* (Westport, CT: Greenwood Press, 1983).

38. Hamar Foster, "Long-Distance Justice: The Criminal Jurisdiction of Canadian Courts West of the Canadas, 1763-1859," *American Journal of Legal History* 34 (1990): 1-48; Hamar Foster, "Sins Against the Great Spirit: The Law, the Hudson's Bay Company, and the Mackenzie's River Murders, 1835-1839," *Criminal Justice History* 10 (1989): 23-76; Lawrence M. Friedman and Robert V. Percival, *The Roots of Justice: Crime and Punishment in Alameda County California, 1870-1910* (Chapel Hill: University of North Carolina Press, 1981); Desmond H. Brown, "Unpredictable and Uncertain: Criminal Law in the Canadian North West Before 1886," *Alberta Law Review* 17 (1979): 497-512; Cornelia Schuh, "Justice on the Northern Frontier: Early Murder Trials of Native Accused," *Criminal Law Review Quarterly* 22 (1979): 74-111.

39. *Farwell v. Boston & Worcester R.R.*, 4 Metc. 49 (1842).

40. Banwell, *Frontier Judge*. See also, Sidney G. Pettit, "The Tyrant Judge: Judge Begbie in Court," *British Columbia Historical Quarterly* 11 (1947): 273-94.

41. William Francis English, *The Pioneer Lawyer and Jurist in Missouri* (Columbia: University of Missouri Press, 1947); John J. McGilora, "The Pioneer Judge and Lawyers of Washington," *Washington State Bar Association Proceedings* 7 (1895): 90-98.

42. That is the adjective in the title of Gordon Morris Bakken, *Practicing Law in Frontier California* (Lincoln: University of Nebraska Press, 1991).

43. Frederick C. Luebke, "Time, Place, and Culture in Nebraska History," *Nebraska History* 69 (1988): 150, 156.

44. See the illustration of Ainsworth, Brown County, showing a "typical" courthouse square located beyond the business district on the edge of town. Ainsworth was named for the chief civil engineer for the railroad. Ibid.

45. Research might begin with courts. For example, the articles on the courts of the Quapaw, Creek, Cherokee and Chickasaw nations published in *Indian Territory Bar Association Proceedings* 4 (1903).

46. Not like the status of slavery or the jurisdictional status conferred by military law. It was, rather, a status of blood which could produce quite unusual legal results, including the possibilty that there would be no court with jurisdiction over a case of homicide. For example, in 1882, a Creek killed an Arapaho during a robbery in the Pottawatonie nation. He was arrested by the Seminole light police who, to avoid condemming the Creek to summary execution by Arapahoes, took him to a United

States Army post. The army asked the attorney general to rule as to the proper authorities to whom the man should be surrendered. There were none. As yet, the Pottawatonie legal system did not deal with acts committed in the Pottawatonie nation by non-Pottawatonies. The jurisdiction of Creek courts was limited to crimes committed within the Creek nation. The attorney general did not think the Arapaho could claim jurisdiction on the basis of the victim's nationality when the homicide occurred outside the Arapaho nation. The Seminole did not claim jurisdiction. The United States did not, as yet, have jurisdiction over crimes committed by one Indian on another Indian in either the Indian Territory or the Indian Country. In this fact situation, no one had jurisdiction.

47. Debts could not be collected: *Clark v. Crosland*, 17 Arkansas 43 (1856). Railroads could not be sued in tort by citizens of the Indian Territory: *Briscoe v. Southern Kansas Railway Company*, 40 Fed 273 (Cir. Ct. W.D. Ark., 1889).

48. See sources cited *supra* note 26.

49. Compare Paul W. Gates, "The California Land Act of 1851," *California Historical Quarterly* 50 (1971): 395-430, to Leonard Pitt, *The Decline of the Californios: A Social History of the Spanish-Speaking Californians, 1846-1890* (Berkeley: University of California Press, 1966).

50. Langum, *Law and Community*, *supra* note 28.

51. Robert R. Dykstra, *The Cattle Towns* (New York: Knopf, 1968).

52. Orma Linford, "The Mormons and the Law: The Polygamy Cases," *Utah Law Review* 9 (1965): 308-70, 543-91.

53. Edwin Brow Firmage and Richard Collin Mangrum, *Zion in the Courts: A Legal History of the Church of Jesus Christ of the Latter-Day Saints, 1830-1900* (Urbana: University of Illinois Press, 1988).

54. "I mentioned earlier the analogy between early Massachusetts and early Utah. The Utah history, too, would provide a fascinating subject for imaginative research into the evolution of legal institutions. It has the advantage of closeness in time and thus probably greater relevance for contempory law. Unfortunately there is also a peculiar difficulty resulting from the fact that the most important of the pertinent records are in the private possession of the L.D.S. Church, which is reluctant to make them freely available to scholars for historical research without an insistence on a right of censorship." Spencer L. Kimball, "Book Review," *Utah Law Review* 7 (1960): 281, 285.

55. Hamar Foster, "Long Distance Justice," *supra* note 38, at 33.

56. It was customary law that included an element of criminal jurisdiction. Although it may be true "that at this time no definitive answer can be given to the question: 'What system of criminal law was in force in the North-West when it was admitted to the Canadian Union?'" (Brown, "Unpredicable and Uncertain," *supra* note 38, at 507), we should be careful not to define either "criminal law" or "jurisdiction" narrowly. We can learn a great deal about company "crimes" such as the offense of desertion, or of company punishments, such as flogging administered by brigade leaders, or economic penalties levied by chief factors. Admittedly, there is much to learn about more coventional criminal-law jurisdictions. For example, Foster, "Long-Distance Justice," *supra* note 38; and Foster, "Sins Against Great Spirit," *supra* note 38.

57. Which have been extensively published. For example, Glyndwr Williams, ed., *London Correspondence Inward from Sir George Simpson 1841-42* (London: Hudson's Bay Record Society, 1973); E.E. Rich, ed., *The Letters of John McLoughlin From Fort Vancouver to the Governor and Committee: First Series, 1825-38* (Toronto: The Champlain Society, 1941).

58. Lois Holliday McDonald, ed., *Fur Trade Letters of Francis Ermatinger: Written to his*

Brother Edward During his Service with the Hudson's Bay Company, 1818-1853 (Glendale, CA: Arthur H. Clark Co., 1980).

59. Some aspects of the legal behavior recorded in these diaries are discussed in John Phillip Reid, "The Beaver's Law in the Elephant's Country: An Excursion into Transboundary Legal History," *Western Legal History* 4 (1991): 149-201.

60. James Edward Fitzgerald, *An Examination of the Charter and Proceedings of the Hudson's Bay Company, with Reference to the Grant of Vancouver's Island* (London: Trelawney Saunders, 1849), 62-84 (on p. 78 the author mentions the "monstrous privileges to which it [Hudson's Bay Company] lays claim").

61. In contrast to the respect the Hudson's Bay Company paid to American and Russian territorial claims, its officers had scant regard for Spanish or Mexican claims. Governer George Simpson explained to the officers of the company in London: "[I]n regard to the Territorial rights of the Mexican Republic, we follow the example of the Spanish functionaries on the Coast, and our opponents [i.e. competition] from the United States, by making no enquiries about them." E.E. Rich, ed., *Part of Dispatch from George Simpson Esqr. Governor of Ruperts Land to the Governor & Committee of the Hudson's Bay Company London: March 1, 1829. Continued and Completed March 24 and June 5, 1829* (Toronto: The Champlain Society, 1947), 52.

62. When the justices of the peace in Rupert's Land and the far West were officers of the Hudson's Bay or the North West Company, committals of persons for trial in Lower Canada "were often made as a matter of company policy." See Brown, "Unpredictable and Uncertain," *supra* note 38, at 501. See also Katherine M. Bindon, "Hudson's Bay Company Law: Adam Thom and the Institution of Order in Rupert's Land 1839-54," in Flaherty, *Essays in the History of Canadian Law, supra* note 8, at 1: 43.

63. In Hudson's Bay vocabulary the term "Snake River" included the Great Salt Lake area, the region of the Humboldt River, and the Sacramento Valley, as well as the reaches of the Snake River.

64. As far as this observer has determined, the only comparable opportunity would be the law of an Indian nation.

65. *McGarrity v. Byington*, 12 California 426, 431 (1859).

66. *Attwood v. Fricot*, 17 California 38, 42 (1860).

67. *English v. Johnson*, 17 California 108, 115 (1860).

68. *Morton v. Solambo*, 26 California 527, 533 (1864).

69. *Merced Mining Co. v. Fremont*, 7 California 317, 326-27 (1857).

70. *St. John v. Kidd*, 26 California 263 (1864); *Gore v. McBrayer*, 18 California 583, 589 (1861); *Prosser v. Parks*, 18 California 47 (1861).

71. *Table Mountain Tunnel Co. v. Stranahan*, 20 California 198, 210-11 (1862).

72. *Harvey v. Ryan*, 42 California 626 (1872); John F. Davis, *Historical Sketch of the Mining Law in California* (Los Angeles: Commercial Printing House, 1902), 35.

73. So little attention was paid to the question that California judges sometimes implied that custom was not "law" even when they were enforcing it. Consider what Chief Justice Beatty meant by the word "law" when urging Congress to clarify the apex rule. "[W]hatever regulation is made," he asserted, "should be made by law and not by local and varying rules." Letter from W.H. Beatty, 21 November 1876, *House Executive Document* 46, 46th Congress, 2d Session, 399-400.

74. The complaint of British Columbia officials was not that miners insisted on their own rules, but that they refused to pay license fees. Letter from Chartres Brew to W.A.G. Young and letter from E. Howard Sanders to Chartres Brew, 30 April 1859, in Frederic

W. Howay, *The Early History of the Fraser River Mines* 117, 119 (Memoir No. VI, Archives of British Columbia, Victoria, 1926). It is wrong to say that American miners in British Columbia were dissatisfied with common law because miners' law allowed them to be governed by their own "common sense." Tina Loo, "The Grouse Creek 'War'," *The Beaver* 70, no. 4 (1990): 24, 32-33. Miners' law could be as technical and as rule-determined as common law. Consider the rule of abandonment. In 1850 on the Trinity River, an American and a Frenchman were partners working a placer claim. As the claim was becoming "constantly poorer," the American proposed to go on "a prospecting Tour" while the Frenchman protected their title to the claim by continuing to work it. The Frenchman provided the American with another, older Frenchman who delayed the American by getting lost, keeping him away over two days. When he arrived back the American found other Frenchmen working the claim. His partner "informed me that he had abandoned the Claim, as it would not pay, and the Frenchmen were then working it, the Mining Law permitting any Person to take possession of an abandoned Claim." The American "saw that I was the Victim of Treachery," but being unfamiliar with the law of equity or the defense of fraud, he thought himself bound by the rule of abandonment and surrendered his share of the claim. See Anne Paschall Hannum, ed., *A Quaker Forty-Niner: The Adventures of Charles Edward Pancoast on the American Frontier* (Philadelphia: University of Pennsylvania Press, 1930), 321-23. The distinction between abandonment and forfeiture was well understood, as was the term "claim jumping" which was a legal act, the physical testing of a forfeiture. See Gregory Yale, *Legal Titles of Mining Claims and Water Rights in California Under the Mining Law of Congress, of July, 1866* (San Francisco: A. Roman and Company, 1867), 66, 81.

75. Davis, *Historical Sketch, supra* note 72, at 19.

76. Rodman W. Paul, "'Old Californians' in British Gold Fields," *Huntington Library Quarterly* 17 (1954): 161, 162.

77. For example, Barry M. Gough, "Keeping British Columbia British: The Law-and-Order Question on a Gold Mining Frontier," *Huntington Library Quarterly* 38 (1975): 269, 278; Howay, *Early History, supra* note 74, at ix, xiii.

78. Hamar Foster, "Shooting the Elephant: Historians and the Problems of Frontier Lawlessness," in R. Eales, ed., *The Political Content of Law: Essays in Legal History* (London: Hambledon Press, 1987), 135, 136n.

79. *New York Times*, 5 April 1990, p. C20, col. 6.

80. Graham Parker, "Canadian Legal Culture," in Louis A. Knafla, ed., *Law and Justice in a New Land: Essays in Western Canadian Legal History* (Toronto: Carswell, 1986), 12.

81. Louis A. Knafla, "From Oral to Written Memory: The Common Law Tradition in Western Canada," in Knafla, ed., *Law and Justice, supra* note 80, at 31.

82. Loo, "Grouse Creek War," *supra* note 74, at 25.

83. Message from Richard Hicks to Governor James Douglas, 30 April 1859, Howay, *Early History, supra* note 74, at 18. Hicks was revenue officer and assistant commissioner of Crown lands. Judge Begbie charged that he, "threw men's minds and titles into discontent and confusion." Letter from Judge Matthew B. Begbie to Governor James Douglas, 3 February 1859, ibid., 39.

84. Letter from Judge Matthew B. Begbie to Governor James Douglas, 3 February 1859, ibid., 39.

85. Letter from Judge Matthew B. Begbie to Governor James Douglas, 18 January 1859, ibid., 29. The miners charged: "That the tyrannous conduct of P.B. Whannell, a

Magistrate in her Majesty's service, in arresting persons without cause, without issuing warrants, and for imprisoning persons merely to gratify his own caprice, and in refusing such persons an examination, as the law directs, and also for levying fines in violation of the Statutes, deserves the severest censure." Resolutions of a Miners' Meeting, Hill's Bar, January 1859, ibid., 30.

86. See documents in ibid., 73-75, and discussions, xiii. The commanding officer of the Royal Victoria Yeomanry Cavalry in Melbourne, Australia, wrote that the resident magistrate at the Yale mining camp in British Columbia was "an absconder and absent without leave." Letter from Jas. H. Ross to C. Standish, 9 May 1859, ibid., 59.

87. Letter from Judge Matthew B. Begbie to Governor James Douglas, 3 February 1859, ibid., 38.

88. The miners at one bar expected violence might be committed against them and "therefore resolved to anticipate violence with violence. It appeared to me that when their violence was reprehendable and punished as it was by me, they acquiesced all the more readliy and cheerfully in my decision because they received at the same time assurance that the same protection sho[ul]d be extended to them in case of need w[hi]ch was now exercised against them." Ibid., 39.

89. Morris Zaslow sees it differently:

> [T]wo diametrically opposite principles for the government of a pioneer environment confronted one another. The American philosophy, exemplified by the mining camps, was libertarian and laissez-faire, based on the matter of squatter sovereignty; the Canadian approach was authoritarian or colonial … it was the duty of the frontier to accept the regulations of the superior authority and the agents sent by the authority to administer the affairs of the region.

Morris Zaslow, "The Yukon: Northern Development in the Canadian American Context," in Mason Wade, ed., *Regionalism in the Canadian Community 1867-1967* (Toronto: University of Toronto Press, 1969), 185-86, quoted in Thomas Stone, "The Mounties as Vigilantes: Perceptions of Community and the Transformation of Law in the Yukon, 1885-1897," *Law & Society Review* 14 (1979): 83, 96.

90. Message from Richard Hicks to Governor James Douglas, 26 October 1858. Howay, *Early History, supra* note 74, at 9.

91. David Ricardo Williams, "The Administration of Criminal and Civil Justice in the Mining Camps and Frontier Communities of British Columbia," in Knafla, *Law and Justice, supra* note 80, at 215.

92. Ibid., 218

93. Many years after the Fraser River Rush, Sir Matthew, while on vacation at Salt Lake City, met one of his former jurymen. The man praised the chief justice saying, "You certainly did some hanging, Judge." Begbie answered: "Excuse me, my friend. I never hanged any man. I simply swore in good American citizens, like yourself, as jury-men, and it was you that hanged your own fellow-countrymen." A.E. Beck, "Sir Matthew Begbie: Terror of Lawbreakers of B.C. Fifty Years Ago," *British Columbia Historical Quarterly* 5 (1941): 131.

94. Williams, "Administration of Frontier Justice," *supra* note 91, at 231.

95. Knafla, "Oral to Written," *supra* note 81, at 62.

96. Ibid., 44.

97. "This vigilante [California] system of [mining] camp criminal justice filled a vacuum. No government body existed to control crime; instead, citizens filled the breach. The

phenomenon was wrongly viewed in British Columbia as a form of anarchy — 'lynch law.' One reads constantly in the reports of colonial officials in British Columbia of their worry that vigilantism would come to British Columbia, by which they meant that chaos would prevail." Williams, "Administration of Frontier Justice," *supra* note 91, at 219.

98. "Criminal law ... was British, not American. But because of its resolute application, colonial law-enforcement officials and the judiciary had an unexpectedly easy time of imposing British justice. The American miners were, in fact, compliant, always a surprise to colonial officials." Ibid., 231.

99. Stone, "Mounties as Vigilantes," *supra* note 89, at 98.

100. Ibid., 101.

101. Hamar Foster, "Shooting the Elephant: Historians and the Problem of Frontier Lawlessness," in Richard Eaves and David Sullivan, eds., *The Political Context of Law: Proceedings of the Seventh British Legal History Conference Canterbury 1985* (London: Hambleton Press, 1987), 142-43. We must be on guard not to carry the dichotomy between American law and British order too far. The British Columbia colonial secretary once wrote of an American camp on the Fraser where "'lynch law' had been established and rules framed." This reference to "lynch law," Williams asserts, "expressed an attitude typical of colonial officials: because camp law was informal it was therefore dangerous. He failed to appreciate as we now can, that precisely the opposite was the case. It was not anarchy but order." See Williams, "Administration of Frontier Justice," *supra* note 91, at 221-22.

102. One, peculiar to American history, the law of the territories, seems less interesting than it was once thought to be. The idea was "that, following separate studies of the original colonies, a study of the laws and legal institutions of the territories as a group will serve to provide and be indicative of the feasibility of a unified approach to legal developments west of the original states." *Michigan Law Review* 61 (1962): 39 (discussing the theories of William Wirt Blume), quoted in Nelson and Reid, *Literature of Legal History, supra* note 1, at 47. The territories are, however, a subject of study too much neglected. "I think it's a great shame that probably 99 percent of the people who train in legal history or call themselves legal historians probably don't read Earl Pomeroy on the territories — or Howard Lamar or Paul Gates, or others who have written on the territorial and early state phases. Names like Philbrick are as little known, I am sure, as the commentators on Hammurabi are to most American legal historians." Harry N. Scheiber, "Western Legal History: Where Are We And Where Do We Go From Here," *Western Legal History* 3 (1990): 127, 128.

103. For the United States, a minor example might be community property, and in both nations there is the matter of Chinese immigration.

104. Donald J. Pisani, *The Fragmented West: Water, Law, and Public Policy, 1848-1902* (Albuquerque: University of New Mexico Press, forthcoming); Donald J. Pisani, "Enterprise and Equity: A Critique of Western Water Law in the Nineteenth Century," *Western Historical Quarterly* 18 (1987): 15-37. For treatment of a very special aspect of western water law, see Michael C. Myers, *Water in the Hispanic Southwest: A Social and Legal History, 1550-1850* (Tucson: University of Arizona Press, 1984).

105. Although many of the studies produced so far do not handle law well. See Fay G. Cohen, *Treaties on Trial: The Continuing Controversy over Northwest Indian Fishing Rights* (Seattle: University of Washington Press, 1986); Daniel Raunet, *Without Surrender, Without Consent: A History of the Nishga Land Claims* (Vancouver: Douglas and McIntyre, 1984).

106. Schuh, "Northern Frontier," *supra* note 38, at 74-111.

107. There is also the vast topic of land law, much of which has been considered, especially in the writings of Paul W. Gates. True, when we think of the history of land in the West, or, at least, in the westward movement, we think of scandals. For example, D.N. Sprague, "Government Lawlessness in the Administration of Manitoba Land Claims, 1870-1887," *Manitoba Law Journal* 10 (1980): 415-41; Roy M. Robbins, *Our Landed Heritage: The Public Domain 1776-1936* (Princeton, NJ: Princeton University Press, 1942), 236-84. There is, however, much that is positive to be told. Consider that when settlers first came to North America, many were concerned about security of title and there was even reluctance to work without some proof on record. So intense was this "peasants' psychosis" that it is believed by some historians to be a factor in the invention of recording in Massachusetts Bay. See George Lee Haskins, "The Beginnings of the Recording System in Massachusetts," *Boston University Law Review* 21 (1941): 281-304. Something fundamental occurred by the nineteeth century. Settlers moving west seemed confident they would enjoy quiet title. A striking instance is the Oregon country. Americans and Canadians, as well as gentlemen and servants of the Hudson's Bay Company, improved claims apparently confident of secured title even though it was not known under which nation, the United States or Great Britain, security would be established.

108. William Cronon, *Changes in the Land: Indians, Colonists, and the Ecology of New England* (New York: Hill and Wang, 1983).

109. Arthur F. McEvoy, *The Fisherman's Problem: Ecology and Law in the California Fisheries, 1850-1980* (New York: Cambridge University Press, 1986).

110. It is unfair to Cronon to compare his book to McEvoy's as he was not writing about law. The premise that he could not answer questions about colonial Indian law to the same degree that McEvoy could answer questions about nineteeth-century native law in California is based on the writer's own experience researching the law of the eighteeth-century Cherokees. However, Cronon did spend time researching *Changes in the Land* in Yale's law library (*supra* note 108, at ix), he made an extensive examination of the colonial law of property (ibid., 233-34), and the book contains enough law, that for the last several years it has been read by law students in an American legal-history seminar at New York University.

111. Aided, of course, by more studies of aboriginal law than can be found of the eastern nations, as for example, one that McEvoy cites — see Alfred L. Kroeber, "Law of the Yurok Indians," *Proceedings of the Twenty-Second International Congress of Americanists* 5 (Part 2, 1926): 511-16.

112. David Grayson Allen, *In English Ways: The Movement of Societies and the Transferal of English Local Law and Custom to Massachusetts in the Seventeenth Century* (Chapel Hill: University of North Carolina Press, 1981).

113. Whereas the only comparable study considered the institutional and legal origins of a single Massachusetts town. Sumner Powell, *Puritan Village: The Formation of a New England Town* (Middletown, CT: Wesleyan University Press, 1963). For citations of other discussions of an early colonial or "transferred" legal culture, and for a discussion of how these studies might relate to western legal history, see Reid, "Some Lessons of Western Legal History," *supra* note 30, at 6-9.

114. Newspapers, court records, and private correspondence are other obvious sources. Indicative of private diaries as a source of western history are the more personal and extensive histories that characterize studies of women in the West. For example, Ruth B. Moynihan, Susan Armitage, and Christiane Fischer Dichamp, eds., *So Much to be Done: Women Settlers on the Mining and Ranching Frontier* (Lincoln: University of Nebraska Press, 1990); Glenda Riley, *The Female Frontier: A Comparative View of Women*

on the Prairie and the Plains (Lawrence: University Press of Kansas, 1988); Cathy Luchetti, *Women of the West* (St. George, UT: Antelope Island Press, 1982); Elizabeth Hampsten, *Read This Only to Yourself: The Private Writings of Midwestern Women, 1880-1910* (Bloomington: Indiana University Press, 1982); Joanna L. Stratton, *Pioneer Women: Voices from the Kansas Frontier* (New York: Simon and Schuster, 1981); Julie Roy Jeffrey, *Frontier Women: The Trans-Mississippi West* (New York: Hill and Wang, 1979).

115. It would appear, from looking at a single source, that Canadian conclusions would not be so much different from conclusions drawn from American sources. Canadian overlanders, like those on the Oregon trail, argued over whether to travel on Sunday, celebrated the Queen's birthday as Americans celebrated the Fourth of July, held elections, voted on rules and regulations, looked forward to arriving at the fur posts, and went in search of gold. See Mark Sweeten Wade, *The Overlanders of '62*, ed. John Hosie (Victoria, B.C.: C.F. Banfield, 1931).

116. Diary entry for 19 November 1849, quoted in John Phillip Reid, "Paying for the Elephant: Property Rights and Civil Order on the Overland Trail," *Huntington Library Quarterly* 41 (1978): 37, 55.

117. For an account of the suffering of 1850 along the Humboldt and its lessons about the legal culture of nineteenth-century Americans, see John Phillip Reid, *Law for the Elephant: Property and Social Behavior on the Overland Trail* (San Marino, CA: Huntington Library, 1980), 228-49.

118. Entries for 2, 3, 4, 7 July 1850, Mendall Jewett, Journal to and from California of Dr. Mendall Jewett (transcript, Denver Public Library).

119. Langum, *Law and Community, supra* note 28, at 267.

120. Ibid., 89, 92, 94.

121. Ibid., 273.

122. Ibid., 140.

123. The concept of a shared legal culture in the West may have wider implications for general legal history. It may help us test some of the unsubstantiated themes recently put forward by a new school of legal historians — such as the argument that rules of property were imposed upon the people of nineteenth-century America by an elitist legal profession serving the greed of a corporate managerial class. When Margaret Ogilvie claimed that "[w]hatever the topic, it may be tritely remarked that we are all Horwitzians now," she must have been speaking for Canadian legal historians only. In the United States, much of the work of this school is received more as poetry than as history, like a bad limerick that does not rhyme. Ogilvie, "Recent Developments," *supra* note 9, at 232. For similar Canadian enchantment with this school see Risk, "Law and the Economy," *supra* note 12, at 118-22; Barry Wright, "An Introduction to Canadian Law in History"; Susan Binnie, "Some Reflections on the 'New' Legal History in Relation to Weber's Sociology of Law," in W. Wesley Pue and Barry Wright, eds., *Canadian Perspectives on Law and Society: Issues in Legal History* (Ottawa: Carleton University Press, 1988), 7-19, 29-42; D.G. Bell, "The Birth of Canadian Legal History," *University of New Brunswick Law Journal/Revue de droit de l'Université du Nouveau-Brunswick* 33 (1984): 312, 313, 318.

124. John Umbeck, *A Theory of Property Rights: With Application to the California Gold Rush* (Ames: Iowa State University Press, 1981).

125. John Umbeck, "A Theory of Contract Choice and the California Gold Rush," *Journal of Law and Economics* 20 (1977): 421, 429.

126. Umbeck, *Theory of Property Rights, supra* note 124, at 70.

127. Ibid., 5.

128. Ibid., 100.

129. Ibid., 101-02.

130. Ibid., 100. As a result, the size of a mining claim and its value were inversely related. The reason was that any small claim decreed by a district had to have a large enough value so that the majority of the mining population would agree to that size and not resort to violence. Of course, the small size would never have been decreed unless a majority agreed as all districts were ruled by majority vote.

131. For a related but much more defendable economic-origins argument, see Gary D. Libecap, "Economic Variables and the Development of the Law: The Case of Western Mineral Rights," *Journal of Economic History* 38 (1978): 338-62.

132. Reid, *Law for the Elephant, supra* note 117, at 129.

133. Henry Drummond Dee, "An Irishman in the Fur Trade: The Life and Journals of John Work," *British Columbia Historical Quarterly* 7 (1943): 229, 231. Work's journals are also discussed by Ray M. Reeder, "John Work," in LeRoy R. Hafen, ed., *The Mountain Men and the Fur Trade of the Far West: Biographical Sketches of the Participants by Scholars of the Subject and With Introduction by the Editor*, vol. 2 (Glendale, CA: Arthur H. Clark Co., 1965).

134. London paternalism and St. Louis individualism gathered each its own fruits. The territory of the Hudson's Bay Company, inhabited by a numerous and diverse Indian population, was an area of peace and order. Throughout its length and breadth the Company's transportation service was maintained, without interruption, by boat crews barely large enough for the requirements of the portage; the murder of a white trader was an event that was infrequent and that was visited when it occurred with prompt punishment; and even intertribal wars yielded at times to the intervention of the Company's officers. On the American side of the line, violence and murder were the order of the day.

Frederick Merk, "Introduction to the Revised Edition: The Strategy of Monopoly" and "Introduction to the First Edition," in Merk, ed., *Fur Trade and Empire: George Simpson's Journal Entitled Remarks Connected with the Fur Trade in the Course of a Voyage from York Factory to Fort George and Back to York Factory 1824-1825* (1931; Cambridge, MA: Harvard University Press, 1968), lix. "Where true monopoly existed in the North ... the chief factors of the Hudson's Bay Company, who had no need to try to beat out anyone, became arms of the government, responsible for the administration of justice." David Lavender, "Some American Characteristics of the American Fur Company," *Minnesota History* 40 (1966): 178, 186.

135. For example, Thomas McKay of Hudson's Bay was in an American camp when he spotted a Blackfoot crouching outside. He sprang on his horse and went after the Indian. It was some time before the Americans, fearful he had ridden into a trap, caught up with McKay. "He was in an excessively bad humor, and grumbled audibly about the 'Blackfoot rascal getting off in that cowardly fashion,' without at all heeding the congratulations I was showering on him for his almost miraculous escape. He was evidently not aware of having been peculiarly exposed, and was regretting, like the hunter who loses his game by a sudden shift of wind, that his human prey had escaped him." Entry for 11 July 1834, John K. Townsend, *Narrative of a Journey Across the Rocky Mountains to the Columbia River, and a Visit to the Sandwich Islands, Chili, &c.* (1839), reprinted in Reuben Gold Thwaites, ed., *Early Western Travels 1748-1846* (Cleveland, OH: Arthur H. Clark Co., 1905), 207-08.

136. Entry for 12 September 1828, Archibald McDonald, *Peace River. A Canoe Voyage from*

Hudson's Bay to Pacific, by the late Sir George Simpson, in 1828, ed. Malcolm McLeod (Ottawa: J. Durie & Son, 1872), 21. The case is not well reported, a fact worth noting as the editor was a barrister. Interested in scenes of travel, he ignores the opportunities available to discuss law, in that respect much like the American historian Grant Foreman and the anthropologist James Mooney, both lawyers who ignored even greater opportunities. In some ways McLeod is worse, as he poked fun at the case, treating it so lightly as to destroy the record by reciting poetry and attempting humor.

137. Entry for 12 December 1825, "The Peter Skene Ogden Journals," ed. T.C. Elliott, *Quarterly of the Oregon Historical Society* 10 (1909): 331, 342. The Vancouver referred to was Fort Vancouver on the Columbia.

138. Entry for 7 January 1826, ibid., 347-48

139. Entry for 5 February 1826, ibid., 352.

140. Entry for 27 September 1830, Francis D. Haines, ed., *The Snake Country Expedition of 1830-1831: John Work's Field Journal* (Norman: University of Oklahoma Press, 1971), 24.

141. Letter from Robert Campbell to Hugh Campbell, 18-19 July 1832, in Charles Eberstadt, ed., *The Rocky Mountain Letters of Robert Campbell* (New Haven, CT: Beinecke Library, 1955), 8-9.

142. It was the duty of the junior officer to accompany the men. Dee, "Irishman in the Fur Trade," *supra* note 133, at 238.

143. Entries for 8, 9, 10, 11 September 1828, "Alex R. McLeod's Journal Southern Expedition," in Maurice S. Sullivan, ed., *The Travels of Jedediah Smith: A Documentary Outline Including The Journal of the Great American Pathfinder* (Santa Ana, CA: Fine Arts Press, 1934), 113-14. Starting on a trapping expedition, John Work left Fort Vancouver to meet his men at the lower sawmill "where they were sent a few days ago to drink the regale. Some of the men being in liquor I deferred starting till tomorrow." Entry for 18 August 1831, William S. Lewis and Paul C. Phillips, eds., *The Journal of John Work: A Chief-Trader of the Hudson's Bay Co. during his Expedition from Vancouver to the Flatheads and Blackfeet of the Pacific Northwest* (Cleveland, OH: Arthur H. Clark Co., 1923), 71.

144. At the start of another avenging expedition — to avenge the killing of Alexander McKenzie and four other men — it was said: "In the evening the men received a *regale* and the Iroquois went through a war dance, in character, before the Hall Door." Entry for 16 June 1828, Journal of Frank Ermatinger, in McDonald, *Letters of Ermatinger, supra* note 58, at 98.

145. William S. Lewis and Paul C. Phillips, "Introduction and Notes" to *Journal of John Work, supra* note 143, at 71 n146.

146. For example, John Dunn, *History of the Oregon Territory and British North-American Fur Trade; with an Account of the Habits and Customs of the Principal Native Tribes on the Northern Continent* (1844; London: Edwards and Hughes, 1846), 154.

147. Merrill J. Mattes, *The Great Platte River Road: The Covered Wagon Mainline Via Fort Kearny To Fort Laramie* (Lincoln: Nebraska State Historical Society, 1969), 482 (quotation attributed to Samuel Parker, July 1835).

148. Entry for 27 July 1835, Samuel Parker, *Journal of an Exploring Tour Beyond the Rocky Mountains, Under the Direction of the A.B.C.F.M. Performed in the Years 1835, '36, and '37* (1838; Minneapolis, MN: Ross and Haines, 1967), 66.

149. By a trapper in the employ of Robert Campbell and the Rocky Mountain Fur Company, June 1833. Charles Larpenteur, *Forty Years a Fur Trader on the Upper Missouri: The Personal Narrative of Charles Larpenteur 1833-1872,* ed. Milo Milton Quaife (Chicago: Lakeside Press, 1933), 25. In 1841 it was described by Rufus B. Sage as "a grand

jollification to all hands ... who soon got most gloriously drunk." Mattes, *Great Platte River Road, supra* note 147, at 483.

150. Entry for 2 January 1801, David W. Harmon, *A Journal of Voyages and Travels in the interior of North America between the 47th and 58th degree of North Latitude, extending from Montreal to the Pacific Ocean, a Distance of about 5000 miles, including an Account of the Principal Occurrence during a Residence of Nearly Nineteen Years in Different Parts of that Country*, ed. Daniel Haskel (New York: Allerton Book Co., 1905), 39.

151. Warren Angus Ferris, *Life in the Rocky Mountains 1830-1835*, ed. Herbert S. Auerbach (Salt Lake City: Rocky Mountain Book Shop, 1940), 153. New Year's Day was marked from the very start of the American fur-trade era on the Missouri. "[A]t Sunset saluted the exile year, the Boys had Whisky and a Dance, all Cares and troubles were forgotten and drowned in oblivity and so concluded again a year with, I may say, a cheerful night." Entry for 31 December 1812, John C. Luttig, *Journal of a Fur-Trading Expedition on the Upper Missouri 1812-1813*, ed. Stella M. Drumm (New York: Argosy-Antiquarian, 1964), 109.

152. "[T]his being a holaday [*sic*] ... We lay by all day." Entry for 1 January 1822, Elliott Coues, ed., *The Journal of Jacob Fowler Narrating an Adventure from Arkansas through the Indian Territory, Oklahoma, Kansas, Colorado, and New Mexico, to the Sources of Rio Grande Del Norte, 1821-22* (New York: Francis P. Harper, 1898), 73.

153. *Adventures of Zenas Leonard Fur Trader* 5 (1839; Clearfield, PA: D.W. Moore, Readex Microprint Edition, 1966).

154. Even Wilson Hunt, leading the overland Astorians on that memorable first journey to the Pacific by an American fur brigade, halted for the day. "My people asked me not to travel on the 1st of January without first celebrating the new year." Entry for 1 January 1812, Hoyt C. Franchère, ed., *The Overland Diary of Wilson Price Hunt* (Ashland, OR: Oregon Book Society, 1973), 52. "[T]he day passed away amidst singing and dancing and feasting most sumptuously upon dogs and horse flesh." D[aniel] Lee and J.H. Frost, *Ten Years in Oregon* (New York: n.p., 1844), 37.

155. For example, at Astoria, see Gabriel Franchère, *Journal of a Voyage on the North West Coast of North America during the Years 1811, 1812, 1813 and 1814*, ed. W.K. Lamb (Toronto: Champlain Society, 1969), 107. On an expedition: Entry for 25 December 1825, E.E. Rich and A.M. Johnson, eds., *Peter Skene Ogden's Snake Country Journals 1824-25 and 1825-26* (London: Hudson's Bay Record Society, 1950), 108; Entry for 25 December 1826, K.G. Davies and A.M. Johnson, eds., *Peter Skene Ogden's Snake Country Journal 1826-27* (London: Hudson's Bay Record Society, 1961), 45; at a Hudson's Bay post: Entry for 25 December 1834, "Journal of Occurrences at Nisqually House, 1833-1835," ed. Clarence B. Bagley, *Washington Historical Quarterly* 7 (1916): 144, 153.

156. Entry for 3 April 1831, Haines, *Snake Country Expedition, supra* note 140, at 90.

157. Entry for 1 November 1830, ibid., 41; Entry for 1 November 1832, Alice Bay Maloney, ed., *Fur Brigade to the Benaventura: John Work's California Expedition 1832-1833 for the Hudson's Bay Company* (San Francisco: California Historical Society, 1945), 13.

158. Entry for 25 December 1801, Harmon, *Journal of Voyages*, 57. "This being the first day of the year, in the morning, I gave the people a *dram* or two, and a pint of rum each, to drink in the course of the day, which enabled them to pass it merrily, although they had very little to eat." Entry for 1 January 1802, ibid., 58.

159. Entry for 1 January 1835, "Journal of Nisqually House," *supra* note 155, at 154.

160. Entry for 1 January 1825, T.C. Elliott, ed., "Journal of Alexander Ross — Snake Country Expedition, 1824," *Quarterly of the Oregon Historical Society* 14 (1913): 366, 388. 1825 was an exception: "The day passed away in feasting and quietness for they had no liquor to

make them troublesome." Entry for 1 January 1825, William Kittson, *Journal of Occurrences in a Trapping Expedition To and From the Snake Country in the Year 1824 and (25) Kept by William Kittson*, printed in "Appendix A" to Rich and Johnson, *Ogden's Snake Country Journals, supra* note 155, at 211.

161. Entry for 1 January 1826, Rich and Johnson, *Ogden's Snake Country Journals, supra* note 155, at 110.

162. Entry for 31 December 1826, Davies and Johnson, *Ogden's Snake Country Journal, supra* note 155, at 49.

163. Entry for 1 January 1831, Haines, *Snake Country Expedition, supra* note 140, at 62.

164. Entry for 1 January 1832, Lewis and Phillips, *Journal of John Work, supra* note 143, at 119.

165. Entry for 1 January 1833, Maloney, *Fur Brigade, supra* note 157, at 24. At Astoria, the first American post on the Columbia, the first New Year's Day there was issued "a small ration of liquor to the men." Entry for 1 January 1812, Franchère, *Journal of Voyage, supra* note 155, at 108. And at the first American post on the upper Missouri, Fort Manuel, "the Boys had a treat of Whisky." Entry for 24 December 1812, Luttig, *Journal of a Fur-Trading Expedition, supra* note 151, at 108.

166. Alexander Ross, *The Fur Hunters of the Far West: A Narrative of Adventures in the Oregon and the Rocky Mountains*, vol. 1 (London: Smith, Elder and Co., 1855), 291. It is a definition much like Maitland's definition of equity: "Equity now is that body of rules administered by our English courts of justice which, were it not for the operation of the Judicature Acts, would be administered only by those courts which would be known as Courts of Equity." F.W. Maitland, *Equity also The Forms of Action at Common Law: Two Courses of Lectures*, eds. A.H. Chaytor and W.J. Whittaker (Cambridge, U.K.: Cambridge University Press, 1936), 1.

167. Dunn, *History of the Oregon Territory, supra* note 146, at 49, 154.

168. Malcolm McLeod, "Notes" to McDonald, *Peace River, supra* note 136, at 54.

169. Kate Ball Power, Flora Ball Hopkins, and Lucy Ball, eds., *Autobiography of John Ball* (Grand Rapids, MI: Dean-Hicks Company, 1925), 79. A historian has said that Etienne Provost "was virtually a free trapper, receiving his outfit from [William H.] Ashley, to whom he was under the obligation of disposing of his furs." Harrison Clifford Dale, *The Ashley-Smith Explorations and the Discovery of a Central Route to the Pacific 1822-1829* (Cleveland, OH: Arthur H. Clark Co., 1918), 93. This statement is omitted from the revised edition of 1941.

170. Trudy Nicks, "The Iroquois and the Fur Trade in Western Canada," in Carol M. Judd and Arthur J. Ray, eds., *Old Trails and New Directions: Papers of the Third North American Fur Trade Conference* (Toronto: University of Toronto Press, 1980), 85, 91-92.

171. "These freemen may be considered a kind of enlightened Indians, with all their faults, but none of their good qualities." Ross, *Fur Hunters, supra* note 166, at 1: 291-92.

172. "There cannot be a better test for knowing a worthless and bad character in this country than his wishing to become a freeman — it is the true sign of depravity." Ibid., 292-93. Sir George Simpson described the freemen as a "worthless and motley crew ... the very scum of the country and generally outcasts from the Service for misconduct are the most unruly and troublesome gang to deal with in this or perhaps any other part of the World, are under no control & feel their own independence they therefore require very superior management to make any thing of them." David E. Miller, "Introduction" to "Peter Skene Ogden's Journal of his Expedition to Utah, 1825," ed. Miller, *Utah Historical Quarterly* 20 (1952): 159, 161-62.

173. When three freemen asked Ogden not to raise camp as their horses were far in the rear,

he agreed "for many reasons and most particularly being in an unknown Country I do not consider it safe to leave any one too far in the rear." Entry for 13 December 1826, Davies and Johnson, *Ogden's Snake Country Journal, supra* note 155, at 40-41.

174. A judgment based on experience and on the fact that Canadians were not up to the standards of English or Americans, and certainly not up to Scots. Giving six men permission to trap ahead of the main camp, Ogden urged them to take every precaution. "They promise fair, but Canadians always do so till fairly off, when they soon become negligent, disagree, separate, and nine times in ten lose their horses." Entry for 27 October 1827, Peter Skene Ogden, *Snake Country Journal 1827-1828*, in Glyndwr Williams, ed., *Peter Skene Ogden's Snake Country Journals 1827-28 and 1828-29* (London: Hudson's Bay Record Society, 1971), 19.

175. Thus the factors of the North West Company's Fort Chipewyan asked the manager of Hudson's Bay's Fort Wedderburn to return two "engaged servants" who "recently deserted their service." Letter from George Keith and Simon McGillivray to George Simpson, 5 January 1821, in E.E. Rich, ed., *Journal of Occurrences in the Athabasca Department by George Simpson, 1820 and 1821, and Report* (Toronto: The Champlain Society, 1938), 209. See also Letter from George Simpson to George Keith and Simon McGillivray, 5 January 1821, ibid., 209-10; Entries for 8 and 9 January 1821, ibid., 212-13; Nicks, "Iroquois and Fur Trade," *supra* note 170, at 92.

176. As in the case of the North West Company and Hudson's Bay (note 175), when a man "deserted" from an American Fur Company's outpost on the Big Horn, the bookkeeper at Fort Union wrote to Robert Campbell, requesting that the man be sent back. "I wrote him an answer stating that the man arrived and applied to me for employment but I declined not knowing his engagements to the Am fur Co and that the man would go up [i.e., return]." Entries for 26 and 28 September 1833, "The Private Journal of Robert Campbell," ed. George R. Brooks, *Bulletin Missouri Historical Society* 20 (1963): 3, 7-8.

177. For example, "Across the Continent Seventy Years Ago: Extracts from the Journal of John Ball of his trip across the Rocky Mountains and his life in Oregon, compiled by his daughter," *Quarterly Oregon Historical Society* 3 (1902): 82, 87.

178. David J. Weber, *The Californios versus Jedediah Smith 1826-1827: A New Cache of Documents* (Spokane, WA: Arthur H. Clark Co., 1990), 23 n29; Harvey L. Carter, "Ewing Young," in Hafen, *Mountain Men and Fur Trade, supra* note 133, at 387. In fact, the behavior of American leaders and men was often indistinguishable from that of Hudson's Bay people:

> For the space of several days past, we have observed an inclination in five or six of our men to leave our service. Immediately as we encamp, we see them draw together in some secluded spot, and engage in close and earnest conversation. This has occurred several times, and as we are determine ... to keep our horses ... we have stationed a sentry near their tent. ... The men we are willing to lose ... but horses here are valuable.

Entry for 21 May 1834, Townsend, *Narrative of a Journey, supra* note 135, at 162.

179. Letter from Nathaniel J. Wyeth to Friend Weld, 3 April 1835, and entries for 10-18 November 1834, in F.G. Young, ed., *The Correspondence and Journals of Nathaniel J. Wyeth 1831-6* (Eugene, OR: University Press, 1899), 148-49, 235; Entry for 23 November 1834, Townsend, *Narrative of a Journey, supra* note 135, at 308; Dale L. Morgan and Eleanor Towles Harris, "A Galaxy of Mountain Men: Biographical Sketches," in Dale L. Morgan and Eleandor Towles Harris, eds., *The Rocky Mountain Journals of William Marshall Anderson: The West in 1834* (San Marino, CA: Huntington Library, 1967), 278.

180. Entries for 21 and 23 August 1832, Journal of Fort Pierre, quoted in Hiram Martin

Chittenden, *The American Fur Trade of the Far West: A History of Pioneer Trading Posts & Early Fur Companies of the Missouri Valley & Rocky Mountains & of the Overland Commerce with Santa Fe*, ed. Stallo Vinton, 2 vols. (New York: Press of the Pioneers, Inc., 1935), 955; Morgan and Harris, *Rocky Mountain Journals, supra* note 179, at 270.

181. See the remarkable comments, François Antoine Larocque, "Yellowstone Journal," reprinted in W. Raymond Wood and Thomas D. Thiessen, eds., *Early Fur Trade on the Northern Plains: Canadian Traders Among the Mandan and Hidatsa Indians, 1738-1818 — The Narratives of John Macdowell, David Thompson, François-Antoine Larocque, and Charles McKenzie* (Norman: University of Oklahoma Press, 1985), 209-10 (see also Entry for 31 July 1805, p. 179); "Charles McKenzie's Narratives," ibid., 259, 290-91; Harmon, *Journal of Voyages, supra* note 150, at 253-57.

182. "Journal of Jean Baptiste Trudeau Among the Arikara Indians in 1795," translated by Mrs. H.T. Beauregard, *Missouri Historical Society Collections* 4 (1912): 9, 29.

183. Alexander Ross, *Adventures of the First Settlers on the Oregon or Columbia River: Being a Narrative of the Expediton Fitted out by John Jacob Astor, to Establish the "Pacific Fur Company;" With an Account of some Indian Tribes on the Coast of the Pacific* (London: Smith, Elder and Co., 1849), 327-28.

184. Entry for 7 August 1812, Luttig, *Journal of a Fur-Trading Expedition, supra* note 151, at 66-67.

185. A Hudson's Bay Company officer wrote of the Carrier nation: "A very common custom, prevailing among the Females, is when in a fit of despondency arising from Jealously — improper treatment &c. — is to commit Suicide by hanging themselves to a Tree — they have occurred frequently within our Knowledge." Report of Joseph McGillivray, 1827, printed in Rich, *Part of Dispatch, supra* note 61, at 207.

186. Entries for 13 and 14 February 1827, Alexander Roderick McLeod, *Journal of a hunting Expedition to the Southward of the Umpqua under the command of A.R. McLeod C.T. September 1826*, in Davies and Johnson, *Ogden's Snake Country Journal, supra* note 155, at 214-15. Even today, it would seem, some historians look at such events in terms of one law, instead of in the context of the multicultural legal world in which they occurred. It is not correct, for example, to analyze as ingratitude the death of a trapper who was killed after an Indian died who had been given medical aid by that trapper. Lewis O. Saum, *The Fur Trader and the Indian* (Seattle: University of Washington Press, 1965), 141-42.

187. When a Cree asked Daniel Harmon at the North West Company's Alexandria post to accept his daughter, Harmon realized that "while I had the daughter, I should not only have the father's furs, but those of all his band." Entry for 11 August 1802, Harmon, *Journal of a Fur-Trading Expedition, supra* note 150, at 70.

188. Letter from George Simpson to Robert McVicar, 26 January 1821, Rich, *Journal of Occurrences, supra* note 175, at 244-45.

189. Sylvia Van Kirk, *Many Tender Ties: Women in Fur-Trade Society 1670-1870* (Norman: University of Oklahoma Press, 1983), 4.

190. "The vigilance of these women has often been instrumental to the safety of the forts, when the most diabolical combinations were set on foot by the natives." Ross, *Fur Hunters, supra* note 166, at 296.

191. Sylvia Van Kirk, "Fur Trade Social History: Some Recent Trends," in Judd and Ray, eds., *Old Trails and New Directions, supra* note 170, at 165. Later, Van Kirk made the point more circumspectly, saying that "through marriage the trader was drawn into the Indian's kinship circle." Van Kirk, *Many Tender Ties*, 29.

192. Peter Ogden, for example, tried to be helpful by writing a book on Indian customs, but

he always has fathers feeling shame should their daughters stray from the path of marriage virtue, and mothers handing a weapon to their eldest son and saying, "Go, my son, go, and revenge your father, whose death the foul machinations of others have occasioned." [Peter Skene Ogden,] *Traits of American-Indian Life and Character* (London: Smith, Elder and Co., 1853), 184, 191. There were societies where these events could have happened, but in a matrilineal nation would it be the father or the mother's brother who was shamed, and would the mother or the son have the right or duty to avenge the father?

193. The experiences of James P. Beckwourth are not helpful. He married Crows, but as he was assumed to be the long-lost son of a Crow, he belonged to a clan. The picture, however, is confused, as it was his "father" who arranged his marriage and he did so by negotiating with the "father" of the woman. Delmont R. Oswald, ed., *The Life and Adventures of James P. Beckwourth as told to Thomas D. Bonner* (Lincoln: University of Nebraska Press, 1972), 145-50. When he and another man adopted one another, Beckworth does note that the relationship barred his new "brother" from marrying into the family, but that assertion is so vague it could mean anything. Ibid., 156. Just how Edward Rose, another famous mountain man, established Crow kinships through his several marriages with Crow women is not asked by his biographer. Willis Blenkinsop, "Edward Rose," in Hafen, *Mountain Men and Fur Trade, supra* note 133, at 9: 335-45.

194. There are many more questions. One would be just how much being married helped a mountain man to promote trade in nations where marriage was generally a temporary alliance. Another would be the legal risk when drawn into a kinship system. George Simpson observed: "It is a lamentable fact that almost every difficulty we have had with Indians throughout the Country may be traced to our interference with their Women or their intrigues with the Women of the Forts ... in short 9 Murders out of 10 Committed on Whites by Indians have arisen through Women." Entry for 26 March 1825, in Merk, ed., *Fur Trade and Empire, supra* note 134, at 127.

Law and Order on the American Frontier: The Western Civil War of Incorporation

Richard Maxwell Brown

Underlying a great deal of the violence and disorder in the frontier West was a particular pattern of conflict. At its core was the conservative, consolidating authority of capital — the commercial, industrial and financial forces that were in Alan Trachtenberg's conception "incorporating" America during the late nineteenth century.[1] In the West this process of incorporation was well underway by 1870. Yet, there were opposing factions and individuals who fought the incorporating trend politically and sometimes violently. The violent resistance to incorporation has recently been traced by scholars: by David Thelen, who traces the "paths of resistance" in industrializing and urbanizing Missouri of the post-Civil War period;[2] by Altina Waller, depicting insurgent feudists of West Virginia and Kentucky in the context of southern Appalachian conditions that resembled those of the West;[3] and by Robert McMath highlighting guerrilla-like resistance in Texas in what Hahn and Prude call "the age of capitalist transformation."[4]

In the West as a whole the incorporation trend resulted in what was really a civil war across the entire region — one fought in many places and on many fronts in almost all of the western territories and states from the 1850s until 1920. This was the "Western Civil War of Incorporation."[5] The campaigns and battles of the Western Civil War of Incorporation were sometimes launched by the aggressive, power-grabbing forces of incorporation and were sometimes initiated by the dissidents who resisted the process of incorporation. This great conflict was not always violent; far more often the incorporating forces carried out their campaigns for the economic and cultural conquest of the West in legislative halls and judicial chambers where they were often opposed. Lawyers and judges were among those at the center of this conflict in both its peaceful and violent phases.

A jurisprudential crucible in the Western Civil War of Incorporation was the San Francisco courtroom of the United States Circuit Court for the Ninth Circuit. A key member of the Ninth Circuit Court was Associate Justice Stephen J. Field of the United States Supreme Court, who periodically returned to his California home to sit on the bench for sessions of the Ninth Circuit Court.[6] Indeed, Field headed a potent clique of Pacific Coast federal circuit and district court judges that included Lorenzo Sawyer of California and Matthew P. Deady of Oregon. For the conservative forces, the issue in the Western Civil War of Incorporation was to bring law and order in its most essential form to the frontier West. This included the law in its technical form of statutes, judicial decisions and legal processes. Yet these legal technicalities were of the greatest importance, and in this sense the judicial clique of Stephen J. Field was a powerful bloc on the conservative side in the Western Civil War of Incorporation.

There is space only to discuss the major characteristics and one particular example of the Western Civil War of Incorporation, but in an appendix to this essay are listed over forty violent episodes in this regional war — a decided undercount, however, of all such events.[7]

In its broadest terms this Western Civil War of Incorporation pitted insurgent or resistant Indians against the squeeze play of political pressure and military force which concentrated them in reservations stippling the vast region.[8] The process of incorporation also pressed relentlessly on the traditional lifeways and livelihoods of the Hispanics of the Southwest who fought back, for example, with banditry in south Texas and the resistant violence of the *gorras blancas* (white caps) in New Mexico.[9] So, too, in the mines, mills and logging camps of what historian Carlos Schwantes has called the "wageworkers' frontier" of the West. Employees resisted corporate industrialists with strikes which frequently ended in violence between labor unionists and the paramilitary and military forces which joined in an alliance of capital and government to suppress the work stoppages and disorder so often characteristic of the farflung work places of the West.[10]

The ubiquitous vigilante movements of the West were often spearheaded by elite incorporating forces, as in the cases of the San Francisco vigilantes of 1856, Granville Stuart's Montana "stranglers" of 1884, and many other such movements.[11]

As farmers and ranchers moved into the prairies, plains, valleys and mountain country of the West, dramatic local conflicts often escalated into such rabid vendettas as those embodied in the Johnson County War in Wyoming and the Mussel Slough conflict in California.[12] In these and many other struggles in the Western Civil War of Incorporation, gunfighters as well as lawyers and judges played crucial roles. Best known are the *glorified gunfighters* whose fame and exploits became a part of the legend of the West; these were some 200 or 300 gunslingers headed by the most noted of all — the likes of Wild Bill Hickok, Billy the Kid and Wyatt Earp.[13] Less known but far more numerous were the thousands of *grassroots gunfighters* whose violent deeds were little or not at all known beyond their own localities. Although generally not as effective as the glorified gunfighters, the grassroots gunfighters could be deadly.[14]

In the range country and boom towns of the pastoral and mining West, gunfighters were the front-line soldiers in the Western Civil War of Incorporation. Whether they were glorified or grassroots gunfighters, these shock troops divided along two lines. Those who brought their gun power to the incorporating side were the conservative *incorporation gunfighters* whose ranks included glorified gunfighters like Wild Bill Hickok of Kansas and Wyatt Earp of Arizona, and grassroots gunfighters like Walter J. Crow of California. On the other side were the dissident *resister gunfighters*, one of whom was Billy the Kid and some of whom, including the Kid, were mythologized, in E.J. Hobsbawm's formulation, as social bandits of the West.[15] It is in these political and ideological conceptual categories of incorporation and resister gunfighters that the reality behind the myth of the western gunfighter is to be found.

The Western Civil War of Incorporation coincided with a trend from 1865 to 1900 in which wealthy and powerful individuals, companies and corporations attempted either to push pioneers off the land or to make them pay dearly for their occupancy. In effect, this was a land-enclosure movement comparable to those which afflicted England from the Middle Ages to the eighteenth century. Especially aggressive in the West were the big ranchers, whose gunfighting cowboys sought to exclude small ranchers and homesteading farmers from the ranges. Also crucial to the land-enclosing trend were the top railroads of the West which, through Congressional land grants to them, tied up huge acreages and set the price of land sales to settlers. It was such a grant to the Southern Pacific Railroad that bred the Mussel Slough conflict in California. Innumerable westerners chafed under the land-enclosing trend. Reformer Henry George of San Francisco believed deeply in the homestead ethic — that the health of American society rested on the small farmer "owning his own acres, using his own capital, and working with his own hands." He denounced the trend of land monopolization in the guise of huge railroad land grants such as that to the Southern Pacific in California, which he saw as making the "many poorer, and few richer." Referring to the "Big Four" owners of the Southern Pacific — Collis P. Huntington, Leland Stanford, Charles Crocker and Mark Hopkins — in whose "few hands" he saw all wealth and power tending more and more to be concentrated, Henry George asked "what sort of a republic will this be in a few years if these things go on?"[16]

One of the principal battlegrounds in the Western Civil War of Incorporation was in the richly irrigated Mussel Slough country thirty miles south of Fresno in California's Central Valley. Here the homestead ethic[17] of the settlers clashed with the capitalistic, individual-enterprise ethic of the Southern Pacific's Big Three (the Big Four having become the Big Three with Hopkin's death in 1878). In dispute were thousands of acres which hundreds of settlers had occupied by invoking the federal land preemption law, but which the Southern Pacific claimed under a federal land grant to it.[18] The dispute went to the Ninth Circuit Court in which Judge Lorenzo Sawyer, a close friend of two of the interested parties (Southern Pacific owners Stanford and Crocker), not surprisingly decided in the railroad's favor in the controversial 1879 case of *Southern Pacific Railroad Company v. Pierpont Orton.*[19]

Legal scholars disagree on whether Sawyer's decision upholding the railroad's land claim was right as a matter of law. John A. Larimore cogently argued that it was while David J. Bederman forcefully contended that it was not but was, rather, the result of Sawyer's personal view that corporations should be given full scope to carry out their activities. Larimore, Bederman, and all authorities agree, however, on the strongly conservative Sawyer's deep sympathy for corporations and the Southern Pacific and its owners. Ambrose Bierce and Josiah Royce (mentioned below) thought that the railroad was legally right but morally wrong, a view held by a great many others. Whichever side was legally and/or morally right in the Mussel Slough conflict, the episode fits the paradigm of the Western Civil War of Incorporation pitting incorporating elements (Sawyer, the Southern Pacific, and the Big Three) against resistant settlers, their legal counsel (who were among the ablest lawyers in California but to no avail in Sawyer's court), and their allies.[20]

The settlers responded with night-riding vigilantism to intimidate local supporters of the railroad, and in a "no-duty-to-retreat" mood they prepared to defend their productive small farms with firearms. The crisis exploded into the greatest small-group gunfight in far western history on 11 May 1880, when settlers resisted a federal marshal's party at work dispossessing them from their homes. With an ultimate toll of seven deaths, the Mussel Slough gunfight far surpassed the three dead of the legendary shootout of Wyatt Earp and his brothers in Tombstone, Arizona, a year later.

The Mussel Slough gunfight of 11 May 1880, a key battle in the

Western Civil War of Incorporation, was entirely the work of seven grassroots gunfighters who, however, were subdivided into the opposing categories of incorporation and resister gunfighters. Both of the incorporation gunfighters of Mussel Slough lost their lives that day but not before one of them, Walter J. Crow, killed all five of the settler-resister gunfighters who confronted them.[21] In so doing, he took far more lives than any of the glorified gunfighters such as Wyatt Earp or Billy the Kid had ever claimed on a single occasion.

National public opinion, as well as that in California, focused on the five slain settlers who were widely seen as martyrs to the defense of their homes against the oppressive policy of the Southern Pacific. The conclusion was drawn that a great American and western corporation, the Southern Pacific, headed by a few millionaires, was not content to deprive hard-working farmers and family men of their homes, but would demand the ultimate sacrifice and have them shot down in cold blood by gunfighting surrogates. In London, Karl Marx avidly followed the California conflict, and after the five farmer fatalities in the Mussel Slough shootout he wrote to an American correspondent that nowhere else in the world was "the upheaval most shamelessly caused" by capitalist oppression taking place "with such speed" as in California.[22]

Although largely forgotten today, the Mussel Slough conflict and its deadly gunfight burned itself into the consciousness of late nineteenth-century Americans. Ambrose Bierce, then a San Francisco journalist, wrote column after column in support of the settlers and against the railroad magnates.[23] Within two decades, four novels based on the Mussel Slough conflict were written — one by a leading American philosopher, the California-born and reared Harvard academic, Josiah Royce,[24] and another, Frank Norris's powerful American classic, The Octopus.[25] Norris's title had long been applied to the Southern Pacific in California.[26] Even more broadly, the image of the octopus was a hostile metaphor for the incorporating forces of the frontier West.

Roundly defeated in both their courtroom and gunfighting battles with the Southern Pacific, the dissident Mussel Slough settlers were decided losers in their phase of the Western Civil War of Incorporation. They had no choice but to leave their farms or pay the railroad to remain; most of them lost their farms. The result was the embittering of a generation in California's Central Valley that was far wider than the hundreds of farmers who had been in direct conflict with the railroad. One outcome was the popular admiration of a famous team of outlaws, Chris Evans and John Sontag, who repeatedly robbed Southern Pacific trains from 1889 to 1892. As both glorified and resister gunfighters, the antirailroad lawbreaking of Evans and Sontag was a violent substitute for seething resentment of the Southern Pacific by a host of peaceful, law-abiding Californians.[27]

The consensus of scholars (in which I join) is that the outcome of the Mussel Slough conflict was a tragedy with the dispossession of the settlers reflecting badly upon the Big Three (previously the Big Four) owners of the Southern Pacific, whatever the railroad's legal rights may have been. To the credit of the Big Four, however, were their (for the times) enlightened views on the rights of racial minorities. Richard J. Orsi has noted that Collis P. Huntington was "a lifelong opponent of racial prejudice" who condemned white oppression of the Chinese, American Indians, Filipinos and Japanese while supporting African-American education and employment in his great industrial enterprises in the South. Significantly, the Big Three (especially Huntington) and their judicial allies — Field, Sawyer and Deady — defended the Chinese against assault and loss of civil liberties.[28]

As emphasized, lawyers and judges played crucial roles in the Western Civil War of Incorporation. Indeed, just as we may speak of incorporation gunfighters and resister gunfighters, we might speak of incorporation lawyers and judges *versus* resister lawyers and judges. But the incorporation lawyers and judges have become far better known because top legal talent was often employed by incorporating forces. Such was the role of the highly conservative Willis O. Van Devanter of Wyoming between his stints as chief justice of the Wyoming Supreme Court, 1889- 90, and associate justice of the United States Supreme Court, 1911-37. The Republican Van Devanter served as the defense lawyer of the incorporation gunfighters, who on behalf of the incorporating big cattlemen of Wyoming had attacked the small ranchers, farmers and rustlers in the Johnson County War of 1892.[29]

Often, too, legal figures were principals in episodes of the Western Civil War of Incorporation, as was true of both Thomas B. Catron and Albert B. Fall of New Mexico. Catron, an immensely ambitious and avaricious lawyer, who headed the infamous Santa Fe Ring and was the Republican political boss of New Mexico in the late nineteenth century. He was the evil genius of law and politics in that turbulent territory. He was a protagonist in three notable episodes of the Western Civil War of Incorporation in New Mexico — the Lincoln County war, the Colfax County War and the Tularosa War.[30] Also in New Mexico, Albert B. Fall started out in the Tularosa War as both a resister lawyer and gunfighter, but his innate conservatism and drive for personal power led him to change sides. By the early twentieth century Fall was one of the most powerful incorporators in New Mexico and had become a reactionary Republican senator from that state.[31] All of this was before his spectacular career collapsed in the disgrace of his corrupt conduct as President Harding's secretary of the Interior.

One sensational but now obscure event in western history was an incident in the Western Civil War of Incorporation which represented a merger of the gunfighting tradition and the legal history of the West. It was the shooting death of Judge David S. Terry in Lathrop, California, on 14 August 1889 by David Neagle, the bodyguard of Stephen J. Field, who was still serving both as associate justice of the United States Supreme Court and as Ninth Circuit Court judge.[32] This was a controversial homicide which, so Neagle and Field claimed, was provoked by Terry's assault on Field at the time of the killing. Neagle was an incorporation gunfighter who had rightly gained a reputation as a tough Tombstone law enforcer in the era of Wyatt Earp.[33] The killing of Terry was indirectly but significantly related to the Mussel Slough conflict. Terry, the stormy petrel of California politics, had strongly supported the Mussel Slough settlers,[34] while Field was a friend and judicial ally of the settler *bête noire*, Lorenzo Sawyer, with whom Field had upheld the Southern Pacific in crucial taxation cases heard in the circuit court.[35]

Terry and Field were political enemies, but it was Terry's threats against Field — growing out of a heated legal and personal dispute stemming from Field's role as circuit judge in the hugely complicated (and hugely significant) Sharon divorce case — that led Field to employ Neagle as his bodyguard.[36] Field headed the economically conservative Pacific Coast federal judicial clique that included Lorenzo Sawyer. Field was the mentor of Sawyer and, like him, was a jurisprudential protagonist of the Southern Pacific as well as a personal friend of Leland Stanford and other railroad leaders. Terry, on the other hand, was a leader of the dominant anti-incorporating wing of the Democratic party in California which, at his behest, had struck a hard blow against the 1884 national presidential ambitions of Field, a strongly conservative Democrat.[37] Terry's murder immediately became politicized in California as local authorities pursued legal processes against Neagle — an effort rebuffed by Sawyer in his important decision in *In re Neagle*, later upheld by the United States Supreme Court with Field as a jubilant abstainer.[38]

From first to last in the 1888-89 feud between them, both Terry and Field had behaved implacably. Field's attitude — very much shared by his surrogate, gunfighter Neagle — was a reversion to his days in the California Gold Rush era when, as a volatile, dynamic and much-threatened young politico and judge, Field had unmistakably let it be known that he would, if need be, defend himself with the firearm he so ostentatiously carried.[39] Much later in his life, Field believed strongly that only his armed, resolute demeanor had saved his life and that such determination both preserved him from violence and made retaliatory violence by him unnecessary.[40] Recent articles in *Western Legal History* are enlarging our knowledge of the Field clique and its relationship to the Western Civil War of Incorporation.[41] Still, fuller study of the clique and its impact is a major need in the field of western legal history.

By 1900 vast stretches of the West were incorporated but the civil war was not over. A militant early twentieth-century labor movement spearheaded by the Western Federation of Miners and the Industrial Workers of the World was uncowed and unincorporated until World War I brought a final, successful surge in the incorporating trend (see Appendix). By 1920 the Western Civil War of Incorporation was over, won by the conservative side. Yet, just how unique was the Western Civil War of Incorporation? Was its equivalent to be found north of the Canadian-American boundary and south of the American-Mexican line?

First, in regard to the south-of-the-border question, a central factor in the long regime of Porfirio Diaz was what might be called the North Mexican Civil War of Incorporation, with its theatre being the states of Chihuahua and Sonora. Here the federal police force — the *rurales* — were the violent protagonists of incorporation and had much in common with the incorporation gunfighters of the American West.[42] The triumphant conservative side in the North Mexican Civil War of Incorporation eventually bred a backlash, beginning with the 1906 labor uprising at the great American-owned Cananea copper company in Sonora that led to the Mexican Revolution of 1910.[43]

As for the north-of-the-border question, I naturally defer to the opinion of specialists on Canada, but it seems to me that what Professor Macleod has written of as "the Canadianizing of the West"[44] resembles to some extent what I have characterized as the incorporating process in the American West. Was Louis Riel's rebellion of 1885[45] an episode in a Western Canadian Civil War of Incorporation?

Even more broadly, was there a nineteenth-century Western Hemispheric Civil War of Incorporation which extended all the way from the cattle ranges of Chile and Argentina to the Prairies of Canada? An affirmative answer is suggested by intriguing evidence in Richard W.

Slatta's recent comparative study of the cowboys of North and South America.[46]

To conclude with a final word on the Western Civil War of Incorporation, there was plenty of brutality and oppression but this should be viewed in perspective. Mitigating the harsh reality of, and coexisting with, much of the Western Civil War of Incorporation was a remarkably open, mobile and expanding society in the West from the 1880s on, which enabled many of lower- or middle-class status not only to avoid the battlegrounds of the regional civil war but to prosper and thrive.[47] Nor should the popularity of the incorporating triumph be overlooked and underestimated, for there was a widespread desire — by no means restricted to the elite — for the more orderly, structured society which was one result of the Western Civil War of Incorporation. Finally, a series of reform movements and significant advances in popular education[48] after 1890 softened the impact of the Western Civil War of Incorporation without greatly diminishing the early- and mid-twentieth-century order and stability that was, in part, its legacy.[49]

APPENDIX
Selected Episodes in the Western Civil War of Incorporation 1850-1919

The listing below is a decided undercount of episodes in the Western Civil War of Incorporation, but it is a representative one. Each of the episodes below is treated in at least one book or article; in most of the cases the sources are abundant. Many of the sources for these episodes appear in Richard Maxwell Brown, "Historiography of Violence in the American West," in Michael P. Malone, ed., *Historians and the American West* (Lincoln: University of Nebraska Press, 1983), chapter 11; and Brown, *No Duty to Retreat: Violence and Values in American History and Society* (New York: Oxford University Press, 1991), chapters 2 and 3.

The episodes are listed in chronological order. The outcome of each of these events in the Western Civil War of Incorporation is indicated by one of the following abbreviations: V = victory for incorporating faction; D = defeat for incorporating faction; A = ambiguous outcome. Additional abbreviations used: IWW = Industrial Workers of the World; WFM = Western Federation of Miners; VIG = Vigilantism was used by incorporating faction.

1. First Round Valley War, northwest California, 1850s-1865. Incorporating white settlers carry on genocidal campaign of dispossession against local Indians. (V)

2. Mexican outlaws' activity, California, 1850s-1860s. Incorporating California rangers suppress guerrilla-like insurgency of native Mexican outlaws. (V)

3. San Francisco vigilantes, 1856. Incorporating mercantile elite of San Francisco vs. Irish-Catholic working-class element. (VIG/V)

4. Montana vigilantes, 1863-65. Incorporating faction of vigilantes of Virginia City and Bannack vs. outlaw gang. (VIG/V)

5. Second Round Valley War, northwest California, 1865-1905. Land-enclosing big ranchers vs. small landholders. (V or A)

6. James-Younger outlaw gang, Missouri, 1866-82. Bank and train-robbing outlaws vs. incorporating industrial, financial, commercial and state-government forces. (V)

7. Williamson County War, Texas, 1869-76. Yegua Notch Cutters outlaw gang vs. Olive family of incorporating big ranchers. (Olives defeat the outlaws but are, in effect, forced to move to the more open range country of Nebraska; see number 12. (A)

8. *Bandido* insurgency, South Texas, 1870s-1910s. Hispanic outlaws vs. incorporating force of Texas Rangers. (V)

9. Kansas cattle towns, 1870s-1880s. Incorporating merchants represented by incorporation gunfighter law enforcers vs. Texas cowboys. (V)

10. Colfax County War, New Mexico, 1875. Incorporating large land company (headed by Thomas B. Catron) vs. local settlers upon whose interests the company impinged. (V)

11. San Francisco, 1877. Incorporating "Pick Handle Brigade" of establishment vigilantes vs. working-class rioters in sympathy with nationwide rail workers strike. (VIG/V)

12. Custer County, Nebraska, 1877-79. Incorporating big ranchers led by Olive family from Texas (see number 7) vs. homesteaders. (D or A)

13. Lincoln County War, southern New Mexico, 1878. This was a special case in that it was a conflict between two incorporating factions which nullified each other; the ultimate victor was New Mexico's top incorporator, Thomas B. Catron. (V)

14. Cochise County War, southeast Arizona, 1878-82. Urban, industrial elite of Tombstone (violently spearheaded by the Earp brothers) vs. a coalition of out-county small ranchers and cowboy outlaws. (V)

15. Mussel Slough conflict, California, 1878-82. Southern Pacific (incorporating force) vs. small-farming settlers. (V)

16. Sand Hills War, northwest Nebraska, 1880s-1890s. Incorporating big cattle ranchers vs. homesteaders. (A)

17. Fence-cutting conflict, central Texas, 1880-1900 (including a peak event, the Fence Cutters' War, 1883-84, afflicting at least twelve counties). Land-enclosing big ranchers vs. small ranchers and farmers. (V)

18. Outlaws vs. law enforcers, Missouri-Kansas-Oklahoma-Arkansas, 1880s-1910s. Law enforcers represent incorporating forces vs. outlaws who often had popular support. (V)

19. Billy the Kid outlaw activity, southern New Mexico, 1880-81. Incorporating big ranchers and business and professional men vs. Billy the Kid's rustling gang. (V)

20. Granville Stuart's Montana vigilante movement of 1884. Incorporating big cattle-ranchers (the vigilante faction led by Stuart) vs. horse-stealing outlaws. (VIG/V)

21. Colorado's "Thirty Years' War," 1884-1914. Incorporating mine owners and managers with state-government allies vs. organized labor. The term and concept of the Thirty Years' War in Colorado is that of historian and former presidential candidate George S. McGovern, who used it in his Northwestern University Ph.D. dissertation (see numbers 29 and 35 for two of the major events in Colorado's Thirty Years' War). (V)

22. Bald Knobbers, southwest Missouri, 1885-87. Incorporating urban-industrial-commercial forces vs. mountaineers of traditional rural culture. (VIG/V)

23. Pleasant Valley War, Arizona, 1886-92. Incoming incorporating, commercially minded, large landholding and ranching elite vs. traditionalistic early settlers (VIG/V)

24. *Gorras blancas* (white caps) conflict, northern New Mexico, 1890. *Gorras blancas*

spearheading traditional Hispanic pastoral villagers vs. incorporating, land-enclosing Anglo and Hispanic elite ranchers and lawyers. (D)

25. Tularosa War, southern New Mexico, 1890s. Incorporating big cattle ranchers and business and professional allies vs. traditionalistic small ranchers and cowboys. (A)

26. Harney County conflict, Oregon, 1890s. Big cattle ranchers vs. homesteaders. (A)

27. Johnson County War, Wyoming, 1892. Elite cattle ranchers and establishment allies vs. small ranchers, homesteaders and cowboy outlaws in the culmination of a long-term conflict. (VIG/A)

28. Coeur d'Alene War, northern Idaho, 1890s. Incorporating mine owners supported by state and federal governments and military forces vs. organized labor (including WFM). (V)

29. Cripple Creek conflict, Colorado, 1894-1904. Incorporating mine owners and managers vs. organized labor (including WFM) (part of Colorado's Thirty Years' War; see number 21). (V)

30. Caldwell, Idaho, assassination of the former governor, Frank Steunenberg, 1905, and its aftermath, 1906-07. Anti-incorporating miners' union (WFM) vs. incorporating forces represented by Steunenberg. Important aftermath is trial of WFM leaders for the assassination. (A)

31. Goldfield, Nevada, conflict, 1907. Incorporating mine owners vs. IWW. (V)

32. Los Angeles, 1910. Dynamiting of *L.A. Times* building by labor-union conspirators results in significant loss of life. *Times* publisher Harrison Gray Otis as spearhead of incorporating forces in southern California vs. labor-union movement. (V)

33. Aberdeen, Washington, 1911-17. Incorporating lumber-mill magnates and town allies vs. IWW. (V)

34. Wheatland, California, riot of hop pickers, 1913. Anti-incorporating IWWs and migrant workers vs. owners of Durst hop ranch. (V)

35. Southern Colorado coal-mining conflict, 1913-14. Rockefeller and other incorporating, mine-owning forces vs. organized labor. Culminates in miner families' loss of life in "Ludlow Massacre," 1914 (part of Colorado's Thirty Years' War; see number 21). (V)

36. San Francisco, bombing of Preparedness Day parade, 1916. Incorporating industrial and business forces vs. organized labor (including its radical fringe). (V)

37. Everett Massacre, Washington, 1916. Conflict between incorporating lumber-mill magnates and allies vs. organized labor. IWW intervention results in the massacre, with labor element's casualties being heaviest. (VIG/V)

38. Bisbee, Arizona, 1917. Conflict between incorporating mine interests and town and law-enforcement allies vs. striking miners (including IWW). (VIG/V)

39. Butte, Montana, lynching of Frank Little, 1917. Little, an antiwar activist and IWW organizer, fell afoul of local vigilantes. (VIG/V)

40. Green Corn Rebellion, eastern Oklahoma, 1917. Uprising of antiwar poor farmers and tenants against incorporating landlords and townspeople. (V)

41. Seattle General Strike, 1919. Incorporating Seattle forces (led by the mayor) defeat the general strike, an event accompanied by turbulence but not violence. (V)

42. Centralia, Washington, massacre and reprisal, 1919. Incorporating town element vs. IWW. (VIG/V)

NOTE: The listing above makes clear that World War I coincided with a final surge of the incorporating trend in the West, a trend that was completed by 1920.

Summary of the forty-two episodes: victory for incorporating faction — 33; defeat for incorporating faction — 1; ambiguous outcome — 6; unclear whether the outcome was a victory or ambiguous — 1; unclear whether the outcome was a defeat or ambiguous — 1. In eleven of the forty-two episodes, incorporating factions employed vigilantism.

The tabulation above shows that three-quarters of the forty-two episodes resulted in victory for the incorporating forces. Yet the remaining nine episodes (including six with ambiguous outcomes) underscore the point that, although the overall result of the Western Civil War of Incorporation was victory for the conservative incorporating forces, the resisting forces were strong.

NOTES

1. Alan Trachtenberg, *The Incorporation of America: Culture and Society in the Gilded Age* (New York: Hill and Wang, 1982.).

2. David Thelen, *Paths of Resistance: Tradition and Dignity in Industrializing Missouri* (New York: Oxford University Press, 1986), chapters 4 and 5.

3. Altina Waller, *Feud: Hatfields, McCoys, and Social Change in Appalachia, 1860-1988* (Chapel Hill: University of North Carolina Press, 1988).

4. Robert C. McMath, Jr., "Sandy Land and Hogs in the Timber: (Agri)cultural Origins of the Farmers' Alliance in Texas," in Steven Hahn and Jonathan Prude, eds., *The Countryside in the Age of Capitalist Transformation: Essays in the Social History of Rural America* (Chapel Hill: University of North Carolina Press, 1985).

5. The concept and term "Western Civil War of Incorporation" is the author's. See Richard Maxwell Brown, *No Duty to Retreat: Violence and Values in American History and Society* (New York: Oxford University Press, 1991), chapters 2 and 3.

6. In this period members of the United States Supreme Court customarily spent a part of each year in the federal circuit court to which they were assigned.

7. See Appendix, Selected Episodes in the Western Civil War of Incorporation, 1850-1919.

8. On white-Indian wars in the West which resulted in the concentration of Indians on reservations see Robert M. Utley, *The Indian Frontier of the American West, 1846-1890* (Albuquerque: University of New Mexico Press, 1984); and Richard White, *"It's Your Misfortune and None of My Own": A History of the American West* (Norman: University of Oklahoma Press, 1991), chapters 3 and 8.

9. Robert J. Rosenbaum, *Mexicano Resistance in the Southwest: "The Sacred Right of Self-Preservation"* (Austin: University of Texas Press, 1981), chapters 3 and 8.

10. Carlos A. Schwantes, "The Concept of the Wageworkers' Frontier: A Framework for Future Research," *Western Historical Quarterly* 28 (January 1987): 39-55. Episodes of violence on the wageworkers' frontier are listed in the Appendix.

11. On San Francisco vigilantes of 1856 see Richard Maxwell Brown, *Strain of Violence: Historical Studies of American Violence and Vigilantism* (New York: Oxford University Press, 1975), chapter 5; Robert M. Senkewicz, *Vigilantes in Gold Rush San Francisco* (Stanford: Stanford University Press, 1985). On the 1884 Montana vigilantes see Oscar O. Mueller, "The Central Montana Vigilantes Raids of 1884," *Montana: The Magazine of Western History* 1 (January 1951): 23-35. On western vigilantism in general see Brown, *Strain of Violence*, chapter 4. On legal attitudes and the role of lawyers and judges in regard to vigilantism see Brown, *Strain of Violence*, chapter 6.

12. On the Johnson County War see Helena Huntington Smith, *The War on Powder River*

(Lincoln: University of Nebraska Press, 1966); Lewis L. Gould, *Wyoming: A Political History, 1868-1896* (New Haven: Yale University Press, 1968), chapter 6. For the Mussel Slough conflict see note 18.

13. On Hickok and Earp see Brown, *No Duty to Retreat*, chapter 2. On Billy the Kid, see Robert M. Utley, *Billy the Kid: A Short and Violent Life* (Lincoln: University of Nebraska Press, 1989).

14. A deadly grassroots gunfighter, Walter J. Crow, is treated below.

15. The concepts and terms of "incorporation gunfighter" and "resister gunfighter" are the author's. Also see Brown, *No Duty to Retreat*, chapters 2 and 3. On social bandits see E.J. Hobsbawm, *Social Bandits and Primitive Rebels* (Glencoe, IL: Free Press, 1959); Richard White, "Outlaw Gangs of the Middle Border: American Social Bandits," *Western Historical Quarterly* 12 (October 1981): 387-408; Utley, *Billy the Kid*, 200, 270.

16. Henry George, *The Complete Works of Henry George* (1883; Garden City, NY: Doubleday Page, 1911), vol. 3, 75; vol. 8, 5, 7, 20, 33-34, 36-38, 71-72, 94-95, 171.

17. On the homestead ethic, see Richard Maxwell Brown, "Back Country Rebellions and the Homestead Ethic in America, 1740-1799," in Richard Maxwell Brown and Don E. Fehrenbacher, eds., *Tradition, Conflict, and Modernization: Perspectives on the American Revolution* (New York: Academic Press, 1977).

18. The following treatment of the Mussel Slough conflict is based on Brown, *No Duty to Retreat*, chapter 3. See also James L. Brown, *The Mussel Slough Tragedy* (n.p., 1958); Richard J. Orsi, "The Confrontation at Mussel Slough," in Richard B. Rice, William A. Bullough and Richard J. Orsi, *The Elusive Eden: A New History of California* (New York: McGraw, 1987), 217-36; and David J. Bederman, "The Imagery of Injustice at Mussel Slough: Railroad, Land Grants, Corporation Law, and the 'Great Conglomerate West'," *Western Legal History* 1 (Summer/Fall 1988): 237-69.

19. *Southern Pac. R. Co. v. Orton*, 32 F. 457 (C.C.D. Cal. 1879). In his will, Sawyer named Crocker to be his executor. On the Sawyer-Stanford friendship see P.O. Ray, "Sawyer, Lorenzo," *Dictionary of American Biography* (New York: Charles Scribner's Sons, 1928), vol. 16, 395-96, and Linda C. A. Przybyszewski, "Judge Lorenzo Sawyer and the Chinese: Civil Rights Decisions in the Ninth Circuit," *Western Legal History* 1(Winter/Spring 1988): 27, 53n.

20. John A. Larimore, "Legal Questions Arising from the Mussel Slough Land Dispute," *Southern California Quarterly* 58 (1976): 75-94; Bederman, "Imagery of Injustice." Virtually all authorities on the Mussel Slough conflict, with the exception of Orsi and Larimore, hold that the settlers were in the right. Orsi, "Confrontation at Mussel Slough," incisively supports his view that the Southern Pacific and its Big Three owners — Stanford, Crocker, and Huntington — were more sinned against (by the settlers and their leader, John J. Doyle) than sinning in the Mussel Slough conflict.

21. Visalia (CA), *Visalia Weekly Delta*, 21 May 1880. See also, Brown, *No Duty to Retreat*, 108-09.

22. Karl Marx and Frederick Engels, *Letters to Americans: 1848-1895: A Selection*, ed. Alexander Trachtenberg (New York: International Publishers, 1953), 126.

23. Bierce's columns appeared in *The Wasp* (San Francisco), 1880-82; some are reprinted in Ernest Hopkins, ed., *The Ambrose Bierce Satanic Reader: Selections from the Invective Journalism of the Great Satirist* (Garden City, NY: Doubleday, 1968), chapters 12 and 13.

24. Josiah Royce, *The Feud of Oakfield Creek* (1887; Manchester, NH: Irvington, 1990).

25. Frank Norris, *The Octopus: A Story of California* (1901; New York: Viking Penguin, 1986). The other two Mussel Slough novels were William C. Morrow, *Blood-Money* (San

Francisco: F.J. Walker and Co., 1882), and Charles C. Post, *Driven from Sea to Sea; or Just a Campin'* (Philadelphia: Elliott and Beezley, 1884).

26. G. Frederick Keller's big cartoon in color in *The Wasp*, 10 July 1880, depicting the Southern Pacific as the octopus cruelly constricting California was probably the first such characterization in print. Predating Norris's *The Octopus* was a nonfiction anti-Southern Pacific exposé, John R. Robinson, *The Octopus: A History of the Construction, Conspiracies, Extortions, Robberies, and Villainous Acts of ... Subsidized Railroads* (1894; Salem, NH: Ayer, 1981).

27. The legal sequence of the dispossession of individual farms may be followed in the case files of 136 settlers (all of whom lost their cases to the railroad) in Old [Federal] Circuit Court (1865-1911) case files (manuscripts in Federal Archives and Records Center, San Bruno, CA). The numbers of the Mussel Slough case files are: 2034-38; 2160-65; 2282; 2317; 2320-22; 2358; 2361-2479. The adverse decisions in these cases, in which about 16,000 acres were in dispute, were all by Judge Lorenzo Sawyer who in each case simply applied his opinion in the *Orton* case of 1879. The township maps of tract-by-tract land occupancy in Thomas H. Thompson, *Official Historical Atlas-Map of Tulare County* (Tulare, CA: County of Tulare, 1882), show the replacement of the displaced settlers by the new occupants who came to terms with the railroad.

    On Evans and Sontag see Wallace Smith, *Prodigal Sons: The Adventures of Christopher Evans and John Sontag* (Boston: Christopher, 1951). In *The Octopus*, Frank Norris based Dyke, an embittered railroader turned train robber, on the outlaw career of Sontag.

28. Richard J. Orsi, "The Big Four: Villains or Heroes?" in Rice et al., *Elusive Eden*, 246-48. On Field see Carl Brent Swisher, *Stephen J. Field: Craftsman of the Law* (Washington: Brookings Institution, 1930), chapter 8. On Sawyer see Przybyszewski, "Judge Lorenzo Sawyer." On Deady, see Ralph James Mooney, "Matthew Deady and the Federal Judicial Response to Racism in the Early West," *Oregon Law Review* 63, no. 4 (1983): 561-637, which focuses on Deady's judicial protection of Chinese rights. See also the essays by John R. Wunder and John McLaren in this book.

29. Smith, *War on Powder River*, 193, 261, 275, 281-82.

30. On these three wars and Catron's role in regard to them: Robert M. Utley, *High Noon in Lincoln: Violence on the Western Frontier* (Albuquerque: University of New Mexico Press, 1987); Jim B. Pearson, *The Maxwell Land Grant* (Norman: University of Oklahoma Press, 1961), on the Colfax County War; and Charles L. Sonnichsen, *Tularosa: Last of the Frontier West* (1960; Albuquerque: University of New Mexico Press, 1980). Also on Catron see Howard R. Lamar, ed., *The Reader's Encyclopedia of the American West* (New York: Thomas Y. Crowell, 1977), 172.

31. See the treatments of Fall in Sonnichsen, *Tularosa*, and in Arrell M. Gibson, *The Life and Death of Colonel Albert Jennings Fountain* (1965; Norman: University of Oklahoma Press, 1986).

32. On the Neagle-Terry-Field episode see text below and note 36.

33. William B. Breakenridge, *Helldorado: Bringing Law to the Mesquite*, ed. Richard Maxwell Brown (1928; Lincoln: University of Nebraska Press, 1992), 175, 178, 181, 200-1, 235-37, 288, 319, 419. Gary L. Roberts, "Neagle, David" in Lamar, *Reader's Encyclopedia*, 807-08.

34. Wallace Smith, *Garden of the Sun* (Los Angeles: Lymanhouse, 1939), 267. See also A. Russell Buchanan, *David S. Terry: Dueling Judge* (San Marino, CA: Huntington Library, 1959).

35. Swisher, *Stephen J. Field*, chapter 9.

36. Although integrally related to Terry, Neagle, Field, Lorenzo Sawyer and the Western

Civil War of Incorporation, the Sharon divorce case is, for lack of space, beyond the scope of extensive discussion in this essay. Sarah Althea Hill claimed to be married secretly to millionaire Senator William Sharon and sued him for divorce and, thus, a share of his immense wealth. Sharon, before his dealth, swore there was no marriage. Terry became an attorney for Hill and later became her husband. As Ninth Circuit Court judge, Field made a crucial ruling against Mrs. Terry; Sawyer and Deady also ruled against her. On the Sharon divorce case see: Swisher, *Stephen J. Field*, chapter 13; Robert H. Kroninger, *Sarah and the Senator* (Berkeley: Howell-North, 1964); Oscar Lewis and Carroll D. Hall, *Bonanza Inn: America's First Luxury Hotel* (New York: Knopf, 1939), chapters 4 and 5; Gary L. Roberts, "In Pursuit of Duty," *American West* (September 1970): 26-33, 62-63, and 87-95; Malcolm Clark, Jr., ed., "My Dear Judge: Excerpts from the Letters of Justice Stephen J. Field to Judge Matthew P. Deady," *Western Legal History* 1 (Winter/Spring 1988): 87-95.

37.   On Field as jurisprudential protagonist of the Southern Pacific and friend of Stanford and other railroad leaders see Swisher, *Stephen J. Field*, chapter 9. On Terry as anti-Field see R. Hal Williams, *The Democratic Party and California Politics, 1880-1896* (Stanford: Stanford University Press, 1973), 47-50, 54; see also Swisher, *Stephen J. Field*, 300-10.

38.   For Sawyer's decision see *In re Neagle*, 39 Fed. 833 (1889), upheld by the United States Supreme Court (Field abstaining) in *In re Neagle*, 135 United States 1 (1890). See also, Swisher, *Stephen J. Field*, 350-61; Kroninger, *Sarah*, chapters 19 and 20; and Roberts, "In Pursuit of Duty," 62-63. In the aftermath of Neagle's killing of Terry, Field allowed himself to be arrested *pro forma*, knowing that Sawyer, as circuit-court judge would nullify the action as, indeed, he did. See Swisher, *Stephen J. Field*, 351-55.

39.   Swisher, *Stephen J. Field*, 37-51.

40.   Ibid, 50-51. A major new study of Field by Charles W. McCurdy is in progress — for example, see McCurdy, "Stephen J. Field and the American Judicial Tradition," in Philip J. Bergan, et al., *The Fields and the Law* (San Francisco: U.S. District Court for the Northern District of California/New York: Federal Bar Council, 1986), 5-19.

41.   On Sawyer see Przybyszewski, "Judge Lorenzo Sawyer," and Bederman, "Imagery of Injustice." On Field, Deady, Sawyer, and the inner history of the Ninth Circuit Court see Clark, "My Dear Judge," 79-97.

42.   Paul J. Vanderwood, *Disorder and Progress: Bandits, Police, and Mexican Development* (Albuquerque: University of New Mexico Press, 1981), chapters 6-11. Vanderwood compares the Mexican federal *rurales* to the Royal Canadian Mounted Police (did he really mean the North-West Mounted Police or both the NWP and the RCMP?; in any case, his essential point remains) and the Texas Rangers (as well as Spain's Guardia Civil, the French gendarmerie, and Italy's carabinieri) — ibid., xii.

43.   Ibid., chapters 12 and 13.

44.   Roderick C. Macleod, "Canadianizing the West: The North-West Mounted Police as Agents of the National Policy, 1873-1905," in Lewis H. Thomas, ed., *Essays on Western History: In Honour of Lewis Gwynne Thomas*, (Edmonton: University of Alberta Press, 1976), 101-110.

45.   Bob Beal and Rod Macleod, *Prairie Fire: The 1885 North-West Rebellion*, (Edmonton: Hurtig, 1984).

46.   Richard W. Slatta, *Cowboys of the Americas* (New Haven: Yale University Press, 1990), 103-110. See also Slatta, ed., *Bandidos: The Varieties of Latin American Banditry* (Westport, CT: Greenwood, 1987), in which some of the bandits resemble the resister gunfighters of the western United States.

47.   Wallace Stegner, *The American West as Living Space* (Ann Arbor: University of Michigan

Press, 1987), 21-22. On California's open, mobile, expanding society, 1880-1920 see Walton Bean and James J. Rawls, *California: An Interpretive History*, 4th ed., (New York: McGraw-Hill, 1982), chapters 18-25.

48. For example, on the regenerative effect of expanded secondary-school education in Everett, Washington, a city that had been sorely afflicted by an episode in the Western Civil War of Incorporation, the Everett Massacre of 1916, see Norman H. Clark, *Mill Town: A Social History of Everett, Washington, from its Earliest Beginnings on the Shores of Puget Sound to the Tragic and Infamous Event Known as the Everett Massacre* (Seattle: University of Washington Press, 1970), 236-37.

49. Ibid., and Michael P. Malone and Richard W. Etulain, *The American West in the Twentieth Century* (Lincoln: University of Nebraska Press, 1989), chapters 1, 2, 4, 5, 6.

Law and Order on the
Western-Canadian Frontier

R.C. Macleod

The idea that frontiers are unusually violent and disorderly places has been around for a very long time. It has been a central concern of historians since Frederick Jackson Turner and, as Richard Maxwell Brown's paper demonstrates, can be easily accommodated in such recent formulations as Alan Trachtenberg's "incorporation of America." Canadian historians have tended to be less comfortable with this kind of sweeping generalization because our frontier experience seems, in some important respects, less homogeneous than that of the United States. To my mind the research and writing on western Canadian history in the last two decades have revealed differences between parts of the region that may be as great or greater than those on opposite sides of the 49th parallel. What I intend to do is outline those intraregional differences and suggest a framework for explaining them.

This is not to say that the grand theoretical approaches of Turner and Trachtenberg are unimportant but that they tend to obscure some important issues in the historical study of violence. The first of these is that at least some violence and disorder has nothing to do with economic or class conflict. Every criminologist knows that family dynamics are one of the most fruitful sources of violence and that these are to a large degree independent of wealth and class. Literary sources from every civilization tell us that violent conflicts are universal. No human society is without what might be called an ambient level of violence, although clearly these levels differ considerably from time to time and place to place. Thus to demonstrate that violence occurred in a particular setting and coincides with the appearance of a new form of economic or legal structure suggests a causal relationship but does not prove it. Historians looking at frontiers need to pay more attention to the ambient levels of violence present before the changes begin. In doing so they must recognize the local and regional variations that are so marked in a pre-industrial world.

The second issue that, to my mind, has been overlooked in the historiography of the frontier is the variety and complexity of the interaction between European capitalism and native societies in North

America. In most of western Canada the initial contacts were between the aboriginal peoples and merchant capitalism, uncomplicated by an agricultural frontier. This relationship lasted nearly a century and a half in some areas. There are important variations in this basic situation even before the arrival of agriculture and industrial capitalist organization. At times the economy was fluid and competitive, at other times monopoly prevailed. These differences produced striking changes in the levels of violence. So did the establishment of an international boundary.

In approaching the topic in this way, I am following the suggestion of Robin Fisher in an article he published in the *Pacific Historical Review* a few years ago, comparing native-white conflict in Washington and British Columbia.[1] Fisher pointed out that the stereotypical peaceful Canadian frontier was based on the prairie experience and did not apply to the region west of the Rockies. He then went on to analyze the history of native-white relations on both sides of the border in terms of native cultural variations and different white approaches to government. A little reflection on this observation led me to the conclusion that for the whole of western Canada from the earliest contacts there must be more than two distinct variants. The number of permutations among the fundamental variables that affect peace and order make that a virtual certainty. I consider these variables to be: first, the different cultures of the various Indian nations; second, the dominant economic base; and finally, the institutional structure imported by the Europeans. Traditionally most historical research has concentrated on the latter, paid some attention to the economic situation and almost none to the Indians. Enough work has been done on the last two in recent years to identify at least six areas within western Canada that had unique combinations of these factors. There may well be more but there are surely not fewer.

The Hudson's Bay Company (HBC) in its two centuries of control over much of what is now western Canada adopted two quite different approaches to the problem of maintaining order in its territories. One applied to its fur-trading operations from Hudson Bay to the Pacific while the other applied only to the Red River settlement for the half century after 1820. The HBC's far western operations on the Columbia River and Vancouver Island may constitute a third separate case, but I do not know enough about them to say. From my limited knowledge I am inclined to lump together the periods of Company rule on the West Coast with the colonial period to 1871. British Columbia as a Canadian province clearly deserves separate consideration. The Prairies after the Canadian takeover in 1870 are the classical Canadian peaceful frontier, so much so that they have become one of the clichés of popular culture by way of a rather dreadful TV series called "Bordertown." The Yukon during the gold rush is the last of the Canadian frontiers.

The HBC charter of 1670 granted the Company virtually sovereign powers within its territories. For all of those territories, apart from the precincts of the Company posts, and for most of the area up to 1870, this was a mere fiction. Order had to be maintained among Company employees, but formal law was scarcely necessary to accomplish that. It is clear that the HBC controlled its employees by a combination of economic pressure, physical intimidation (it was useful for a Company factor to be handy with his fists) and the ingrained deference of a society with deep class divisions. If all else failed the offending employee was shipped back to England.

On two occasions the British government passed legislation that attempted to strengthen the Company's power to maintain order: the Canada Jurisdiction Act of 1803 and the Act for Regulating the Fur Trade and Establishing a Civil and Criminal Jurisdiction within Certain Parts of North America, 1821.[2] The Canada Jurisdiction Act was aimed specifically at providing a solution to the increasingly violent rivalry between rival Montreal-based fur traders. It permitted the governor of Lower Canada to appoint justices of the peace for the Indian territories including Rupert's Land. The justices of the peace could commit lawbreakers to trial in the courts of Lower Canada and anyone was given the power to arrest individuals and take them back for trial. Both companies immediately recognized the act as a useful device for harassing the enemy and hauled off key opposition employees on trumped-up charges whenever the opportunity offered.[3] The ultimate illustration of the futility of the legislation as an instrument of peace and order arose from the so-called Seven Oaks Massacre of 1816, in which twenty-one of the Scottish settlers brought to Red River by Lord Selkirk were killed by Métis connected with the North West Company.[4] Selkirk had been warned of impending trouble and had attempted to meet it by having himself appointed a justice of the peace for Rupert's Land and hiring a group of ex-soldiers to protect his settlement. Arriving too late to prevent the killings, Selkirk seized the North West Company inland headquarters at Fort William, arrested a large number of Nor'Westers and sent them back for trial.

The North West Company was too well connected with the Colonial Office and the government of Lower Canada to submit meekly to this challenge.[5] It persuaded the governor, Sir John Sherbrooke, to appoint a two-man commission to investigate the incident and the charges arising from it. The commissioners, William Coltman and John Fletcher, both had ties to the North West Company.[6] A warrant for Selkirk's arrest was obtained and served on him but he refused to accept it. When word of this reached England the colonial secretary ordered Sherbrooke to arrest Selkirk and bring him to trial immediately. By the time this order had crossed the Atlantic, Selkirk was in the United States making a rather leisurely return to Canada via St. Louis, Louisville and Washington, D.C. His arrival set off a remarkable series of trials in both Upper and Lower Canada that lasted for most of the next year. A complete description of the trials would fill volumes but let me summarize. Selkirk personally was acquitted of various charges including resisting arrest, theft, assault and false imprisonment. Five HBC employees were also acquitted of a variety of charges. Various Nor'Westers faced a total of forty-two murder charges, eighteen of arson, nine of burglary, sixteen of robbery and numerous lesser offenses.[7] Only one conviction resulted from approximately 150 charges and that occurred because a Nor'Wester named Charles de Reinhard confessed to the murder of an HBC employee. Even in this case the guilty party was eventually released because of doubts about the jurisdiction of the court that convicted him.[8] The legal costs came close to bankrupting both parties.

The amalgamation of the rival fur companies in 1821 restored the monopoly position of the HBC and removed the major source of white versus white violence in western Canada. It has usually been assumed that peace once more descended upon the region, but this conclusion crumbles altogether in the face of recent scholarship which focuses on the Indian side of the fur trade. There was, of course, an almost total absence of formal legal activity. As Hamar Foster has shown in a recent article, the HBC made only one effort after 1821 to exercise its authority in its territories outside Red River.[9] The prosecution of three Company employees for the mass murder of eleven Hare Indians in 1835 was prompted as much by the need to demonstrate its good faith at a time when the Company charter was up for renewal as any real interest in upholding the law.

The response of the HBC to violent encounters with the native population was complex and varied from place to place. Large-scale thefts and killings were often simply ignored. In June 1794 the Gros Ventre attacked and burned South Branch House, killing three Company employees and wounding two others; there was no response by the Company.[10] In 1810 Fort Edmonton reported losing 650 horses to Cree and Assiniboine raids, and again nothing was done.[11] In 1852 Fort Selkirk at the junction of the Pelly and Yukon rivers was attacked by a group of

Tlingit, forcing the factor, Robert Campbell, to flee for his life. The Company reaction was to close the post and seek a more hospitable environment for its operations in the Yukon.[12] These examples could be multiplied many times. Under George Simpson's management after 1821 the HBC adopted a more aggressive stance but even that consisted mostly of trying to persuade Métis "freemen" in the vicinity of the larger posts that it was in their interests to attack the enemies of the Company.[13] The HBC also tolerated a high level of what might be called "recreational" violence among its employees.[14] If the circumstances seemed to require it, the HBC sometimes met violence with violence, or used economic pressure to persuade other band members to punish offenders.[15] Successful fur traders avoided violence if possible and attempted to tailor their responses to the customs and expectations of the bands they were dealing with.[16]

The question of what we are to make of all this is of more than passing scholarly curiosity given the current status in the courts of aboriginal rights. Legal orthodoxy since the St. Catharine's Milling case in 1885 has been that the arrival of the HBC in 1670 immediately extinguished all native sovereignty.[17] Obviously the reality for most of western Canada right up to the time the Company relinquished its monopoly was quite different. This has led Hamar Foster to conclude that the territories ostensibly controlled by the Company were, "subject largely to Indian law."[18] If by this he means some agreed-upon set of rules and customs that applied to all aboriginal inhabitants, or even to tribes, this seems to me as much a fiction as universal HBC sovereignty. If, on the other hand, he envisages each band as maintaining such a body of law, that seems quite in accord with the historical evidence. John Milloy's comment on the centrality of the band for the Plains Cree could apply to other Indian nations as well:

> The system of complete transferability of membership among the bands gave the Cree social structure the elasticity to absorb, among other shocks, the blows of war and disease. As well, internal social pressures were given vent when a disaffected member could easily join another band. Aspiring warriors could fulfil their leadership ambitions without having to disrupt the existing political structure. Although there is no evidence of "democracy," the band members' freedom of movement enforced a code of acceptable behaviour on the leadership, and made the leaders seek consensus as the basis for decision making.[19]

There were thus dozens of systems of law coexisting in this period. Conformity to the law was essential for anyone living within it, but no band would have considered attempting to enforce its laws on someone outside the band. Relations with outsiders were quasi-diplomatic rather than legal. They were governed, in other words, by considerations of group self-interest and self-preservation rather than by agreed-upon rules. The HBC posts fitted into this system without much friction, behaving simply as if they were additional bands with their own internal laws. If anything, the Company presence reduced the overall level of violence. Warfare hindered trade, and the HBC from its earliest ventures inland tried to use its economic leverage to arrange truces and settlements. The Métis people when they emerged in the late eighteenth century fit into the system in the same manner, creating kin-based groups of up to several hundred individuals.[20]

As Robin Fisher has noted, one of the most durable clichés of Canadian history, going back at least to Parkman, is that the fur trade promoted peaceful relations between Indians and whites.[21] But there were clearly circumstances under which this was not true. During periods of intense competition the trade actually promoted violence. The HBC's Snake Country expeditions, for example, were anything but pacific. The most that can be said is that, unlike agriculture, the fur trade did not require the immediate importation of a European legal system that implied the exclusion of Indian systems. Interracial conflict and violence were not uncommon during the fur trade but they were not an outgrowth of the clash of two incompatible legal systems. Serious conflict was relatively easy to avoid where the population was sparse and an effective monopoly existed.

The beginning of agricultural settlement at Red River in 1811 immediately introduced a new legal concept to western Canada, the idea that there could be a single system of law attached to a particular territory that, at least in some respects, asserted a supremacy over all other laws. The 116,000 square miles granted to Lord Selkirk by the HBC, known as Assiniboia, was treated quite differently from the rest of the lands covered by its charter. Almost at once (1815) the Company published its first code of penal laws. These were to apply only to Company employees but since all the Selkirk settlers were enrolled as Company servants it was clearly meant to apply to them.[22] The HBC had, after all, managed for a century and a half without such a code. The actions of the first governor of Assiniboia, Miles Macdonnell, made it clear that the laws of the colony were to apply to all within its borders. His proclamation of January 1814, prohibiting the export of pemmican from Assiniboia, was aimed explicitly at the Métis employees of the North West Company.[23] The significance of this challenge to the existing order and the fact that its importance went well beyond mere economic rivalry was apparent to the Métis. Their answer was to assert their political identity as the "New Nation," and to undertake an escalating campaign of violence, culminating in the killings at Seven Oaks, intended to drive out the settlers.

After this inauspicious beginning, the Red River settlement was to be a remarkably peaceful place for the next thirty-five years. Selkirk signed treaties with the Assiniboine, Cree and Ojibway, extinguishing their title to the land to his satisfaction if not entirely to theirs.[24] The Indians were from this point on part of the legal system as far as land and property were concerned. They remained outside it for some time as far as criminal matters involving only their own people were concerned.[25] The Métis, on the other hand, were fully within the new legal regime in spite of their earlier protests. This was of crucial importance since they formed a majority of the population of the settlement until the 1870s. There appear to be several reasons for their acceptance of European-style law. The HBC shrewdly co-opted the Métis leader, Cuthbert Grant, giving him an annual salary and a title, "Warden of the Plains." The population of the settlement grew very slowly, leaving plenty of room for all who wished to acquire a river-lot farm on the Red or the Assiniboine, thus eliminating competition for land as a source of conflict.[26] Finally, the vigorous and successful efforts of the Roman Catholic church undoubtedly helped accustom the Métis to a European rather than an Indian concept of law.

The machinery of law in Red River was rudimentary at first. HBC regulations passed in 1822 gave the governor and his council the power to enroll and arm any male inhabitants to uphold their authority. With a jury, governor and council could try all noncapital cases.[27] This arrangement worked well until the mid-1830s when George Simpson decided that the growing complexity of land transactions required a more formal structure. Like the decision to prosecute the Hare Indian murders this was also done with an eye to convincing Parliament that the company was living up to its administrative responsibilities. In 1835 Assiniboia was divided into four judicial districts, each with a magistrate to deal with minor cases. More serious cases remained with the governor and council who sat as the General Quarterly Court.[28] In 1839 the Company appointed a recorder of Rupert's Land who sat as a member of the council and provided general legal advice. The first recorder, Adam Thom, was a Scot who had made his way to Lower Canada where he worked as a journalist before articling in the office of James Charles Grant. His violently anti-French pamphlets and articles were one of the contributing factors to the 1837 rebellion in Lower Canada. In the aftermath of the rebellion Lord Durham recruited him as part of his staff, where Thom served as assistant commissioner for Municipal Affairs.

Thom lasted eleven years as recorder before being forced to resign by the company. He made no secret of the fact that he considered the Métis inferior and refused to use French in his court. Since the Métis formed the majority of the population and had a well-developed tradition of acting to eliminate their grievances, it is not surprising that pressure from them finally forced the company to get rid of Thom. What is surprising is that the pressure took so long to develop. There was no resistance to the law code that Thom drew up for the settlement and that the Company approved in 1841, even though he made no effort to consult the community.[29] Most of the time there was only petty crime to occupy the courts. From 1840 to 1844 there were no offenses serious enough to justify calling together a grand jury.[30] In 1845 Thom ignored the 1821 act which required capital cases to be sent to Canada, and tried a Saulteaux Indian for murdering a Sioux. A jury found him guilty and he was hanged at once. The Indians were well aware that this marked a departure from the old policy of ignoring violence that did not involve whites. They threatened to hang the recorder in retaliation but nothing came of it.[31]

The trouble that did arise had its roots, not in the use of the new legal system to impose order, but in the effort by Thom to use it to uphold the Company's trade monopoly. The appearance of American traders in Minnesota and the Dakotas in the 1840s gave the Métis population of Red River both an alternate market and a source of trade goods. Thom's efforts to halt the activities of the free traders were unsuccessful, apart from a brief period between 1846 and 1848 when troops were stationed in the settlement as a result of the Oregon crisis, but his uncompromising defense of the Company's position created growing resentment among the Métis. The famous Sayer trial of 1849 brought matters to a head. Faced with the trial of one of their number for defying the monopoly, several hundred armed Métis appeared at the courthouse. They denied the validity of the Company charter and refused to allow Sayer to appear. The jury found Sayer guilty but recommended mercy. The court wisely declined to punish him and dropped all outstanding charges against other free traders.[32] The Métis petitioned the Company to remove Thom and he was eased out of the position of recorder within a short time.

With the monopoly and the crusty recorder effectively removed, the settlement reverted to its accustomed tranquillity during the 1850s. For one entire year in the middle of the decade the General Quarterly Court dealt with only a single case, while the lower courts handled eleven.[33]

The decade of the 1860s, however, was to be very different. Gerald Friesen sees the period from 1840 to 1880 on the Prairies as one of transition to an industrial capitalist society.[34] So fundamental a change creates severe strains, and for the only substantial settlement in the region the 1860s were unquestionably the time of most rapid change. Regular steamboat service to Minnesota was in place by the start of the decade and hundreds of newcomers from Canada and the United States began to appear. They quickly came to dominate the business community at Red River as well as the only newspaper. The political and legal systems of Assiniboia remained under the control of the old inhabitants, with no decisive shift until near the end of the 1870s.[35] On the other hand the Canadians quickly perceived and exploited the weaknesses of the government.

Since the Sayer trial the courts at Red River had neither the will nor the means to enforce unpopular decisions. This was dramatically illustrated by the Corbett case in 1863. Corbett was a popular clergyman who was charged with attempting to procure an abortion for his servant, Maria Thomas, whom he had made pregnant. He was found guilty and sentenced to six months imprisonment. Corbett spent only a few days in jail before a group of his friends, led by a school teacher named James Stewart, broke him out. Stewart was then arrested but he too was freed by an armed group of his friends. The justices of the peace in a letter to the governor admitted that they were powerless to remedy the situation and recommended that no further action be attempted against Corbett or Stewart.[36] Over the next few years there were several similar incidents involving mainly the Canadians at Red River defying the decisions of the courts and rescuing their friends from jail at gunpoint.[37] The uprising against the transfer of the territory to Canada led by Louis Riel at the end of the decade is usually described in terms of its political causes and consequences. It can also be seen as the logical outcome of the decline and fall of the HBC's legal system and the failure to replace it with any machinery to keep order.

There were important differences in the experience of the HBC west of the Rockies. For one thing it was much shorter. The land-based fur trade was not established until the first decade of the nineteenth century and it lasted little more than a generation as the dominant economic activity. Much, perhaps even the more important part of the fur trade in British Columbia, was conducted from ships over a somewhat longer period.[38] The situation of quasi-diplomatic relations and coexisting legal systems was not only brief in British Columbia, but there was no counterpart of the Red River experience in which the Indians were drawn gradually under the influence of English law in at least one small part of the region. In spite of these differences, the pattern of events was not significantly different; the Company made no attempt to impose on the native population the laws it applied to its own employees. Company justice within its posts was often perfunctory and governed more by considerations of economy than law, even when the well connected were involved. When the son of Chief Factor John McLoughlin was murdered in a drunken brawl with one of his men at Fort Stikine in 1842, Governor Simpson dismissed it as "justifiable homicide."[39] As elsewhere, relations between Indians and the Company were governed by economic self-interest.

The inception of direct colonial rule on Vancouver Island in 1849 produced no disruptions of the peace. The extension of direct British control to the mainland in 1858 as a result of the Fraser River gold rush led indirectly to one serious incident, the so-called Chilcotin uprising of 1864.[40] The principal reason why the British government was prepared to take over direct rule on the West Coast when it was unwilling to do so on the Prairies was the strategic significance of the former as a naval base. Warships stationed at Esquimalt spent much of their time backing up the new government's efforts to begin the process of eliminating the widespread practice of slavery among the coastal peoples.[41] Robin Fisher suggests that the ability to use sailors and marines to enforce the law, rather than local volunteers, helped keep violence under control.[42] He is also undoubtedly correct in asserting that of even greater importance was the fact that James Douglas, the governor from 1851 to 1864, was an HBC man with long experience of peaceful dealings with the Indians. Even though the HBC arrived late in British Columbia its employees brought over the mountains a well-tested set of policies that needed little adjustment.

At the beginning of the 1870s all these territories with reasonably peaceful antecedents but weak institutional structures came under Canadian control — Red River, Rupert's Land, the North-West Territories and British Columbia. For a country of less than four million people with no experience in colonial administration and, as the Red River uprising demonstrated, wholly ignorant of conditions in the area, the task of integrating the territories in an orderly fashion was daunting to say the least. It was a prospect that created a state of near panic in Alexander Morris, the second lieutenant governor of the North-West Territories and the first Canadian government official to confront the problem face to face. Writing to Ottawa in 1873 he said, "[t]he most important matter of the future is the preservation of order in the North

West and little as Canada may like it she has to stable her elephant."[43] As I have written elsewhere, orderly development of the new western territories was an absolute necessity in the eyes of the Canadian government. Any serious and prolonged disruption could bankrupt the government and bring the vision of a transcontinental empire to an abrupt end.

The prime minister of Canada, Sir John A. Macdonald, had a plan to overcome these difficulties. In principle it involved keeping the tightest possible federal control over the new territories while the process of settlement was taking place.[44] The centerpiece of the scheme was a federal police force, the North West Mounted Police.[45] The plan could not be applied uniformly to the whole region because Louis Riel had forced the creation of the province of Manitoba in 1870, while British Columbia entered Confederation as a province the following year. Since the constitution made policing a provincial responsibility, the Mounted Police did not operate in Manitoba and British Columbia except on a restricted and temporary basis until the twentieth century.

The timing of the Canadian takeover of the West was crucial in terms of finding an effective solution to the problem of order. The English historian of the Mounted Police, Clive Emsley, points out in his comparative study, *Policing and Its Context 1750-1850*, that modern police forces only began to come into their own in the 1850s. London's metropolitan police date from 1829, of course, but it was not until 1856 that legislation required all English counties to have similar modern forces. The French began to copy the English reforms systematically in the 1850s and 1860s.[46] The new police were full-time professionals operating under tight discipline. They helped to overcome an inevitable public suspicion and hostility by astute use of publicity and through welfare work at a time before the existence of social work. The police were conspicuously uniformed on the assumption that their visible presence would prevent crime and maintain order, although as Emsley suggests their success in maintaining order might have been more apparent than real.[47]

Sir John A. Macdonald was aware of the recent developments in British and European policing. As early as the 1850s when he was attorney general of Upper Canada he had attempted to set up a new style of police for the whole of the colony.[48] That effort had failed but in 1873 he was prime minister and could put his plan into effect, even if his cabinet colleagues did not fully understand what he was doing.[49] The Mounted Police had all the essential characteristics of the new police of the mid-nineteenth century.[50] The challenges they faced in the 1870s and 1880s were of an entirely different order from those of the HBC era. Immigration was slow at first but reached tens of thousands by the end of the century. The buffalo and the whole Plains Indian economy based on the hunt disappeared with startling suddenness in the early 1880s. Through this great transformation the Mounted Police were outstandingly successful in maintaining order until the rebellion of 1885. It could be argued that the very completeness of their success — they did not have to fire a shot in anger through the whole of their first decade in the West — led to the carelessness in Ottawa that allowed the rebellion to occur. Perhaps the most striking feature of the rebellion when it did occur was that only a few bands elected to join Riel and the Métis although all the Indians of the Prairies had very real grievances.[51]

The high point of Mounted Police success came during the Yukon gold rush. By that time the police had two decades of experience and they had no trouble dealing with a situation that was in many respects less difficult than that farther south. The native population was less warlike and far less numerous; it could be, and in fact was, largely ignored. The fact that there were only a few practical routes into the Klondike made it easy to apprehend offenders.[52] The gold miners were interested in getting rich and were quite happy to give up their own system of justice through miners' meetings as long as the Mounted Police could provide a minimally fair and consistent substitute. Even the harshness of the environment was an advantage because knowledge of how to survive in winter made the police an indispensable source of information for the incoming prospectors. One of the most interesting comparative studies of the subject was published in 1988 by the anthropologist Thomas Stone. He points out that the gold claims themselves were always quite orderly whether controlled by miners' meetings, the United States Army or the Mounted Police. The significant differences came in the urban centers that sprang up to service the rush.[53] Skagway and Nome were lawless and violent while Dawson was very little different from southern Canadian cities; everything closed on Sundays and the Mounted Police strictly enforced the law that prohibited riding bicycles on the sidewalks.[54]

Even if one discounts the Rose Marie image of the Mounted Police so assiduously promoted by the force itself over the years, it is evident that they were a highly successful operation. Their experience strongly suggests that the role of the state is crucial in the maintenance of order. One could perhaps make a much stronger statement if it could be demonstrated that Manitoba and British Columbia after 1870, without the

Mounted Police, had higher levels of violence and lawlessness than the rest of the region with them. I know of no single study to suggest that this was the case. My reading of the history of those provinces in the late nineteenth century leads me to believe that the differences were not great. A comparative study would be a formidable undertaking. There is the universal problem of the vagaries of nineteenth-century criminal statistics. The very different economies of British Columbia and the Prairies complicate comparisons. Most of the recent scholarship on the history of crime and policing stresses the centrality of the urban experience. British Columbia, with its population heavily concentrated in Victoria and Vancouver, was a much more urbanized society than the Prairies. This must have had an important effect but what it might be we can only guess since there are almost no studies of crime and law enforcement in western Canadian towns and cities.

Some years ago in my study of the Mounted Police I said that they were responsible for keeping order in the West, thereby making possible the extension of Canada across the continent. I am less sure of that conclusion today. I still believe it is valid but I do not think it can be demonstrated with the present state of scholarship. I would be more inclined now to stress the psychological importance of the Mounted Police. By that I mean that even if the police did not do everything they were supposed to, the government and public believed they did. The Mounted Police were, if you like, the most modern and up-to-date technology available for dealing with the problem of order when they were created, and their existence gave the government the confidence necessary to undertake a task that might otherwise have seemed impossible.

The western Canadian frontier experience over three centuries shows no monolithic pattern of legal change leading to violent conflict. If there is any consistency it lay in a sensitivity to how much law (and law enforcement) was necessary in a given set of circumstances. The HBC was content for most of its history to allow its legal system to coexist on a basis of equality with those of the native peoples. With the beginning of agricultural settlement at Red River, the new law needed to accommodate this economic change was strictly limited in both its scope and geographical extent. After 1870, when the time came for a wholesale introduction of Canadian law, the government, benefiting from the American experience and perhaps from that of British Columbia as well, recognized that half measures would be likely to produce more conflict. By creating the most powerful law enforcement agency it could devise, the government hoped to keep violence to a minimum, not by avoiding change but by implementing it as quickly and thoroughly as possible.

NOTES

1. Robin Fisher, "Indian Warfare and Two Frontiers: A Comparison of British Columbia and Washington Territory During the Early Years of Settlement," *Pacific Historical Review* 50, no. 1 (1981): 31-51.

2. 43 Geo. III (1803), c. 138; and 1 & 2 Geo. IV (1821), c. 66.

3. E.E. Rich, *The Hudson's Bay Company, 1670-1870* (London: Hudson's Bay Record Society, 1959) vol. 2, 274.

4. Ibid., 318-28.

5. One of the North West Company partners, Edward Ellice, was a member of Parliament and acted as an informal, but highly influential, advisor on Canadian affairs to the Colonial Office. See "Edward Ellice," *Dictionary of Canadian Biography* (Toronto: University of Toronto Press, 1976), vol. 9, 233-39.

6. Gene M. Gressley "Lord Selkirk and the Canadian Courts," in J.M. Bumsted, ed., *Canadian History Before Confederation: Essays and Interpretations* (Toronto: Irwin-Dorsey, 1972), 287-304.

7. Ibid., 301.

8. "Owen Keveny," *Dictionary of Canadian Biography*, vol. 5, 465-66.

9. Hamar Foster, "Sins Against the Great Spirit: The Law, the Hudson's Bay Company, and the Mackenzie's River Murders, 1835-1839," *Criminal Justice History: An International Annual* 10 (1989), 23-74.

10. John S. Milloy, *The Plains Cree: Trade, Diplomacy and War, 1790 to 1870* (Winnipeg: University of Manitoba Press, 1988), 33.

11. Ibid., 83.

12. Kenneth S. Coates and William R. Morrison, *Land of the Midnight Sun: A History of the Yukon* (Edmonton: Hurtig, 1988), 25.

13. Marcel Giraud, *Le métis canadien, son role dans l'histoire des provinces de l'Ouest* (Paris: Institut d'ethnologie, 1945), vol. 2, 1024-26.

14. John Foster, "Paulet Paul: Métis or 'House Indian' Folk Hero?" *Manitoba History* 9 (Spring 1985): 2-8.

15. Shepard Krech III, "The Beaver Indians and the Hostilities at Fort St. John's," *Arctic Anthropology* 20, no. 2 (1983): 35-45.

16. Theodore Binnema, "Conflict or Cooperation?: Blackfoot Trade Strategies, 1794-1815" (M.A. thesis, University of Alberta, 1992), 52-53.

17. *R. v. St. Catharines Milling and Lumber Company* (1885), 10 O.R. 196; *R. v. St. Catharines Milling and Lumber Company* (1886), 13 O.A.R. 148; *St. Catharines Milling and Lumber Company v. The Queen* (1887), 13 S.C.R. 577; *St. Catharines Milling and Lumber Company v. The Queen* (1888), 14 A.C. 46.

18. Foster, "Sins Against the Great Spirit," 27.

19. Milloy, *Plains Cree*, 75.

20. R.F. Beal, J.E. Foster, and Louise Zuk, "The Métis Hivernement Settlement at Buffalo Lake, 1872-1877" (Edmonton: Alberta Historic Sites, Alberta Culture, 1987), 14.

21. Fisher, "Indian Warfare and Two Frontiers," 37.

22. E.H. Oliver, ed., *The Canadian North-West: Its Early Development and Legislative Records,*

Minutes of the Councils of the Red River Colony and the Northern Department of Rupert's Land, 2 vols. (Ottawa: Publications of the Canadian Archives, 1914-15), 1285-87.

23. W.L. Morton, *Manitoba: A History*, 2nd ed., (Toronto: University of Toronto Press, 1967), 50.

24. Chief Peguis, one of the principals involved, claimed repeatedly as late as 1860 that he had not intended to sell the land to Selkirk. See Rich, *Hudson's Bay Company*, vol. 2, 814.

25. In 1824 the governor and council tried a Saulteaux who killed his wife, found him guilty, then released him with a warning. See Dale Gibson and Lee Gibson, *Substantial Justice: Law and Lawyers in Manitoba, 1670-1970* (Winnipeg: Peguis Publishers, 1972), 21.

26. The total population was about 7,000 by the mid-1840s. See Gerald Friesen, *The Canadian Prairies: A History* (Toronto: University of Toronto Press, 1987), 90.

27. Kathryn M. Bindon, "Hudson's Bay Company Law: Adam Thom and the Institution of Order in Rupert's Land 1839-1854," in David H. Flaherty, ed., *Essays in the History of Canadian Law* (Toronto: The Osgoode Society, 1981), vol. 1, 46-47.

28. Roy St. George Stubbs, *Four Recorders of Rupert's Land* (Winnipeg: Peguis Publishers, 1967), 5.

29. D.H. Brown, "Unpredictable and Uncertain: Criminal Law in the Canadian North West Before 1886," *Alberta Law Review* 17 (1979).

30. Stubbs, *Four Recorders*, 19-20.

31. Bindon, "Hudson's Bay Company Law," 61.

32. Morton, *Manitoba*, 77.

33. Gibson, *Substantial Justice*, 44-45.

34. Gerald Friesen, "Homeland to Hinterland: Political Transition in Manitoba, 1870 to 1879," Canadian Historical Association, *Historical Papers*, 1979.

35. Morton, *Manitoba*, 196-97.

36. Stubbs, *Four Recorders*, 147-54.

37. Gibson, *Substantial Justice*, 54-58; Dale Gibson, *Attorney for the Frontier: Enos Stutsman* (Winnipeg: University of Manitoba Press, 1983), 77-96.

38. Robin Fisher, *Contact and Conflict: Indian-European Relations in British Columbia, 1774-1890* (Vancouver: University of British Columbia Press, 1977).

39. Margaret Ormsby, *British Columbia: A History* (Toronto: Macmillan, 1958), 79. See also the essay by Hamar Foster in this book.

40. Edward Sleigh Hewlett, "The Chilcotin Uprising of 1864," *BC Studies* 19 (Autumn 1973): 50-72.

41. Barry Gough, "Send a Gunboat! Checking Slavery and Controlling Liquor Traffic Among Coast Indians of British Columbia in the 1860's," *Pacific Northwest Quarterly* 69, no. 4 (October 1978): 159-68.

42. Fisher, "Indian Warfare and Two Frontiers," 48.

43. National Archives of Canada, John A. Macdonald Papers, vol. 252, Morris to Macdonald, 17 January 1873.

44. Lewis Herbert Thomas, *The Struggle for Responsible Government in the North-West Territories 1870-1897*, 2nd ed. (Toronto: University of Toronto Press, 1978).

45. S.W. Horrall, "Sir John A. Macdonald and the Mounted Police Force for the North West Territories," *Canadian Historical Review* 53, no. 2 (1972): 179-200; R.C. Macleod,

The North West Mounted Police and Law Enforcement 1873-1905 (Toronto: University of Toronto Press, 1975).

46. Clive Emsley, *Policing and Its Context 1750-1850* (London: Macmillan, 1983), 78-97.

47. Ibid., 146.

48. Nicholas Rogers, "Serving Toronto the Good: The Development of the City Police Force, 1834-1880," in Victor L. Russell, ed., *Forging a Consensus: Historical Essays on Toronto* (Toronto: University of Toronto Press, 1984), 122.

49. As long as he was prime minister, Macdonald always kept the Mounted Police under his personal control. See R.C. Macleod, "The Mounted Police and Politics," in Hugh A. Dempsey, ed., *Men in Scarlet* (Calgary: McClelland and Stewart, 1975), 95-114.

50. For the police use of publicity see Keith Walden, *Visions of Order: The Canadian Mounties in Symbol and Myth* (Toronto: University of Toronto Press, 1982). For police welfare work see Macleod, *North West Mounted Police and Law Enforcement*; and Carl Betke, "Pioneers and Police in the Canadian Prairies, 1885-1914," *Canadian Historical Association Papers* 9 (1980): 15-16.

51. Bob Beal and Rod Macleod, *Prairie Fire: The 1885 North West Rebellion* (Edmonton: Hurtig, 1984).

52. William R. Morrison, *Showing the Flag: The Mounted Police and Canadian Sovereignty in the North, 1894-1925* (Vancouver: University of British Columbia Press, 1985), 47.

53. Thomas Stone, *Miner's Justice: Migration, Law and Order on the Alaska-Yukon Frontier, 1873-1902* (New York: Peter Lang, 1988), 274.

54. Morrison, *Showing the Flag*, 47.

Aboriginal Rights and the Canadian Legal System: The West Coast Anomaly

Paul Tennant

First as colony within the empire, then as province within Canada, British Columbia has remained a distinct arena in the playing out of political and legal contests over aboriginal rights in Canada. When British Columbia joined Canada in 1871, its officials brought with them attitudes and policies that were sharply different from those established east of the Rockies. Subsequently, Canadian federal politicians[1] supported the new province's continuing to deny aboriginal rights and to act as though the principles applied elsewhere in the country did not apply west of the Rocky Mountains. Moreover, both federal and provincial politicians were resolutely agreed that the aboriginal peoples and their leaders should be excluded from the political process.

For their part, and despite their great cultural and political diversity, the aboriginal peoples of British Columbia accepted the province as the appropriate unit for their common political action. Thus, the white politicians and the Indians[2] both accepted the province as something of a separate political realm. In matters of aboriginal rights, as in so many other aspects of Canadian life, the Rockies were a notable boundary.

How did colonial British Columbia come to have an Indian policy that differed from that developed east of the Rockies? How did the province of British Columbia manage to preserve its separate policy after it joined Canada? How did the federal government's treatment of aboriginal claims differ east and west of the Rockies? These are the fundamental historical questions.

Today, however, the old pattern is crumbling. It began to come apart in the late 1960s as aboriginal British Columbians turned to new sorts of political action and began as well to take their claims to court. How were the British Columbia Indians able to involve the courts in their struggle for aboriginal rights? What have been the issues in the major court cases and how have the decisions affected aboriginal rights? These are the fundamental contemporary questions.

In seeking answers to all these questions, one must begin with the Royal Proclamation of 1763.[3] Having taken Quebec and now seeking to control the fur trade and further other imperial interests westward to the Pacific, the British intended the proclamation to be the basis of good relations with the Indians. The proclamation recognized the "nations or tribes" of Indians to the west of the colonies as continuing to own their lands under the new British sovereignty and protection, and directed that the Indians be left undisturbed on those lands. It thus recognized existing collective land rights and, it could be argued, the right to community or tribal self-government, as continuing under the British Crown.[4] The extension of British sovereignty was thus not regarded as canceling pre-existing rights. Aboriginal rights, however, were subject to limitations. Indians could not sell their lands until they were brought within a colony, and then they could do so only to the Crown, and only through collective public action.[5] As Brian Slattery has stated:

> In technical terms, the Indian interest constitutes a legal burden on the crown's ultimate title until surrendered. ...
>
> The Royal Proclamation of 1763 has a profound significance for modern Canada. Under its terms aboriginal peoples hold continuing rights to their lands except where those rights have been extinguished by voluntary cession.[6]

In 1763 Europeans already had almost three centuries of contact and control in the eastern and southern portions of the continent, but no white contact had yet been made in the future British Columbia. The vast area was at this time home to several hundred thousand inhabitants in some thirty separate tribal nations. The coastal peoples lived in dense concentrations, their unique and complex civilizations depending upon the giant cedar tree and the rich marine environment. The peoples of the interior, less numerous and more egalitarian, lived generally in smaller communities and had less complex societies.

Europeans arrived in the 1770s. For the next sixty years, the fur trade was the principal mode of Indian-European interaction. There was no attempt at colonization. The Indians gained the benefits of trade goods, and they suffered catastrophic epidemics of new diseases, but they experienced no formal challenge to their existing ways of governing their lands, their resources, and themselves. By the 1840s, James Douglas, son of a Scot trader and a Caribbean woman of color, and himself married to a Canadian Indian woman, was one of the leading western officials of the Hudson's Bay Company (HBC). The colony of Vancouver Island was established in 1849, the Company was given charge of land settlement and Douglas was soon appointed governor of the colony.

Douglas's superiors, in the Company and in the British Colonial

Office, accepted the principle of preexisting aboriginal land ownership; their instructions to him, in accord with the proclamation, assumed that he would purchase Indian land title in advance of white settlement. From 1850 to 1854, Douglas arranged fourteen treaties in which he purchased a small fraction of the land in the colony from its Indian owners. The Indians ceded title in return for payment in blankets; they retained the right to carry on their fisheries in perpetuity, and to hunt on the treaty lands until settlement took place.[7] According to the literal wording of the treaties, the Indians retained their original ownership of their "Village Sites and Enclosed Fields," but subsequently these places, which amounted to only a few acres per capita, were simply treated as reserves[8] belonging to the Crown.

At this same time, officials in the colony of Canada had recently completed treaties with Indians along Lakes Huron and Superior. These treaties were more generous than the Douglas treaties in reserve acreage, allowing eighty acres for each Indian family of five,[9] but both sets of treaties recognized Indian title only to extinguish it. Tribal or community self-government under the Crown was not even considered by the white officials to be a possible aboriginal right. The Douglas and the Canadian treaties were essentially vehicles that recognized preexisting land rights but ensured that Indian title and self-government did not continue. The Canadian officials were explicitly and consciously following the principles set out in the Royal Proclamation. Douglas, however, gives no evidence of having been aware of the proclamation, and, indeed, he and company officials regarded New Zealand treaty policy as their model.[10]

James Douglas arranged no treaties after 1854. Most of Vancouver Island remained devoid of any agreement by the Indians that their lands be used for settlement. On the mainland, which became the new colony of British Columbia in 1858, Douglas made no land purchases of any sort. (Douglas became governor of both colonies and gave up his position of chief factor of the HBC.) The conventional academic explanation of this aspect of Douglas's policy has been that Douglas desired to purchase Indian title, but lacked the funds to do so. The cost of the fourteen treaties had been minimal, however, and Douglas could easily have diverted the necessary sums for further purchases without substantially impairing his other spending priorities, one of which was road construction into the mainland interior.

On Vancouver Island, under pressure from the elected legislators and newspaper editorials to deal fairly with the Indians on the Indian land question, Douglas continued rhetorically to acknowledge the Indians as having rights to the land. On the mainland, facing no legislature and no contrary white public opinion, Douglas did not even acknowledge the issue, despite the explicit mention of treaties in the first instructions sent to him by the Colonial Office concerning the new colony.

Douglas's departing from his earlier principles and coming to ignore in practice not only aboriginal land title but also all other land-based aboriginal rights in both colonies was the first critical step in British Columbia's divergence from the policies of the Royal Proclamation (much less those applied in New Zealand). What explains Douglas's new policies?

By the 1850s public concern in Britain over the treatment of aboriginal peoples was declining and the British government was becoming less concerned with the internal affairs of the North American colonies. Indeed, as governor, Douglas was freer of control by superiors than he had been as a HBC official. In these circumstances he was able to develop and implement his own policies and to sidestep the initial Colonial Office expectation that he would proceed with more treaties in accord with established British policy.[11]

Well aware of the physical and social ills that were the lot of many Indians, Douglas believed that aboriginal salvation lay in assimilation. Douglas's views must not be mistaken. His vision showed none of the mean-spirited bigotry that characterized the assimilation policy of later times; his was a vision of assimilation with equality and dignity. Aboriginal traditions and aboriginal rights, however, had no place in that vision. Individual Indians would become regular British subjects. Douglas's "system," as he called it, had two principal objectives. The first was the transformation of the Indians through Christian conversion and basic education. This task would be accomplished by Christian missionaries.

The second objective was the dismantling of Indian communities and the assimilation of individual Indians and families. While Douglas must have intended that many Indians would become nonagrarian workers, it was free-hold farming that his system emphasized. Indians were to have the same land rights as white settlers, and on the same legal foundations — under authority granted by the British Crown, individuals could pre-empt unsurveyed Crown land and, by developing and living on the land, obtain fee simple ownership. This policy would be applied on the remaining nontreaty portions of Vancouver Island and on the mainland.

In both theory and practice, Douglas's system denied any basis for aboriginal rights. Any positive relevance of the aboriginal past was denied in the intent to convert the Indians, to educate them in British ways, and to have them leave their collective, nonagrarian culture in favor of individual, largely agrarian, pursuits. The new land rights that Indians were to have were to be granted by the British Crown and exercised on land that was regarded as unencumbered Crown land. In practical and legal terms, there was simply no recognition that there was any unsurrendered and unextinguished Indian interest constituting any burden on the Crown's title.

Douglas's policy was a denial of aboriginal title and of the principles of the Royal Proclamation. This profound but simple fact has hitherto been overlooked, in part because of Douglas's liberality of outlook toward the Indians, and in part because Douglas never acknowledged that he was denying Indian land title and other preexisting rights.

Douglas dealt with aboriginal rights not by explicitly extinguishing them (as through further treaties or expropriation) but by ignoring them. It was Douglas who laid the foundation for the doctrine to which all future British Columbia governments would adhere — that aboriginal rights either had never existed or had been extinguished by the very fact that they had been ignored by the new regime.[12]

Closely related to Douglas's preemption policy was the matter of Indian reserves. After abandoning the treaty process, Douglas unilaterally allotted very small reserves, typically of no more than ten acres for each Indian family. The creation of these early reserves in British Columbia involved neither formal Indian negotiation and consent, nor any formal recognition of Indian right, whether that right was pre-existing or granted by the new regime. The reserves were government creations and Douglas was clear in stating that they could be reduced or sold by government. The small size of the reserves can be understood fully only in light of Douglas's preemption policy. Indians were to obtain their land not in reserves, but by quitting their communities to become individual homesteaders. In so doing, they would have access to the same amounts of land as individual white settlers.[13] In Douglas's system the reserves were mere way stations; once the Indians were converted and educated they would find their future off the reserves.

Douglas retired in 1864. Over the next decade and more the most influential official was Joseph Trutch, who served as chief commissioner of Lands and who was responsible for the colony's side of arrangements for union with Canada, which occurred in 1871. It was Trutch who first enunciated the British Columbia government position that Indian title had never existed and never been recognized. Trutch disposed of the Douglas treaties by having them viewed as friendship pacts in which the Indians had been paid to stop enunciating their unjustified claims.

Later students have tended to be critical of Trutch, seeing him, quite correctly, as an ill-informed "red-neck," and also viewing him as reversing Douglas's Indian·land policies. As far as Indian title was concerned, however, Trutch was merely bringing Douglas's implicit, *de facto* denial of title into open acknowledgement. Trutch's denial of title was accepted in part because of the groundwork already laid by Douglas, but also because of the emerging white myth that Indians were primitive creatures with neither the experience nor the mental capacity to have held sophisticated understandings of property in land. In this view there was no more need to arrange treaties with Indians than with beavers or chipmunks.

Nevertheless, if Trutch and Douglas were alike in denying pre-existing aboriginal rights, it was under Trutch that the withdrawal of equal rights under the Crown began. The two colonies were united into the single colony of British Columbia in 1866, and one of the first acts of the legislature was to prohibit preemption by "any of the Aborigines of this Colony or the Territories neighbouring thereto."[14] So far as ready access to land was concerned, Indians were now confined to their reserves, whose small size had been justified in the first place only by the Indian ability to preempt elsewhere. Despite the new circumstances, Trutch continued generally to enforce the ten-acre formula in laying out new reserves.

While little record was kept of the negotiations over union between British Columbia and Canada, it is evident that aboriginal matters were not of high concern to either party. There is some evidence that Canadian officials assumed that the principles of the proclamation had been followed west of the Rockies, and that reasonable reserves had been laid out following treaty negotiations, and there is no evidence that the Canadian prime minister, Sir John A. Macdonald, distrusted Trutch's assurances that Indians had been treated fairly and liberally. In any event, the terms of union completely ignored aboriginal rights, including land title, and dealt only with Indian reserves.

The British North America Act gave the Canadian Parliament jurisdiction over Indians and Indian reserves, once the reserves had been constituted, but provided Parliament with no power to expropriate provincial land for reserves or to compel a province to provide it. As reserves had been laid out in only a few areas of British Columbia by

1871, it was essential that the terms of union ensure that the province would provide land for further reserves. Article 13 of the terms of union left the province with the upper hand, for in it the province agreed only to "a policy as liberal as that hitherto pursued," and to convey "tracts of land of such extent as it has hitherto been the practice of the British Columbia Government to appropriate for that purpose."[15] This wording meant that the province could not be compelled to exceed its established ten-acre formula. In addition, as the article provided no ready means of arbitrating federal-provincial differences in approach, the province would have to consent to the creation of every reserve and was thus left with a veto power in the process of reserve creation.

Union thus brought British Columbia Indians under federal jurisdiction which, for most purposes, meant supervision by Indian agents operating under the federal Indian Act, but did not extend the principles of the Royal Proclamation into British Columbia. The terms of union assumed that aboriginal rights were irrelevant, and entrenched the province's Indian reserve policy. The possibility remained that the federal executive would try to protect Indian interests by using its power of disallowing provincial statutes. Although the power would be used on occasion for this purpose, it would not have any substantial effect on the province's Indian policies.

As important as the institutional safeguards provided to the province by the terms of union were the informal political arrangements which were entered upon. Trutch returned from Ottawa as Macdonald's main British Columbia cohort and confidant. Macdonald appointed him the first lieutenant governor and had him knighted. Over the next quarter century the Conservatives were in power in Ottawa for all but five years. During those five years, 1873-78, the Liberal government did put pressure on the province, mainly to establish a more generous reserve policy, but the matter of treaties and title was also raised. During this same interval the loose opposition to Trutch in the provincial legislature pressed for larger reserves, but Trutch was easily able to deflect both federal and local efforts. It was also at this time that the legislature withdrew the provincial franchise from Indians.

Having acquired Rupert's Land and the North-West Territories, the Canadian authorities had already begun to negotiate treaties in accord with the principles of the proclamation. Indeed the first major prairie treaties were being actively negotiated while the British Columbia delegation was in Ottawa, and they were signed in the same year that British Columbia joined Canada. During the remainder of the 1870s the

Canadian authorities continued the treaty-making process across the southern Prairies, and at the turn of the century arranged further treaties covering the remaining area west of the Rockies north to the 60th parallel.

For the most part the prairie treaties were completed, reserves were established and the surrendered lands were surveyed before white settlement was permitted, and, with the partial exception of Manitoba, before provinces were created. Local white public opinion was thus hardly a factor in government policy, as the process was in most cases completed not only before the whites had any representative institutions at the local or provincial level, but also before most white settlers had even arrived. Friction on the Prairies was further reduced because of the reserve acreage formula which, as in Treaty 8, generally allocated Indians a per-family reserve acreage that was comparable to the acreage available to settler families in the same area.

In British Columbia the pattern was the reverse. On Vancouver Island from 1854 to 1864 white settlers had been present and in support of further treaties; James Douglas had resisted that pressure. After 1864, as white immigration continued, the views represented by Joseph Trutch became firmly implanted in the white population. British Columbia was now assumed to have been an empty land awaiting white "discovery"; Indians were taken as inferior and as incapable on their own of conceiving of title in property; white agitators were therefore blamed for the fact that Indians were claiming aboriginal title and other rights; Indians who made claims were depicted as conniving and venal.[16]

A further and important factor, present until the 1940s, was the white assumption that the Indians were a vanishing race whose members would lose their identity through assimilation or through the population decline that continued until the 1920s (when there were fewer than 30,000 registered Indians remaining in the province). The Indian peoples and the issue of aboriginal rights were given neither substance nor honor in white British Columbia history or politics. From 1871 to the 1980s no white member of any provincial cabinet ever demonstrated a full understanding of the bases for aboriginal claims in the province.[17]

Yet British Columbia Indians did not disappear and the tribal nations did not lose their identity — and there were Indian protests from the earliest indications that white settlers were proceeding to take up land without Indian agreement. In 1887 a delegation of Nisga'a and Tsimshian chiefs traveled from the north coast to Victoria to meet with government officials. The chiefs demanded recognition of aboriginal title, the making of treaties to legitimize white settlement and to guarantee adequate Indian reserves, and the allowing of Indian community or tribal autonomy under the British Crown. The chiefs also demanded a public inquiry into the whole land question.

Premier William Smithe dismissed the notion of Indian title, telling the chiefs that the Queen had generously given reserves "to her Indian children because they do not know so well how to make their own living the same as a white man," and that "[w]hen the whites first came among you, you were little better than the wild beasts of the field."[18] However, fearing rebellion, the federal and provincial governments set up a joint commission of public inquiry, which dismissed the consistent Indian demands for treaties and for control over natural resources as the misguided products of white agitation.[19]

In accepting the commission's report, the government of Canada sanctioned the British Columbia government's denial of aboriginal title and abandoned the principles of the proclamation as far as British Columbia was concerned. Even before 1887, however, the federal authorities had shown themselves willing to curtail Indian traditions that hindered assimilation. Among the coastal peoples, the great feast or potlatch was the major social, political and economic institution, and its continuation was a practical assertion of an Indian right to self-government; the potlatch was outlawed by the federal Parliament in 1884.[20]

During the 1880s and later, however, as has been indicated, federal officials continued to arrange Indian treaties east of the Rockies in accord with the proclamation. One of these, Treaty 8, actually included the portion of British Columbia that lies east of the Rockies. Anxious to quell threats of Indian violence in connection with the overland flow of gold seekers to the Yukon in 1898, the Canadian authorities, without provincial participation, used the regular treaty process to have some Indian communities in the northeastern portion of the province cede their title. The problem of provincial intransigence over reserves and reserve size was solved by granting reserves from land that the province had turned over to Canada to encourage railway construction. The Treaty 8 reserves allowed 640 acres (one square mile) for each Indian family, that is, more than sixty times the acreage normally allowed elsewhere in the province by the British Columbia government. Applying as it did the principles of the proclamation, and thus escaping the strictures of the terms of union, Treaty 8 remains the major anomaly within the anomaly.[21]

Denied the principles of the proclamation, and confined to their small reserves, Indians in the remainder of the province now turned towards sustained political action. Communities and tribal nations were now mounting their separate protests, always focusing on the land question. By 1910 there were intertribal political associations on the coast and in the southern interior, and in 1915 they came together to form the first provincewide Indian political organization. Henceforward, with a brief hiatus from 1927 to 1931, there would be a continuous presence of intertribal political organizations in the province.[22]

In 1907, the provincial legislature had further curtailed Indian civil rights by amending the Land Act to prohibit Indians from purchasing surveyed land owned by the province.[23] In 1912 the provincial and federal governments took the first steps towards the eventual "cutting-off" from a number of reserves of land regarded as highly desirable by whites. The "cut-offs" were made, in 1924, despite repeated government reassurances that the Indian Act's provision requiring Indian consent for reserve reductions would be respected. The Allied Indian Tribes of British Columbia pressed Ottawa and Victoria for treaties and adequate reserves, and hoped to have the land claims considered in London by the Judicial Committee of the Privy Council, which now seemed supportive of similar claims in other parts of the empire. The federal government agreed only to a special parliamentary committee of inquiry.[24] The committee summarily denied any need for treaties or larger reserves, blamed white agitators for the claims, and recommended that agitators be curbed.

Parliament responded by outlawing Indian claims activity. It did so indirectly, but effectively, by making it illegal for any person to receive money, or promise of money, from any Indian for any claims-related activity.[25] At times the provision would later be depicted as intended only to prevent payments to lawyers, but the provision in fact made it illegal for any Indian or other person to receive money from any Indian, and so, in practice, made it illegal for any Indian political organization to pursue land claims or any other claims to aboriginal rights. Payments to lawyers for claims purposes were certainly now prohibited, and thus, any practical possibility of getting the claims to court was now illegal.

The anti-claims provision remained in effect until 1951, when it and, as it happened, the anti-potlatch provision were both dropped. Two years earlier the Supreme Court of Canada had replaced the Judicial Committee of the Privy Council as Canada's highest court of appeal. While there is no evidence that federal officials considered there to be any possibility that British Columbia Indians would once again take up the land-claims issue, any official who did consider the possibility would have been reassured by the comforting fact that Canadian judges would now be the final arbiters should any aboriginal claims get to court.

The Canadian courts had to this time served only to buttress the twentieth-century view that all rights were created and granted by the Crown or Parliament. The courts enforced the treaties east of the Rockies but regarded aboriginal rights, as well as the treaties, as continuing at the pleasure of the Crown. Aboriginal concerns were not acknowledged as an important category within Canadian jurisprudence. Judges had the same outlook as the politicians.

As for British Columbia provincial politicians, the possibility of Indian land-claims activity was no longer even a matter of conscious awareness. There was, however, some postwar unease about racial discrimination, and as a result Indians regained the provincial franchise in 1949, while in 1953 the prohibitions against Indian preemption and purchase of Crown land were repealed. The Douglas treaties had long since been forgotten by provincial officials. From time to time on Vancouver Island Indians were arrested and fined or jailed for hunting out-of-season or without a provincial license on unoccupied treaty land, and the fishery interests of the treaty Indians were ignored by industry and governments.

Indian pursuit of land claims resumed in British Columbia within a few years of the legalizing of claims activity. In 1955 the north coast Nisga'a[26] formed the province's first tribal council; other tribal councils and new political organizations soon followed. In 1969, with the final provocation provided by the federal government's celebrated "White Paper" proposal to terminate Indian status, a provincewide organization was formed to continue pressing for a claims settlement. While that organization[27] and others would spend great effort over the next two decades lobbying both levels of government, the lobbying itself produced few direct results. The major changes that did occur in government policy were induced, rather, by the courts; and, in a nice irony, the Canadian courts would not have awakened to the significance of aboriginal rights when they did had it not been for the surviving hand of James Douglas, who had been the first to deny aboriginal rights in British Columbia.

As has been noted, the Douglas treaties stated that the Indians were allowed "to hunt over the unoccupied lands ... as formerly," but the provincial government had come to ignore that right. In 1963, two Nanaimo Indians, Clifford White and David Bob, shot deer on unoccupied treaty land, and were arrested for killing the deer without a provincial license and out-of-season. Thomas Berger, a young lawyer just starting practice, defended the two, arguing that the Douglas agreements were valid treaties that acknowledged and continued the preexisting aboriginal right to hunt, and that the Royal Proclamation guaranteed aboriginal rights in British Columbia. The province's lawyers argued that the agreements were private Hudson's Bay Company transactions rather than treaties, and that the proclamation had not been intended to apply west of the Rockies.[28]

In a 3-2 decision, the British Columbia Court of Appeal ruled that the agreements were valid treaties, and therefore acquitted White and Bob. Only one member of the majority, Mr. Justice Tom Norris, concerned himself with the deeper principles; in his opinion "the aboriginal rights as to hunting and fishing affirmed by the *Proclamation of 1763* and recognized by the Treaty ... still exist."[29] As Douglas Sanders has pointed out, Berger's legal assertions and Norris's confirming opinion "had the effect of reviving the aboriginal rights issue" among legal scholars and in the courts of Canada.[30]

As a direct consequence of Berger's success in the *White and Bob* case, the Nisga'a tribal council hired him to take their land claim to court, seeking a declaration against the province that the Nisga'a had held title to their land at the time the colony was established, and that the title continued in the absence of any explicit action specifically intended to extinguish it. The courts in British Columbia ruled that the Nisga'a had never held title,[31] because the proclamation had not applied west of the Rockies, but that even if they had held title it would have been extinguished by the fact of the province's having ignored it. The views of British Columbia judges and prevailing white assumptions remained in complete accord.

The Nisga'a appealed to the Supreme Court of Canada, all of whose members at the time were from east of the Rockies. Seven judges heard the case, but only six gave opinions on its merits. They agreed unanimously that the Nisga'a had held title to their land when British Columbia was created.[32] This ruling was a major moral victory for the Nisga'a and an outright rejection of the province's arguments, but the practical question was whether the Nisga'a still held title. On this question the six judges split evenly, with three judges holding that implicit extinguishment was sufficient and three that explicit action was necessary. Here too, with three judges of the highest court siding with them, the Nisga'a had won a moral victory, but the tie in opinions meant that the Nisga'a would obtain no court declaration of present-day ownership. The tie did mean, however, that no precedent had been set. The province had not won either.

The Supreme Court outcome added enormously to the strength of the moral claim of the Nisga'a; they had lost a legal battle but won a major political victory. The practical results were soon evident when the federal government, under Prime Minister Pierre Trudeau, announced that it would now negotiate treaties with Indians west of the Rockies. Trudeau made clear that his own views had been altered by the opinions of the judges. Trudeau assumed, or at least hoped, that British Columbia would join in the negotiations. The Nisga'a and federal officials began negotiations in 1976, but the province declined to participate.

The next major case had its beginnings in the 1950s, when federal officials arranged for the lease of part of the Musqueam reserve, in Vancouver, to the Shaughnessy Golf and Country Club. Chief Delbert Guerin later discovered that the true appraised value of the land had been withheld from the Musqueam, and realized that the officials had been acting on behalf of the club rather than the Indian band. The Musqueam case seemed hopeless, but they hired lawyer Marvin Storrow who guided the case to the Supreme Court of Canada, which in 1984 confirmed the lower court award of $10 million in damages to be paid by the federal government to the band.

The Supreme Court's ruling rested not simply on regular civil law notions of breach of trust, but also on the doctrine of aboriginal title, which the court now clarified, in part by revising the generally understood implications of the Nisga'a decision. Chief Justice Brian Dickson now affirmed that aboriginal title was "a legal right derived from the Indians' historic occupation and possession of their tribal lands"; that the Indians' "interest in their lands is a pre-existing legal right not created by Royal Proclamation, by ... the Indian Act, or by any other executive order or legislative provision"; and that the legal right applied whether the lands in question were a reserve or "traditional tribal lands" that were outside reserves and on which aboriginal title remained "unrecognized."[33]

It was precisely traditional tribal lands outside reserves that were at this time the subject of protests and blockades on the part of Indians attempting to protect those lands from provincially authorized resource development. Most of the active tribal nations had by this time prepared and presented their formal statements of land claim to the federal government, in accord with the federal policy developed following the

Nisga'a decision. But the claims were getting nowhere as long as the province refused to recognize their validity and to respond by agreeing to negotiate.

The blockade by Nuu-chah-nulth Indians to halt logging on Meares Island was getting underway when the *Guerin* decision was delivered. A judge of the Supreme Court of British Columbia denied the Indians' application for an injunction to halt the logging, but in early 1985 the Court of Appeal granted the injunction pending the outcome of the Nuu-chah-nulth land claim. In effect, the court gave a higher priority to the Indian interest in nontreaty land than to the province's right to govern resource development on that land. Mr. Justice Peter Seaton presented the court's main opinion:

> The trial judge thought the claim to Indian title so weak that he could safely conclude that it could not succeed. I do not agree with that view... The proposal is to clear-cut the area. Almost nothing will be left. I cannot think of any native right that could be exercised on lands that have recently been logged... I am firmly of the view that the claim to Indian title cannot be rejected at this stage of the litigation... The Indians have pressed their land claims in various ways for generations. The claims have not been dealt with and found invalid. They have not been dealt with at all. Meanwhile, the logger continues his steady march and the Indians see themselves retreating into a smaller and smaller area. They, too, have drawn the line at Meares Island. The island has become a symbol of their claim to rights in the land... It is important to the Indians' case that they be able to show their use of this forest. I do not mean to suggest that the Indians ought to continue using the forest only as they used it in the past. The importance of the evidence of extensive use is that it may demonstrate a right to continued use... There is a problem about tenure that has not been attended to in the past. We are being asked to ignore the problem as others have ignored it. I am not willing to do that.[34]

Those who had been ignoring the rights and claims of Indians were the provincial government politicians. The courts were now putting the politicians on notice that they no longer had the field to themselves. Over the next few years some half dozen similar injunctions were granted in various parts of the province, giving reassurance to Indians and anxiety to resource companies. The provincial government politicians tried at first to shape non-Indian public opinion against the land claims and against any need for the province to negotiate. But with a new premier, William Vander Zalm, in 1986 and a new, larger and more moderate group of appointed officials in the Ministry of Native Affairs, the provincial outlook began to adjust to the new reality being imposed by the courts.

During 1990 two major developments, one in the courts, the other on roads and rail lines, occurred that forced the province to act. Section 35(1) of Canada's new Constitution of 1982 states that "[t]he existing aboriginal and treaty rights of the aboriginal peoples of Canada are hereby recognized and affirmed." A similar statement had been removed at the last minute from the draft version; it was reinserted as a result of protests by Indian groups and others, but with the word "existing" added to it. It was evident that a number of premiers accepted section 35(1) only because they believed that nontreaty aboriginal rights no longer existed. They took the same position that British Columbia had been taking in court, that any such rights had been extinguished implicitly — by being ignored or superseded in provincial or federal statutes or regulations. Neither the Nisga'a nor the *Guerin* case was affected by the section as both had arisen before 1982.

In 1984 Ronald Sparrow, a Musqueam, was arrested, in traditional waters of his people, for fishing with a net longer than federal regulation allowed. The location was not part of a reserve and was, like all of mainland British Columbia west of the Rockies, not subject to any treaty. The Musqueam band again hired Marvin Storrow and argued that the length restriction violated the Musqueams' collective aboriginal right to fish as now recognized and affirmed by section 35(1). The federal government, joined by the province, argued that the Fisheries Act and its regulations had served to extinguish any aboriginal right to fish, and had done so prior to 1982 — that is, that by taking control of the Indian fishery Parliament had extinguished any aboriginal right to fish, even though the act did not state that it was extinguishing the right. The provincial and the county court judges accepted the federal assertions and convicted Sparrow.

The British Columbia Court of Appeal reversed the lower courts, however, and in the late spring of 1990 the Supreme Court of Canada upheld the Court of Appeal ruling with a unanimous decision that an aboriginal right to fish did exist in British Columbia in 1982. The principles and strictures set out by the Supreme Court make the *Sparrow* decision the single most important aboriginal-rights ruling yet made in Canada. Those principles and strictures came increasingly to be seen by observers in British Columbia as the death knell for any lingering provincial government hope that the direction of the Nisga'a and *Guerin* cases would be halted.

The court flatly rejected the principle of implicit extinguishment. The Fisheries Act had not "demonstrated a clear and plain intention to extinguish the Indian aboriginal right to fish." More generally,

> [h]istorical policy on the part of the Crown is not only incapable of extinguishing the existing aboriginal right without clear intention, but is also incapable of, in itself, delineating that right. The nature of government regulations cannot be determinative of the content and scope of an existing aboriginal right.[35]

Aboriginal rights are, indeed, to be seen as a distinct aspect of law, and one that is not subordinate even to the most cherished of Anglo-Canadian legal concepts:

> Courts must be careful ... to avoid the application of traditional common law concepts of property as they develop their understanding of ... the "sui generis" nature of aboriginal rights.[36]

While the federal government is entitled to "regulate the exercise" of an aboriginal right, the court indicated that negotiations with the affected group are the appropriate means of determining the content of regulations.[37] In addition, the section is to be "construed in a purposive way. When the purposes of the affirmation of aboriginal rights are considered, it is clear that a generous, liberal interpretation ... is demanded."[38] In accord with this principle, the key word "existing," which the premiers had added to sanitize the section, is not to be interpreted merely in terms of rights or practices that were actually being exercised by any particular group in 1982 (in which case different peoples in different places would possess different rights, and groups would have lost their rights because they had obeyed the law). "Existing" is to mean "unextinguished," and the term "existing aboriginal rights" is to be "interpreted flexibly so as to permit their evolution over time."[39] Aboriginal rights in Canada are not frozen in the past nor are they to be static in the future.

While the court did not specifically consider the application of the *Sparrow* principles to aboriginal title (and, indeed, the clear separation by the courts of fishing rights and land-based rights must be pointed to as significant in itself), there could be no doubt that these principles were precisely the ones that Indians had been advancing and that the province had been denying since the Nisga'a had brought the first land claim to court. The province could no longer make any credible defense of its own historic position.

By the spring of 1990 the second major land claim trial, brought by the neighbors of the Nisga'a, the Gitksan-Wet'suwet'en, was nearly finished in the Supreme Court of British Columbia.[40] Even before the *Sparrow* decision, senior provincial officials, together with a varied assortment of journalists, lawyers, Indian leaders, and academics (including the author) had come to anticipate that Chief Justice Allan McEachern,[41] who was hearing the case, would recognize unextinguished aboriginal title as having some degree of present-day force, thus leaving the province with no choice but to negotiate with the Indians to reach an agreement. The *Sparrow* decision served to strengthen those anticipations.

The other major development during 1990 began in June in Quebec, when provincial police escalated the Mohawk road blockade into an armed confrontation, generating daily headlines and endless television footage across Canada and provoking supportive road and rail blockades by other Indian communities, most of them in British Columbia. The express purpose of the British Columbia blockades, however, was to pressure the province of British Columbia to join the federal government in negotiating land claims with the Indians.

In August, after the premier of British Columbia had met with a number of the tribal nations, the historic reversal occurred. The premier announced that the province would enter the negotiations, and before the end of the year the province had in fact formally joined the still ongoing negotiations with the Nisga'a. The province, however, went only half way; it agreed to negotiate but it still refused to admit that aboriginal title was an existing right. In December a seven-member task force (with two members appointed by the federal government, two by the provincial government, and three by a representative meeting of Indians) was established to make recommendations concerning the substance and conduct of the negotiations. The task force was assigned the deadline of July 1991.

In March 1991 Chief Justice McEachern gave his decision in the Gitksan-Wet'suwet'en case. The decision was a stunning defeat for the Indian claimants. McEachern ruled that the precontact Indian groups could not be regarded as developed and sovereign societies. At contact, the groups had

> rights to live in their villages and to occupy adjacent lands for the purpose of gathering the products of the lands and waters for subsistence and ceremonial purposes. These aboriginal interests did not include ownership of or jurisdiction over the territory.[42]

The rights that did exist, however, did not survive the colonial period, for, McEachern found, the Royal Proclamation of 1763 had never applied to the territory of the province and, to clinch the matter,

> [t]he pre-Confederation colonial enactments construed in their historic setting exhibit a clear and plain intention to extinguish aboriginal interests in order to give an unburdened title to the settlers, and the Crown did extinguish such rights to all the lands of the colony.[43]

Evidently Chief Justice McEachern took the Supreme Court of Canada's "clear and plain intention" criterion (enunciated in the *Sparrow* decision) to mean that any colonial intention had only to be clear and plain retrospectively to judges in 1991 — and did not need to be clear and plain to Indians or others when the events were unfolding in the colonial period.

As intriguing as the substance of the judgment was its belittling treatment of Indian life and culture. Critics found much to suggest that McEachern's outlook and values had been formed in an earlier age and were almost untouched by attitudes and assumptions that could be considered politically correct in the modern era.[44]

Surprisingly perhaps, the British Columbia government did not seek any political advantage from the McEachern decision. The premier and the minister of Native Affairs (both new in 1991 and neither with any prior record of support for aboriginal causes) reiterated the province's commitment to negotiate aboriginal claims, while the federal minister of Indian Affairs gave similar reassurances. The tripartite task force issued a unanimous report in July, recommending a set of principles and guidelines for the negotiation process that was immediately and enthusiastically endorsed by an assembly representing most of the Indian groups in the province. Both ministers gave their general approval almost as quickly. Thus, there was every indication that broad-scale tripartite negotiations concerning aboriginal land title and other rights would soon commence in British Columbia.

What then is to be concluded about aboriginal rights and the legal system in British Columbia? After an initial policy of recognizing aboriginal title and other rights, British Columbia came to have a colonial policy of denying those rights. Britain was willing to allow James Douglas to proceed with his "system" which denied aboriginal rights, in favor of the noble, if misguided, goal of egalitarian assimilation. Joseph Trutch was at the forefront as predominant white opinion turned to a denial both of Indian rights and of Indian equality, and embraced the doctrine that to ignore aboriginal rights was to erase any that might somehow have survived. Trutch's greatest achievement was arranging terms of union that omitted any mention of aboriginal rights and preserved British Columbia's ungenerous reserve policy. Thereafter, despite occasional lip service, the Canadian authorities were unable or unwilling to press to have the principles of the Royal Proclamation enforced west of the Rockies, and in 1927 the Canadian Parliament took the ultimate action, aimed directly at British Columbia Indians, of outlawing claims-related activities. Judicial redress was thus made legally impossible.

The established pattern began to crumble in the late 1960s as the courts themselves became willing to depart from the assumptions of the white politicians. A new sector of Canadian jurisprudence emerged, focusing upon aboriginal rights, and for two decades the courts largely supplanted the politicians as the aboriginal-rights decision makers. During the late 1980s, through the various injunctions and through the *Sparrow* decision, the courts replanted the principles of the Royal Proclamation west of the Rockies. The courts, however, made clear their expectation that the politicians would resume their political role.

In 1990, following the Indian protest blockades, the politicians did resume control of the aboriginal-rights political agenda. In 1991, the political process withstood the shock when none other than the chief justice of the province departed from the established judicial trend by seeking to uproot the proclamation west of the Rockies. The federal and provincial politicians were no longer willing to exempt British Columbia from the principles long applied elsewhere in Canada. Moreover, the aboriginal leaders were by now accepted as major and legitimate participants in the political process. As far as aboriginal rights were concerned, the Rocky Mountains were at last beginning to subside.

NOTES

The author is grateful to Hamar Foster, Tina Loo, John McLaren and Douglas Sanders for comments on the initial draft of this paper.

1.   In this paper I include politicians and officials within the meaning of the term "legal system."

2.   In accord with common British Columbia usage, I use the words "aboriginal," "Indian" and "native" synonymously.

3.   The proclamation continues to be published as the oldest document among the statutes of Canada. "Appendix No. 1; The Royal Proclamation, October 7, 1763," *Revised Statutes of Canada 1970* (Ottawa: Queen's Printer, 1970), 123-29. (Cited hereafter as Proclamation.)

4.   Despite its fundamental constitutional importance, however, the proclamation has been largely ignored in Canadian education and remains largely unknown to the Canadian public; it has thus not been allowed to influence general non-Indian historical or normative understandings.

5.   As the proclamation stated, "If at any Time any of the Said Indians should be inclined to dispose of the said Lands, the same shall be Purchased only for Us, in our Name, at some public Meeting or Assembly of the said Indians." Ibid., 128.

6.   Brian Slattery, "The Hidden Constitution," in Menno Boldt and J. Anthony Long, eds.,

The Quest for Justice: Aboriginal Peoples and Aboriginal Rights (Toronto: University of Toronto Press, 1985), 121-22.

7. I deal in more detail with Douglas's land policies in Tennant, *Aboriginal Peoples and Politics: The Indian Land Question in British Columbia, 1849-1989* (Vancouver: University of British Columbia Press, 1990), chapters 2 and 3. A more comprehensive examination of British outlook and policies to 1890 is provided in Robin Fisher, *Contact and Conflict: Indian-European Relations in British Columbia, 1774-1890* (Vancouver: University of British Columbia Press, 1977). The impact of colonial policies on one major tribal nation is examined in Joanne Drake-Terry, *The Same as Yesterday: The Lillooet Chronicle the Theft of Their Land and Resources* (Lillooet, B.C.: Lillooet Tribal Council, 1990).

8. Indian "reserve," not "reservation," is the Canadian term.

9. Such acreage figures were simply formulas used in determining reserve size, and do not indicate that individual families were assigned particular plots. Reserves, in both British Columbia and Canada, were assigned collectively to Indian communities, or "bands" as they are formally styled.

10. James Hendrickson, "The Aboriginal Land Policy of Governor James Douglas, 1849-1864" (paper presented at BC Studies Conference, Simon Fraser University, 4-6 November 1988).

11. This is not to suggest that Douglas's subsequent policies were concealed from his superiors. Douglas kept them informed and they endorsed his initiatives without further insistence on treaties or other formal means of recognizing aboriginal rights.

12. Even though the government of British Columbia agreed in 1990 that it would negotiate land claims, it continued to decline to recognize formally the principle of aboriginal title.

13. In fact, primarily along the lower Fraser River, some Indians did proceed to preempt. In face of white hostility, Douglas publicly defended his policy, doing so in one of his last acts as governor, in his opening address to the first session of the new mainland legislature, in January 1864.

14. British Columbia, "An Ordinance further to define the law regulating the acquisition of Land in British Columbia," 31 March 1866. A further amendment in 1870 extended the prohibition to "any of the Aborigines of this continent." The government was empowered to provide exemptions from the prohibition in specific cases.

15. British Columbia, *Sessional Papers*, 1871, 12.

16. From the 1880s through to the present, provincial government politicians have continually believed that Indian claims were a recent phenomenon, with the assertions typically being that claims were fifteen or twenty years old, and with their origin equated with some outside stimulus, such as the arrival of a white sympathizer or, most recently, with the granting of land claims preparation funding by the federal government in 1971.

17. The Honorable Jack Weisgerber, minister of Native Affairs in 1990 when the province agreed to negotiate land claims, stands as the first ever white member of a British Columbia cabinet to demonstrate a thorough understanding of the issue.

18. British Columbia, *Sessional Papers*, 1887, 257, 264.

19. British Columbia, Commission Appointed to Enquire into the Conditions of the Indians of the North-west Coast, *Papers relating to the Commission...* (Victoria: Government Printer, 1888), 1-12.

20. The authoritative treatment of the potlatch law and the Indian response to it is contained in Douglas Cole and Ira Chaikin, *An Iron Hand Upon the People* (Vancouver: Douglas and McIntyre, 1990).

21. For more detail concerning the treaty, see Tennant, *Aboriginal People and Politics*, 65-67. Not all Indian communities in the area of B.C. east of the Rockies did adhere to the treaty, but even so the federal authorities took the whole area as having been surrendered.

22. Ibid., chapter 7.

23. Drake-Terry, *Same as Yesterday*, 243, 298. The existing pre-emption prohibition already prevented Indians from acquiring unsurveyed Crown land; in effect, the 1907 amendment closed a remaining loophole. Both prohibitions were removed in 1953.

24. Canada, House of Commons, Special Committees of the Senate and House of Commons ... to Inquire into the Claims of the Allied Indian Tribes of British Columbia..., *Proceedings, Reports and the Evidence* (Ottawa: King's Printer, 1927).

25. Indian Act, 1927, section 141.

26. Until the late 1980s the usual spelling was "Nishga."

27. For details concerning the 1969-1989 Indian political activity in the province, see Tennant, *Aboriginal Peoples and Politics*, chapters 12-15.

28. For the province's arguments, see ibid., 216.

29. *Regina v. White and Bob* (1964), 50 D.L.R. (2d) 613 (B.C.C.A.), at 647.

30. Douglas Sanders, "Pre-existing Rights: The Aboriginal Peoples of Canada" (unpublished paper, Faculty of Law, University of British Columbia, 23 October 1987).

31. The chief justice of the province headed the appeal court panel himself, and did not appoint Norris to it.

32. Three judges held that the proclamation did extend west of the Rockies; three held that it did not but that it was not the source of title in any case. Also hearing the case was a seventh judge who ruled against the claimants on a legal technicality and expressed no opinion on the merits of the claim. *Calder v. Attorney-General of B.C.*, [1973] S.C.R. 313; (1973), 34 D.L.R. (30) 281.

33. *Guerin v. R.*, [1984] 2 S.C.R. 335; [1984] 6 W.W.R. 481 at 495, 497.

34. *MacMillan Bloedel Ltd. v. Mullin; Martin v. R. in Right of B.C. et al.*, [1985] 3 W.W.R. 577 (B.C.C.A.) at 583-93. Leave to appeal refused [1985] 5 W.W.R. lxiv.

35. *Regina v. Sparrow* (1990), 56 C.C.C. (3d) 263 (S.C.C.), 282.

36. Ibid., 290.

37. "Section 35(1) at the least, provides a solid constitutional base upon which subsequent negotiations can take place." Ibid., 285.

38. Ibid., 286.

39. Ibid., 276.

40. *Delgamuukw v. British Columbia* (1991), 79 D.L.R. (4th) 185 (B.C.S.C.).

41. At the start of the trial he was chief justice of the Supreme Court of British Columbia; during the trial he had been promoted to the position of chief justice of the Appeal Court for the province.

42. *Delgamuukw v. British Columbia* (1991), 79 D.L.R. (4th) 185 (B.C.S.C.), 196.

43. Ibid., 197.

44. In a joint statement, Anglican, Lutheran, Mennonite, Presbyterian, Quaker, Roman Catholic and United Church leaders in the province criticized the tone and substance of the decision as "a tragic commentary on the continuing colonial attitudes that pervade our legal system." *Project North B.C. Newsletter* (Spring 1991).

Tee-Hit-Ton and Alaska Native Rights

Stephen Haycox

In 1955 the United States Supreme Court handed down one of the most significant historic statements ever made by the American government on the constitutional rights of native Americans to their aboriginal land. The case was *Tee-Hit-Ton Indians v. United States*, a matter involving a band of Alaska's Tlingit Indians, wherein the Court held that Indian title rights, while permitting Indians exclusive occupancy of aboriginal land, did not represent a property right the extinguishment of which required compensation under the fifth amendment.[1] The fifth amendment prohibits the taking of land without just compensation, and has been held to mean that interest must be paid as well. One of several cases involving Alaska native rights which moved through the courts in the 1940s and 1950s, *Tee-Hit-Ton* was highly important to the question of how to handle aboriginal lands, for it overturned a line of interpretation which had begun in a 1923 case, *Cramer v. United States*, and had been reinforced in a 1941 decision, *United States ex re. Hualpai Indians v. Santa Fe Railroad*.[2] These cases confirmed the principle that abandonment of Indian land did not constitute extinguishment of title, a finding under which, in the right circumstances, most United States lands might be subject to aboriginal title. Lawyers for Indians both in and out of government looked to these decisions to support claims for compensation for Indians whose lands had been taken by the government for various reasons. And the court met the expectation of compensation in a landmark case in 1946, *United States v. Alcea Band of Tillamooks, Tillamook I*, following which the Court of Claims awarded $3 million for a nineteenth-century taking of Tillamook lands, and a potential $17 million interest calculated from the time of the taking.[3] Indian attorneys were elated with *Tillamook I*, and many began assembling cases through which they hoped to gain for their tribal clients sufficient financial resources to counteract the malaise of Indian dependence, poverty and despair.

But their optimism was short-lived. The government appealed *Tillamook I*, and in a disturbing decision the Court found in 1951 in *United States v. Alcea Band of Tillamooks, Tillamooks II*, that the Court of Claims had erred in the compensation award, for the recovery had not been based on the fifth amendment, but rather on a jurisdictional act;

accordingly, no interest was warranted.[4] To justify interest, the Court ruled, the title must have been recognized in some way, principally by jurisdictional act or by treaty. Disappointed lawyers understood that the nineteenth-century value of taken lands was but a fraction of the interest awards they had begun to count on. *Tee-Hit-Ton* seemed to dash completely any lingering hope that large awards could be expected by judicial decision.

The optimism generated by *Tillamook I* had already received some jolts before *Tillamook II* was decided. In an Alaska case, *Miller et al. v. United States* in 1947, the Ninth Circuit Court of Appeals had found that the Alaska purchase treaty had extinguished aboriginal title by implication.[5] And in another Alaska case, *Hynes v. Grimes Packing Company* in 1949, this one involving native fishing rights, the United States Supreme Court had held that the Karluk Indians of Kodiak Island were not entitled to compensation for lost fishing grounds because as a specific group they had no treaty with the United States.[6] This was particularly disturbing to Alaska natives because no Alaska groups had treaties with the government; Indian treaty making had been terminated in 1871, just a few years after the Alaska purchase treaty, and therefore the status of all Alaska natives was unclear, though few doubted that it was different from the status of the western American treaty Indians.[7] Though they did not have a treaty, the Karluk people did have a reservation, a fact which they hoped would substitute. But the court was unimpressed, finding that title to nontreaty Indian land existed "by the will of the sovereign," and was subject to "the unfettered will of [the] Congress."

The *Tee-Hit-Ton* finding has always been controversial, sparking considerable debate among commentators.[8] The decision has been criticized on a number of grounds, including political motivation. Generally the courts have not followed it, voluntarily awarding compensation in many instances where takings have been challenged.[9]

The *Tee-Hit-Ton* case was instigated by one man, though it was brought in the name of an Alaska Indian tribe, the Tee-Hit-Ton, which at the time of the case was comprised of approximately sixty-five individuals. The architect of the suit was William Lewis Paul, Sr., a former president of the Alaska Native Brotherhood (ANB), and long a significant leader among the Tlingit and Haida Indians who had fought for political and legal recognition of their rights as Indians, and had advanced their cause significantly.[10] That Paul should have started the suit was ironic in a number of contexts. He was at the time of the case disbarred from the practice of law in Alaska; the principal attorneys of record were his two sons, William Paul, Jr. and L. Frederick Paul. Paul, Sr., had long been associated with the view that Indians were fully equal citizens of the United States, and as such were entitled to no special treatment or compensation. More important, he was opposed in the mid-1950s by a majority faction within the very organization through which he had made his reputation, and through which in former times he had wielded considerable power, the ANB. The *Tee-Hit-Ton* case was in fact Paul's "last hurrah." He had been at odds with other Indian leaders in Alaska for some time, and after the decision was handed down would no longer play a primary role in the decisions made by those leaders. The story of Paul's role in *Tee-Hit-Ton* is a fascinating one, and is as important to the history of Alaska native advocacy as the case is to the history of the adjudication of native land rights in America. Unlike *Tee-Hit-Ton*, however, Paul's story and the history of the ANB, and how *Tee-Hit-Ton* and its related Alaska cases were generated, is unknown save to those principals still living, and a few readers of obscure historical documents.[11]

Born in 1885 of two Tlingit mixed-blood parents, William Paul and two brothers had been raised by a widowed mother who worked as an interpreter and lay missionary at the Sitka (Presbyterian) Industrial (Indian) Training School, and at other Presbyterian mission sites in southeast Alaska. Sent to Richard Pratt's Carlisle Indian School, Paul adopted Pratt's philosophy that Indians were no different from other people, and that their equality was fully guaranteed and protected by the fourteenth amendment.[12] He eschewed special status or treatment for Indians, insisting only that Indians control their transition from aboriginal to western culture, not whites. After graduating from Whitworth College, then in Tacoma, Washington, Paul completed a law degree through correspondence while working at a bank and trust company in Portland. He returned to Alaska permanently in 1920, and with his brother Louis took over the leadership of the ANB, a Presbyterian- and government-inspired native self-help group founded in 1912 and dedicated to acculturation of all Alaska's native people. The Pauls dominated the ANB throughout the 1920s. William Paul served as secretary of the organization in 1921 and 1922, during which years his brother Louis was president. Louis succeeded William as secretary for 1924 and 1925, and was elected president again in 1927. William was elected president in 1928 and 1929. From 1924 to 1927, William also served in the territorial legislature, the first Alaska native to do so. By assembling a large bloc of Indian voters, many of whom were illiterate, he won election in 1924 and again in 1926. Though he wielded considerable political influence, a circumstance which generated significant white opposition, he failed in his bid for the legislature in 1928, largely because of last-minute charges of corruption. He also failed in campaigns for election as territorial attorney general in 1930 and 1932.[13]

Throughout the 1920s, as leader and principal spokesman for the ANB, Paul testified before a number of Congressional committees, and successfully brought suits challenging discrimination against Natives in public schooling and the denial of the natives' right to vote. In the legislature he fought for widows' and orphans' benefits for natives, and for their eligibility for the territorial pioneer home. In 1934, when Alaska natives were excluded from the New Deal Indian Reorganization Act (IRA) because their status was held to be different from that of continental Indians, Paul worked with Interior Department officials and Alaska's territorial delegate to Congress to fashion an amended IRA for Alaska which was adopted in 1936.[14] At the same time, he helped to lobby through Congress a jurisdictional act authorizing Alaska's Tlingit and Haida Indians to bring a suit in the Court of Claims for ownership of the seventeen million-acre Tongass National Forest.[15] In the summer of 1936 a subcommittee of the Senate Interior Affairs Committee held hearings in Alaska on the condition of natives there. Paul served as the chief counsel and aide to the committee. He was soon to be appointed Bureau of Indian Affairs (BIA) field representative in Alaska for implementation of the IRA. Then, at the height of his career, he hoped to use his influence and contacts to obtain an appointment as director of the IRA credit fund in the territory, a position of considerable power.[16]

Paul was not without critics, however, within as well as outside the native community. He was very strong-willed, independent, and often aggressive. More than one acquaintance characterized him as arrogant and domineering. Many resented and some feared his power. In 1925 the territorial legislature passed a voters' literacy act designed to eliminate Paul's political base. Paul succeeded in attaching a rider preserving the franchise for all previous voters, effectively vitiating the measure. Beginning in 1928 his leadership was contested by the Peratrovich family of Klawock, directly in the annual ANB conventions, and indirectly through an attempt to establish a rival organization, at which they failed. Then, soon after Paul's appointment as IRA field representative in 1936, his enemies persuaded a committee of the Alaska bar to bring formal charges against him for unethical conduct. A year later Paul was found to have embezzled an Indian client's settlement in a lien case, and was disbarred.[17]

Though his power was greatly reduced, Paul still was a significant ANB leader. All past presidents of the ANB served as voting members of the body's executive committee. Paul continued to work for Indian rights, most particularly on the Tlingit-Haida land suit over the Tongass forest. The 1935 jurisdictional act provided that should the land suit be won, any compensation awarded must be distributed by a central council of all the Tlingit and Haida Indians. The manner of the distribution was not specified. Paul sought to control the central council, and at an *ad hoc* convention in 1941 gained control of the proceedings and secured election as the council's president.[18] In 1939 and 1940 Paul's sons earned their law degrees at the University of Washington, and joined their father in Alaska to help with the land suit. At the same 1941 convention, Paul succeeded in securing their appointment by the central council as attorneys for the suit, subject to the approval of the Interior Department. They were to serve with a Washington, D.C. attorney in the office of James Curry, a veteran tribal attorney who held a large number of Indian contracts throughout the United States, and would soon serve as general counsel of the National Congress of American Indians (NCAI). The appointment of Paul's sons exacerbated the internecine struggle within the ANB.

Although he sought to use the IRA for his own political purposes, Paul did not agree with its general philosophy of collective, tribal identity and organization of natives. In this regard, his association with the IRA and the BIA was at least pragmatic if not cynical. Schooled at Carlisle in Richard Pratt's notion of the absolute equality of all Indians and rapid assimilation through education, Paul maintained all his career that the path to Indian equity lay in eliminating special status and privilege for Indians. He opposed reservations, tribal identity, native sovereignty and federal trusteeship. Under John Collier, of course, the BIA endorsed and advanced the collective, tribal identity of American Indians and Alaska Natives. This put Paul on a collision course with the BIA, and his relationship with federal officials was always strained. At times he appeared to accommodate to the New Deal approach, but because his style was always pragmatic, his motives were open to question.[19]

The fact that there were no treaties with Alaska natives confirmed Paul in his thinking that Indians should be seen as individuals fully equal on constitutional terms with all other Americans. Their protection under the fourteenth amendment was not compromised by the trustee relationship implied by treaties. This led Paul to the conclusion that in their dealings with the federal government, Alaska natives must act as individuals, not collectively as members of any group, tribe or community. The only way Alaska natives could be assured of benefits under the suit would be to sign as individual plaintiffs, and pay a fee to the attorneys as an earnest of their intention.[20] Not surprisingly, the BIA and the Interior Department rejected this approach, insisting that proof of kinship with any Indian group occupying lands covered by the suit constituted qualification for benefits, and arguing that payment of a qualification fee was a hardship for many who might qualify.[21] Some accused the Pauls of attempting to establish a fund for their own benefit; the Pauls responded that some initial funding was necessary to begin an enrollment process. Attorneys for the Indians also criticized Paul's theory. If he were to prevail, NCAI counsel Curry argued, the land claims suit would be impossible to pursue. Separate suits would need to be entered for individuals and small groups with sufficient commonality as a class to argue a collective benefit. Curry wrote a number of letters taking Paul to task for his meddling, and warning that theory had the potential to disrupt the land-suit process, a warning seconded by the area office of the BIA.[22]

This difference of interpretation played to the Peratroviches' strength, and they sided with the BIA. Throughout the 1930s, Peratrovich supporters had captured the presidency of the ANB, and Roy Peratrovich, one of two sons of the Peratrovich patriarch, was elected president for five successive years from 1940 to 1944. However, Paul's membership on the executive committee helped him retain a sufficient base in the organization for him to keep his chairmanship of the central council. Moreover, William Paul, Jr., was elected secretary of the ANB for most of those years, while Paul's sons continued to serve as land-claims attorneys until they resigned in 1944, blocked from further action by the BIA's refusal to validate their father's interpretation of native status, and more directly by the Interior Department's refusal to confirm them as attorneys for the suit because of their inexperience. By then, Paul had devised a new strategy; he would bring a suit in federal court to test his interpretation.[23]

Miller et al. v. United States was the first of a series of cases brought officially by the Paul brothers but written by their father to test his theories of the interpretation of the status of Alaska natives and their land rights. That series would end with *Tee-Hit-Ton*. By then, the issues had become larger than Alaska land rights alone, bringing further national legal attention to the question of universal native rights in America. But this was not the Pauls' intention, and it was not the principal focus of their efforts. *Miller* involved an appeal by several Tlingit Indians living at Juneau, Alaska, protesting a wartime condemnation of land on the waterfront there by the federal government for construction of wharfage facilities.[24] Paul, Sr., decided that he would claim the land for the Indians by virtue of aboriginal title, but as individuals rather than as a tribe or group. The court had first to rule on the question of aboriginal title, and then on the question of whether individual Indians could hold such title. If they could, Paul's contention that suits needed to be brought in the name of individual Indians would be greatly strengthened. The attorneys of record for the case were Paul's sons; they asked $80,000 in damages for the taking. In Alaska District Court, Judge George Alexander denied the protest, granting the government's demurrer that the Indians had no interest in the property since aboriginal title was not compensable. Paul had anticipated the decision, and his sons immediately appealed.

As secretary of the ANB, William Paul, Jr., informed the body's executive committee of the suit; since the native community in Juneau was small and clannish they would have learned of it anyway through the local ANB camp.[25] It is not clear, however, that the ANB leadership understood the implications of the action for a compensatory award under the land claims suit. Paul, Sr., was selective in explaining matters he dealt with which had implications for the organization and for all natives, a mode of operation which contributed to his reputation as a manipulator. The various filings for the suit in the district court were somewhat protracted, with petitions in the summers of 1943 and 1944. The circuit court handed down its judgment in February 1947, reversing the district court. The Alaska purchase treaty, the justices argued, granted to the United States all property in Alaska except that held by "individual property holders."[26] Since no Indian land had been explicitly reserved, the court found that no collective Indian land existed. In other words, the court found that the Indians had no aboriginal title in Alaska, a judgment of profound implication, and one which ignored the implications of the 1941 *Hualpai* decision on the permanence of aboriginal title. There was a mitigating finding in the case. The first Civil Government Act for the territory, adopted in 1884, declared that "the Indians or other persons in said district shall not be disturbed in the possession of any lands actually in their use or occupation or now claimed by them..."[27] The Court found that this language constituted direct Congressional recognition of the Indians' title, thereby restoring it. But they held the land only *as individuals,* not as members of any aboriginal group. This was a novel and remarkable finding; not only did it note the extinguishment of aboriginal title without an explicit declaration, but it also suggested that the collective, tribal delineation of Indians which was at the core of the New

Deal notion of Indian self-determination had no currency in Alaska.[28] For the moment, Paul seemed to have won his point. If there were to be compensatory payments under the claims suit, they would have to go to individuals, since there were no recognized Indian groups, according to *Miller*. In fact, the *Miller* decision turned out to be an aberration; the Supreme Court twice explicitly disapproved it.[29] But in the euphoria of celebration, victory seemed within William Paul's grasp.

Not surprisingly, Indian attorneys expressed dismay at the Court's judgment, and confidence that it would soon be overturned. In Washington, James Curry was furious over the decision. Paul had set back the cause of Indian rights in Alaska by decades, he wrote to ANB president Roy Peratrovich, and perhaps had made any settlement under the jurisdictional act an impossibility. The ANB should have nothing to do with Paul; he was "dangerous and out of control."[30] Curry also attempted to divide Paul's sons from their father. Both chafed under his domination, and William, Jr., had a number of independent attorney contracts with native villages, causing him concern over the impression that he was his father's pawn. Curry wrote to him that his father's ideas were "absolutely untenable," and that the senior Paul was "a meddlesome and divisive force" from which the younger Paul would do well to distance himself.[31] But both of Paul's sons continued to work with their father, and soon found themselves hard at work assembling new briefs.

The court of appeals remanded the case to the Alaska District Court with the finding that the appellants might sue for compensation, and Paul immediately set to work to pursue a judgment. His sons again helped him prepare the case. The retrial was held before a newly appointed judge. Paul amended the original protest to include a larger area than in *Miller*, but otherwise did not change it.[32] The new case was styled *United States v. 10.95 Acres of Land in Juneau, et al.* However, the new judge, a longtime Alaskan named George Folta, again found against the appellants. There was no direct succession of usage, and therefore of property right, whatever it may previously have been, between holders of the tideland before 1867 and after 1884, Folta judged, and based his denial on those grounds. In his dictum Folta noted the *Miller* finding that a possessory right is compensable. Such a right, he argued, "must be notorious, exclusive and continuous," and must leave "visible evidence ... so as to put strangers upon notice that the land is in the use or occupancy of another."[33] It was impossible to tell from the testimony, Folta wrote, whether the defendants claimed the possessory right as individuals or as a community. This was somewhat true, for Paul had made both arguments in the brief. He had argued that the 1884 act confirmed rights which had existed since time immemorial. Folta noted that such rights sounded more like an assertion of aboriginal title than individual title. And in any case, he did not feel compelled to rule on that question. Folta was an old enemy of William Paul, and the Indian leader had essentially written off the case when he saw that Folta had been appointed.[34]

In the meantime, the *Hynes v. Grimes* case was decided at the Supreme Court. The Pauls were not directly involved in this case, but it had a significant bearing on their approach to the questions of Indian title and compensatory awards, and they followed it closely. In 1944 the secretary of the Interior created several new Indian reservations in Alaska, at Hydaburg, Kake and Klawock in the southeast, at Karluk on Kodiak Island, and a 1.4 million-acre reservation for the village of Venetie in the interior. The reservations were created pursuant to authorization in the Alaska amendments to the IRA. The Karluk reservation included traditional coastal fishing waters, which was the principal interest which Paul had in the case. If coastal waters could be protected in a reservation, perhaps they could also be included in the definition of aboriginal title. There was significant opposition to the creation of the reservations, which were seen as a threat to Alaska's economic development. At hearings held in Hydaburg and Klawock, attended by Felix Cohen, associate solicitor in the Interior Department and Indian rights activist, anti-Indian sentiment ran high among those offering testimony. One southeast Alaska newspaper printed a special forty-four page "Anti-Reservation Issue." The ANB was ambivalent on the issue, both endorsing and opposing reservations at different times. The ambivalence reflected both the opposing factions within the organization, headed by Paul and by the Peratroviches, and also considerable uncertainty as to whether reserves, which would protect native lands, might bring with them a level of paternal trusteeship by the federal government which Alaska natives had largely escaped. William Paul had supported the creation of reservations when he served briefly as BIA field officer in 1937; his argument then had been that through their IRA constitutions, Indians could control their own affairs. Subsequently, however, he opposed them, and wrote numerous letters attacking the BIA. Klawock, the home village of the Peratroviches, rejected its reservation, as did Kake, but both Hydaburg and the northern villages of Karluk and Venetie accepted theirs. The Hydaburg reservation later was found by the Supreme Court to have been faultily created, and was disallowed.[35]

Hynes v. Grimes stemmed from complaints brought in Alaska District

Court against the authority of the secretary to create new reservations, and against the enforcement of exclusion of any but Karluk villagers from the Karluk reservation. Both the Alaska District Court and the Court of Appeals upheld an injunction against exclusion. The canneries, represented by the general counsel to the Alaska Packers' Association, W.C. Arnold, appealed to the Supreme Court. Felix Cohen filed an *amicus curiae* brief on behalf of the village of Karluk, urging reversal. But the Supreme Court also upheld the injunction, though it did find that the secretary was authorized to create the reservation; the injunction was upheld on grounds that the exclusion of nonvillagers violated legislation guaranteeing a nonexclusionary fishery. Unusually, the Court also commented on the *Miller* finding that the 1884 Alaska Civil Government Act recognized an individual, compensatory land right. The Court dissociated itself with the *Miller* finding. "With all respect," Justice Stanley Reed wrote, the Court could not "express agreement with that conclusion." It was based on *Tillamooks I*, Reed noted, and "[t]hat opinion does not hold the Indian right of occupancy compensable without specific legislative direction to make payment." Justice Reed also asserted that compensation was mandated only when there had been "definite intention by congressional action or authority to accord legal rights, not merely permissive occupation."[36] Neither the purchase treaty nor the 1884 Civil Government Act constituted such "recognition," a direct repudiation of *Miller*.[37]

The Court did not address specifically Paul's issue of individual rather than collective responsibility. But the Court's explicitly negative view of the case raised a cloud over it. Paul realized immediately that in the face of that cloud, he could not base his cause on the *Miller* finding. Still, there was a slim hope for Paul, for the finding that exclusions from the fishery were unconstitutional supported his argument that no special consideration could be afforded Alaska natives, suggesting the possibility that compensatory awards would need to be paid individually.

During the protracted journey of *Hynes v. Grimes* through the courts Paul had written letters to Cohen and to the various Interior secretaries, and a number of circular letters to ANB camps arguing that the secretary did not have the authority to create reservations in Alaska.[38] Even though Kake and Klawock rejected their reservations, village leaders considered Paul's letters meddlesome.[39] He did not hesitate to attack individuals in his circular and personal letters, a characteristic which did nothing to encourage an objective appraisal of his arguments.

One of his favorite targets was James Curry. Two years after Paul's sons had resigned as land-suit attorneys for the ANB in 1944, the ANB, under Roy Peratrovich's leadership, had hired Curry to take their place. Curry had come to Alaska for the 1946 ANB convention and had clashed with Paul openly and in private. Paul renewed his charge that if the suit were to proceed on Curry's and Cohen's theory of collective title, any chance of getting a just settlement for the Indians would be lost.[40] Curry received a hearing while he was in Alaska, but after his departure Paul kept up his attack continuously, and won a number of Indian leaders to his point of view.

Paul was useful as an ally, then, when Curry came under attack in Washington, D.C. In 1950, Senator Clinton Anderson of New Mexico began an investigation of Curry. Holding half of all United States Indian attorney contracts at the time, Curry subcontracted most of the actual work, taking a percentage fee as principal attorney. This may have been a justifiable practice, since some of the subordinate attorneys might not have qualified with the Interior Department, and as general counsel of the NCAI Curry had statistical and support resources which were unavailable to many tribal attorneys. But to Anderson, Curry seemed like a profiteer, and with Dillon Myer, commissioner of Indian Affairs, he set out to expose and discredit him. Formal hearings were held in Washington in 1952,[41] and Alaska's delegate to Congress, E.L. "Bob" Bartlett, sitting with the committee as a courtesy since a large number of Alaska villages as well as the ANB had contracts with Curry, subpoenaed William Paul to testify about Curry. The executive committee of the ANB, led mainly by the Peratroviches, objected strenuously.[42] They feared, perhaps correctly, that in Washington Paul would represent himself as a spokesman for the ANB. The executive committee sent telegrams to Bartlett, Clinton and the members of the committee proclaiming that Paul did not speak for the organization. But in Washington Paul correctly stated that he was an immediate past secretary of the ANB, as a past president was a member of its executive committee, and that as an attorney who practiced in Alaska, and a Tlingit Indian, he had an opinion. In the face of his direct testimony, the technical point as to whether he officially represented the ANB made litte difference. In his testimony not only did Paul argue that Curry's legal position on Tlingit-Haida land claims was flawed, but he also revealed that while Curry had claimed never to have received any payment for his services to the ANB, he had in fact been advanced over $5,000 in expenses.[43] After the hearings, Commissioner Myer refused to renew any of Curry's contracts, and he soon retired from practice. Back in Alaska, the ANB executive committee held an extraordinary two-day meeting at which they grilled Paul on his statements in Washington, and on his legal activities. Paul was circumspect in his responses, allowing that he had not denied "that he was a member of the executive committee," and had told the committee that as he and his sons were the only Tlingit attorneys in Alaska, they probably understood the legal implications of Curry's suit better than any other ANB members. He could not, Paul said, provide information on whether the senators viewed him as a representative of the ANB. He refused to discuss his direct testimony on the grounds that as it was subpoenaed, it was privileged.[44] This meeting was a low point in Paul's fight with the Peratroviches and with the leadership of the ANB. In separate letters individual leaders told Paul to give up his suits, as his legal machinations might damage the land suit and the opportunity for a settlement. Paul answered that as a private individual represented by attorney — his sons — he could pursue whatever course he might, and the executive committee could not stop him. When he won, he asserted, they would thank him.

It was in this context, then, that William Paul decided again to attempt to test the theory of collective aboriginal title with the *Tee-Hit-Ton* case.[45] In light of the Court's disapproval of the *Miller* findings, Paul decided to bring his new suit in the name of a small group, each identified and enrolled individually by name, but acting as a class. In this way he hoped to avoid the possibility that the suit might be seen as a repeat of *Miller*, yet still satisfy his theory that the claim needed to be brought by specified individuals. It was not entirely clear how a small group of Tlingit differed in its collective character from the larger group of all Tlingits.[46] The protest group was comprised of the members of Paul's extended family, which included about sixty-five members. The Tee-Hit-Ton were identified in the suit as a tribe, but that usage was somewhat problematical. The principal organizational unit for natives in Alaska was the village; the traditional use of the term tribe, as represented in the IRA, did not exist. This fact had been one of the reasons the original IRA was not applied to Alaska. The clan house was the central social unit, with kinship defined matrilineally. Because of intermarriage, different clans were represented in several villages. There were members of a number of clans in any one village, but no village had representatives of all the clans. As he defined it, Paul was of the Raven phratry or lineage (moiety), the village of Wrangell, the Kiks-uddy clan, and the Tee-Hit-Ton family, which had had a major clan house in Wrangell since "time immemorial."[47] It is not in fact clear that all Tlingits would have accepted this taxonomy, but Paul persuaded the court that it was legitimate; the court recognized the Tee-Hit-Ton as a valid native group.

Tee-Hit-Ton Indians v. United States was generated by the sale of timber in the Tongass National Forest, with seventeen million acres, the largest forest in the federal system. Congress had opened the forest to timber sales by joint resolution in 1947, over the protests of the ANB, the NCAI, James Curry, and other spokesmen for the cause of aboriginal rights, including Felix Cohen and former Interior Secretary Harold Ickes.[48] The protesters claimed, on the basis of the 1941 Haulpai case, that the Tlingit owned all of the forest. Even though the 1947 act called for sales proceeds to be held in escrow until the question of title should be decided, the Tlingit charged that the cutting of timber permanently altered the forest, and with it, resources upon which the Tlingit depended. With Governor Ernest Gruening, the Forest Service had requested the opening in order to guarantee a supply of timber for pulp mills projected to be built in southeast Alaska. The first sales were made in 1951, and Paul soon after devised his suit.

ANB leaders were unhappy about Paul's actions. The suit authorized by the 1935 jurisdictional act was still pending, and the central council was on the verge of hiring yet another attorney to pursue it. A suit on behalf of one family would be divisive, and more so if they won. It might well occlude the question of title so much as to eliminate the possibility of other Indian units making similar claims. The suit would inevitably contribute to the factional strife which already beset the ANB, and it would certainly confuse most Indians. And Roy Peratrovich wondered about Paul's motives. Paul appeared to be forsaking his long-stated commitment to all Alaska's natives, acting solely on his own for the benefit of himself and his family, an interpretation given credence by Paul's 1937 disbarment, and his apparent willingness to interpret circumstances to his own benefit.[49]

Paul responded that his only interest lay in making sure that the opportunity not be lost to salvage something from the appropriation and destruction of native lands. He repeated his conviction that the collective definition of land title would be disallowed by the courts in the final analysis, despite the rejection of the Miller decision by the Supreme Court. The fact that the circuit court had found for individual compensation suggested that legal opinion was divided, and could as easily go in Paul's favor as against it. Paul resented the charge that his real motivation was personal. In a biting letter to Peratrovich he recounted his long history of achievements for Alaska natives, including successful challenges over school discrimination, voting rights and widows' benefits. He took credit for introducing the ANB resolution which led to the land-claims suit in the first place, and reminded ANB leaders of his work to have the IRA extended to Alaska and of its many benefits. Peratrovich was not convinced. Paul's accomplishments were real ones, he admitted, but his reputation for machination was also based on something real.[50]

In testimony before the court, Paul was the principal witness. He noted that he was the chief of the Tee-Hit-Ton, whose numbers were considerably reduced from earlier times. He indicated a number of locations in the 350,000 acres claimed by Tee-Hit-Ton which he said had been used and occupied since time immemorial; these included the existing town of Wrangell and the abandoned site of Tongass village, several houses in different locations, and a traditional salmon fishing and smoking site. Paul noted that some of the individual locations were sheltered winter habitations while others were summer locales. He said that he learned of all the Tee-Hit-Ton sites, and the boundaries of their lands, when he returned from Carlisle Indian School in the summer of 1904 for the salmon fishing season. In the court's summary of this testimony Justice Reed noted dryly that use of these areas by other Tee-Hit-Tons was "sketchily asserted."[51]

In fact, the whole fabric of the Tee-Hit-Ton brief could be said to have been "sketchily" conceived, and Paul's motives for the case were rightly susceptible to question. Though clan organization still exerted some influence among the Tlingit, all of these Indians were well acculturated by 1951 when the suit was brought, and the immediate family, and the village and town were the principal units of social identity. Until Paul decided to identify and enroll all the members of the Tee-Hit-Ton family for the suit, no attempt had been made to distinguish clearly all members of the group, who thought of themselves more as residents of Wrangell village and members of the Kiks-uddy clan than as members of the Tee-Hit-Ton family. Other extended families in Kiks-uddy were not clearly identified; nor were the families in the other Tlingit clans. Moreover, as the court noted, use of the lands asserted by Paul to be Tee-Hit-Ton lands by family members other than Paul was not clear. It is not unlikely that other Tee-Hit-Ton members might not have known about or been able to describe the lands in question. Paul's careful delineation of the Tee-Hit-Ton family seems to have been prepared specifically for the suit.

In fact, isolated by his continuing carping and criticisms, and unwilling to compromise and cooperate, Paul seems to have determined to strike out entirely on his own. Yet, as they often had, Paul's actions could be construed to be simultaneously serving both his personal cause and the broader interest of the native people. If he won the Tee-Hit-Ton suit, and compensation was paid for the destruction of the Tee-Hit-Ton portion of the Tongass Forest, Paul and his immediate family would have clear title to the claimed Tee-Hit-Ton lands and their resources, and they would be the beneficiaries of some kind of monetary settlement. But the other Tlingit families would have the successful suit as a model for their own claims. This was how he represented his actions to other ANB leaders.[52] They clearly saw Paul as a maverick and gadfly, and Roy Peratrovich and his supporters wrote strong letters to Paul again questioning his motives. Paul countered that he had many supporters of his own still in the organization and accused Peratrovich of opposing him for personal rather than objective reasons. In a circular letter, Paul again listed his lifetime accomplishments for Alaska natives and for the ANB. He also pleaded for unity, and an end to internal bickering.[53]

Paul's suit generated renewed effort within the ANB to pursue the original Tlingit-Haida land suit. With the demise of James Curry's contracts, the Tlingit-Haida central council had had to hire yet another attorney. They settled on Israel S. Weissbrodt of Washington, D.C., then one of the principal Indian attorneys in the United States. Weissbrodt began assembling his suit in 1954, the same year the court of claims heard Paul's brief on *Tee-Hit-Ton*.[54] Concern over whether the court would link the two suits was not without merit.

As noted at the beginning of this paper, and as is well known among students of the evolution of federal Indian policy and its adjudication, the claims court found, and the United States Supreme Court later affirmed, that the Tee-Hit-Ton did not have a recognized and compensable claim to the 350,000 acres in the Tongass forest, as William Paul had advanced. At the same time, the Supreme Court again commented on the *Miller* decision, reviewing its own commentary on that case in *Hynes v. Grimes*, and again confirming its view in *Tillamook II* that the taking of aboriginal title is not compensable without a prior explicit recognition of the title by the government.[55] Because of this review, and because of its timing, after *Tillamook II* and in confirmation of it, *Tee-Hit-Ton* entered the canon of significant twentieth-century cases on federal Indian law. Since the Tee-Hit-Ton title was not recognized by direct Congressional action, the taking of the Tongass National Forest "did not give rise to an immediate claim for just compensation" in the words of Archibald Cox, attorney for the Passamaquoddy and Penobscot tribes of Maine in their celebrated land suit in 1975.[56] This forced Indian advocates to rely on the broad trust responsibility of the Congress toward Indians, and complicated the matter of seeking compensation for takings of aboriginal land.[57]

In Alaska, *Tee-Hit-Ton* also had a major impact, for it discredited William Paul as a competent legal interpreter of Indian rights. The *Miller* decision might have had that effect had Paul been less well known, and had he not over the years had so many successes in defense of Indian rights, whatever his personal interests. But the *Tee-Hit-Ton* case, again because of its timing, pitted Paul against the ANB and the Tlingit-Haida land suit, and isolated him from his people and his tradition of service to them. And with its repeated repudiation of *Miller*, the decision erased any confidence in Paul as a useful legal advocate. Not surprisingly, this was the last major case on Indian rights which Paul would assemble.

William Paul would always be a noted Tlingit. But his reputation now rested entirely on his past deeds, not his present abilities. He was respected as an elder, but not taken seriously as a current major player. His old supporters rallied behind him immediately after the *Tee-Hit-Ton* decision was announced and secured enough backing to elect him president of the ANB at the November 1955 convention. But it was clearly an honorific gesture. Ignored by the executive committee, he was able to do little to influence the direction or activities of the organization.

At the same time, the momentum of events also began to eclipse Paul. In 1958 Alaska became a state, and a new generation of native leaders represented native Alaskans in their relationship with the new government, culminating in the formation of a truly statewide native political organization in 1965, the Alaska Federation of Natives. And in 1959, the United States Court of Claims handed down its decision in the Tlingit-Haida land suit, proposed by William Paul in 1928 and authorized by the Congress in 1935.[58] Paul had no part in the final presentation of the case, but Weissbrodt and the other attorneys on the brief utilized much of the work Paul had done for *Tee-Hit-Ton* in their preparation, identifying twenty-five extended family groups (called tribes in the suit) and their traditionally used territories, for example. In its finding, the court found that the Tlingit and Haida had had clear aboriginal title to all the Tongass lands at the time of the Alaska purchase treaty in 1867 and thus at the time of the taking of the forest in 1905. This decision further repudiated *Miller*, finding that the purchase treaty extinguished aboriginal title. Subsequently, in 1968, contrary to the finding in *Tillamook II* and *Tee-Hit-Ton*, the court awarded compensation for the taking, based on the value of the resources in 1905.[59] That compensation was paid to the Tlingit and Haida people collectively, and was distributed and invested by the Central Council of Tlingit and Haida Indians of Alaska, the land suit committee which Paul and his sons had controlled in the early 1940s and from which his sons had resigned in

1944 over their disagreement with the federal government. It was a bittersweet moment for Paul, watching his people win a victory in a matter he had begun, but the pursuit of which had been based on principles he utterly eschewed.

Born in 1885, William Paul lived until 1978, witnessing not only the success of the Tlingit-Haida land suit, but also passage of the landmark and monumental Alaska Native Claims Settlement Act of 1971. Though often referred to by the new native leadership for his historic contributions, Paul had no significant active role in the new native organization or its activities. For all intents and purposes his effective career as a native leader ended with *Tee-Hit-Ton*. Fortunately for Alaska natives, successful prosecution of their land claims and other rights did not.

Legal scholars do not always have the time or opportunity to learn of the practical circumstances which give rise to significant cases. Their focus is usually on the law established by such cases, and how it relates to previous and subsequent law, a consideration which transcends the particular situations which give rise to the suits initially. But most law suits involve real people in real circumstances, and their development and resolution have real consequences in the settings from which they arise. *Tee-Hit-Ton* has earned a permanent place as a chapter, or perhaps a footnote, in the history of federal Indian law. In 1955 when the Supreme Court decided the case, the country was in the throes of a repudiation of the federally supported self-determination policy which characterized the Indian New Deal; termination was the new policy. But it did not last. After 1960, under Attorney-General Robert Kennedy and a liberal Congress, the United States was recommitted to self-determination, and the courts as well as the Congress generally have confirmed aboriginal title, and have paid compensation for previous takings when challenges have arisen. In so doing they have not followed the precedent or the implications of *Tee-Hit-Ton*. But *Tee-Hit-Ton* represents an important development in the evolution of modern Indian law in the United States, as its inevitable presence in historical surveys of the law indicates.[60] And because of its impact there, as well as its significance in the region, it should also have a permanent chapter in the history of Alaska, and particularly in the story of the development of Alaska native rights.

NOTES

1.   120 F.Supp. 202 (1955); 177 F.Supp. 452 (1959).
2.   261 U.S. 219 (1941).
3.   329 U.S. 40 (1946).

4.   341 U.S. 48 (1951).

5.   159 F.2nd 997 (1947); for the Alaska context for these cases, see David S. Case, *Alaska Natives and American Laws* (Fairbanks: University of Alaska Press, 1984), 61-67.

6.   337 U.S. 86 (1949).

7.   Felix S. Cohen, *Handbook of Federal Indian Law* (1942; Charlottesville: Michie Bobbs-Merrill, 1982), 217-20.

8.   See, for example, Nell Jessup Newton, "At the Whim of the Sovereign: Aboriginal Title Reconsidered," *Hastings Law Journal* 6 (1980): 1215-85; Henderson J. Youngblood, "Unraveling the Riddle of Aboriginal Title," *American Indian Law Review* 5 (1977): 75-137.

9.   For example, *Tlingit and Haida Indians of Alaska v. U.S.*, 389 F.2nd 778 (1959), in which the court awarded the Tlingit and Haida Indians of Alaska $7.5 million for the 1905 taking of the Tongass National Forest. Perhaps the most significant recent example occurred in Maine where the Passamoquoddy Indians sued for compensation for an ancient taking and were awarded $81.5 million in compensation for 12.5 million acres: *Joint Tribal Council of Passamaquoddy Tribe v. Morton*, 528 F.2nd 370 (1982); see also Paul Brodeur, "Annals of Law," *New Yorker*, 11 October 1981; see note 55 below. The Puyallup Indians of Washington recently agreed to a court-approved settlement of $140 million in compensation for several acres of the Tacoma waterfront.

10. William L. Paul, Sr., "The Real Story of the Lincoln Totem," *Alaska Journal* 4 (1971): 3-15; Stephen Haycox, "William Paul, Sr., and the Alaska Voters' Literacy Act of 1925," *Alaska History* 2 (1986-87): 22-32; "Alaska Native Brotherhood Conventions, 1912-1959," *Alaska History* 4 (1989): 39-46.

11. The author is completing a book-length manuscript history of the Alaska Native Brotherhood and William Paul, 1912-1959.

12. See Francis Paul Prucha, *The Great Father: The United States Government and the American Indians* (Lincoln: University of Nebraska Press, 1984), 2, 681-86, 793-94.

13. See note 10.

14. Kenneth Philp, "The New Deal and Alaskan Natives, 1936-1945," *Pacific Historical Review* 50 (1981): 309-27.

15. Act of June 19, 1935, 49 Stat. 388, ch. 295.

16. University of Washington Archives (UWA), William Paul Papers (WLPP), file "ANB Historical," William Paul (Sr.) to Louis Paul, 23 March 1936.

17. *United States ex rel. Folta v. Paul* 9 Alaska Reports 189 (1937).

18. The jurisdictional act called for a central council; Act of June 19, 1935, 49 Stat. 388, ch. 295. The ANB established several versions of this under the title of land claims committee, the first under Paul's leadership at the 1939 convention. In 1941, a land claims convention was held at Wrangell under BIA auspices; delegates from all eighteen Tlingit and Haida villages were represented. It was at this meeting that Paul engineered his election as president of the committee, or central council; Sealaska Heritage Foundation (SHF), Curry-Weissbrodt Papers (C-WP), William Paul circular letter, 4 April 1941, file C3:6. (The Curry-Weissbrodt Papers consist of the office files of James Curry and Israel Weissbrodt, filmed by the Sealaska Heritage Foundation, Juneau, Alaska, 1983, Joaqlin Estus and Glenda Choate, editors.)

19. Officials in the Juneau Area Office complained constantly about Paul's failure to follow instructions, as revealed in letters in the National Archives (NA), Records of the Office of the Secretary of the Interior (SI) Central Office File, "Alaska".

20. UWA, WLPP, file "Land Claims," William Paul circular letter, 15 December 1941.

21. NA, SI, "Alaska," Secretary of the Interior to Don Foster, BIA, JAO, 22 July 1941.

22. National Anthropological Archives (NAA), Smithsonian Institution, James Curry Papers (JCP), file "Land Suit," James Curry to William Paul, 12 March 1942.

23. UWA, WLPP, file "Land Claims," Roy Peratrovich to William Paul, 3 March 1944; Roy Peratrovich, interview with the author, 7 August 1988.

24. 159 F.2nd 997 (1947).

25. UWA, WLPP, file "Land Claims," William Paul circular letter, 7 April 1944.

26. Article VI.

27. Section 8.

28. However, in dicta in section 5 of the decision, note the Court's finding: "It seems quite clear, therefore, that whatever 'possession' the Tlingit Indians had 'from time immemorial prior to' the year 1867 was a tribal and not an individual right..." The individual right established by *Miller* was solely from the language of the 1884 civil government act.

29. *Tee-Hit-Ton v. U.S.*, 348 U.S. 294 (1955); it is interesting, though not a particularly unusual sort of inconsistency, that the court should have found against an obligation of compensation while at the same time criticizing the *Miller* decision on the 1867 extinguishment of title. Also, *Tlingit and Haida Indians of Alaska v. U.S.*, 177 F. Supp. 452, 147 Ct. Cls. 388 (1959); this case explicitly upheld the survival of Tlingit and Haida aboriginal claims to the Tongass National Forest (sixteen million acres) pursuant to the Alaska purchase treaty, and thus directly repudiated *Miller*. It is interesting that William L. Paul, Jr., in a thesis at the University of Washington in 1940, argued that the U.S. had not purchased the aboriginal title because it had never been extinguished by the Russians, and therefore was not the Russians' to sell; 147 Ct. Cls., 385-192, findings, No. 58-62. See also D. H. Hunter, *The Alaska Treaty* (Kingston, Ontario: The Limestone Press, 1981), 71.

30. NAA, JCP, file "Alaska, 1947," James Curry to Roy Peratrovich, 13 March 1947.

31. SHF, C-WP, file C3-3.1, James Curry to William Paul, Jr., 24 March 1947.

32. 75 F.Supp. 841 (1949).

33. *United States v. 10.95 Acres of Land in Juneau, et al.*, 75 F.Supp. 844 (1949).

34. UWA, WLPP, file "Land Claims," William Paul to Louis Paul, 3 November 1946.

35. *United States v. Libby, McNeil and Libby*, 107 F.Supp. 697 (1952).

36. 337 US 86 (1949).

37. Ibid., 106 (n. 27).

38. NA, SI, file "Alaska Claims," William Paul to Felix Cohen, 26 October 1948.

39. NAA, JCP, file "Alaska, 1948," Frank Peratrovich to James Curry, 11 July 1948.

40. SHF, C-WP, file C2-4, James Curry, memo to file, 22 November 1948.

41. U.S. Congress, Senate Report No. 8, 83rd Cong., 1st Sess., "Attorney Contracts with Indian Tribes," 2-25.

42. NAA, JCP, file "Alaska, 1952," Joe Williams, Pres., ANB, to Sen. Clinton Anderson, 3 March 1952.

43. Ibid., file "Committee Hearings," James Curry to Roy Peratrovich, 30 September 1952.

44. UWA, WLPP, file "Alaska Native Brotherhood," William Paul to Frances Paul, 24 September 1952.

45. 120 F.Supp. 202 (1955).

46. UWA, WLPP, file "Land Claims," William Paul, Sr., to William Paul, Jr., 21 August 1953.

47. Paul, "Lincoln Totem," 3.

48. Stephen Haycox, "Economic Development and Indian Land Rights in Modern Alaska: The 1947 Tongass Timber Act," *Western Historical Quarterly* 21 (1990): 21-46.

49. Roy Peratrovich, interview with author, 7 August 1988.

50. UWA, WLPP, file "Alaska Native Brotherhood," William Paul to Roy Peratrovich, 12 December 1953.

51. 120 F.Supp 286 (1955).

52. UWA, WLPP, file "Alaska Native Brotherhood," William L. Paul circular letter, 15 December 1953.

53. Ibid., Roy Peratrovich to William Paul, 2 February 1954; William Paul circular letter, 23 March 1954.

54. SHF, C-WP, File W4-5.

55. 120 F.Supp 283 (1955).

56. *Joint Tribal Council of Passamaquoddy Tribe v. Morton*, 528 F.2nd 370.

57. David H. Getches, Daniel M. Rosenfelt and Charles F. Wilkinson, *Cases and Materials on Federal Indian Law* (St. Paul: West Publishing Co., 1979), 248.

58. *Tlingit and Haida Indians of Alaska v. United States*, 147 C. Cls 315, 177 F.Supp. 452 (1959).

59. *Tlingit and Haida Indians of Alaska v. United States*, 389 F.2nd 778 (1968).

60. See, for example, Getches et al., *Cases and Materials*, 248; Willliam C. Canby, Jr., *American Indian Law*, 224, 226.

Killing Mr. John:
Law and Jurisdiction at Fort Stikine, 1842-1846

Hamar Foster

We are now in a complete fix as brother Jonathan would say. If these men cannot be tried by the Russians, what is to be done with them?

Archibald Barclay to George Simpson, 18 November 1843

In attempting to piece together a picture of daily life in the fur trade during the period in which the Hudson's Bay Company's (HBC) licensed monopoly extended all the way to the Pacific Coast (1821-1858), one is immediately confronted with the question of sources.[1] The problem is not that there are none — the HBC Archives alone are a treasure trove — but that, like most sources, they are largely one-sided: British rather than Canadian, management rather than labor, European rather than aboriginal. In addition, and notwithstanding the relative abundance of post journals, correspondence and the many other documents that the Company seems to have delighted in producing, the precolonial fur trade lacks a source that later periods enjoy in abundance: court records. Not only does this make it difficult to explore the patterns of conflict in the trade, but it deprives historians of a great deal of other valuable material. Whatever the deficiencies of the common-law trial (and there are many), it is a wonderful producer of paper and information.

Where native peoples are concerned this is especially a problem. Their internal conflicts were solely a matter of Indian law and, for the most part, clashes between Indians and traders were also beyond the jurisdiction of what little European law there was. Instead, the HBC settled such incidents by the adoption of a "blood for blood" policy against the immediate wrongdoers or, occasionally, by a form of economic retaliation against their communities as a whole.[2] The situation is little better with respect to most transgressions involving traders alone, which the Company regarded primarily as matters of corporate discipline, and dealt with informally.[3] Only if the offense were a serious one, such as murder, did a real possibility exist that a more formal legal regime might apply, and this was because of an imperial statute usually referred to as the Canada Jurisdiction Act.[4]

147

There were of course no law courts in the Indian Territories. The Canada Jurisdiction Act therefore provided for trials of offenses committed there, or in "other Parts of America not within the Limits of" the Canadas or the United States, to take place in the courts of Lower or, exceptionally, Upper Canada. Prior to 1821 the act was invoked on a number of occasions by the Hudson's Bay and North West companies, both of which sent men east to be tried for offenses connected with the bloody incidents associated with Lord Selkirk's efforts to colonize Red River.[5] After 1821 it was used only once, when the HBC sent three employees (engagés) to Trois Rivières on a charge of murdering eleven Hare (North Slavey) Indians near Great Bear Lake in 1835.[6] However, even though the act was resorted to but rarely, serious matters usually required detailed, written deliberation, so the mere fact that the statute existed meant that the possibility that it might be applied had to be taken into account. As a result, the paper trail in the Selkirk and Great Bear Lake cases includes legal opinions written by a number of eminent British barristers. The killing of John McLoughlin, Jr., did not attract quite this sort of attention, but it did spawn a voluminous correspondence and a sheaf of depositions. The politics of the fur trade, the clash of great personalities, and a father's grief demanded no less.

This documentation enables one to argue that McLoughlin's death is of historical interest for a number of reasons. In the first place, it was the only case from west of the Rocky Mountains that the HBC considered sending to Canada for trial.[7] Secondly, it presents an excellent example of the financial, jurisdictional and evidential problems involved in cases that arise out of frontier incidents that are sent for trial in distant metropolitan centers. This is mainly because it was a candidate for prosecution in not merely one but three jurisdictions, which accounts, in part, for the amount of paper it generated.[8] Only one scholar has investigated the affair in any depth, and W. Kaye Lamb did so primarily to assess its impact upon the career of the dead man's father, Dr. John McLoughlin, the senior HBC officer on the Pacific slope. My perspective is rather different, but I am indebted to Lamb's work, especially his careful sequencing of events and marshaling of sources.[9]

A third reason for attaching some significance to the case is that it reveals a great deal about the difficult labor relations in the Company at that time, at least insofar as its operations in the Far West were concerned. The cultural diversity of the fur trade and the HBC's hiring and disciplinary practices were two important reasons for this. Not only were the men at Fort Stikine a small, foreign island in a sea of indigenous peoples who regarded them as no more than tenants at will; they were themselves a somewhat volatile ethnic mix. They certainly had little in common with their bosses, and often not much more with many of their fellow *engagés*. Indeed, after McLoughlin was killed the Canadians and the Iroquois at Stikine were inclined to accuse each other. Strained relations both within and without the isolated little post were therefore important factors in what happened there.

Finally, the fate of young John McLoughlin is not only a fascinating, if somewhat pathetic, narrative, but it fits comfortably with the transboundary theme of the conference that produced this collection of essays. His death at Fort Stikine in April 1842 occurred at a British post in Indian Country, on land leased from the Russians.[10] Although the site is now the town of Wrangell, Alaska, it is also within the traditional territories of the southern Tlingit, whose claim for compensation for their lost resources was dismissed by the United States Supreme Court in 1955.[11] In short, McLoughlin's death at Stikine is a story, not only about law for elephants and beavers, but for bears and ravens, too.[12]

***

Mr. John has bad white men at Stikine.

> Indian report received by Chief Factor John Work at Fort Simpson before the killing

Redoubt St. Dionysius was a post established in 1833 by the Russian American Company at a point on the southeastern coastal strip of Alaska that is now called the Panhandle. Located at the north end of the Duke of York's Island, a few miles south of the point where the Stikine River flows into the ocean, its geographical designation is 56°33′ north latitude and 132°14′ west longitude. It was erected as a protective measure, in response to the HBC's proposal to build an establishment in territory claimed by the British further up the Stikine, closer to the sources of fur. When the Company attempted in 1834 to do just that, the Russians ordered their men at the Redoubt to block them, and the HBC vessel *Dryad* retreated. Because the Company took the view that this action violated the treaty of 1825 between their respective nations, it filed a claim for damages and negotiations commenced.[13]

These negotiations eventually merged with a more broadly based attempt to regularize trade on the Northwest Coast, and in 1839 the two companies entered into an arrangement whereby the Russians undertook to lease the coastal strip — except for the islands where Fort Archangel (Sitka) was located — to the British for 2,000 otter skins per year. This agreement was supposedly designed to eliminate the Americans from the Alaska trade, but overhunting had largely achieved that end already. Its real purpose, so far as the Russians were concerned, was to alleviate their increasingly disadvantageous trading position by requiring the HBC to sell them all its land furs. For its part, the HBC wanted guaranteed access to the furs coming from the interior and to have the Russians buy produce from its farms in the Columbia, rather than from American ships.[14] Accordingly, in June 1840 Chief Factor James Douglas accepted possession of Redoubt St. Dionysius, along with the rest of the Alaska Panhandle, and renamed it Fort Stikine. He also presided over the building of a new HBC post, Fort Durham, further north.[15] That, in any event, was its official name; in practice it was nearly always referred to as Taku, after the river where it was situated.

Stikine was not, apparently, much of a prize. Certainly no one seems to have had much good to say about it. The following description by Sir George Simpson, North American governor of the Company, is fairly typical, and is a good illustration both of contemporary attitudes and Simpson's own uncompromising style. It comes from the published account of his voyage around the world in 1841-42, in the course of which he visited Fort Stikine three times:

> The establishment, of which the site had not been well selected, was situated on a peninsula barely large enough for the necessary buildings, while the tide, by overflowing the isthmus at high water, rendered any artificial extension of the premises almost impracticable; and the slime, that was periodically deposited by the receding sea, was aided by the putridity and filth of the native villages in the neighbourhood, in oppressing the atmosphere with a most nauseous perfume. The harbour, moreover, was so narrow, that a vessel of a hundred tons, instead of swinging at anchor, was under the necessity of mooring stem and stern; and the supply of fresh water was brought by a wooden aqueduct, which the savages might at any time destroy from a stream about two hundred yards distant.[16]

Simpson's graceless remarks about the local people were a reference to the Stikines, one of several Tlingit tribes occupying the coastal strip. A matrilineal society divided into two phratries or moieties, Raven and Wolf, the Tlingit were organized in villages composed of members of different clans. There were eight, perhaps nine of these clans represented at Stikine, where the different lineages or house groups (hit-tan) lived in multifamily wooden lodges. The fur traders understood little of this taxonomy and appear to have confused tribes with clans; it is therefore often difficult to reconcile their records with the writings of anthropologists. For his part, Simpson referred to the Stikines as the "Secatquonay," and stated that they obtained the furs they traded at the fort mainly from the Nahani and other interior tribes, some of whom frequented Company posts as far away as the Mackenzie River district.[17] According to James Douglas, the Secatquonay were about 600 in number, and "cheerfully" supplied the fort with deer and salmon, on one occasion trading "500 carcasses of Deer ... in 15 days" with the Russians.[18] Douglas had not stayed at Stikine for any length of time, and is probably not the best judge of how cheerful everyone was; but his report does indicate the extent to which the fort's complement relied upon the Stikines for its provisions.

Generally, relations between the Tlingit and the Russians, like those between the British and the native peoples within their trading territories, were peaceful. But there had been intermittent conflict, and in 1802 the Tlingit had attacked and burned Sitka.[19] They had also consistently resisted the Czar's somewhat feeble assertions of sovereignty, perhaps most notably by forcing the authorities to abandon all attempts to impose taxation.[20] By 1840, the situation appears to have been tense at Stikine. When the Russians handed over possession, they told the clerks taking charge that the HBC would need more men than they had in order to hold the fort.[21] On 17 June, two days after the departure of the Company's steamship *Beaver*, the meaning of this warning became clear. The post journal records that the Stikines informed the traders that, if they did not agree to exchange goods for furs at the lower, Fort Simpson, tariff, they should all leave. The HBC had no rights there, said the chiefs, because the land did not belong to them. Two days later, some of the Indians began to "cut down the works about the [fort's] mill."[22]

Although the record is uneven, relations did not improve quickly, and when the traders balked at lowering the tariff the Stikines took their furs directly to Fort Simpson. Roderick Finlayson, a young clerk who was with the party that handled the transfer of Fort Stikine to the Company, reports two unsettling incidents in his unpublished memoirs.[23] The first occurred in June 1840, when the men in the fort had to "fire on some ... Indians who attempted to scale the stockade with a view to taking the place." Finlayson suggests that the assault was prompted by the discovery that the fort's complement "was less than that kept by the Russians," and adds that the latter were of the view that the situation was especially tenuous because the chiefs had a large number of slaves "who were bound to do their bidding on the pain of being shot." In fact, no one was killed, although some of the defending force were wounded. Finlayson does not — as the post journal does — mention the tariff issue as a contributing cause, but it clearly was. Nor does he mention the aquaduct described by Simpson, perhaps because that was a later addition. He does say that, during his subsequent posting to Stikine in 1841, the Indians destroyed the bridge to the mainland that the men used to get their water. In response, the traders took a chief hostage and kept him until the Indians repaired the damage. Peace was made and the hostage returned, but in anticipation of further difficulties the men dug a well inside the fort. It yielded "brackish" water.

The post journal tells a similar tale. The first man to take charge was William Glen Rae, an Orkneyman. He was a son-in-law of Dr. John McLoughlin, known as the "Emperor of the West" because he answered only to Simpson and the governor and committee in London. Assisting Rae was McLoughlin's son, also named John, who would take over the post in the autumn of 1841 when Rae was transferred to California. Both shared Finlayson's and the Russians' concerns about their new fort's defensive position. According to Rae, the local Indians continually pressed him on the tariff issue, and backed up their demands by the attack on the mill. They were, he reports, "by no means in good humour with us." Given that the fort was within Tlingit territory and that its occupants were ignoring the Indians' complaints, this seems hardly surprising. Perhaps the fact that Rae was forced to use a woman who spoke only a little of the Chinook trade jargon as an interpreter was also part of the problem. No one at Stikine could speak or understand "a syllable" of the local language. Another factor was related to their relatively small numbers: not only were several of Rae's men sick or injured, but the "Awyhees" (Hawaiians) did not know how to handle firearms. As the Indians well knew, noted Rae, "our means of defence are very humble indeed."[24]

Rae's first journal entry, a perusal of which confirms the linguistic and ethnic diversity referred to earlier, underlines these concerns. There were twenty-two men in all: eleven Kanakas ("Awyhees") from the Sandwich Islands, and eleven Canadians, Métis ("half-breeds"), and Iroquois.[25] Nearly all had little or no experience on the Northwest Coast, and some, notably the Kanakas (ten of whom had arrived from Hawaii only two months before), also had little fur-trade experience. Rae comments in the journal on many of these men. This is noteworthy because some of them were involved in the killing of McLoughlin nearly two years later, and many more participated in the subsequent cover-up of what had happened. For example, Rae describes Iroquois Pierre Kanaquassé as a "blackguard," and notes that Antoine Kawenassé, another Iroquois, was "a good man before he had the fever but has been sickly ever since." One of the Canadians, Benoni Fleury, Rae says is a "half fool, or in other words very stupid," and some of the other Canadians were severely disabled by injury. Nearly all the Kanakas could "neither work, understand or be understood."[26] In two comments that are of particular interest in light of subsequent events, Rae describes François Pressé as "a half-breed and passable," and Urbain Heroux as a "good man."[27]

These passages suggest that, even allowing for the fact that Rae possessed the standard prejudices or worse, he was in command of a rather weak and possibly unreliable garrison that had yet to establish a secure relationship with its Indian neighbors. Dr. McLoughlin probably had some appreciation of this. When he decided early in 1841 to send Rae to the Company's post at Yerba Buena and to put John in charge of Stikine, he also had Roderick Finlayson brought down from Taku. His son needed a "gentleman" as second-in-command, and Finlayson was a "congenial and competent" young man who went on to enjoy a highly successful career in the Company's service.[28] During his six months as the younger McLoughlin's assistant, and for some time afterwards, Finlayson appears to have said nothing to his superiors that was critical of McLoughlin's conduct.[29]

He did, however, report in the post journal at least one example of the sort of incident that was not unusual west of the mountains, and which involved two key elements turned up by the subsequent investigation: discipline and alcohol. It involved Benoni Fleury, who had earlier impressed Rae as stupid and who acted as the fort's steward. Apparently he "got intoxicated ... by helping himself rather too plentifully without permission out of some spirits remaining in the cupboard, for which he got a few well merited cuffs from Mr. John."[30] Much later, the elder McLoughlin was to maintain that Rae and his son had been selected to take charge of Stikine for a reason. They were both big men, he said, and could keep order "without being obliged to have recourse to dangerous weapons."[31]

Had Simpson not been on the coast that year, Finlayson might have stayed on as the younger McLoughlin's assistant and, quite possibly, the latter might not have died.[32] But Simpson *was* on the coast, in the course of a voyage around the world. On his tour of inspection from Fort Vancouver to Sitka and back, he visited Stikine in September, on his way north, and formed a favorable opinion of the manner in which Finlayson and McLoughlin were running the establishment. When he revisited in October on the return leg and learned that one of the officers at Fort Simpson was due for a furlough, Simpson decided that Finlayson should be his replacement.[33] This of course meant that "Mr. John" was now in sole command of Fort Stikine. His journal entry for 3 October, written sometime after the *Beaver* had steamed south at 5:00 A.M. with Simpson and Finlayson on board, reveals his thoughts: "I am here left alone with two assistants who cannot speak the language or make themselves understood. I endeavour to battle the watch as well as I can until someone is sent."[34]

***

If you have any the least affection for your father mother or brothers you will retire to some distant far country that you may never more be heard of.

Dr. Simon Fraser to his nephew, John McLoughlin, Jr., 12 January 1836

Reporting in 1843 to a friend about the elder McLoughlin's reaction to his son's death, one fur trader noted the insult that had accompanied this injury. *"The Big Doctor,"* he wrote,

is in a deplorable state, poor man, what anxiety he has experienced about that young man, and to be murdered at last with such a character as his murderers have given him...[35]

Historians seeking to understand the events at Fort Stikine, and the reaction to them, have therefore sought an explanation as to what sort of man the younger McLoughlin was. In particular, they have examined his early life to discover some clue as to his disposition and habits, some indication of instability or intemperance.[36] Such inquiries can of course give only partial answers, and this case is no exception. The evidence has some significant gaps, and although it reveals that McLoughlin was a man quick to anger, uncertain of his goals and probably ill-suited to command, it does not entirely resolve the question of whether the character "his murderers [had] given him" was a complete picture. Instead, it raises doubts about whether, notwithstanding his character, he had acted quite as badly as some of his killers alleged.

McLoughlin was born on 18 August 1812, probably at Fort William (formerly Kaministiquia), when his father was in the employ of the North West Company. His mother, Marguerite Wadin, was half Cree, and had married the elder McLoughlin *à la façon du pays* after her first husband left her to join the Astor expedition.[37] Nothing has been unearthed about his early years, but when the HBC, his father's new employer, transferred the family to the Columbia district in 1824, neither young John nor his sister, Elisabeth, accompanied them. Instead, John remained in a boarding school at Montreal, under the care of his uncle, Dr. Simon Fraser.[38] In the years to come he would continue his education both in Montreal and in Paris, where another uncle, David McLoughlin, was a physician. He therefore saw very little of his father and mother from the time he left for school, probably around age nine or so, until he was employed by the HBC and sent to the Columbia in 1837, when he was twenty-five. The explanation for this lies mainly in the great distances involved, but also in the elder McLoughlin's opposition to John entering the fur trade. Concerned about the increasingly limited prospects for men of mixed blood in the new Company, he devoted money and resources to educating his son in both medicine and commerce, notwithstanding that it meant they would be separated for so long.

But this is not the whole story. In addition to his general concerns about the future of children born of "country marriages," Dr. McLoughlin was also worried that John's character and abilities made him an especially poor risk. The details of the young man's life in Lower Canada and Paris are sufficiently documented elsewhere, but they can be summarized by saying that his progress was uneven, at times non-existent.[39] In 1834 his uncle sent him back to Montreal from Paris for some unforgivable but unnamed offense, and as the years went by John neglected his studies and ran up such heavy debts that he was arrested by his creditors. By 1836 the other relatives, and the agent in Montreal, that his father had charged with keeping an eye on John, had all lost patience with him. His father was bitterly disappointed: "There never was so far as I know a Young Man from this Country who had so fine a Prospect to begin life with and now he has thrown it away."[40] Perhaps because by then it seemed to be his only option, John applied to the HBC for a passage to the fur country. When that was refused, he asked for employment. That too was refused, and his father was not sorry:

> Is he such a fool as to suppose that people will Engage a person in this Service who has shown so Untractable a Desposition as to Disagree with his Relations and Guardians ... to shew you the little spirit he has ... on seeing he could not get a passage to come up to this Country nor be taken in the service he offered to come up as a Common Engagé.[41]

Yet perhaps this was a sign, not that he lacked spirit, but that he wanted desperately to earn the absent "Doctor's" love and respect by being with him, and by going about his father's business.

Rejected by the HBC, John found a different sort of adventure. He joined a remarkable "filibustering" expedition which originally seems to have been associated with an attempt to help the Texans in their war of independence with Mexico. Little is known about its "general," whose name was James Dickson and who styled himself "Liberator of the Indian Nations." But a number of other "half-breed" sons of fur traders signed up in his cause, and in August 1836 the "Indian Liberating Army" left Buffalo, New York, fifty or sixty strong. When Dickson and his men arrived at Sault Ste. Marie, Chief Trader William Nourse learned that they planned to travel west via Red River instead of south. He thought it advisable to send word to his superiors, reporting that Dickson intended to recruit more men at Red River and Pembina. The army would then

> proceed to the junction of the Yellow Stone River with the Missouri ... [and] continue till they reached the Southern pass of the Rocky Mountain... He says that while at Washington he saw many of the Chiefs of various Indian Tribes ... and made arrangements with them (particularly the Cherokees) to join him at a designated point ... his object is to obtain possession of California, for the Indians now about to be removed from the United States and make it an independent kingdom.[42]

The army did not have permission to go through Rupert's Land, and the HBC took a dim view of these events; therefore Nourse's summary may not be entirely reliable. But, given what was happening in the United States at that time, Dickson's goal — if not his methods and capabilities — is understandable. One of the results of President Jackson's Indian policy was the forced expulsion of the Cherokee and the other "civilized tribes" from their lands, and the ensuing "Trail of Tears." Indeed, five years before Nourse wrote his report, no less a figure than Alexis de Tocqueville had observed a band of Choctaws crossing the Missouri at St. Louis, a picture of suffering that he said would "never fade from [his] memory."[43]

Young John soon found himself a major in Dickson's army, which pleased him not least because it was accompanied — theoretically — by a pay increase. He also ordered a fancy uniform with silver epaulets and gold lace.[44] But the expedition soon fell apart. By the time Dickson and his men left Sault Ste. Marie, desertion and illness had taken their toll, and probably only about one-third of the men were left; even fewer eventually reached Red River. McLoughlin described the ordeal in letters to a cousin, John Fraser, detailing the near foundering of his boat, the intense cold, and the lack of provisions.[45] One passage in a letter written after crossing the lakes, but before embarking on the last leg of the journey, is revealing. Declaring that he knew that more hardships were to come, he wrote:

> [T]hese men that I had was the worst of all those living under the face of

Heaven I could not get them to work without hard treatment, I assure you that before I get to the red river I shall break some of their bones, and I will do it with the greatest pleasure for they deserve it, they give me more trouble than they are worth.[46]

He then asked if it were true that his father would be in Montreal that fall. In his reply Fraser expressed the family's distress at John's situation, and urged him to abandon Dickson's "degraded" expedition. He also told him that his father was now most anxious for his "lost son" to come to the Columbia. "[G]o and return to him," urged Fraser, "he will receive you will his arms open, he will soothe the pain and suffering you are feeling, he will restore you to yourself and make a new man of you..."[47]

Governor Simpson, who had taken something of an interest in John's progress — or rather lack thereof — now intervened. He had formed an unfavorable opinion of the young man years earlier, when on a visit to John's school he had seen him engage in a violent display of temper. Simpson probably also knew the nature of what John had done in Paris to justify being expelled from his uncle's home.[48] Given his jaundiced views of "country born" children, and with the example of the "Indian Liberating Army" before him, Simpson must have been sorely tempted to leave the young man to his own devices. He was, however, determined to scatter the remnants of Dickson's force in order to protect the interests of the HBC. He therefore sent instructions to Chief Factor Alexander Christie, the officer in charge of Fort Garry, to give Dickson no assistance. Instead, Christie was to do his best to get the men quarreling amongst themselves and generally to hasten the force's disintegration. "Towards this end," Simpson authorized him to employ John McLoughlin and another fur trader's son. "[B]y detaching them," he wrote, "you will have less difficulty in managing the others."[49]

So it was that, at last, John McLoughlin, Jr., became a clerk and surgeon of the "Honourable Company," engaged for three years at a salary of £100 per year. Originally assigned by the Council of the Northern Department to Fort McLoughlin (now Bella Bella), his father chose to keep him closer at hand, at Fort Vancouver. It seems that by March 1840 he was doing well: he wrote John Fraser to tell him that he had learned more about transacting business working at Fort Vancouver than he ever would have in Montreal. They were at it, he said, from 6:30 A.M. until 9:00 P.M. He added that soon he would heading north to help establish Fort Stikine, a post in the newly acquired Russian territories.[50]

***

"[Stikine] has been a hell upon Earth with a Sink of Pollution Ever since Rae left it..."

Simpson to Chief Factor Rowand, quoted in Rowand to McLoughlin, 11 March 1843

Two years later, the logbook entry for the *Cowlitz* on 25 April 1842 notes that the ship, with Governor Simpson on board, arrived at Stikine in the evening and anchored in eight fathoms of water.[51] Simpson had been at Sitka, waiting for passage to Siberia, when he decided to visit Taku and Stikine one more time, perhaps because he had already given orders that Taku should be closed the following year.[52] According to the log, he proceeded ashore in the longboat and discovered that "Mr. McLoughlin, Jr., the gentleman in charge of the fort, was shot by one of his own men in an affray."[53] Simpson's account in his letter to the deceased's father is more elaborate:

> On arrival (from Taco on the Evening of the 25th) off the little Anchorage at this place, my mind was filled with apprehension that all was not right, by observing that both the English and Russian Flags on the Fort were half mast high, and that Mr. John McLoughlin, the Gentleman left in charge, did not appear on the platform; the stillness that prevailed on shore, — one man only belonging to the Establishment having made his appearance at the gate, evidently showing that there was a mournful tale to relate, and on landing I was more shocked than words can describe to learn that Mr. McLoughlin was no more, having fallen on the night of the 20/21 Instant in a drunken fray, by the hand of one of his own men.[54]

When Simpson inquired as to how McLoughlin had been killed, the men he spoke to painted a sordid picture of an alcoholic, irrational commander who had severely abused them and neglected his own duties. According to Thomas McPherson, the young man who had replaced Finlayson, the evening of 20-21 April was an especially drunken one, primarily because McLoughlin, contrary to regulations, had freely distributed liquor to the Iroquois and the Canadians. By midnight he was wildly out of control, and responded to what he saw as threats by fetching his rifle, which he accidentally discharged when he fell. Too drunk to reload it himself, he sought McPherson's help, and then set off to find the men who had threatened him. In the course of this search, Urbain Heroux, whom Rae had earlier described as a "good man," shot McLoughlin in self-defense.[55]

The course of action that Simpson took in response to this story was, in every sense of that overused word, fateful. After speaking to a number of the men on 25 April and taking some formal depositions the following day, he departed for Sitka on the 27th, leaving Charles Dodd in charge, and handed Urbain Heroux and the depositions over to the Russians.[56] That he appears to have uncritically accepted the version contained in the depositions is not too difficult to explain. He did not know the men of the fort very well, and therefore did not doubt their credibility as much as others soon would. But he did know McLoughlin's personal history, and if the young man had turned over a new leaf since joining the Company, the only evidence that Simpson had seen of it was the apparently good order the fort had been in when he had visited the previous autumn, when Finlayson was still there. In the face of his long-standing doubts about the man's character and the testimony that the witnesses to McLoughlin's death were giving, he must have concluded that the young man's character flaws had reasserted themselves when confronted with the isolation and tensions of Fort Stikine. Accordingly, Simpson decided to look for evidence that the post had not been run well and, not surprisingly, seemed to find it. Not only did he accept what he was told about McLoughlin's violence and drinking, but he discovered, among other things, that the books and accounts were in an "irregular" state and that one pile of bear skins had been so neglected that it had overheated to the point of near-combustion.[57]

What all this meant was that the Company had an exceptionally ugly case on its hands. Its twenty-one-year license to trade had been renewed only four years before, and only the outbreak of rebellion in Upper and Lower Canada, which had diverted attention from its application to renew, saved it from having to engage in a lengthy defense of its record. Neither the Company nor its monopoly were popular, especially at Red River, and rumors of how harshly it treated both the Indians and its *engagés* were common.[58] If one of its clerks had so abused his men that they had killed him in self-defense, a trial in Canada would be (what today is termed) a public-relations disaster. Simpson knew this, and eventually said so in a letter written to the governor and committee in London in 1844, after it had become reasonably clear that there would be no prosecution.[59] In it, he proposed that the Company should take no action beyond sending those most seriously implicated in McLoughlin's death out of the fur country upon expiration of their contracts. He was concerned, however, that Dr. McLoughlin had sent a number of the men involved all the way to Norway House and might prosecute the case personally if the HBC did not. Simpson concluded:

> In the whole case our aim has been to assume as little responsibility as possible and at the same time to facilitate the prosecution by every

means not incompatible with the rights and feelings of innocent parties. Neither by this course, nor by any other practicable course, can the Hudson's Bay Company expect to avoid popular censure in this most untoward business; and if, as I firmly believe, the prisoners either escape unpunished or receive at most a trifling punishment, Mr. McLoughlin will hardly find in his own feelings any compensation for the odium which he will have heaped, and the injury which he will have inflicted, on the honourable company... I have requested [him] to make up a statement of all the expenses of the investigation, so that your honours may be able to decide whether the burden is to fall on the Fur trade or on Mr. McLoughlin himself...

This letter, written in June 1844, seems a rather good indication of what Simpson's plan of action, formulated probably within hours of his arrival at Stikine a few days after McLoughlin's death, had been all along. The fort was in Russian territory, so they had jurisdiction. Let them investigate the case, and let them conclude, by examining the depositions and interrogating Heroux, that there was insufficient evidence of murder to justify a trial. This conveniently antiseptic solution of conceding jurisdiction to Russia was a rather neat attempt at damage control, but it quickly ran into problems.

Perhaps if Simpson had chosen his words more carefully when he wrote to McLoughlin to tell him of his son's death, the affair would not have become so acrimonious. But he did not. As we have seen, he informed the dead man's father that John had been killed in a "drunken fray." And then, in a passage remarkable for its callousness, he went on to conclude that the younger McLoughlin's conduct and management had been "exceedingly bad." Simpson said nothing about the fact that the previous autumn he had apparently been sufficiently impressed with the state of the post to send Finlayson south and leave McLoughlin on his own. Instead, he informed the father that his son's violence "when under the influence of liquor, which was frequently the case, amount[ed] to insanity." This in a letter to a man who believed that his wayward son had finally found himself. With respect to the incident in question, Simpson opined that the shot was fired by Urbain Heroux "under the influence of terror, as a measure of self-preservation," and that any court trying the case would reach a verdict of "Justifiable Homicide."[60] In any event, he told McLoughlin, because Stikine was in Russian territory he could take no legal action, but he would take Heroux with him to Sitka and turn him over to the authorities there. Interestingly, Simpson also ordered that Pierre Kanaquassé be sent in irons to Fort Vancouver. Once there, he was "to be forwarded to Canada, as a worthless character and not to be re-admitted to the Service."[61]

Had Simpson stopped there, the letter would have been bad enough. But, in addition to returning to the topic of the younger McLoughlin's mismanagement, he noted that the Indians were now some 2,000 strong, attracted to the area by the oolachan fishery. They knew that the clerk in charge had been killed by his men and, Simpson wrote, if he had not arrived with the *Cowlitz* and the Russian steamer, they might have attacked the fort. "I consider it due to the people to say," he added, "that as a body, their conduct throughout has been fully better than could have been expected under such inhuman treatment as they were frequently exposed to." Simpson never formally retreated from his view, formulated on the spot, of what had happened at Fort Stikine.[62] But this statement about the men's behavior would soon cause him particular discomfort, because not long after he reported the incident a number of new facts came to light, all of which pointed strongly to the conclusion that his assessment of what had happened was not only hastily conceived but seriously flawed.

It was the elder McLoughlin who pried most of this information loose, motivated as he was by grief and, possibly, by guilt over not having sent his son an able assistant when Finlayson was transferred. The sources of this rather different picture of life at the post include Kanaquassé, the Iroquois Simpson wanted out of the service; the younger McLoughlin's correspondence with Finlayson and Chief Trader Work, both of whom were stationed at Fort Simpson; McLoughlin's "wife" at Stikine; and a number of other, lesser informants, most of whom were reluctant to get involved.[63] Almost as important, when Dr. McLoughlin was able to have his son's accounts examined it was discovered that they had been posted up to the day of his death, and the journal had been completed up to 19 April.[64] Moreover, only an inconsequential amount of supplies was unaccounted for, and the younger McLoughlin's personal liquor allowance was found to be "almost in the same state as when Mr. Finlayson left."[65]

Dr. McLoughlin knew that the men at the post, whose conduct Simpson had so generously praised, were among the least reliable on the coast, and he was not slow in apprising the governor and committee of this fact.[66] Pierre Kanaquassé, he said, was "one of the Greatest villains in the country ... whom necessity alone has obliged us to employ," and it was subsequently learned that he had been accused of robbery and murder in Canada. Urbain Heroux was a convicted felon, "addicted to liquor," who had been prosecuted in Canada, by his own relatives, for burglary and robbery; they dropped the case only because, while in prison, Heroux promised to leave Canada and come to the fur country.

François Pressé had been "turned out of the Southern Department" of Rupert's Land for trying to shoot a man at Moose Factory, George Heron was a "Blackguard ... who does not know his prayers," and so on. "Is it surprising," McLoughlin asked in a subsequent despatch, "if such men are brought to the Country; that people are murdered in it?"[67]

In 1844, when the quality of personnel and discipline on the Northwest Coast had really become a sore point in the case, McLoughlin alleged that some of these men had been sent to Stikine, not only because no one else wanted them, but also because no replacements were available and they could not desert from there.[68] And as early as June 1842 he had learned enough about what had happened to include some details about the behavior of these men on the night of his son's death. Antoine Kawenassa, for example, was reported to have "painted himself with the Blood of the Deceased and said to an Indian Laughing — It was the blood of a Deer." And Heroux, the man who fired the fatal shot, was said by one of the Kanakas to have "put his foot on the neck of his prostrate victim, writhing in the Agonies of death," to ensure that he would die.[69]

The "break" in the case had come quickly, in the person of Pierre Kanaquassé, whom Simpson had sent down to Fort Vancouver. McLoughlin's low opinion of the man prompted him to detain him on board the schooner *Cadboro*, with a view to sending him up to Fort Simpson pending further investigation. Kanaquassé seems to have regarded the HBC's authority over Iroquois generally and himself in particular as even less legitimate than that of the Canadian government he had left behind. Bored by his captivity and not in the least intimidated by the Company or anyone else, he therefore decided to tell Chief Factor Douglas what he knew. Informed of this, McLoughlin ordered that an inquiry be convened at Fort Nisqually before Douglas, Chief Trader Donald Manson, Captain William McNeill and the Reverend Jason Lee, so that Kanaquassé's allegations could be thoroughly examined. He did this, he said, because he was concerned that if he immediately examined Kanaquassé himself it might be said that he was too biased in favor of his son. In the meantime, he instructed Manson to go to Stikine to examine the rest of the men there, and then to send any suspects to join Heroux at Sitka.[70]

At the inquiry, Kanaquassé told a strange story that cast a rather different light upon the version reported by Simpson. He said that he had never seen McLoughlin drunk, nor was he aware of any incidents in which men had been wrongly punished, including the punishments he received.[71] The reason they all hated McLoughlin, he said, was that he would not allow them to have Indian women within the fort, or to leave it at night in order to visit the women. Nevertheless, some of the men — including Thomas McPherson — regularly left against orders and stole from the fort's stores. Most important, Kanaquassé asserted that all of the men but one — a Kanaka named Pouhow — had signed a paper agreeing to kill McLoughlin if he were not removed from command, and confirmed that he had himself tried to shoot McLoughlin on three separate occasions. That was why Simpson had sent him south in irons. Indeed, Chief Trader Work had already told Simpson that, prior to McLoughlin's death, he had "heard from the Natives of some irregularities at Stikeen and that two of the Iroquois Peter [Kanaquassé] and Antoine [Kawenassa] had fired at the deceased."[72] But because he had a letter from McLoughlin at about that time that made no mention of this, "and as we can seldom rely on the reports of Indians I did not credit it, more especially as on enquiry at Mr. Finlayson who I am sure could not tell a lie, nothing of the kind had occurred during his residence there..."[73]

Strangest of all was Kanaquassé's description of the confusing and almost surreal events on the night that McLoughlin was killed. Whatever the true import of the paper signed by the men, there is little doubt that some of them intended to kill McLoughlin that night, and that he knew it. For a while he played a demented sort of cat-and-mouse game with the fort's complement, making it clear that he knew what was up and virtually challenging them to act, even as he sought allies. Fortified with liquor and determined to go down fighting, he eventually bid a tearful farewell to his Indian wife and went out into the darkness, gun in hand, to hunt those who were hunting him. Although he had concluded long ago that he could trust no one, he took Antoine Kawenassa with him and headed for Urbain Heroux's room. McLoughlin told Kawenassa to approach from one side while he took the other, and to shoot any Canadians he might see. McLoughlin himself moved forward "in a stooping position looking very intently before him." At this point a shot was fired, and then several more. One of these hit McLoughlin high in the chest, breaking his spine.

The Kanakas were first on the scene, just in time to see Heroux emerge from behind a wall only a few paces from the corpse, and they asked him who had killed "the master." "*Vous n'avez pas besoin de demander qui est ce qui la tué,*" he replied. Kanaquassé then arrived and, finding all of the fort's complement assembled around the body, he remarked that they had done what they had all long intended to do. But when he suggested that they carry the body to the main house, Heroux, Lasserte, Bélanger and "the other white men" who were there said: "*Quand on tue un chien on le laisse là.*" Only the Kanakas would help him. By morning, Heroux was threatening violence against McPherson, whose allegiance he clearly doubted, and the Iroquois were angry because the Canadians ordered everyone to stay in the fort. Kanaquassé wanted to go see his woman, and he told Kawenassé that Heroux was as bad as McLoughlin, because they both kept the men prisoners. "I see we must raise the devil again with these Canadians," he said, "before we can get our liberty."[74]

Some of Kanaquassé's evidence was subsequently corroborated to a degree by John Rowand, an elderly chief factor who had accompanied Simpson on his tour of the coast in the autumn of 1841. Because Rowand was unwell, Simpson had left him at Stikine while the rest of the party visited Sitka, and Rowand told Dr. McLoughlin that during this time he had never seen his son drink or beat his men. He also said that he had thought it rather strange to have left McLoughlin all alone in charge of such a place, especially because McPherson was not a fit second.[75] Rowand had apparently said nothing about this to Simpson, and the latter reacted rather testily to the news, suggesting that the old man's state of health may have "prevented his paying the proper attention."[76] Rowand thus found himself caught in an escalating controversy, and took the hint: if McLoughlin had behaved badly, Rowand told Simpson in a private letter, he had indeed probably been too sick to notice. "I wish," he rather wearily concluded, "I had acted as some of my Columbian friends, they took great care not to touch upon that affair at all..."[77]

Kanaquassé's revelations led McLoughlin to probe further. The post journal had already revealed his son's concern about Indian attacks and the quality of the men, one entry noting that no work had been done that day "in consequence of the men being rather out of their senses after their drinking last night."[78] The younger McLoughlin's letters to Chief Trader Work and to his departed assistant at Fort Simpson, Roderick Finlayson, were to the same effect. He told the former that he was overworked and short on sleep, and that he would not renew his contract unless he were sent an able assistant.[79] Even before Finlayson had left, McLoughlin had complained to Work (in terms reminiscent of his letter to John Fraser five years earlier) that many of the men were "useless," especially when it came to the hard labor needed to complete the fort's defenses.[80] A few months later he made a progress report:

> Since I had the pleasure of writing you last I have managed to get new

pickets to one side of the Fort — not without much trouble. The more I see of the men the more I have to complain of them. I am obliged to mark every thing that is to be done — if not I am sure that it will be spoiled I have tried them in every way — and I am sorry to say that it is from my strict discipline that I get them to attend to their duty. If I had men that understood anything about *work* I should have had the Fort surrounded by this time.[81]

Possibly because Work might draw negative conclusions about his capacity as a leader, McLoughlin did not report his worst fears. But his letters to Finlayson were more direct. In December 1841 McLoughlin wrote that he was pleased that the gallery was finally finished because "when I get the Blue Devils I can stretch my legs at nights." And, more ominously: "I am still amongst the living of this troublesome post though reports says that I am going to be dispatched to the *Sandy Hills* — all that does not trouble me much — but it keeps me on my guard."[82] In the letters written in February 1842, the last before his death, he reminds Work of his decision to leave if he is not given a competent assistant, and tells Finlayson that he has "had all the troubles that a man could have since I have been alone." And, finally, "I cannot trust to no one."[83]

Finlayson was in a somewhat awkward position. He clearly knew that the situation at Stikine had deteriorated, yet he kept silent. Even after McLoughlin's death, he appears to have said only that there was no alcohol abuse while he was there. But once allegations surfaced that McLoughlin had taken "liberties" with Heroux's wife on the very night he was killed, Finlayson decided that he needed to explain why he did not tell his superiors earlier about "certain of" the deceased's other "habits." It seems that rumors were circulating that he had joined in McLoughlin's alleged excesses, and Finlayson was concerned that Simpson might believe them. Because his character was "at stake," he wrote in May 1843, he had to speak out.[84]

In this letter Finlayson comes across as an extremely proper young man, virtuous, religious, perhaps even a little self-righteous, and very worried about his job. He did take a little spirits and water with the deceased on two or three occasions, he admitted, but only out of politeness. However, he would not join McLoughlin in having sexual relations with the Indian women, and when he made that clear young John never again "troubled me with such a proposal. ... Mr. McLoughlin, tho' he was my master, could not divest me of my self control." He did not report any problems, he said, because

I never saw the deceased drink or ever have the least appearance of being influenced with liquor or unable to perform the duties of the place

... the only thing I had to bring forth was his criminal connexion with Indian women. Rather then see my name guilty of such base and unmanly Conduct I would rather quit the Service & trust to fortune elsewhere. ... The consequence attending a report of mine on the deceased's conduct would be an accusation against me for plotting against my master & probably create enemies for myself throughout the Country...

Thus, much of what Finlayson had to say made Simpson's version of what had happened appear unreliable. In particular, both he and Rae maintained that some of the incidents of drunkenness cited in the depositions Simpson had taken never occurred. As Lamb points out, this was consistent with the record of the deceased's youth: however badly McLoughlin may have behaved in Montreal and Paris, there was never any suggestion that he abused alcohol, and Finlayson specifically disputed what McPherson had said on this score in his deposition before Simpson.[85] Finlayson also advised Work that much of the rest of what McPherson had sworn to was probably false, including the allegation that McLoughlin had distributed the rum that night; in fact, it subsequently turned out that it was McPherson, not McLoughlin, who had done so.[86] This, in a way, was corroborrated by McPherson himself. On the day after McLoughlin's death, he wrote a confusing letter to John Work in which he expressed the fear that the men who killed McLoughlin "will do to me the way they did to him."[87] This suggests that between writing this letter and swearing his deposition he may have been subjected to a certain amount of pressure.

What Finlayson really thought about all these events is unclear. Probably he shared what he called "the general opinion," which was that McLoughlin's violence and his appetite for women had provoked a number of the "ruffians" in the fort's complement to rid themselves of him. Certainly he implies that, after he left Stikine, both McLoughlin and his men reverted to form. "The deceased's good Conduct while I remained with him," he wrote,

may be mainly attributed to the influence of my example in resisting many temptations which if I had indulged in would now have given me much reason to blush with shame and my constant adherence to the religious principles in which I have been reared... All hands in the Fort, as soon as they were rid of my presence, began to pick & steal every description of property on which they could lay their hands & deal it out ... to their indian paramours. ... I [therefore] consider it hard that I should be dismissed the Service Upon So Slender a blame as not to have reported the deceased's attachment to women, which was well known to Sir George & others before I came to the Country.[88]

It must have been one of the most stressful incidents in Finlayson's life, and he described it as "an affair ... involved in mystery which will I dare say soon be unravelled." David McLoughlin, the deceased's younger brother, was not so optimistic. In a letter to the same cousin that John had written to during his stint in the "Indian Liberating Army," David agreed that there was a mystery, but doubted that it would be easy to unearth the truth. Time proved his prediction closer to the mark. In the unpublished memoir Finlayson wrote years later, he passes over McLoughlin's death with barely a mention, and says nothing at all of his own, painful role.[89]

A third important source was the deceased's Indian wife, whom Dr. McLoughlin asked Chief Factor Work to question. Work had earlier dismissed reports from Indians that "Mr. John" had "bad white men" with him at Stikine, and the elder McLoughlin was not impressed with the way Work had carried out his part in the investigation.[90] Nonetheless, Work did ensure that the woman was questioned, and she swore a deposition before Chief Trader Manson. She was a daughter of Quatkie (or Quatkay), a chief who was friendly to the HBC, and said that the deceased had told her shortly before his death that "[i]f the Steamer does not come soon I will not see her."[91] She "persist[ed] in denying" that he

> Drank as Represented by the men when Sir George Simpson was at Stikine she says she wished to speak to him on the subject But had no Body to speak for her But Hanega Joe whom she knew was such a notorious Liar that he would not tell the truth and she was Deterred on that account from saying any thing...[92]

McLoughlin argued that this was important because "Indians do not view drunkenness as improper" and he had never seen an Indian woman "attempt to screen the drunkenness of her husband..."[93] However accurate that remark may be, it unjustifiably underestimates the possible significance of the affair to the Stikine Indians. There may well be factors at work here beyond our sight, and instability in the fort could only help the Stikines in their continuing and generally successful campaign to ensure that trade was on their terms. In any event, by the time the evidence of McLoughlin's wife was obtained, the governor and committee had long since come to the conclusion that the death of John McLoughlin, Jr., was anything but a "justifiable homicide."

***

Antoine Kawanassé [told] Mr. Manson that ... he had heard Heroux state some hours before that he would shoot my Son like a Dog ... and Lasserte saw him shoot my son...

Dr. McLoughlin to the governor and committee, 10 November 1844

As Lamb points out, the initial reaction of the governor and committee to the news from Fort Stikine was cautious.[94] The elder McLoughlin's assault on the facts deposed to before Simpson raised serious doubts about the deponents' credibility, so he was requested to respond to McLoughlin's concerns. But Simpson never really retreated from his original position, nor would he apologize for the insensitivity with which he had advanced it. As a result, the relationship between the two men, which had already deteriorated because of disagreements over whether some of the coastal forts should be closed, worsened. McLoughlin's long, haranguing letters to the governor and committee did persuade them that a murder had occurred, because he marshalled solid evidence in support. However, those parts of the letters that attacked Simpson's conduct raised questions about McLoughlin's judgment that would soon damage his credibility with the HBC.

By mid-1843 McLoughlin's new evidence had arrived in London, and in June the Company's secretary, Archibald Barclay, wrote privately to Simpson about the matter.[95] The "new light" shed on the case showed that the "crime was clearly long pre-mediated," said Barclay,

> and if ever men deserved hanging, Urbain Heroux, Pierre Kanaquassé and the scoundrel McPherson, ought to be *strung up*. It is evident that the charges of habitual intoxication and excessive severity were trumped up after the deed was committed as a screen to the villainy of the culprits.[96]

This new evidence, he added, was to be sent to the Russian governor at Sitka in order that the culprits could be properly dealt with according to Russian law. But in fact very few of them were at Sitka. Although McLoughlin had ordered both Chief Trader Manson and James Douglas to send them there, neither had done so.[97] Douglas did send Kanaquassé and François Pressé to join Heroux, but the others were distributed among Stikine, Fort Simpson and the new Fort Albert (Victoria), to be held "under watch and ward."[98] There they would remain until the Company decided what to do with them.

In September 1843 Barclay wrote to Simpson again. He repeats his conclusion that the deceased was not a habitual drunkard and adds that the punishments the young McLoughlin "inflicted ... although irregular and not perhaps conducted with the due decorum but in an *off-hand* style (as I fear is too much the custom there) were not of excessive severity…"[99] More importantly, he tells Simpson that he differs with him about the case. There was indeed a plot, he says, and the deceased was killed while attempting to arrest "the Canadians implicated chiefly" in it.[100] He concedes that the "evidence taken since you were at Stikine is no doubt loose, irrelevant often little to be depended upon, but it is not nearly so bad as that given before yourself at Stikine." Lamb, whose interest in the case was largely confined to its effect upon the struggle between the "Big Doctor" and the "Little Emperor," observes that these words must have shaken Simpson: they came "perilously near to being a complete acceptance of McLoughlin's point of view."[101] But Barclay did not hold Simpson personally responsible, nor did he think that proceedings should be taken against all the conspirators. Kanaquassé's written agreement could not be found, and without it the case against all but Kanaquassé and Heroux was weak. "[T]heir punishment," declared Barclay, "whether it affect their lives or liberty would be a most salutary, I may say necessary measure under all the circumstances — and this is the determination which the Board have come to." As for McLoughlin, Barclay assured Simpson that he had been reprimanded on a number of counts, including his personal attacks on Simpson. "He has not been allowed to triumph."

But the plan to have the men tried by the Russians was already unraveling. At about the same time that Barclay was writing to Simpson, Adolphe Etholine, the governor of the Russian American Company's territories, wrote McLoughlin from New Archangel (Sitka). He agreed with McLoughlin that it was surprising that he had as yet received no instructions from St. Petersburg regarding Heroux, but said that he expected he would hear soon. He must have hoped so, because Heroux had "shewn himself here to be a man of ferocious disposition, having attempted to murder his keeper, who prevented his escape."[102] Two months later, the governor of the HBC in London, Sir John Pelly, advised Simpson that he now doubted that the Russians would be holding any trial. Baron Wrangel had informed Pelly that, because Stikine was "in that part of the Russian dominions given in Bail to the Hudsons Bay Comp.," the Russian government would not assume jurisdiction over the case. As a consequence, Governor Etholine had been ordered to send the prisoners back to McLoughlin.[103]

Barclay was not impressed. He believed the talk about jurisdiction to be "more fudge alleged to get rid of the business," and told Simpson:

> We are now in a complete *fix* as brother Jonathan would say. If these
> men cannot be tried by the Russians, what is to be done with them? B.
> Wrangell says they will be sent back to the Columbia, to be dealt with
> according to the tender mercies of McLoughlin. They might be tried in
> Canada but what an expense and inconvenience to get them and the
> witnesses transported thither, — and what an exposure too! To let them
> loose without trial would be a most dangerous example to others.[104]

Suggesting that money was the real reason the Russians were refusing to
act, Barclay then wondered whether the Company should offer to pay for
a trial at Sitka whereby the convicts could then be banished to Siberia.
But nothing ever came of this, possibly because it appears that the
Russians at Sitka had no criminal jurisdiction, which meant transporting
the accused and all the witnesses to Siberia for trial.

Instead, an increasingly frustrated and embittered McLoughlin
ignored Simpson's order to release the men held under house arrest at
the forts, maintaining to the governor and committee that the men were
confined under "the Warrant of a Magistrate" (presumably that of
McLoughlin, or perhaps of Douglas or Work). In such circumstances, he
said, "until instructions come from England, how Sir George, who is
himself only a Magistrate, can take on himself to order their liberation, I
know not."[105] When the Russians returned Heroux, Kanaquassé and
Pressé in February 1844, all the men involved in the killing at Fort Stikine
were sent down to Fort Vancouver.[106] Then, consulting neither Simpson
nor the governor and committee, McLoughlin sent Heroux, Kanaquassé,
a dozen or so "witnesses" and an interpreter to Rupert's Land to await
transportation to Canada. He instructed his agent in Montreal that, if the
HBC and the Canadian authorities were both unwilling to prosecute, he
should commence proceedings himself.[107]

This action brought everyone's wrath down on McLoughlin's head.
The governor and committee had already chastized him for his personal
attacks on Simpson; they now advised McLoughlin that sending so many
men to Norway House was "an irregular and injudicious proceeding" for
which he would be held personally and financially responsible. His
fellow officers were not so harsh, but they too were heartily sick of the
affair and of the effect it had had upon McLoughlin, who seemed to feel
compelled to vindicate his son's character as well as to avenge his death.
In April 1843 the chief factor at Fort Colville wrote that the "pile upon
pile of papers the unhappy father has laboured to fill up upon this
harassing question to prove his son to have been what in my opinion he
was not, is truly astonishing." He added: "I cannot however disguise my
dread of the attack that will be made upon me this Summer if I go down,

to bring me into his own way of thinking as I believe is his habitual practice with every one with whom he comes in contact."[108] Two years later Chief Trader John Tod told a friend that "I fear the Dr. has not only compromised his dignity in this affair but has also failed to excite the Sympathy of the greater part of his friends, from his very excess."[109]

Eventually, even McLoughlin ran out of energy, and funds. He explained to a friend in 1846 (his last year of active service) that because the only place the men could be tried was England, he would have to let the matter drop. He could not afford the approximately £10,000 that such proceedings would cost.[110] It is unlikely that McLoughlin felt any differently about how the case had been handled than he had in February 1844, when he wrote what was probably his last letter on the subject to Simpson. Reproduced in a Hudson's Bay Record Society volume, it takes up twenty-eight single-spaced printed pages in which he replies, point by point, to Simpson's arguments. Stung both by Simpson's strategy of blaming the victim and by his willingness to cover everything up, the grieving father asks how anyone who had conducted such a cursory investigation could write to the parent of a dead man, praising the conduct of his killers.[111] He also could not understand how Simpson could continue to assert his view that it was a case of justifiable homicide, once the new evidence had come to light:

> I was astonished More than I can Express when I first read with what confidence you assert that a Jury would pronounce a Verdict of Justifiable Homicide when the depositions you had before you on the mens own showing are that the punishment [sic] were not more severe than their Bad conduct deserved What is an officer to be murdered with impunity because he flogs a thief or a Sentry who sleeps on his watch because as is well known the safety of the whole Establishment depends on his Vigilance...[112]

Guilt was a question that should be decided, not "according to your or my conviction but by the authorized tribunals who are appointed by competent authority and are Responsible before God and man for their decision." Yet, "even now you are perfectly silent as to the measures that are to be adopted towards the murderers of my Son..."[113]

***

I am no Lawyer But ...

Dr. McLoughlin to the Governor & Committee, 10 November 1844

In his letter to Simpson of 1 February 1844, McLoughlin makes an obvious, if somewhat imperial, point. Surely, he said, it was reasonable to presume that "there is no place under Christian Dominion where a British subject is murdered but it will be Enquired into Especially when the murderer and his associates are in the power of the authorities of the Country."[114] Yet "the murderer and his associates" were not tried, notwithstanding that both the Russians and the Company, at one time or another, had them in their power. The short explanation for this is that, once the Russians declined jurisdiction, the expense involved in bringing the case to trial was more than the Company was willing to incur. Bad publicity was virtually certain, but convictions were not; and although the governor and committee initially disagreed with the view that the younger McLoughlin was "hardly worth the trouble," when it became clear that it would be their trouble and not the Russians' they eventually came around to it.[115] To put all this in context, it is necessary to examine whether Fort Stikine really was "under Christian Dominion," that is, whether the legal conclusions reached by the Company were justified, and what other considerations were brought to bear on the ultimate outcome of the case.

That the Company and the Russians might regard Stikine as within the jurisdiction of one or the other — or perhaps both — of their governments is to be expected. It was located on territory claimed by the Czar, whose representatives had been exploring and trading in the region since the mid-eighteenth century, and Britain had recognized that claim by treaty in 1825. The British case for jurisdiction was even older, although not territorial: it was based upon the current version of what was originally a Tudor statute authorizing the trial, in England, of acts of homicide committed by subjects abroad, even in lands outside the Crown's dominions.[116] The third alternative, trial in Canada, was authorized by the Canada Jurisdiction Act of 1803. According to it, if the accused were British subjects they could be tried in Canada, even if the offense "appeared" to have been committed in a "Colony, Settlement or Territory belonging to any European State."[117] Given that the Russians declined jurisdiction, this left two expensive but apparently legal alternatives — a trial in either England or Canada.

A third alternative — that Tlingit law applied — was never considered. Throughout this period the Tlingit believed that their concepts of justice should be extended to Europeans within their territories, especially when the dignity of high-ranking individuals was affected. One of the most serious offenses was to visibly injure the face, and the journals of Forts Stikine and Simpson reveal a number of instances where traders paid compensation in blankets and furs, or exceptionally rum, for having done this. Such was Tlingit law, and the law of many North American aboriginal societies. The Tlingit outnumbered the Europeans on the Panhandle by about 8,000 to 500 and had no cause to believe that anyone had seriously challenged their sovereignty, so if this law had been ignored, the consequences could have been serious.[118] Nonetheless, they did not attempt to interfere with what happened at Stikine; it did not involve any of their own people, and it confirmed the relative weakness of the Company in Alaska.

There were therefore good reasons not to involve Tlingit law or, due to distance and expense, British courts. But were the reasons that Heroux and Kanaquassé avoided trial in Canada purely practical and financial? The answer to this question depends upon the weight one is inclined to give some remarks made by Simpson in his despatch to the governor and committee in June 1844. Referring to a legal opinion that he had sought from Adam Thom, the HBC's recorder at Red River, Simpson told his superiors in London that Thom was "clearly of the opinion that Canada has no jurisdiction beyond the [Rocky] mountains..."[119] This, of course, is the position Simpson had taken all along, a fact that should come as no surprise. In July 1842 he had written to the governor and committee from Okhotsk, in Eastern Siberia, explaining that although Stikine was situated on Russian territory, and was "consequently beyond [his] jurisdiction as a Magistrate for the Indian Territories," he had examined some of the men anyway, out of a desire to get at the truth.[120] Moreover, even if Canada did have jurisdiction in Russian America, this would extend only to British subjects. Because Kanaquassé was Iroquois, Thom advised, the "liberal and indulgent principles of penal interpretation" would probably lead to the conclusion that he could not be considered a British subject.[121]

In fact, although both propositions are plausible, they are probably wrong. There was, even then, case law that strongly supported the view that the Canada Jurisdiction Act applied west of the Rockies, including — so long as the prisoner was a British subject — Russian America. And only five years earlier the assize court at Trois Rivières had at least implicitly ruled that, although "mere" Indians were not British subjects for the purposes of the act, those employed by the Company were.[122] So if Pierre Kanaquassé had been Tlingit rather than an Iroquois *engagé*, the Company might well have attempted to execute him itself; or, if it was unable to secure the cooperation of the Stikines in this, obtain compensation of some kind instead.[123] But it was Heroux the HBC was really after, and because he was Canadian his prosecution should have raised no such difficulty. It was a simple case of one trader killing another or, more dramatically, an employee killing his boss. As such, it was just the sort of case that the Canada Jurisdiction Act had been designed to catch.

Thom was clearly aware of some of these precedents, so it does not seem unreasonable to conclude that he was, to a certain extent, tailoring his advice to fit the requirements of his client and employer. In the end, he said he thought that only England had jurisdiction, but that even this might have been "rendered inconsistent with the spirit of the [law] by the proceedings in Russia." What this meant is unclear, especially as there really had been no proceedings. In all likelihood, the British government had made it known that, as Britain was not especially interested in making any claim to territory or governmental authority in Russian Alaska, it was equally unwilling to help the Company try Kanaquassé and Heroux in Middlesex. In any event, if one were betting that on this view of the law even McLoughlin was unlikely to pursue the matter so far, they would — as we have seen — be right.

Given the uncertainties in Thom's legal advice, other reasons must be sought for the Company's reluctance to go to court, and most of these have been alluded to already. In the first place, the case against the accused had some significant weak spots. When Simpson took the depositions at Stikine he did not cross-examine the deponents, defending himself against McLoughlin's angry complaints about this by asserting that he had no power to do so: the depositions were simply voluntary statements under oath.[124] No doubt Douglas, Work and Manson had fewer qualms in this regard, and that is why the statements made before them contradicted the earlier ones so significantly. However, although these contradictions helped to establish that much of what Simpson had been told was false, they also raised serious doubts about the credibility of most of the deponents. Many had a motive to falsify, many of the incidents allegedly involved alcohol, and some of the most important witnesses, the Kanakas in particular, spoke very little English. When they gave evidence before Simpson they did so through a Kanaka sailor aboard the *Cowlitz* who was sufficiently fluent to act as an interpreter. The Canadians were examined in English, but some replied in French.[125] Moreover, if the conspiracy theory were true, all but one of the men at the fort were accomplices to one degree or another, hence in law their testimony would be suspect on that ground as well. The fact that the document alleged to have contained evidence of the conspiracy had disappeared was also a problem, because the oral evidence of its contents conflicted.[126] None of this meant that a case of murder could not be made out against Heroux, or attempted murder against Kanaquassé, but it was an expensive hypothesis to put to the test.

A second and possibly even more worrying problem for the Company was that the question of why the men west of the mountains were so troublesome had become, internally, a major issue. A trial would make this public, and expose the HBC's labor policies to scrutiny. Ever since the merger with the North West Company in 1821 and the cutbacks it entailed, Simpson had been trying to run the HBC's operations as if he had access to a real labor market. Surplus workers were settled at Red River so they could be hired on a short-term basis, and the HBC's monopoly was relied upon to prevent these men from engaging in private trade. Because the monopoly could not be enforced, the Company ended up with a deficient stock of long-term employees as well as an inadequate pool from which to draw short-term replacements. As one historian put it:

> [T]he advantages to employers of a capitalistic market were sought before the market really existed. What Simpson actually did was to produce profits out of the unrecognized corrosion of the magnificent labour force bequeathed him by the [North West] Company. When the demoralization of that labour force had become complete, about 1850, the Company could no longer command labour at the times and places desired and had to content itself with a very inferior quality of employee.[127]

The McLoughlin case suggests that some of the work force was "demoralized" long before 1850. The Company's employment policies not only helped to lower the quality of the men it attracted, but led, in turn, to increased emphasis upon ethnicity in hiring. This was done both to increase the potential labor pool by casting the net more widely, and to make managing the men easier by keeping the numbers of so-called troublemakers low. For example, the Scots and the Irish were, in Simpson's view, especially "inclined to form leagues and cabals which might be dangerous to the peace of the Country," so they were to be hired in smaller numbers and placed with different ethnic groups.[128] Most of these already had their own, well-developed sense of identity. They had lived apart before entering the service, and separated "by mutual consent" when encamped; "the Iroquois had a fire; the French Canadians had a fire,"[129] and the officers had a fire. Simpson hoped that such polyglot bands would decrease the likelihood of harmful "combinations," but the exceptional events at Fort Stikine show that this was not always the case. However tense relations between the Iroquois and the Canadians were before and after McLoughlin's death, they shared an antipathy for him that proved potent enough when the time came.

To complicate matters further, McLoughlin's loyalty to the Company, which would normally guarantee discretion, was also becoming suspect; this made the possibility of publicity even more worrying. There was already a tendency to regard him as a "radical" whose political sympathies were increasingly American and republican rather than British and corporate, and disputes with Simpson over trade policy and the death of his son at Stikine would soon end his career.[130] The debate about the quality of the men under McLoughlin's command had arisen naturally out of the latter incident, and he had complained to the governor and committee about the "impropriety of the people in Canada Engaging for this Country men under Criminal prosecution and Re-engaging men who had been turned out of the Service. I am also informed that Jourdain one of the Mackenzie River murderers has been Re Engaged and returned last year to the Country."[131]

It was Simpson who replied first to McLoughlin's complaints, and he did so by blaming him for permitting "a System of Terror" to prevail in his department, telling him that "I have as you know always Believed Kindness to Be the Best Disciplinarian."[132] The governor and committee seemed to agree. "We have learned from other sources," they told McLoughlin,

> that there is an insurmountable reluctance on the part of respectable labourers to accept employment on the West side of the Mountains, occasioned by the reports circulated by those who have returned from that quarter... They may be the fabrication of worthless or malicious persons, but unfortunately the effect is the same as if they were well founded: the service is injured, men of good character are deterred from entering it.[133]

They went on to recommend that any corporal punishment that was necessary "be administered with coolness [and] moderation," and that proper records be kept of such occurrences, to be forwarded to London. They underlined their concern by threatening a course of action that was clearly designed to impress McLoughlin, who had quarreled with Simpson about the relative effectiveness of coastal forts versus trading by steamer. Unless better men were employed, they said,

> we should prefer having no posts at all. It would be infinitely better to recur to the old system (rude as it was) of visiting the coast once or twice a year for the purposes of trade, than that such scenes as those, which occurred at Stikine should be witnessed by the Natives.[134]

There were other comments in this despatch that must have stung McLoughlin, but he was careful to confine his criticism primarily to

Simpson, whom he rather sarcastically accused of having "become all at once very sensitive about striking the men." On at least two occasions, he pointed out, Sir George had himself inflicted floggings and beatings, and on a third he "tickled" a man's shoulders "with a canoe pole" until he had to be restrained from beating the man further.[135] In the very long letter that McLoughlin wrote directly to Simpson in February 1844 he was even less restrained.[136] Referring to Simpson's assertion that he believed kindness to be the best disciplinarian, McLoughlin reminded him that he was addressing someone who had spent forty years in the fur country, and angrily accused Simpson of "writing for Effect on others."[137] He then recited a further three or four incidents of Iroquois and other *engagés* plotting to kill officers in various parts of the Company's territories. It is therefore hardly surprising that Simpson was worried that McLoughlin's actions, let alone a public trial, would embarrass the Company, and he can have been little comforted by McLoughlin's response to this concern. "I do not understand what you mean by Embarassing," wrote McLoughlin. "Is murder not to be punished because it is Embarassing?"[138]

Apparently, it was not. Simpson had already experienced what a Canadian trial of a fur-country murder was like, in the "Mackenzie River murders" case to which McLoughlin had himself referred when he raised the question of the quality of the men he was being sent.[139] The men charged in the earlier case, and especially the interpreter, Baptiste Cadien, were not unlike Pierre Kanaquassé. Cadien's mother was Dogrib, and, like Kanaquassé, he had been repeatedly warned by the postmaster at Fort Norman not to frequent the local Indian lodges in search of women. These injunctions were disobeyed. In December 1835 Cadien, two other *engagés* and two Dogrib went to an encampment at Lake Puant, a nearby fishery, and stole the woman he wanted. In the course of doing so they killed eleven people, mainly women and children. When they returned to the post Cadien was allegedy bent on killing the postmaster as well, but the latter was warned in time.

When Cadien was tried at Trois Rivières in 1838, the Company, traditionally rather obsessed with privacy, received too much of just the sort of attention it did not want. The newspapers vociferously debated the case, and the local clergy and a number of citizens petitioned against the death sentence Cadien received. Even one of the presiding judges lobbied to have it commuted. Eventually it was, and several years later Cadien died aboard a prison hulk in England, awaiting transportation to a penal colony in Van Dieman's Land. Only two witnesses had been sent out with Cadien, yet — according to Simpson — trying him in Lower

Canada had been very expensive.[140] By way of comparison, the Stikine case involved at least two accused, and perhaps as many as a dozen witnesses.

In some respects, the similarities between the two incidents are close, and both McLoughlins were probably familiar with the details of the earlier case. As the father put it, after his son's death:

> [I]n 1840 in going up the Columbia at the Dalles the people were ordered not to go to the Indian Lodges but Pierre [Kanaquassé] Attempted to go in Defiance of the officers when [my son] knocked him Down and obliged him to Remain and while Mr. Rae was in charge of Stikine Pierre left his watch, left the Port Hole opened and went to the Indian Lodges after a woman for which he was Deservedly flogged — as he had afforded an opportunity to the Indians if so Inclined to cut off the whole Establishment — If Pierre would act this way when there were two officers what would he do when there was only one.[141]

Kanaquassé was every bit as determined to spend time with the Tlingit at Stikine as Cadien had been to visit the North Slavey at Lake Puant, and he resented McLoughlin's refusal to allow him to do so. Kanaquassé told Douglas that, on the very day McLoughlin died, the latter had forbidden him to bring his wife into the fort. This rule, he said, was the "real cause of [the men's] enmity to the deceased."[142]

The Company had always strictly forbidden the common *engagés* from taking part in short-term, potentially exploitative sorties in search of Indian women. These were perceived as security risks, because sexual jealousy, alcohol or disease could, individually or combined, quickly bring down the wrath of the native community upon the traders' heads. Years earlier, when Simpson first visited the region west of the Rockies, problems with another "disaffected" interpreter had led him to comment that:

> It is a lamentable fact that almost every difficulty we have had with Indians throughout the Country may be traced to our interference with their Women or their intrigues with the Women of the Forts in short 9 Murders out of 10 Committed on Whites by Indians have arisen through Women.[143]

The man in question had been "severely reprimanded" for "over intimacy" and "indiscreet amours" with the local women. Because he had attempted to seek revenge by inciting the tribes against the traders, Simpson's response was a harsh one: he met with the chiefs in council in order "to dispose of the Interpreter without giving umbrage to the Indians."[144]

This rule against unregulated "fraternization" with local native populations did not change over time, although it was never easy to enforce. But the Company did allow more formal, long-term relationships, especially in the remoter areas. Simpson had himself given permission to a number of the men at Stikine to marry when he visited in 1841, a point he noted in his published account of his travels:

> Fourteen or fifteen of the men of the establishment asked permission to take native wives: and leave to accept the worthless bargains was granted to all such as had the means of supporting a family. These matrimonial connections are a heavy tax on a post, in consequence of the increased demand for provisions, but they form, at the same time, a useful link between the traders and the savages.[145]

At such places there was no one else to marry, and the result of this graceless permission was that several did so. They apparently moved their new wives into the fort, and proceeded to have children and to engage in other domestic pleasures and, occasionally, disputes. All this afforded the Stikine Tlingit much more information about HBC society and its foibles than the Company wanted them to know, and certainly much more than the Company knew about the Tlingit.[146]

It seems likely that the distinction between trade wives and other sexual partners may have eluded some of the HBC's *engagés*, especially those with Indian blood. Nonetheless, it was the elder McLoughlin's opinion that his son had reaped a bitter reward — an unavenged death coupled with posthumous defamation — for attempting to enforce the rules. He told Simpson this,[147] and made the point again when he responded to the committee's remarks about the "scenes" at Stikine:

> If [by scenes] you mean a licentious intercourse with Indian women, my deceased son only allowed the number of men he was instructed to take Indian wives, and in justice to him I must say he is the only Officer of the three Posts who followed his instructions on this subject, and would not allow the men to bring women from the Indian camp for the night into the Fort, and on account of danger allowed the men as little Intercourse as possible with the Indians, and this is what the men considered the greatest grievance, because they had more indulgence at the other places.[148]

Unfortunately, it is not entirely clear what his son's instructions were, or how he conducted his own sexual relations. For example, if he did forbid Kanaquassé from bringing his wife into the fort, was this because he felt he should exclude all women except his own, or because the Iroquois's marriage had not been approved by Simpson? Alternatively, was it because McLoughlin was punishing Kanaquassé for plotting against him or for some other infraction, or because they disagreed upon who was an approved wife and who was not? Or was it for some other reason, one we cannot see?

The Company's practice in such matters was never a model of consistency and, as the nineteenth century progressed, the privileges of rank must have become increasingly irksome to *engagés* who did not enjoy them; if McLoughlin was abusing his, this would have been resented. Perhaps his father was right and young John really was the only officer who had followed orders. If so, Finlayson's account of his character and habits suggests that this too may have been part of the problem. Of all the clerks on the Northwest Coast, John McLoughlin, Jr., was probably the least qualifed to demand that the rules of "proper" sexual behavior be observed.[149]

***

You will no doubt learn from other more authentic sources, the particulars of the melancholy fate of poor John McLoughlin. — They are to blame, I think placing the young man in a situation for which his well known propensities rendered him so totally unfit.

Chief Trader John Tod to James Hargrave, 15 March 1843

So in the end no one stood trial in Canada, or anywhere else. The men who were to be witnesses received all their back wages, which McLoughlin had stopped when he learned of the conspiracy, and some returned to the Company's service. Much to McLoughlin's distress, one even got a raise, and another was sent back to work in the Columbia.[150] The Kanakas also went back, but they played a very minor role in the affair; they may even have been allied with the younger McLoughlin when he died.[151] The rest of the men were sent out as "retiring servants" upon completion of their contracts of employment, including, it seems, Urbain Heroux and Pierre Kanaquassé. Nearly all of them had renewed these contracts with the younger McLoughlin in October 1841, about six months before his death. Some may have done this because of their newly forged family ties, but in the result they spent most of their time away from Stikine, under house arrest and doing no work.[152]

The careers of the northern coastal forts were also near their end. Taku was dismantled in 1843 in order that the men there could go south to build a new post at Camosun (Fort Albert, soon renamed Victoria), and so was Fort McLoughlin.[153] Stikine remained open long enough to fill a few more despatches with news about another plot against officers' lives, giving McLoughlin an opportunity to explain to the governor and committee that the boldness of the men was due to the perception that, like Heroux, they would not be punished.[154] Then, in 1849, Stikine was also abandoned, to enable the men to take part in establishing Fort Rupert at the northern end of Vancouver Island. The new post's journal reveals that among these was Captain Cole, one of the Kanakas who had been at Stikine in 1842.[155]

Soon after young John McLoughlin's death there was trouble further south as well. In July 1842 two men swore depositions that, while engaged in splitting shingles near Cowlitz Farm about five weeks earlier, they had spoken of the murder at Stikine with a third man, Narcisse Mousette.[156] According to them, Mousette had proposed that, if they all agreed, he would help to kill the officer in charge at Cowlitz, Charles Forrest. They "rejected the proposal with horror," they said, and one of them, Hilaire Gilbeault, went to Forrest immediately after work to tell him what had transpired. When confronted, Mousette maintained that he was only joking, but McLoughlin had him sent out of the country anyway. In a display of good judgment that should have done him credit, he declined to take any further action, as it would "not be worth while to send evidence to prosecute him."[157] But he did have James Douglas advise the posts along the way not to employ Mousette, and was very angry to learn two years later that someone had engaged the man anyway. Because McLoughlin also discovered that Simpson took Mousette's side in this dispute, he decided to complain to the governor and committee. On this occasion, his earlier good sense deserted him. Alleging that, had he not sent Mousette away, more of the Company's officers would have been murdered, he ascribed the Mousette's boldness to the careless way in which Simpson had investigated his son's death. This was an allegation of which there is not a hint in the depositions, however plausible it might otherwise have been. It could only have done him further injury.[158]

But by then McLoughlin's grief and anger were taking their toll. Soon his world would darken even further, as it became clear that there would be no trial, and that his position in the Company had been irreparably damaged. Although technically he did not leave its employ until 1849, in June 1845 he was told that he would no longer be in charge west of the mountains, and he was on furlough and leave of absence from mid-1846. At about the same time, he also learned that William Glen Rae, the son-in-law who had been transferred from Stikine to California to take over the HBC's post at Yerba Buena, had collapsed under the strain of work and alcoholism, and killed himself.[159]

Now both of the clerks who had established the HBC post at Stikine were dead. This blow came too late to worsen McLoughlin's already mortally wounded position in the Company, but as one historian has written, "it was nonetheless a bitter experience to have the murder of his son followed by the suicide of his son-in-law, under circumstances that gave ample range to his critics."[160] The historian is of course W. Kaye Lamb, in an essay introducing the third and final volume of McLoughlin's Fort Vancouver Letters. Attempting to summarize the effect on McLoughlin's career of the years between 1839 and 1844, he quoted McLoughlin's "bitter words" to Sir John Pelly, written after his demotion: "Sir George Simpson's Visit here in 1841 has cost me Dear."[161] It had cost Simpson, on the other hand, nothing at all. Although it was he who had transferred Finlayson to Fort Simpson, who had taken the misleading depositions at Stikine, and who appears never to have adequately explained just what his instructions concerning Indian wives there had been, his career was unimpaired. The difference is that Simpson was indispensable, McLoughlin was not.

It seems appropriate to conclude the present essay, not with the unhappy father, but with the murdered son and his men. It was their actions, after all, that raised the questions of law and jurisdiction that so afflicted the case. According to Pierre Kanaquassé, after the murder he and the Kanakas washed and dressed the body in the main house, but the men refused to pray over it, and then quarreled about who was going to obey whom, now that McLoughlin was dead. In the morning one of them made a coffin, which he completed at around 11:00 A.M. When the body had been placed in it, it was removed from the carpentry shop and put in the bathhouse. Afterwards, McPherson gave the men a dram.

The following day, 23 April, the "corpse was carried to the grave by Lasserte, Pressé, Leclaire and some Kanakas, but Urbain did not touch it." Then the men had another dram.[162] The complete post journal entry for that day is a simple one:

> Weather as yesterday. The men were employed digging the grave for the body and about 12:00 at noon it was deposited in the ground, firing at the same time the salute of a gun. Traded today five black bear skins for various articles. Several canoes arrived from up the river.[163]

"Poor John," wrote David McLoughlin a year later, "he had a great deal of trouble the short time he was in this world, & if he had remained in Canada this would never have happened ... Our people here are such beasts..."[164] When asked about the incident in 1878 by a researcher for historian Hubert Howe Bancroft, one retired fur trader had a different response, unencumbered by a brother's love.[165] By then a Washington Territory probate judge, George B. Roberts said that young McLoughlin was "too young and hotheaded for such a service." According to Roberts, he should not have been left in charge of Fort Stikine.

NOTES

1. Throughout this paper the term "HBC" will be used interchangeably with "the Company" and the "Hudson's Bay Company."

2. See, for example, Shepard Krech III, "The Beaver Indians and the Hostilities at Fort St. John's," *Arctic Anthropology* 20, no. 2 (1983): 35-45. In retaliation for the killing of some of their employees in 1823 the Company closed Fort St. John's and Fort Dunvegan, and considered closing the rest of the posts in the area.

3. Although sometimes this did lead to adequate documentation, especially where legal proceedings of some kind were contemplated: see for example, Foster, "Mutiny on the *Beaver*: Law and Authority in the Fur Trade Navy, 1835-1840," in Dale Gibson and W. Wesley Pue, eds., *Glimpses of Canadian Legal History* (Winnipeg: Legal Research Institute, 1991), 15-46.

4. An Act for extending the Jurisdiction of the Courts of Justice in the Provinces of Upper and Lower Canada, to the Trial and Punishment of Crimes, and Offences within certain parts of North America adjoining to the said Provinces, 43 Geo. III (1803), c. 138 (UK). This statute extended to all offenses, but was in fact applied only to serious ones. It was supplemented several years later by 1 & 2 Geo. IV (1821), c. 66, but no cases appear to have been sent east under the latter statute.

5. It was used on one or two other occasions, as well. See generally, Foster, "Long-Distance Justice: The Criminal Jurisdiction of Canadian Courts West of the Canadas, 1763-1859," *The American Journal of Legal History* 34 (1990): 1-48.

6. See Foster, "Sins Against the Great Spirit: The Law, the Hudson's Bay Company, and the Mackenzie's River Murders, 1835-1839," *Criminal Justice History: An International Annual* 10 (1989): 23-76.

7. It appears that in 1817 the North West Company sent a murder case to Montreal from what is now British Columbia: see Foster, "Long-Distance Justice," 31-32.

8. Unfortunately, except for a few letters (originals in French) collected by the Hudson's Bay Record Society, I have been unable to consult Russian sources. However, I am advised by Prof. R.A. Pierce of the University of Alaska at Fairbanks that approximately 60,000 documents of the Russian American Company are currently being indexed (personal communication, 11 October 1990).

9. See W. Kaye Lamb, "Introduction," in E.E. Rich, ed., *The Letters of John McLoughlin from Fort Vancouver to the Governor and Committee: Second Series, 1839-44* (London: Hudson's Bay Record Society, 1943), xi-xlix.

10. In a twist that is also relevant to the conference theme, Judge Matthew P. Deady held in *United States v. Seveloff*, 27 F.Cas 1021 (D.Ore 1872) that Alaska was *not* "Indian Country," as that term is understood in American law: see Sidney L. Harring "The Incorporation of Alaskan Natives Under American Law: United States and Tlingit Sovereignty, 1867-1900," *Arizona Law Review* 31 (1989): 284-85. *Seveloff* was the first Alaskan criminal case to reach the United States federal courts.

11. *Tee-Hit-Ton Indians v. U.S.*, 348 US 272 (1955). The Tlingits' relationship to the Company is examined in Laura F. Klein, "Demystifying the Opposition: The Hudson's

Bay Company and the Tlingit," *Arctic Anthropology* 24 (1987): 101-14, which includes a brief discussion of the killing of McLoughlin at Stikine. See also the essay by Stephen Haycox in this book.

12. The reference to the Russian bear is obvious; the raven is one of the two moieties into which the Tlingit, like the Haida, divided themselves. On the laws of the Tlingit, see Kalervo Oberg, "Crime and Punishment in Tlingit Society," *American Anthropologist* 36 (1934): 145-56.

13. Sir George Simpson to the governor and committee, 25 November 1841, in Glyndwr Williams, ed., *London Correspondence Inward from Sir George Simpson, 1841-42* (London: Hudson's Bay Record Society, 1973), 62; and Stephen M. Johnson, "Wrangel and Simpson," in Carol M. Judd and Arthur J. Ray, eds., *Old Trails and New Directions: Papers of the Third North American Fur Trade Conference* (Toronto: University of Toronto Press, 1980), 208-09. For an account of the *Dryad* incident by one who was there, see *The Journals of William Fraser Tolmie, Physician and Fur Trader* (Vancouver: Mitchell Press, 1963), 283-86.

14. Johnson, "Wrangel and Simpson." See also John S. Galbraith, *The Hudson's Bay Company as an Imperial Factor, 1821-1869* (Berkeley: University of California Press, 1957), 152-53; and James R. Gibson, "The Russian Fur Trade," in Judd and Ray, *Old Trails and New Directions*, 217-30. To secure the agreement, the Company implied that they would establish the proposed inland fort and intercept the supply of furs before it reached the coast. However, Simpson knew how jealous the Tlingit were of their status as middlemen and regarded establishing a post upriver as a last resort. His caution was justified in 1852 when a different Tlingit tribe destroyed Fort Selkirk because it violated their ban on direct trade between traders and Athapaskans: Frederica De Laguna, "Tlingit," in Wayne Suttles, ed., *Northwest Coast*, vol. 7 of *The Handbook of North American Indians* (Washington: Smithsonian Institution, 1990), 209.

15. Lamb, "Introduction," xii. Fort Durham was 162 miles north of Stikine — see Roderick Finlayson, "A History of Vancouver Island and the Northwest Coast" (Bancroft Library, P-C 15, p. 17).

16. George Simpson, *Narrative of a Journey Round the World, 1841-1842* (London: Hudson's Bay Record Society, 1847), quoted in Williams, *London Correspondence*, 62n.

17. Simpson to governor and committee, 25 November 1841, in Williams, *London Correspondence*, 63, and see Laguna, "Tlingit," 212, and 226-27. The HBC "Census of Stikine Population 1845" (Hudson's Bay Company Archives [hereafter HBCA], B.209/Z/1, fo.4) speaks of eight groups, and I have put some possible contemporary and modern equivalents in parentheses: the *Stik na hut ti* (Secatquonay?), the *Ka as ki ti tán*, the *Na nu a a ghe*, the *Te i ti tán* (Tee-Hit-Ton?), the *Kas ke que té* (Kiks-uddy?), the *Talkth que ti*, the *Kik set i*, and the *Kady ét i*. The first three were probably Wolf clans, the remainder, Raven — see Laguna, "Tlingit," 227, who lists nine clans. It is also possible that some of the clans enumerated by the HBC (for example, the *Te i ti tan*) are actually house groups, because the Company may not have appreciated the importance of family identification in Tlingit society — see Klein, "Demystifying the Opposition," 107; and the essay by Stephen Haycox in this book.

18. Ibid, 63n., citing HBCA, B.223/b/28, fo. 48d. Douglas wrote this in 1840, before the incident at Stikine. The 1845 HBC census (see preceding note) indicates that there were 1,574 inhabitants in a total of sixty-four lodges. (This figure includes 166 slaves, some of whom may have been non-Tlingit.)

19. Harring, "Incorporation of Alaskan Natives," 282.

20. Ibid., 280. Although the Russians asserted title against other European nations, they did not make such claims directly to the Tlingit.

21. Finlayson, "History of Vancouver Island," 9. The Company had about eighteen men, whereas the Russians had had twenty-five: HBCA, B.209/a/1, Post Journal for Fort Stikine [hereafter "Post Journal"], 1840-1842, entry for 13 June 1840.

22. Post Journal, entry for Wednesday, 17 June, and Friday, 19 June 1840.

23. Ibid., entry for Sunday, 21 June 1840; and Finlayson, "History of Vancouver Island," 18, referring to the period prior to his formal assignment to the fort.

24. Post Journal, entry for Wednesday, 17 June and Friday, 19 June 1840. Klein, "Demystifying the Opposition," 111, is correct in saying that the men unduly feared attacks and that the Tlingit "capitalized" on this fear and on their fierce reputation. But it is not true (see p. 110) that there were no actual attacks — Finlayson's memoirs and the post journal show that there were, and that some injuries resulted.

25. Post Journal, entries for Monday, 15 June and Friday, 19 June 1840. Hawaiians were also referred to as Sandwich Islanders or "Kanakas."

26. McLoughlin to John Fraser, 12 April 1843, in Burt Brown Barker, *The McLoughlin Empire and its Rulers* (Glendale: The Arthur H. Clark Company, 1959), 250. On the terminological difficulties involved in doing fur-trade history, see Jennifer S.H. Brown, "Linguistic Solitudes and Changing Social Categories," in Judd and Ray, *Old Trails and New Directions*, 147-59.

27. Post Journal, entry for 13 June 1840. Klein, "Demystifying the Opposition," 104, reads "passable" as "palatable." On Company attitudes to "half-breeds" generally, see Jennifer Brown *Strangers in Blood: Fur Trade Company Families in Indian Country* (Vancouver: University of British Columbia Press, 1980).

28. Lamb, "Introduction," xxx. For details of Finlayson's later career see note 88 below.

29. See HBCA, B.134/c/55, fos. 348-51, Finlayson to John McKenzie (at Lachine), 20 May 1843; and text accompanying note 84 below. In a private letter written at Fort Simpson a year after McLoughlin's death, in which Finlayson explained why he did not speak up.

30. Post Journal, entry for Saturday, 4 September 1841. The men all referred to the younger McLoughlin as "Mr. John," and his response to Fleury's offense was not an unusual punishment for liquor transgressions. Just such an incident was one of the contributing factors in the "mutiny" aboard the *Beaver* in 1838.

31. Dr. McLoughlin to governor and committee, 20 November 1844, in E.E. Rich, ed., *The Letters of John McLoughlin from Fort Vancouver to the Governor and Committee: Third Series* (London: Hudson's Bay Record Society, 1944), 49. This letter takes up forty-five printed, single-spaced pages.

32. HBCA, D.5/7, Work to Simpson, 5 July 1842. Chief Factor John Work, who was in charge of Fort Simpson (named after Captain Aemilius Simpson of the *Cadboro*) said in a private letter to Sir George Simpson that he was "convinced that had [Finlayson] remained at Stikine the catastrophe there would not have taken place." According to Finlayson, this was the general opinion — see Finlayson to McKenzie, above note 29.

33. Rich, *Letters, Third Series*, 177-78. James Douglas to Simpson, 5 March 1845. The officer was John Work, who was in poor health.

34. Post Journal, entry for Sunday, 3 October 1841.

35. J.E. Harriott to James Hargrave, 2 December 1842, in G.P. De T. Glazebrook, ed., *The Hargrave Correspondence, 1821-1843* (Toronto: The Champlain Society, 1938), 416 (emphasis in original).

36. See, for example, Lamb, "Introduction," xxii-xxx; and Barker, *McLoughlin Empire*, chapter 5.

37.   Barker, *McLoughlin Empire*, 38. In his capacity as a justice of the peace, James Douglas married the couple in a civil ceremony at Fort Vancouver, because McLoughlin was concerned about allegations of impropriety. He and Marguerite were remarried in a religious ceremony on 19 November 1842, seven months after the death of their son, John — see Sylvia Van Kirk *"Many Tender Ties": Women in Fur-Trade Society, 1670-1870* (Winnipeg: Watson and Dwyer, 1980), 155-57.

38.   Barker, *McLoughlin Empire*, 44. The previous year McLoughlin had written to Fraser, thanking him "for the Kind attention you have … shown my little Boy I hope he minds what you say to him — I wish you would have the Goodness to make him write me a letter … this spring…" (McLoughlin to Fraser, 2 January 1823, in Barker, ibid., 173-74).

39.   See sources cited in note 36, above.

40.   McLoughlin to John Fraser, 14 February 1836, in Barker, *McLoughlin Empire*, 220-22.

41.   Ibid., McLoughlin to Dr. Simon Fraser, 232-35. See also Brown, *Strangers in Blood*, 190-91, and Lamb, "Introduction," xxvi.

42.   Brown, *Strangers in Blood*, 191. If sufficient men joined him at Red River, Dickson intended to take Santa Fe and then California, establishing a military government and not allowing any non-Indians to own land. He failed, but his efforts are remembered in song and story in the Métis community. See, for example, M.M. Lee, *The New Nation — Christ's Chosen People* (n.p., 1987), chapter 13.

43.   J.P. Mayer, ed., *Democracy in America* (New York: Doubleday, 1969), 324. De Tocqueville saw this scene in 1831, a year before the United States Supreme Court handed down its decision in *Worcester v. Georgia*, 31 US (6 Pet.) 515 (1832). "It was then the depths of winter," he reports, "and that year the cold was exceptionally severe… The Indians brought their families with them; there were among them the wounded, the sick, newborn babies and the old men on the point of death… Neither sob nor complaint rose from that silent assembly. Their afflictions were of long standing, and they felt them to be irremediable…"

44.   John McLoughlin, Jr., to John Fraser, 1 September and 11 October 1836, in Barker, *McLoughlin Empire*, 228-31.

45.   Ibid., 8 August 1837, 239-41.

46.   Ibid., 1 September and 11 October 1836, 230.

47.   Ibid., John Fraser to John McLoughlin, Jr., 16 April 1837, 238-39.

48.   Lamb, "Introduction," xxx.

49.   Ibid., xxvii. Simpson also wrote personally to young John in September of 1836, noting that in the spring his father had requested Simpson to employ him.

50.   John McLoughlin, Jr., to John Fraser, 15 March 1840, in Barker, *McLoughlin Empire*, 244-45. For a different view of how hard life was at Fort Vancouver, see Michael Payne, *The Most Respectable Place in the Territory: Everyday Life in Hudson's Bay Company Service York Factory, 1788 to 1870* (Ottawa: National Historic Parks and Sites Branch, National Parks Service, 1989).

51.   HBCA, No.257, reel 2M14, *Cowlitz* log.

52.   After his visit to Sitka and the northern posts in the autumn of 1841, Simpson had gone to California. Because he would not be returning to Fort Vancouver, he arranged to meet the elder McLoughlin at Honolulu to discuss trade policy, then he sailed for Sitka to complete his voyage around the world via Siberia — Lamb, "Introduction," xviii and xxii.

53.   HBCA, No. 257, reel 2M14, *Cowlitz* log.

54. Simpson to McLoughlin, Sr., 27 April 1842, in Rich, *Letters, Second Series*, 343. Taco is of course Taku (Fort Durham).

55. This abbreviated account is from the deposition of Thomas McPherson, sworn at Stikine before Simpson on 26 April 1842 — see ibid., 341-43 and the Post Journal, entry for 21 April 1842. Like the deposition, the journal entry was written — with the help of HBC clerks Blenkinsop and Dodd — a few days after the fact, and it is reproduced in Klein, "Demystifying the Opposition," 105.

56. Simpson took depositions from McPherson, Philip Smith, Benoni Fleury, Captain Cole, George Heron and Kekipi — see Rich, *Letters, Second Series*, 43n. Cole and Kekipi were Kanakas. For details of how Simpson proceeded, see note 125, below, and accompanying text.

57. Rich, *Letters, Second Series*, 344-45.

58. No source is required for this assertion, but a recent and useful one is Barry Cooper, *Alexander Kennedy Isbister: A Respectable Critic of the Honourable Company* (Ottawa: Carlton University Press, 1988).

59. Simpson to the governor and committee, 21 June 1844, in Rich, *Letters, Second Series*, xlvi-xlvii. The Great Bear Lake case, referred to in the text accompanying note 6 above, was tried at Trois Rivières in the brief period between the rebellions of 1837 and 1838.

60. In a private note to McLoughlin (referred to in McLoughlin to governor and committee, 24 June 1842, Rich, *Letters, Second Series*, 43), Simpson confirmed that Heroux had fired the fatal shot, but added that he thought that "it was better not to bring it home to him." He also spoke in terms of justifiable homicide when he reported to the governor and committee, describing the younger McLoughlin's conduct and management as "disgraceful" and describing him as "a slave to licentiousness and dissipation..." (Simpson to governor and committee, 6 July 1842 in Williams, *London Correspondence*, 162).

61. Ibid., and Rich, *Letters, Second Series*, 344.

62. He maintained that it was a case of "justifiable homicide" even before the Parliamentary Select Committee of Inquiry into the Hudson's Bay Company in 1857 — see Report from the Select Committee (Ottawa: House of Commons, 1857), Question 1400 [hereafter "Report"].

63. I have placed the word, "wife," in quotation marks because it is unclear whether the relationship qualified as a "country marriage," that is, a long-term arrangement pursuant to Indian law or custom — see notes 143-149, below, and accompanying text.

64. McLoughlin, Sr. to governor and committee, 18 November 1843 and 20 November 1844, in Rich, *Letters, Second Series*, 153, and Rich, *Letters, Third Series*, 27.

65. McLoughlin to governor and committee, 15 November 1843, in Rich, *Letters, Second Series*, 138.

66. Ibid., 24 June 1842, 46. See also the letter of 20 November 1844, Rich, *Letters, Second Series*, 16, and the "List of Stikine men, April 1842," HBCA, B.223/b/29, 31-32d.

67. Letter of 18 November 1843, Rich, *Letters, Second Series*, 172.

68. McLoughlin to governor and committee, 1 February 1844, in Rich, *Letters, Second Series*, 364, and Burns to Simpson, 16 August 1844, quoted by Lamb, "Introduction," xln.

69. Letter of 24 June 1842, Rich, *Letters, Second Series*, 47, and editor's annotation to the plan of Fort Stikine (HBCA, E.13/1, fo. 291) showing details of the death of John McLoughlin, Jr., in Williams, *London Correspondence*, opposite p. 170. There are two other copies in the HBCA, E.13/1, fo. 76 and B.209/z/1, fo. 1, respectively. I have examined the latter, and it is substantially the same as the one in E.13/1, fo. 291.

70. Lamb, "Introduction," xxxiv-xxxv.

71. See the quite detailed narrative recorded by Douglas (and obviously edited by him) aboard the *Cadboro* on 21 June 1842 and Kanaquassé's lengthy interrogation under oath at Nisqually on 16 July (HBCA, B.223/b/29, 48-61d). That Kanaquassé felt these punishments to have been deserved is interesting, because he swore to a long list of floggings and beatings. Most were for stealing things which the men then gave to Indian women, but there were other offenses as well. For example, on two separate occasions McLoughlin beat Kanackanui and William Lasserte for "staring him in the face." According to Kanaquassé, McLoughlin first asked Lasserte, "do you wish to kill me with your eyes?"

72. HBCA, D.4/7, Work to Simpson, 1 May 1842.

73. Ibid.

74. The skeletal account in these two paragraphs is based upon some of the facts alleged by Kanaquassé in the narrative and deposition referred to in note 71.

75. Rowand to McLoughlin, 11 March 1843, in Rich, *Letters, Second Series*, 355-56.

76. Simpson to governor and committee, 5 January 1843, in ibid., 351. In this letter Simpson advances, as an example of the younger McLoughlin's violence, an incident when the latter struck a "person or persons" without cause aboard the *Beaver*. He neglects to mention, perhaps because he did not know, that the man was Kanaquassé.

77. Rowand to Simpson, 16 August 1844, quoted in ibid., xxxix. On Rowand generally, see J.G. MacGregor, *John Rowand: Czar of the Prairies* (Saskatoon: Western Producer Prairie Books, 1978).

78. Post Journal, entry for 5 October 1841; see also entries for 3 October 1841, 13 December 1841, and 29 March 1842.

79. John McLoughlin, Jr., to Work, 2 December 1841, quoted in Lamb, "Introduction," xxxvi.

80. John McLoughlin, Jr., to Work, 3 March 1841, a letter bequeathed to the University of British Columbia library by the late Judge Howay, quoted in Lamb, "Introduction," xxxv.

81. Ibid., John McLoughlin, Jr., to Work, 3 June 1841, also in the Howay collection, emphasis in original.

82. John McLoughlin, Jr., to Work, 2 December 1841, quoted in Lamb, "Introduction," xxxvi, emphasis in original.

83. John McLoughlin, Jr., to Roderick Finlayson, 14 and 26 February 1842, quoted in ibid., xxxvii.

84. HBCA, B.134/c/55, fos. 348-51, Finlayson to John McKenzie at Lachine. The material in the next paragraph is all from this letter, and it may provide a clue as to what McLoughlin had done in Paris that so outraged his uncle.

85. Deposition of John O'Brien, 4 June 1842, deposing to Finlayson's denial that he had ever seen John McLoughlin, Jr., intoxicated while he was at Stikine, and that McPherson now maintained that he did not understand the questions put to him by Simpson in April — see Rich, *Letters, Second Series*, 345-46; and Lamb, "Introduction," xxxvii.

86. John McLoughlin, Sr., to John Fraser, 12 April 1843, in Barker, *McLoughlin Empire*, 250. Yet he may have done so on McLoughlin's instructions. A close reading of Kanaquassé's deposition (see note 71) suggests that McLoughlin may have been trying

to get the dangerous men drunk and all in one room, so that he would have the edge when they made their move.

87. McPherson to Work, 21 April 1842, in Rich, *Letters, Second Series*, 340-41. As was often the case, this letter was delivered by a party of Stikine Indians, traveling by canoe. Ironically, McPherson also said in this letter that he was afraid that the Stikines might attack the fort.

88. HBCA, B.134/c/55, fos. 348-51, Finlayson to McKenzie. He was of course not dismissed, and went on to become a chief trader in 1850 and ultimately a chief factor. He married John Work's daughter, Sarah, in 1849, and was a member of the council of Vancouver Island from 1851 to 1863. He became mayor of Victoria in 1878, and died in 1892.

89. See David McLoughlin to John Fraser, 19 March 1843, in Barker, *McLoughlin Empire*, 249, and Finlayson, "History of Vancouver Island," 18-19.

90. McLoughlin to governor and committee, 4 December 1843 and 20 November 1844, in Rich, *Letters, Second Series*, 182, and Rich, *Letters, Third Series*, 25.

91. McLoughlin to governor and committee, 31 October 1842, in Rich, *Letters, Second Series*, 85.

92. McLoughlin to governor and committee, 10 November 1844, in Rich, *Letters, Third Series*, 7-8. Hanega Joe, who was said to have been educated in the United States, was employed by the Company as an interpreter because he spoke "a little English." On one occasion McLoughlin had fired, and then rehired, him (see ibid., 8n. and Klein, "Demystifying the Opposition," 105).

93. McLoughlin to governor and committee, 31 October 1842, in Rich, *Letters, Second Series*, 86.

94. Lamb, "Introduction," xli.

95. The new depositions, taken by Manson and Douglas, were voluminous — see HBCA, E.13 and reels 4M20-4M21.

96. Quoted in Lamb, "Introduction," xli, emphasis in original.

97. Ibid., xliv.

98. Ibid. The quoted words are those of Charles Ross at Fort Victoria, in a letter dated 10 January 1844, part of which is reproduced by Lamb at xliv-xlv. "[T]he murderers still remain in limbo," he wrote. "We for our share have got five of them here ... which adds not a little to our other embarrassments."

99. Barclay to Simpson, 4 September 1843, quoted in ibid., xlii, emphasis in original.

100. In his letter to the governor and committee dated 18 November 1843 McLoughlin counters Simpson's view that there was no plan to murder his son by wondering whether Simpson had not heard of the Iroquois plan to murder Donald McKenzie in the Snake Country in 1819, "merely because he wanted to make them do their duty" — see Rich, *Letters, Second Series*, 174.

101. Lamb, "Introduction," xlii. For a relatively recent biography focusing on this aspect of Simpson's personality, see John S. Galbraith, *The Little Emperor: Governor Simpson of the Hudson's Bay Company* (Toronto: Macmillan, 1976).

102. Governor Adolphe Etholine to John McLoughlin, 1 September 1843, in Rich, *Letters, Second Series*, 329 (trans. from the French). When Simpson had taken Heroux to Sitka he had told Etholine not to take any measure that would "affect the life" of Heroux until both governments had been consulted — see Williams, *London Correspondence*, 164n.

103. Pelly to Simpson, 3 November 1843, quoted in Lamb, "Introduction," xlv. McLoughlin believed that the Russians would not prosecute because the depositions taken by Simpson made such a prosecution appear pointless.

104. Ibid., Barclay to Simpson, 18 November 1843 (private), emphasis in original. "Wrangell" is Baron Ferdinand von Wrangel. He had been the governor at Sitka, and by the late 1830s was an adviser to the board of directors of the Russian American Company — for details, see Johnson, "Wrangel and Simpson."

105. McLoughlin to governor and committee, 18 November 1843, in Rich, Letters, Second Series, 156. See also HBCA, D.5/10, McLoughlin to Simpson, 1 February 1844.

106. Lamb, "Introduction," xlv-vi.

107. McLoughlin to governor and committee, 20 November 1844, in Rich, Letters, Third Series, 19-20. Pressé was not sent east because he had been injured. But along with Kanaquassé and Heroux, McLoughlin sent William Lasserte, Antoine Kawenassé, Charles Bélanger, Captain Cole, Kakepé, Simon Aneuharazie, Benoni Fleury, George Heron, Louis Leclaire, Philip Smith, and Thomas McPherson as witnesses. They were, he wrote, "all implicated in the misdeeds ... at Stikene." Each could testify either that Heroux premeditated the shooting or that they saw him shoot the younger McLoughlin. He also sent Olivier Martineau, presumably to testify about Kanaquassé's earlier attempts to shoot his son, and William Spencer to interpret for the Kanakas when they reached York Factory. (In fact, the men were detained when they got to Norway House.)

108. Archibald McDonald to Simpson, 27 April 1843, quoted in Lamb, "Introduction," xliv.

109. Ibid., Tod to Edward Ermatinger, 10 March 1845.

110. Ibid., xlviii, McLoughlin to Ermatinger, 16 February 1846.

111. McLoughlin to Simpson, 1 February 1844, in Rich, Letters, Second Series, 375.

112. Ibid., 365-66. The reference to sleeping on watch is to an incident when his son did punish one of the men.

113. Ibid., 367.

114. Ibid., 380.

115. The phrase in quotation marks is E.E. Rich's, in his The History of the Hudson's Bay Company 1670-1870 (London: Hudson's Bay Record Society, 1959), vol. 2, 714.

116. 9 Geo. IV (1828), c. 31, s. 7 (U.K.). The Tudor statute was 33 Hen.VIII (1541), c. 23 (U.K.), and included treason.

117. 43 Geo. III, c. 138, s. 5. See note 4 for title and description.

118. Klein, "Demystifying the Opposition," 108, and Harring, "Incorporation of Alaskan Natives," 294. Even by 1880 only 430 (excluding the military) of Alaska's 33,426 inhabitants were Caucasian — Claus-M. Naske, "The Shaky Beginnings of Alaska's Judicial System," Western Legal History 1, no. 2 (1988): 163.

119. See note 59. This is in marked contrast to Thom's expansive view of his own jurisdiction, which he saw as extending beyond Rupert's Land proper, and to Indians as well as Europeans: Foster, "Long-Distance Justice," 38n, 45.

120. Williams, London Correspondence, 162.

121. The text of this opinion has not been found, but the argument is still being made today, for example, by the Mohawk at Oka in the summer of 1990, and by the Lil'wat Nation in B.C. (A.G.) v. Mount Currie Indian Band, [1992] 1 C.N.L.R. 70 (B.C.S.C.).

122. See Foster, "Long-Distance Justice," 15, 31-32; "Sins Against the Great Spirit"; and

"Forgotten Arguments: Aboriginal Title and Sovereignty in Canada Jurisdiction Act Cases," *Manitoba Law Journal* (in press). There was a small but not insignificant body of legal opinion to the effect that even Indian employees were outside the statute. Another problem was how to secure jurisdiction over the body of a prisoner who was not within British territory.

123. Compare with the killing of Chief Trader Samuel Black at Kamloops in 1841 by a nephew of Chief Tranquille. The Company always demanded blood when one of their officers was killed, and Tranquille's nephew was shot during an escape attempt by a party made up of both whites and Indians. Whether they could have managed this at Stikine is another question.

124. McLoughlin also criticized Simpson for not having his son's corpse exhumed and examined — see McLoughlin to Simpson, 1 February 1844, in Rich, *Letters, Second Series*, 381.

125. Simpson to governor and committee, 5 January 1843, in ibid., 349. The procedure adopted by Simpson in taking the depositions is described in a letter from John O'Brien to McLoughlin, Sr., 2 June 1845, in Rich, *Letters, Second Series*, 172-73. Nothing was committed to paper on the 25th. On the 26th Simpson went to the dining room of the Big House and took the depositions of the men he had examined by dictating "the substance" of what they said to a clerk. O'Brien was not certain whether what had been written down was read over to the deponents before Simpson required them to swear to it.

126. The paper was probably a petition for the younger McLoughlin's removal, wherein the men agreed to abandon the fort if he were not. However, Kanaquassé had said that it was an agreement to murder the clerk if their demands were not met, and the elder McLoughlin maintained that if the men had been more vigorously questioned they would have admitted this — see McLoughlin to governor and committee, 18 November 1843 and 10 November 1844, in Rich, *Letters, Second Series*, 168, 172, and Rich, *Letters, Third Series*, 10. The real "plot" was probably formed on the day the younger McLoughlin was killed, but aside from Heroux and possibly Pressé, the rest may have contributed only by deciding not to reveal what they knew. Apparently only one man had warned McLoughlin that he was to be killed that night, and he did not want his identity known.

127. H. Clare Pentland, *Labour and Capital in Canada 1650-1860* (Toronto: J. Lorimer, 1981), 32-33, citing the work of Harold A. Innis in support.

128. Simpson's words are quoted in Carol M. Judd, "'Mixt Bands of Many Nations': 1821-1870," in Judd and Ray, *Old Trails and New Directions*, 131. The first Irish employees had been recruited by the Company to counter the violence of the Northwesters prior to 1821, but the commissioned officers found them difficult to control.

129. See Payne, *Most Respectable Place in the Territory*, quoting Philip Goldring, "Papers on the Labour System of the Hudson's Bay Company, 1821-1900: Volume II," (Ottawa: Parks Canada, 1980), Manuscript Report Series, No. 412.

130. In his famous "Character Book" compiled a decade earlier, Simpson described McLoughlin as a man who "would be a Radical in any Country — under any Government and under any circumstances" — see Glyndwr Williams, ed., *Hudson's Bay Miscellany 1670-1870* (Winnipeg: Hudson's Bay Record Society, 1975), 176. McLoughlin sympathized with the rebels of 1837 and was regarded as being too ready to help American settlers in Oregon.

131. McLoughlin to governor and committee, 24 June 1842, in Rich, *Letters, Second Series*, 53.

Jourdain was one of the three men implicated in the Great Bear Lake case — see Foster, "Sins Against the Great Spirit." On the hiring patterns in the Company during this period see Judd and Ray, *Old Trails and New Directions*, 128.

132. This excerpt, from a despatch from Simpson to McLoughlin dated 21 June 1843, is quoted in McLoughlin to Simpson, 1 February 1844, Rich, *Letters, Second Series*, 363. Simpson's capacity to speak from both sides of his mouth may be seen in the following passage about the events at Stikine, taken from his published account of his travels in 1841-42. There he said that "it was to the treacherous ferocity of the neighbouring tribes, that the recent catastrophe was indirectly to be imputed, inasmuch as the disposition in question rendered *necessary* such a strictness of discipline as would, in a great measure, account for Mr. McLoughlin's premature death." Williams, *London Correspondence*, 162n., emphasis added.

133. Governor and committee to McLoughlin, 27 September 1843, Rich, *Letters, Second Series*, 307-08.

134. Ibid., 309.

135. McLoughlin to governor and committee, 18 November 1843, in ibid., 175-76. See also McLoughlin to governor and committee, 20 November 1844, in Rich, *Letters, Third Series*, 15-16, where he ascribes some of the problems to the "nominal" reduction in wages since merger with the North West Company, and to Simpson's decision to relocate the Company's recruiting office to Lachine.

136. McLoughlin to Simpson, 1 February 1844, in Rich, *Letters, Second Series*, 375.

137. Ibid., 363.

138. Ibid., 368.

139. See Foster, "Sins Against the Great Spirit."

140. Report, Q.1020.

141. McLoughlin to governor and committee, 24 June 1842, in Rich, *Letters, Second Series*, 46. Later on, McLoughlin was to maintain that his son was the only officer among the three northern posts who followed his instructions regarding Indian woman, and "this is what the men considered the greatest grievance, because they had more indulgence at the other places. " McLoughlin to governor and committee, 20 November 1844, in Rich, *Letters, Third Series*, 18.

142. McLoughin to governor and committee, 18 November 1843, in Rich, *Letters, Third Series*, 154. In his narrative of 21 June 1842 (HBCA, B.223/b/29, 52), Kanaquassé — as transcribed by Douglas — had said that "one principle cause of [the men's] dislike to Mr. John & their plots against his life was the strictness with which he prevented their sallying from the fort in quest of women." It may be significant that both Cadien and Kanaquassé used the term "wife," whereas to the Company's officers the relationships may have had a different complexion.

143. Journal entry for 26 March 1825, in Frederick Merk, ed., *Fur Trade and Empire: George Simpson's Journal 1824-25* (1931; Cambridge, MA: Harvard University Press, 1968), 127.

144. Ibid.

145. Quoted in Klein, "Demystifying the Opposition," 111. Prior to Simpson's governorship, long-term relationships with Indian and Métis women were generally encouraged, but Simpson had effected a change in this policy in 1830 by marrying a white woman, and by expressing his disapproval of officers who continued in the old ways, especially at Red River — see generally Brown, *Strangers in Blood*, and Van Kirk, *Many Tender Ties*. As Brown points out, prior to his formal marriage Simpson "had fathered at least five children by four different women," three of whom were of mixed blood.

146. Klein, "Demystifying the Opposition," 111-12; and see documents in HBCA, E.13. However, Klein refers to Manson as "Mason," and incorrectly describes McLoughlin as a chief trader. In what is probably a typographical error, she also has him writing a letter to Finlayson dated July 1842 — which is of course three months after his death.

147. McLoughlin to Simpson, 1 February 1844, in Rich, *Letters, Second Series*, 381. As he put it, the men were hostile to his son because "from an Anxious desire to do his duty ... according to his Instructions he kept them in the Fort and would not allow them to go about as much as they wished and is an officer because he does his Utmost to fulfil his Instructions to be murdered with impunity because his conduct is disagreeable to Common Men."

148. McLoughlin to governor and committee, 20 November 1844, in ibid., 18, responding to their despatch of 27 September 1843, ibid., 309.

149. See text accompanying notes 84 and 88. Van Kirk points out (*Many Tender Ties*, 41, 45) that until the latter end of the eighteenth century having an Indian wife was a function of rank.

150. McLoughlin to governor and committee, 20 November 1845, in Rich, *Letters, Third Series*, 115-16, and Klein, "Demystifying the Opposition," 106.

151. He had called out for them to shoot Heroux, or whomever else was shooting at him.

152. Post Journal, entry for 4 October 1841.

153. McLoughlin to governor and committee, 2 August 1843 and 15 Novermber 1843, in Rich, *Letters, Second Series*, 109, 136. In his letter to McKenzie (see HBCA, B.134/c/55, fos. 348-51), Finlayson tells him that he is to be transferred to the "grand establishment" that was to be built that summer (1843) on southern Vancouver Island.

154. McLoughlin to governor and committee, 20 November 1844, Rich, *Letters, Third Series*, 47-49.

155. HBCA, B.185/a/1 (1849-1850). According to ex-HBC man George B. Roberts' 1878 "Recollections," the northern posts had never been remunerative (Bancroft Library P-A83, 9).

156. McLoughlin to governor and committee, 19 August 1842, Rich, *Letters, Second Series*, 66. Rich states in an editorial note (66n.) that the deposition taken by Chief Factor Douglas "has not been traced," but in fact it is at HBCA, B.47/Z/1 and is dated 30 July 1842.

157. Rich, *Letters, Second Series*, 67. Forrest had been in charge of Fort Norman immediately prior to the incident there in 1835 (see text accompanying notes 139 and 140), so he was well acquainted with plots.

158. Ibid., 49-51.

159. W. Kaye Lamb, "Introduction," in Rich, *Letters, Third Series*, lix; and ibid., McLoughlin to governor and committee, 19 July 1845, 75.

160. Ibid., xxix.

161. Ibid., McLoughlin to Pelly, 12 July 1846, 171. Roberts, in "Recollections," said that the "Chary way in which Sir George behaved about the death of [young John] envenomed the doctor against him."

162. Pierre Kanaquassé, narrative and deposition: see note 71 above.

163. Post Journal, entry for 23 April 1842. McLoughlin had the body disinterred and reburied at Fort Vancouver in October of 1843.

164. David McLoughlin to John Fraser, in Barker, *McLoughlin Empire*, 249.

165. Roberts, "Recollections," 25.

Controlling the Army of Occupation: Law Enforcement and the Northwest Defense Projects, 1942-1946

Kenneth S. Coates
William R. Morrison

Many Canadian nationalists would argue that one of the single most shameful incidents of abandonment of Canadian sovereignty in modern times took place during World War II, when the government of Mackenzie King gave the United States a virtual *carte blanche* to pursue its strategic objectives in the northwestern part of the country, unhampered by Canadian regulations or even by Canadian observers. Ottawa literally did not know, nor apparently did it much care, what the Americans were doing in the Northwest in 1942, except in the most general way, and this ignorance persisted until Malcolm MacDonald, the British high commissioner, wrote an alarmist report that forced the government to take some official notice of the Americans' activities in the region.

Of all the aspects of the American activities in the Northwest, the question of legal jurisdiction and law enforcement is perhaps the most troubling from the point of view of Canadian sovereignty, for these two fields are important manifestations of a country's sovereign rights; weakness in this area can thus take on vital national significance. Canadian indifference to the region predated the war; before 1940 it had been largely ignored, governed absent-mindedly by a distant metropolitan power. Except for the furious but brief activity of the Yukon gold rush, the Northwest had been left to itself, its law enforcement handled by the Royal Canadian Mounted Police (RCMP) in the Yukon, Northwest Territories and northern Alberta, and by the British Columbia Provincial Police in the northern part of that province. Most of the police detachments were in native communities, where police officers not only enforced the law but acted as representatives of various government departments, serving as the main contact between government and the people. The administrative structure of the region hardly changed between 1910 and 1940.

Suddenly, and almost without warning, the Canadian Northwest was jolted from its somnolence by the arrival of tens of thousands of American soldiers and civilians, who appeared in the spring of 1942 to build the Alaska Highway, the Canol pipeline, and a number of airfields and ancillary projects. The Americans, believing these projects to be vital to the defense of Alaska, gave them high priority, and Canada quickly gave the necessary permission to build across Canadian soil. The arrangement was essentially that the United States would build and pay for the projects, while Canada would permit the use of raw materials and grant right-of-way across Crown land. Yet an important legal aspect of the projects — the question of who should have jurisdiction over crimes committed by American troops and civilians working on them — was not discussed at the time they were being planned, in the early months of 1942.[1] It was not until April of that year, when the first Americans were already arriving in Edmonton, that the subject was first considered by the Permanent Joint Board on Defence, though no action was taken at the time. When the subject was finally aired, it was discovered that the American position was that its citizens, military as well as civilian, working in Canada should have a total right of extraterritoriality; that is, that Canadian courts should have no jurisdiction over Americans, nor even over Canadian citizens working for American contracting firms.

This was a large pill to swallow, even for the King government, which was notably — or notoriously — anxious to please its American friends in matters of continental defense. Nevertheless, it did swallow the pill, though not in one gulp. In April 1941 Ottawa issued the "Foreign Forces Order, 1941," which provided for "limited exercise of jurisdiction in Canada by forces of certain designated countries,"[2] and the regulation was made applicable to the United States at the end of June. This order gave American military courts in Canada the power to deal with all offenses except murder, manslaughter, and rape, which remained under Canadian control. The order also outlined the principle of concurrent jurisdiction, stating that the Canadian courts retained "concurrent jurisdiction over offences committed by U.S. military personnel against any law in force in Canada."[3]

The Americans immediately began to press their case for extended judicial powers. In July 1942 Canada agreed to their request for concurrent jurisdiction in cases of murder, rape, and manslaughter. The Americans then requested complete criminal jurisdiction over its military personnel serving in Canada. By Privy Council Order of 20 December 1943, the Canadian government granted this request; as of that date the United States military courts had "jurisdiction to try all members of its forces in Canada in respect of every offence committed by any of its members in Canada."[4] Because all the thousands of American civilians working in the Northwest were also subject to military law, this meant that the great majority of those who worked on the defense projects fell outside the jurisdiction of the Canadian courts. Canadian civilians working for the Americans could also be arrested by American military police, and in theory tried by United States military courts, though in practice they were turned over to the Canadian courts for prosecution. The only right the Americans did not claim was the authority to arrest local residents, except those that "may be apprehended only under general rules pertaining to arrests by private individuals."[5]

The rules as they applied to civilians working in the Northwest were summarized in a United States War Department General Order of July 1943:

> 1. Regardless of citizenship, civilian employees of the United States Government, or of contractors, working under and in physical proximity to the United States Army, including those United States citizens in the above categories discharged from their employment who are awaiting transportation to the United States, are persons accompanying or serving with the armies in the field and are subject to military law and discipline under Article of War 2 (d) and triable by general and inferior Courts-Martial...

> 2. As a matter of policy, Commanding Officers will turn over civilian employees of Canadian citizenship to Canadian authorities for trial unless such authorities expressly waive jurisdiction.

> 3. Other civilian employees, regardless of citizenship, subject to the Articles of War, will be held and tried by Courts-Martial unless Canadian authorities insist upon their delivery for trial.

> 4. Requests by Commanding Officers to Canadian authorities for delivery of civilians, regardless of citizenship, except Canadians, for trial by Courts-Martial will be made but not insisted upon.

> 5. In cases of requests by Canadian authorities for delivery of military personnel as defined by Article of War 2 (a) to them for trial, such requests will be submitted to this headquarters by the most expeditious means practicable, the authority requesting such delivery being advised of such action and the individual retained in United States Military custody pending decision.[6]

Canadians who recoil at such a surrender of sovereignty might note that similar arrangements were common in other allied countries during the war, and that the United States passed legislation extending similar privileges to Canadian troops — though not civilians — stationed in the United States, but there were not many of these.

Within this legal framework, the Canadian and American authorities worked out their own arrangements, sometimes informal ones. Minor offenses, like drunkenness and fighting, were quite often dealt with informally, without any charges being laid. And in practice the lines of jurisdiction were often blurred by the principle of concurrence, as the authorities cooperated to bring what was sometimes *ad hoc* justice to the region.

The fact that the thousands of American civilians working on the defense projects were subject to military law (though they could not be charged with purely military offenses, such as mutiny) was to the advantage of project managers, for it gave them an unusual degree of control over their work force. An officer of the United States Army Corps of Engineers noted:

> Generally, it would not be considered desirable to resort to court martial in case of offences but if this office has authority to notify employees they are subject to military law and, in particular, to Article of War 89, a very desirable control would be thus attained over contractors' personnel.[7]

Another official document made the same point:

> [W]here the security of our forces and the accomplishment of our mission are threatened such measures should be taken with relation to apprehension, trial and punishment of civilian offenders as may then and there be necessary to assume success of our operations.[8]

As these and other statements make clear, the legal system was to a degree an adjunct of the overall management structure in the Northwest, serving as a means to keep the workers dedicated to the task at hand. That the private contractors saw the advantage of this arrangement is clear from the fact that they all seem to have accepted it without complaint.[9]

Thus during the Americans' stay in the Canadian Northwest, an additional layer of law enforcement and courts was added to the existing system. The main American agent of law enforcement was the military police, almost universally unpopular with soldiers and civilians, American and Canadian alike.[10] The presence in the region of units of the Royal Canadian Air Force Provost Marshall's Office and the United States Air Corps Military Police (who operated independently of the army's military police) complicated the question of authority, as did the continuing activities of the RCMP and the British Columbia Provincial Police. Along with the prewar court system was a judicial structure consisting of American general courts-martial, established when needed by the senior officer in Whitehorse and Edmonton, and special courts-martial and summary courts-martial, appointed by post or camp commanders.[11] Then, for at least part of the period, there was the ill-defined question of concurrent jurisdiction.

With such a welter of legal authority in the region, it is perhaps surprising that there was not more friction and bad feeling than occurred, and indeed there was a good deal of official unhappiness, particularly in British Columbia and Alberta, where the provincial governments resented the loss of authority over legal matters. In the fall of 1942 a rape case in Alberta involving an American serviceman brought a protest from Lucien Maynard, the province's attorney general. The case had dragged on, with Canadian federal and American authorities unable to decide what should be done with it. In a meeting with an American lawyer, Maynard demanded to know when officials would reach a decision, afraid that "the Provincial Government [would be put] in a position where the people of the Province felt their Government was negligent."[12]

The idea of shared legal responsibility through concurrent jurisdiction might perhaps have seemed fine in theory, but it caused a number of problems in practice. Alberta's deputy attorney general complained that the American military's legal system was too different from the Canadian criminal law for the two to harmonize effectively. The United States military caused endless delays, did not have the proper charges in its code to cover the range of offenses committed in the Northwest, operated under different rules of evidence, and had very different penalties than did the Canadians for the same offenses. Under American military law, the maximum penalty for rape was death; in Alberta the offense was punishable by life imprisonment and whipping. He also noted that "it is contrary to the well established principles of criminal law that an accused person should be placed in jeopardy twice for the same offence which is the situation under our present arrangement." He requested preliminary consultations on all such cases, with the suspect liable only to one legal system.[13]

Another irritant was the Canadian suspicion that the Americans were not taking offenses seriously enough. Late in 1943 a series of incidents occurred in which the offenders — American service personnel — were arrested by the American military police and spirited out of the country before proceedings could start, or were tried by military courts and given sentences that were considered far too lenient.[14] In one instance, a man tried for rape on strong evidence was convicted instead of the much lesser offense of giving liquor to a minor. After a series of confrontations over the matter, Canadian officials declared their intention in December 1943 to force the issue by holding the next American charged with a major offense.[15] The Americans responded by making an effort to remind the troops that they were guests in a foreign country, suggesting more recreation and athletic activity as antidotes to the impulses that led to rape, and calling their attention to the "ill effects of such offences upon [the] reputation and interests of the United States."[16]

These events occurred during the period when Canadians and Americans had concurrent jurisdiction over much of the law enforcement in the Northwest, and when the Americans were pressing for complete power in this area. The compromise of concurrent jurisdiction pleased neither country,[17] and means were sought to resolve the situation. In the spring of 1943 the matter was put before the Supreme Court of Canada, but the five justices who considered the case gave four different opinions, and the question was finally solved by the Canadians giving the Americans the jurisdictional power they wanted.[18]

There was criticism of this solution, particularly from Alberta, which charged that it would deprive Canadians of some of "the protection of Canadian law and Canadian courts, and subject them to American military law and the administration of U.S. courts-martial" in cases where members of the American forces committed offenses against Canadians or their property.[19] Special Commissioner Major-General W.W. Foster dismissed Maynard's complaints as "cheap politics"; the United States Consul in Edmonton commented that "it is considered good political strategy in this part of Canada to bait the Dominion Government on every occasion."[20] Whatever the political ramifications of this decision may have been, the practical effect was to establish parallel legal systems in the Canadian Northwest, one for American soldiers, civilians and Canadian civilians working for Americans, and the other for the rest of the population.

American citizens residing in the region who were not working for the military or one of the defense contractors fell, of course, under Canadian civil jurisdiction. When such people found themselves in trouble with the law, their interests were cared for by the American consular service in Edmonton. When, for example, an American waitress working in Dawson Creek was charged in January 1944 with murdering her husband, she was arrested by the British Columbia Provincial Police and arraigned in a provincial court. The consular office found a lawyer for her and arranged to have an American official present at the hearing. It was necessary to do this, "since the Service Command had accorded a like privilege to Provincial officers where trials concerning Canadian citizens took place before military courts."[21]

No agreement, however, no matter how amicable, could eliminate all the difficulties that were bound to arise in a situation where two parallel legal systems existed, and it was difficult for the Canadian police to accept the fact in practice that Americans working on the defense projects were beyond the reach of Canadian courts (after December 1943; before that date the matter could be negotiated), even if they accepted it in principle. It galled the RCMP and the British Columbia Provincial Police to have the power to arrest a suspect off his base, but then to have to turn him over to the American authorities, though in such situations Canadian authorities were permitted to have an observer at the trial.[22] If an American soldier reached the sanctuary of a United States military establishment, Canadian requests to surrender him were firmly but politely denied. However, the Americans gave guarantees that if *prima facie* evidence of a crime were presented, the suspect would be arrested and tried by court-martial. American civilian workers faced a divided system of justice; they could be tried under either Canadian or American law, depending on how the authorities decided to dispose of the case.

Perhaps the most notable feature of the system of justice in the Northwest was its flexibility. Before the Canadians and Americans had agreed on division of legal responsibilities, and even after, police and other legal officials had problems in deciding who should enforce what law, and on whom. A case at Camp Canol in the Northwest Territories in the summer of 1943 is an example of the operational flexibility of northwest justice. An American civilian worker assaulted another man, giving him a bad beating. Under the Canadian-American agreement then in place, the man should have been charged before a United States court-martial, but the Americans chose not to proceed in that fashion. The accused, who had a previous conviction for buggery, was unpopular in the camp, so the American authorities turned him over to the Canadians, who brought him before Dr. J.P. Harvey, justice of the peace at Fort Norman for arraignment.[23] Another example is the case of Eugene Patterson, a civilian working for the United States Army, who was charged in October 1944 with the murder by stabbing of Lester Cieluch, a resident of Whitehorse. This case took place after the Americans had won exclusive jurisdiction over such matters, and Patterson was arraigned in Whitehorse before a general court-martial of five American officers. He was, however, defended by a Canadian civilian — George Black, the Yukon's member of Parliament, whose experience with courts-martial consisted of a series of Canadian cases after World War I. Patterson was found guilty of the lesser charge of manslaughter and received a ten-year sentence.[24]

Most residents of the Northwest were not interested in the complications of a joint legal system. What rubbed them the wrong way was the substantial and sometimes aggressive presence of the American military police in their country. The military police seemed to be everywhere — controlling line-ups in the liquor store, patrolling the streets, asking politely or not so politely for identification from drivers who were proceeding on innocent errands, minding their own business. A minor refrain of the war in the Northwest was the question "just whose country is this, anyway?" One of many examples of the friction that could arise involved a man named T.H. Callahan, a Canadian working for the R. Melville Smith construction company in Fort St. John. While driving on the highway in the fall of 1943 he was stopped by the military police and charged with exceeding the thirty-five-mile-per-hour speed limit. Over his protests he was taken to an American summary court in Dawson Creek, where he was ordered to pay a $10 fine. To make things worse, his attempt to pay the fine in Canadian dollars was rejected; he was told to pay in American money, or failing that, to pay $11 Canadian.[25] Callahan paid, again under protest, and went to complain to the British Columbia Provincial Police; he found them "much insensed [sic] over the authority which these United States military police have taken upon themselves."[26] Nonetheless, no formal protest was made. Many American soldiers also disliked the military police, of course. One man characterized them nearly fifty years later as "horse's butts"; the RCMP, on the other hand, were "fine, professional people."[27]

Incidents of conflict between the American military police and Canadian civilians seem to have taken place quite frequently, though most of them were fairly minor in nature. C.K LeCapelain visited Dawson Creek in the summer of 1943 and reported ten incidents which had occurred in just over a month, indicating, he said, "a regrettably strained situation":

> a) On July 11th, 1943, B.C. Provincial Police Corporal McIndoe accompanied by two constables, all in uniform, were proceeding within the town limits of Dawson Creek to answer a fire alarm, when they were stopped by a U.S. Military Policeman and told that they were travelling at too great a speed and ordered to report immediately to U.S. Military Police headquarters, which they did not do.

b) Mrs Ollinger a local Canadian housewife who lives within but near the town limits of Dawson Creek has been stopped and checked several times when proceeding home in her own private car and within the town limits by U.S. Military Policemen. She is naturally very wrathy over the matter.

c) On July 19th, U.S. Military Police arrested M— T— for drunkenness at a public dance outside the town limits of Dawson Creek. They took her to Military Police headquarters, searched her and took certain articles from her and later turned her over to the B.C. Provincial Police with the articles. It is alleged that this woman is a prostitute.

d) On July 2nd, S— M—, a suspected bootlegger was arrested by U.S. Military Police at a carnival outside the town limits for trying to sell liquor to the military policemen. M— states that he refused to sell any to the military policeman, recognising him as such, and was beaten and clubbed by the policeman and then struck back in self defense. M— was taken to U.S. Military Police headquarters where he was again mauled and rough handled and, after several hours was turned over to the B.C. Provincial Police who prosecuted him but the case was dismissed.

e) On July 1st, B.C. Provincial Constable J. Gunn who had stopped his car on the provincial highway about two miles from Pouce Coupe and then drove it off the side of the highway while he spoke to a friend, was checked, reprimanded and insulted by a U.S. Military Highway Patrol who stated "As long as we are controlling these highways law and order is going to be kept."

f) Recently a man whose name I did not note, drove his car to the top of a hill on a country side road near Dawson Creek, in the evening in order to get what he considered better radio reception, when a U.S. Military Policeman told him to move on in no uncertain terms.

g) Recently Mr Ross, bridge superintendent for R.M. Smith Coy., arrived in Dawson Creek from the Liard River not knowing of the increased activities of the U.S. Military Police. He borrowed a light delivery truck, the property of the U.S. Government, to get a suit from the cleaners. While in the store, a military policeman entered and demanded to know what he was doing there. This took Ross by surprise and he asked what it was all about, upon which the soldier man-handled him, arrested him and took him to Military Police headquarters where he claims he was beaten with a club and insulted being called "Yellow" and told he should be in the army. Mr Ross saw active service during the War 1914-18. He was later released by the military police.

h) On August 10th, Mr C.K. Watters, head electrical engineer for the R.M. Smith Coy., stopped his truck outside the Alaska Restaurant in Dawson Creek and went inside. While there he noticed through the window, a U.S. Military Policeman searching his truck. He then went outside to see what was going on and noticed a pair of gloves missing from the cab, which he mentioned to the soldier, who thereupon grabbed him by the throat and threw him around and said "Don't you accuse me of stealing you Son of a Bitch."

i) On July 29th, ten restaurants in Dawson Creek were placed "out of bounds" for all U.S. Army personnel and civilian contractors' employees, owing to their dirty and unsanitary condition. Most of them having tidied up, have since been placed in bounds. When the ban was placed on these restaurants military police pickets were posted at the doors and everyone attempting to enter was questioned as to his or her identity. In some cases no one was allowed to enter certain restaurants. This led to much resentment on the part of the Canadians and a very explosive situation in that many brushed the soldiers aside and walked in. The chief complaint seems to be and, I believe it is justified, in the manner in which a few soldiers carried out their instruction, behaving somewhat in the manner of bullying thugs. ...

j) There has also been much resentment over the U.S. Military Police picketing the Provincial Government Liquor Store at Pouce Coupe and demanding identification from all civilians who enter and in attempting to stop Canadian employees of R.M. Smith Coy., from purchasing liquor without their permission.[28]

The most notorious case of American bullying of civilians took place in Whitehorse in January 1945. A group of military police stopped a car driven by Dr. Franks, a local dentist, and he and the other people in the car were forced out, manhandled, and placed under arrest. Both the women in the car sustained slight injuries. When the men protested, they "were told that if they didn't get into the car they'd be shot." Eventually they were released, and went to the RCMP detachment to complain. While they were there a young Canadian civilian, George Klinck, was brought in unconscious, his face bruised and bloodied. No charges were laid against any of the Canadians. George Black, protesting the "injustice," wrote "[i]t is patent that the conduct, if as described, was that of thugs and gangsters, amounted to criminal assault and those responsible for it should forthwith be tried by Court Martial."[29] This case was too flagrant to be ignored, and the officer in charge of the detachment of military police at the time was disciplined for "disobedience of standing orders and for inefficiency." Apologies were offered to the people involved in the incident. Nonetheless, Black was informed that the Americans were "exempt from prosecution by Canadian authorities for criminal acts committed while in Canada." Black was not mollified, and continued to protest, on one occasion referring to the "U.S. Army Gestapo ... still being obnoxious," but to no avail.[30] He and others would grumble about American insensitivity and aggressiveness until the final military police officer of the army of occupation left the Yukon in 1946. In fairness it should be added that not all the complaints about the American military police were valid. In March 1944, two military police stopped a car being driven erratically along the Alaska Highway. When the police questioned the driver, his wife and the other passengers bombarded them with abusive language; the wife called them "scum." Reporting on the incident, the sergeant in command of the local RCMP detachment commented:

> Our relations with the U.S. Army 254th Military Police Company here have been excellent, and I have found all of their men to be courteous and efficient. Very close cooperation is maintained between this Det. and the Military Police, and the system has worked very well to date.[31]

On some levels there was a good deal of cooperation with the American military police. A basic fact of law enforcement in the Northwest was that despite jurisdictional disputes, the Canadian and American police were more allies than competitors — in fact, as W.W. Foster commented in reply to C.K. LeCapelain's list of irritants, the Canadians had asked the Americans to increase the strength of their police in northern British Columbia to "control what was felt by the ... authorities to be a serious menace."[32] Although the official policy was that the military police could not arrest civilians, this was often ignored, and the RCMP found the military police very helpful in assisting them with some of their cases. One Canadian official praised them for their helpfulness:

> It is well known that in various parts of northwest Canada American Military Police work in very close and harmonious cooperation with Canadian civil police and that on numerous occasions American MP's have simply offered their friendly assistance to the Canadian police in maintaining civil law and order. The civilians picked up by the American MP's are promptly turned over to the civil police.[33]

Others suggested that local businesses welcomed the assistance of the military police in helping to maintain public order, with the crowds wanting to get into the liquor stores, for instance: "Ninety percent of those concerned are Americans and if the MP were not present half of the customers would never be served — a fruitful cause of irritation and fights." Police Commissioner Parsons, commenting on the situation in northern British Columbia, wrote:

> On the whole police are doing very well, and although 40,000 people have passed through the area during the past 18 months — there has not

been a single murder and only some 4 or 5 assaults upon women — all dealt with. Almost if not quite a world record?[34]

Given the circumstances of the war, the police found themselves with a diverse range of tasks. Canadian and American agencies readily exchanged information and conducted joint investigations into people applying for jobs where security was sensitive, those reported to have made unpatriotic comments, and those of questionable ideological viewpoints. Smuggling was a perennial problem. The police were convinced that most of the smugglers and bootleggers in the Northwest were civilians, though the soldiers provided an eager market for their wares.[35] There were frequent customs investigations, and the searches often uncovered contraband. Many of the smuggling offenses were minor ones, such as sending PX supplies home through the mail, and penalties were small. The Northwest provided almost unlimited opportunities for theft and pilfering; there was so much material lying about, and records of supplies were so poorly kept, that it was impossible to prevent the disappearance of tools, equipment and material. Although little could be done to control petty theft, the authorities acted quickly to investigate reports of large-scale criminal rings. One rumor involved a ring supposedly formed at the end of the war to exploit large caches of abandoned construction supplies; the ring members were said to use a concealed detour which permitted them to bypass highway checkpoints.[36]

The greatest problem facing the police in the Northwest, however, was the control of alcohol. The use and misuse of liquor disturbed the authorities for several reasons: bootlegging defrauded the Canadian treasury; drunkenness harmed productivity and the war effort and posed the possibility of social disorder; and bootlegging rings might bring organized crime to the region. The official attitude towards the consumption of beer and liquor by military and civilian workers was ambivalent. On the one hand, it posed dangers, but on the other it could, if controlled, provide a useful form of recreation. Since the workers were denied most of life's pleasures, it might benefit them and the projects if they let off steam once in a while. This was the reasoning behind the more or less officially sanctioned "beer bust," a periodic feature of camp life, in which large quantities of beer were brought in and everyone got drunk as quickly as possible — in retrospect it sounds rather dispiriting, but it was considered therapeutic at the time. What the authorities would not permit was unsanctioned drinking, which is why public drunkenness, particularly in permanent civilian communities, and supplying liquor to Indians, were swiftly and severely punished.[37]

One factor controlling drinking in the Northwest was the shortage of alcohol. Though neither the Yukon nor the Northwest Territories were subject to the formal wartime liquor rationing in force in the Canadian provinces, difficulties of supply and transport meant that stocks were never sufficient to meet the demand, and quotas had to be introduced. These, however, were much more generous than those in the provinces. At first, the Yukon liquor stores were allocated 300 bottles of spirits per day, and each customer was permitted to buy one bottle,[38] with no limit on the purchase of wine and beer. In the Northwest Territories the limit was one bottle per day to a monthly maximum of 165 ounces; two bottles of wine could be purchased per day, but only ten per month. A case of beer could be bought each day, but not on the same day as spirits were bought.[39] British Columbia residents had a much smaller quota: forty ounces of liquor, a gallon of wine and twelve pints of beer per month; the figures for Alberta were twenty-five ounces, half a gallon, and twelve pints. But these generous allotments were too much for the supplies, and the limits had to be reduced on several occasions;[40] eventually the ration in Alberta was thirteen ounces of spirits, a bottle of wine, and twelve pints of beer per month. Such were some of the Byzantine regulations that governed the consumption of alcohol in Canada two generations ago.

There were even more restrictions. In an attempt to curb the booming black market in liquor, officials in the Yukon began issuing liquor permits, a system already in existence in some of the provinces.[41] The idea was to make sure that no customer exceeded his quota, but the result was to increase the size of the lines in front of the liquor stores. As George Jeckell noted, "[w]e find out that the patronage of Liquor Stores has greatly increased since the introduction of rationing. Many many people who were never known to enter a Liquor Store now have individual permits and appear to get the maximum quantity."[42] The permit system did not end bootlegging, but rather democratized it, as nondrinkers realized the profit to be made in obtaining and reselling their liquor allotment. In 1943 it was estimated that $15 worth of liquor (three bottles at 1943 prices) bought in Pouce Coupe could be sold in Dawson Creek for over $100.[43] One man reported being offered $100 for a "mickey" of liquor in Dawson Crossing.[44] Though wages were high in the Northwest, the fact that a bottle of liquor could bring such prices — two days' wages or more — shows how strong the demand was. The permits were often sold on the black market; one man was found carrying fourteen of them. In Fort Smith in 1942, a local resident, known to be a nondrinker, was found purchasing liquor at the local store and reselling it to American soldiers. He was charged and convicted, and put on an interdiction list for two years.[45]

The American authorities lent a hand in the control effort by requiring each permit holder to have his permit authorized by his immediate superior; civilians working under the authority of United States law had to appear before the provost marshal at Edmonton, Dawson Creek, Fort Smith or Whitehorse for authorization.[46] There the American men had to produce draft cards, the women social-security cards, and Canadians their registration certificates before the permits were issued.[47]

The main factor keeping the price of bootleg liquor high was the fact that supply fell so short of demand.[48] Under the terms of the Wartime Alcohol Beverages Order of 1942, the Yukon's allotment for 1942-43 was based on shipments of liquor to the territory between November 1941 and October 1942. Given the tremendous increase in population in the region in the spring of 1942, this amount was hopelessly inadequate. Thus black-market prices rose and home brew appeared in the camps and civilian settlements.[49] The price of a bottle of "hooch"[50] was $25, about half the cost of smuggled commercial spirits. Shipments of alcohol were regularly pilfered, particularly on the railroad between Skagway and Whitehorse.[51] Truck drivers on the highway were in a good position to profit from the black market and the temptation to do so was great; secret compartments on trucks could easily hold ten bottles, bought for $50 and retailed for $1,000. Some entrepreneurs hollowed out loaves of bread and hid small bottles in them. One of the primary functions of the checkpoints on the Alaska Highway was to check for illegally transported liquor. Pilots and their crews, particularly those working for civilian companies, were able to earn extra money by smuggling liquor.[52] There was also a certain amount of small-scale bootlegging for individual use. One man who worked for the Public Roads Administration recalled that his boss, the resident engineer, had a still in the back of his office where he made alcohol from dried fruit he got from the kitchen.[53]

There was some squabbling about how to deal with those who broke the liquor laws. When soldiers on the Canol project began buying liquor from local civilians who had purchased it legally, the RCMP decided they would prosecute only the sellers and not the buyers. Dr. Urquhart, the local magistrate, disagreed with this policy, and announced that he would dismiss all cases where the seller and purchaser were not both charged.[54] Local-level negotiations ensued, resulting in Urquhart backing down.[55]

Although the absence of United States Army military-police records makes detailed analysis of crime difficult, it is clear that the American occupation of the Canadian Northwest during World War II was not accompanied by an orgy of lawlessness and violence. The Americans and the Canadians recruited to work in the region proved relatively, even surprisingly, law-abiding. Most of the crime that occurred in the Northwest during the war can be categorized as crime of social control — nonviolent offenses, chiefly involving liquor or gambling, which threatened to impair the efficiency of the war effort, or affronted conventional standards of behavior. There were comparatively few crimes of violence, and little real civil or military disorder in the region. It was, to cite an old and not always reliable stereotype, a Canadian rather than an American frontier, though most of the people and much of the law were American.

Canada, like other allied countries experiencing a peaceful occupation during World War II, surrendered portions of its legal sovereignty to the armed forces of the United States. In doing so, the Canadian government acknowledged the legitimate needs of the Americans to exert authority over their own nationals. Potential conflict was generally averted, through a combination of American eagerness not to offend the host nation, Canadian indifference to the far northwest, and the close cooperation between American military and Canadian civilian authorities. That Canada and the United States shared a common cause in the prosecution of the allied war effort also ensured the close cooperation of the different legal systems.

The extraterritoriality of American troops remained an issue in the postwar period. The pattern of allied occupation set between 1941 and 1945 was not completely reversed after the war. In other countries, particularly non-Western ones, the American military earned an unenviable reputation in this regard; from Korea to Vietnam to the Philippines, and now presumably to Saudi Arabia, the question of how to control American troops overseas has remained a matter of pressing concern. Certainly, few of these occupations have worked as successfully as the American occupation of the Canadian Northwest during World War II. That this is so says much about the legal, cultural and racial compatibility of Canada and the United States. The legal occupation of major portions of this country during the war, accomplished with surprisingly little strife and considerable good will, stands as a testament to the fact that elephants and beavers can sometimes share the same bed, and, if as in this case the elephant has departed leaving the beaver a bit ruffled, its integrity and sovereignty seem to have remained essentially intact.

NOTES

1. The tangled history of American extra-territorial rights in Canada is summarized in S.W. Dziuban, *Military Relations Between the United States and Canada 1939-1945* (Washington: Office of the Chief of Military History, Department of the Army, 1959). On military crime, see C. Bryant, *Khaki-Collar Crime* (New York: Free Press, 1979).

2. Dziuban, *Military Relations*, 297.

3. Ibid., citing Privy Council 5484. The idea of concurrent jurisdiction was that either the Canadian or American military court could try an offense, depending on the circumstances of the case.

4. Ibid., 300, citing Privy Council 9694.

5. National Archives of Canada (NAC), RG 338, box 1, 010.6, Military Laws, C.B. Peck to Commanding Office, Dawson Creek, 29 May 1943.

6. NAC, RG 338, NWSC Roll #2, General Orders, "Courts-Martial Procedure for Trial of Civilians in Northwest Service Command," General Order No. 34, 31 July 1943.

7. NAC, RG 338, box 1, 010.6, Military Laws, Hayes to Division Engineer, 20 May 1943.

8. Ibid., Military Laws, Administrative Memorandum, No. 63: Jurisdiction Over Civilian Personnel, 5 May 1943.

9. Ibid., District Engineer to Commanding General, 8 June 1943.

10. There are unfortunately no records extant for the military police relating to the North West Service Command. According to American archivists, very few military police records of any type from World War II have been preserved.

11. NAC, RG 338, NWSC, box 9, General Orders, 1944, General order, No. 34: Courts-Martial Procedure for Trial of Civilians in Northwest Service Command, 31 July 1943.

12. NAC, RG 59, 811.203/352, PS/ATB, American Consul to J. Graham Parsons, 12 November 1943.

13. NAC, RG 338, box 2, Fort St. John, General, Deputy Attorney General to Brig. Gen. J.A. O'Connor, 10 November 1943.

14. NAC, RG 59, file 811.203/365, Robert English to Secretary of State, 11 December 1943.

15. NAC, RG 338, box 1, NWSC, 0.92, Foreign Affairs and Relations, NOSIG to CG NWSC, 12 December 1943.

16. Ibid., 20 April 1943.

17. NAC, RG 59, file 811.203/365, Robert English to Secretary of State, 11 December 1943. See also NAC, RG 338, Box 2, Fort St. John, General, Conference on Civil-Military Legal Jurisdiction, 11 December 1943 for notes of the meeting.

18. Dziuban, *Military Relations*, 299, states that "The opinions are contained in *Reference re Exemption of U.S. Forces From Canadian Criminal Law* (1943)," S.C.R. 483. For a synthesis of these opinions, see Archibald King, "Further Development Concerning Jurisdiction Over Friendly Foreign Armed Forces," *American Journal of International Law* 40 (1946): 272-74.

19. *Edmonton Bulletin*, 30 December 1943.

20. NAC, RG 59, file 811.203/376, Robert English to Secretary of State, 31 December 1943.

21. Ibid., 811.203/389, American Consular Service, Edmonton to J. Graham Parsons, 18 January 1944.

22. Yukon Territorial Archives (YTA), NWSC, Roll 2, "U.S. Agreements," Military Personnel, 6 April 1944.

23. NAC, RG 85, vol. 960, file 13528, Inspector Sault to Commissioner, RCMP, 16 July 1943. Dr. Harvey had the powers of a magistrate and could hear such cases.

24. *Whitehorse Star*, 20 October 1944.

25. The Canadian dollar was worth considerably less than the American dollar during the war.

26. NAC, RG 36/7, vol. 40, file 28-23, pt. 2, T.H. Callahan to A.D.P. Heeney, 17 November 1943.

27. Questionnaire answered by Hampton Primeaux, Indian Bayou, Louisiana.

28. NAC, RG 85, vol. 958, file 13439, LeCapelain to Col K.B. Bush, Chief of Staff, NWSC, Whitehorse, 18 August 1943.

29. NAC, RG 36/7, vol. 40, file 28-23, part 1, George Black to Brig. General F.S. Strong, 5 January 1945.

30. Ibid., Strong to Black, 25 January 1945; Black to Strong, 27 January 1945.

31. NAC, RG 85, vol. 960, file 13560, Re: Chester Neff: Failure to yield right of way when meeting another motor vehicle, March 1944.

32. Ibid., vol. 958, file 13439, W.W. Foster to R.A. Gibson, 24 August 1943.

33. NAC, RG 338, box 2, Fort St. John, General, Conference on Civil-Military Legal Jurisdiction, 11 December 1943.

34. NAC, RG 22, vol. 107, file 84-32-6, pt. 1, Alaska Highway Survey 1943, 21 December 1943.

35. NAC, RG 338, box 4, file 5-2, Intelligence Reports, Intelligence Report, 11 February-28 February 1945, Issue no. 2.

36. NAC, RG 36/7, vol. 36, file 11-23, F. Whiffin: Service Investigation Criminal, 30 July 1946; Conclusion of Case Report, Criminal-Theft (Major) U.S. and Canadian Gov't Equipment, 24 October 1946. The investigations were inconclusive.

37. Liquor offenses outstripped all other forms of illegal behavior in the Northwest during the war years.

38. The Canadian liquor bottle of that day — the "26er" — held 26 Imperial ounces, or somewhat more than the American quart.

39. Special allocations were made for Norman Wells and Eldorado Mines, and residents could also order a certain amount of liquor through the mail.

40. YTA, YRG 1, series 1, vol. 61, file 35404, part 1, Liquor Regulations Amendment, 17 May 1943; ibid., part 2, Jeckell to Gibson, 13 November 1943.

41. During the Depression, people applying for welfare assistance in some Canadian jurisdictions were compelled to surrender their liquor permits.

42. YTA, YRG 1, series 1, vol. 61, file 35405, part 2, Jeckell to Gibson, 26 February 1944.

43. NAC, RG 36/7, vol. 40, file 28-23, part 2, W.E. Sanderson to Division Engineer, Northwest Division, 23 September 1943.

44. Interview with Cale Roberts, New Westminster, B.C., June 1988. For American readers, or those Canadians brought up under the metric regime, a mickey is a bottle holding 13 Imperial ounces. It would have cost a couple of dollars in 1942. A fiftyfold increase in price seems fanciful, but there is no doubt there were considerable profits in bootlegging.

45. NAC, RG 85, vol. 945, file 12806, F— R—, Fort Smith, NWT, Interdiction Of: Territorial Liquor Ordinance, 15 August 1942.

46. NAC, RG 338, NWSC, box 9, Numbered Memoranda, 1943, Memorandum No. 143, II: Liquor Control, 21 July 1943.

47. Ibid., box 44, Office Memoranda, District Circular Letter No. 39, Liquor Permits, 28 February 1944.

48. YTA, YRG 1, series 1, vol. 61, file 35405, part 1, Liquor Restrictions in Canada, 31 March 1943.

49. NAC, RG 85, vol. 948, file 13076, Liquor Conditions — Watson Lake, YT, 22 June 1943. See also, *Whitehorse Star*, 3 September 1943.

50. The word comes from the region — the coastal Indians made a liquor they called "hoo-chin-oo."

51. NAC, RG 338, box 42, Monthly Historical Reports, Historical Report for February 1943 describes the loss of forty-two cases of liquor at Skagway. See also NAC, RG 338, NWSC, box 18, Staff Meetings, 1943-1944, Conference Notes on Meeting, 10 June 1943; ibid., Staff Meeting, 24 November 1944.

52. NAC, RG 85, vol. 949, file 13094, Re: Liquor Conditions, Watson Lake, Y.T., 18 November 1942.

53. Questionnaire answered by Alex Forgie, Edmonton.

54. He later denied making the statement, although a number of witnesses reported hearing him voice his displeasure with the inconsistent punishments. NAC, RG 85, vol. 949, file 13094, Re: F— M—, Fort Smith, N.W.T., Infra., Section 99, N.W.T. Act, 8 December 1942.

55. Ibid.

Anti-Chinese Violence in the American West, 1850-1910

John R. Wunder

> American Laws, more ferocious than tigers:
> Many are the people jailed inside wooden walls,
> Detained, interrogated, tortured,
> Like birds plunged into an open trap —
> What suffering!
> To whom can I complain of the tragedy?
> I shout to Heaven, but there is no way out!
> Had I only known such difficulty in passing
> the Golden Gate...
> Fed up with this treatment, I regret my journey here.[1]

This poem was written by an unknown Chinese resident of San Francisco's Chinatown around 1910. It contains telling words, words of frustration, resignation and regret, but also words describing the brutality of the failure of American law to stem the wrath of the crowd toward America's newest immigrants of the late nineteenth century.

Almost from the first moment Chinese came ashore at San Francisco, anti-Chinese violence occurred. This violence took a variety of forms.[2] Foremost in the public eye was the anti-Chinese riot or movement. It consisted of groups of armed non-Chinese, usually whites, who wantonly attacked Chinese individuals or groups. Crimes of arson, assault, robbery, burglary, kidnapping and murder were frequent by-products of this action.

Very little attention has been drawn to this particular aspect of American history. A number of scholars have written brief essays about the anti-Chinese movement in specific places and times, but minimal analysis of it has occurred. Recent texts have also included sections about anti-Chinese riots. No summary of existing secondary sources exists, and some riots that cry out for original source documentation have never been perused by historians.[3]

Moreover, basic questions have not been investigated. How many anti-Chinese movements were there? Where did they occur? When did they occur? Are there trends that can be identified that flow from the geographical and temporal demarcation of anti-Chinese riots? The specific victims of the violence need to be identified and personalized. Who were they? What was done to the victims? What was the nature of the violence? How many Chinese were murdered and displaced? What was the Chinese reaction to the violence? These questions require answers as do many others about anti-Chinese violence.

ANTI-CHINESE VIOLENCE: PLACE AND TIME

There has been no systematic cataloguing of anti-Chinese violence in the American West. In part this is due to the only recent discovery by historians of American law and historians of the American West of this phenomenon. Two recent works have attempted a limited survey of major anti-Chinese riot locations. In 1987, Sucheng Chan, in her introduction to *Bitter Melon: Stories from the Last Rural Chinese Town in America*, recorded seventy-one outbreaks of violence in nine states (Arizona, California, Washington, Idaho, Montana, Oregon, Wyoming, Utah and Nevada).[4] One year earlier Shih-Shan Henry Tsai, in his text, *The Chinese Experience in America*, identified fifty-five anti-Chinese riots in nine states (Alaska, California, Colorado, Hawaii, Nevada, Oregon, South Dakota, Washington and Wyoming).[5]

Research in the secondary literature and several primary sources has yielded 153 examples of anti-Chinese violence in the American West ranging through fourteen states (including those five states held in common by Shih-Shan Henry Tsai and Sucheng Chan — California, Nevada, Oregon, Washington and Wyoming; the four states examined by Shih-Shan Henry Tsai — Arizona, Idaho, Montana and Utah; the four states discussed by Sucheng Chan — Alaska, Hawaii, South Dakota and Colorado; and the additional state of New Mexico not previously observed). The time frame covers from 1852 and the first outbreak of anti-Chinese violence in San Francisco to the last major acts of violence in 1903 in Tonopah, Nevada, and the destruction of a Chinatown in Reno in 1908.[6] This compilation lends itself to examining and identifying several new generalizations about anti-Chinese movements in the nineteenth-century American West.

THE GEOGRAPHY OF ANTI-CHINESE VIOLENCE

Much can be gained from asking basic questions about the distribution of anti-Chinese violence. Where this violence took place is important in understanding why it happened. In addition, the nature of the violence needs cataloguing. This is not an easy task as the literature available does not always include this kind of information. Nevertheless, the number of murders per anti-Chinese outbreak and estimates on the dislocation of Chinese can be ascertained from Table 1.[7]

TABLE 1
Anti-Chinese Violence in the American West, 1852-1908

State	Number of Outbreaks	Number of Chinese Murdered	Number of Chinese Dislocated
Alaska	1	0	100
Arizona	11	13	100
California	63	29	4,066
Colorado	6	2	631
Hawaii	1	0	400
Idaho	11	25	528
Montana	9	4	250
Nevada	16	5	1,250
New Mexico	4	0	200
Oregon	11	31	675
South Dakota	1	1	20
Utah	1	0	175
Washington	12	5	1,130
Wyoming	6	28	1,000
Totals	**153**	**143**	**10,525**

Table 1 suggests a variety of surprises. First, it should be noted that these figures are underestimates. Chinese were reluctant, as were African Americans and Native Americans, two other groups subjected to significant racial violence in the United States during the nineteenth century, to report accurately their numbers. Indeed, in both primary and secondary sources, writers were oftentimes estimating displacements and deaths of Chinese based on firsthand or second- and thirdhand knowledge.

The greatest number of situations of anti-Chinese violence occurred in California. This is not surprising since the largest migration of whites and Chinese came to California. More unexpected is the fact that the second highest number of anti-Chinese incidents is a tossup among Nevada, Washington, Arizona, Idaho and Oregon. Neither Arizona, Idaho nor Oregon had significant numbers of Chinese, and where the actual violence took place was in isolated rural areas.

Clearly, anti-Chinese outbreaks in specific states do not correlate with the number of recorded murders from the riots. The most killed were in Oregon, not California, with Wyoming a close third. This is because most of the anti-Chinese movements in California were devoted more to the destruction of Chinese property and to forcing Chinese into a refugee status. The high numbers for Oregon and Wyoming come from two particularly violent outbreaks. In Oregon in 1887 seven whites, cowhands on nearby ranches, came upon a group of about forty Chinese miners northeast of Enterprise near the Snake River and the Idaho border. Thirty-one Chinese were murdered, and the murderers took $10,000 in gold dust. Eventually four of the seven were apprehended. The three that were not escaped to Latin America. Of the four arrested, one died in jail, and at the trial a local jury acquitted the others.[8]

Wyoming's anti-Chinese violence has become much more famous. It stems from the Rock Springs Massacre many historians incorrectly attribute as the beginning of anti-Chinese sentiment and riots in the American West. In the late 1860s coal mines were opened in western Wyoming by Union Pacific Railroad. At first the mines were staffed by miners from Ireland, Wales and Scandinavia. However, a bitter strike in 1875 resulted in Union Pacific hiring Beckwith, Quinn & Company from Evanston, Wyoming Territory, to supply strikebreakers. They did so with Chinese labor.

By 1885, 500 miners resided in Rock Springs, 150 were white and 350 were Chinese. An additional 100 unemployed white miners were living in the town. On 2 September, a conflict over work assignments occurred at the No. 6 Mine. This led to the formation of a mob of approximately 150 white miners who, armed with rifles, opened fire on the Chinese section in Rock Springs. Houses and stores were set aflame. By the next morning twenty-eight Chinese were killed and fifteen were wounded, while 500 more Chinese fled for their lives into the hills. Approximately $150,000 worth of damage to Chinese property had occurred; seventy-nine buildings were torched.

The railroad took the refugees to Evanston. There it decided that this form of labor violence had to be resisted at all costs. Thus, on 9 September 1885, 700 Chinese boarded the train in Evanston and returned to Rock Springs. They were joined by federal troops who were based at Rock Springs to maintain order. On 21 September, the mines were reopened. Whites were encouraged to leave the area. The railroad replaced Chinese homes, and the troops stayed in Rock Springs for nearly fourteen years. Eventually the United States sent $147,000 to China as payment for the losses sustained in the Rock Springs Massacre. Later that year a grand jury met in the neighboring community of Green River to consider indictments against sixteen whites arrested for the Chinese murders, but it decided that none should be charged. There were no trials and no convictions.[9]

The Rock Springs Massacre and the Snake River Massacre both

occurred in rural areas of the West. This highlights another important generalization that can be made from Table 1. Massacres of Chinese occurred with equal frequency in rural and urban areas. Ten or more Chinese were murdered in or near Tubac, Arizona Territory (1873), Los Angeles (1871), Loon Creek, Idaho Territory (1872), Enterprise, Oregon (1887), and Rock Springs, Wyoming Territory (1885).

Over 10,500 Chinese were driven from their homes and businesses during the era of anti-Chinese upheavals in the West. The dislocation of Chinese residents was, of course, much greater in urban areas. Most significant among these upheavals were the anti-Chinese outbreaks in Los Angeles (1871), San Francisco (1877), Denver (1880), Tacoma (1885), Seattle (1886), and Portland (1886). Each of these cities participated in a significant attempt to force its Chinese residents to leave. The most common form of criminality used to force out the Chinese was arson. Other more creative means involved cities declaring Chinatowns unsafe or unsanitary. Robbery, threats and mass public meetings were also used effectively. Chinese displacements in western cities have been estimated from 200 Chinese in Los Angeles to over 1,000 Chinese in Tacoma and Seattle.

Although Seattle and Tacoma are cities in close proximity and they both participated in the anti-Chinese hysteria of the mid-1880s, they approached the matter differently. In 1884 anti-Chinese agitation began in Tacoma when a water company hired Chinese to lay pipe in the city despite increasing white unemployment from the lumber mills. The local newspaper published rabid editorials condemning the Chinese. The Workingmen's Union was formed by 125 laborers, and it quickly became involved in local politics, eventually electing a Sinophobic mayor, R. Jacob Weisbach. On 28 September 1885, an anti-Chinese congress convened in Seattle, presided over by Mayor Weisbach of Tacoma. The congress included delegates from all over western Washington. Labor organizations were well represented. The delegates declared that the Chinese must leave western Washington by 1 November. To accomplish this demand, the congress encouraged communities to set up anti-Chinese cells or "ouster committees."

On 3 October, a mass meeting was held in Tacoma. It selected a Committee of Fifteen and instructed its members to plan the exodus of the Chinese to occur by the 1 November deadline. On 3 November, one month later, 500 whites went to Chinatown and demanded that the Chinese leave Tacoma. The mob began forcibly ejecting the Chinese from their homes and businesses. What few possessions they could retrieve were dumped in wagons. Chinese Tacomans were then forced to walk in the cold and rain to the railroad depot where they were sent on their way to Portland. Two Chinese died during this ordeal.

Immediately after the Tacoma riot, other communities near the Puget Sound sought to implement the "Chinese Must Go" campaign. Puyallup (Pierce County), Issaquah (King County), Port Townsend (Kitsap County), Everett (Snohomish County), Anacortes (Skagit County), and Bellingham (Whatcom County) accomplished what were called "peaceable expulsions," and Seattle began to consider what it should do. On 8 November, United States troops were sent to Seattle to protect the Chinese. Unlike the Rock Springs detachment that stayed for over a decade, troops in Seattle remained in place for barely a week. The sheriff of King County, John McGraw, and Seattle businessmen reassured the governor, federal troops and Seattle's Chinese community that no anti-Chinese riot would occur in Seattle. They were wrong.

In January 1886, the Tacoma Committee of Fifteen was placed on trial in Seattle for conspiring to deny Chinese their civil rights. The committee was acquitted. In February, the committee and its followers decided to inspect Seattle's Chinatown for sanitary law violations, but the primary goal was to force the Chinese onto a steamer set to sail to San Francisco. With the acquiescence of Seattle's police force, 400 Chinese were forced to the Seattle docks. The captain of the boat demanded fare for the Chinese; the crowd came up with enough money to put about 100 on board. Finally Sheriff McGraw, the fire department, and a group of University of Washington college students stopped the forced exodus and gained control of the dock. The Chinese were asked if they wished to stay or leave, but by this point most preferred to leave Seattle; all but fifteen left that week, presumably for San Francisco. Thus, by the end of March 1886, most of the Chinese had been forced to leave western Washington, the two largest contingents coming from Seattle and Tacoma.[10]

Rural areas also participated in the removal of the Chinese. Major efforts to force out Chinese residents were made in Chico, California, in 1877; Eureka, California, in 1885; and Bonners Ferry, Idaho, in 1892. Chico, located in the Sacramento Valley of north-central California, experienced many vicious efforts to remove its Chinese residents. An early center of anti-Chinese activities in the 1850s and 1860s, its newspaper, the *Butte County Free Press*, changed its name to the *Chico Caucasian* to emphasize its opposition to the Chinese. Several attempts were made in the 1870s to burn down Chico's Chinatown, and approximately 300 Chinese were displaced by 1877. That same year nine

Chinese were murdered in attacks on Chinese gardeners, woodchoppers, and miners in or near Chico.[11]

Eight years later along the northern California coast in Eureka, a city councilman was killed by a stray bullet from the gun of one of two Chinese having a dispute. The *Humboldt Times* editorialized advocating removal, and a citizens' committee organized. On 8 February, two days after the councilman's death, a rally was held in Eureka and a riot ensued whereby 480 Chinese were forced to leave Eureka and the surrounding communities. The Chinese in Eureka were not about to leave without compensation. Wing Hing sued the city of Eureka for restitution of the value of his property. A hearing was held in San Francisco, and federal district court judge Lorenzo Sawyer found in *Wing Hing v. Eureka* that no claims for damage to any property could be claimed, because the Chinese could own no real estate in Eureka.[12]

A similar situation happened to the Chinese in northern Idaho in 1892. Bonners Ferry, on the Kootenai River, was founded by miners and assisted by the Great Northern Railroad that came to the region in the 1890s. The railroad brought Chinese workers who settled in shacks on the town's outskirts. In June 1892, a mob assembled and issued a declaration that the Chinese were a nuisance. Several hundred whites marched to the laundries and Chinese homes and informed their residents that they had two hours to pack. At least fifty, and as many as 200, Chinese left Bonners Ferry crammed into several boxcars. No physical violence occurred.[13]

Thus, the geography of anti-Chinese violence takes on a diverse character. Chinese dislocations, like murders, occurred in urban and rural areas with equal harshness. Large cities of the West were not immune to anti-Chinese riots, nor were small villages. Each state experienced some form of anti-Chinese violence, with California providing the setting for most of the outbreaks.

TEMPORAL CONSIDERATIONS IN ANTI-CHINESE MOVEMENTS

Anti-Chinese violence began almost at the same time that Chinese migrated to the American West. The first recorded outbreak occurred in San Francisco in 1852. Mass meetings were called to protest increased Chinese immigration, and a Committee of Vigilance was formed. Riots occurred, property was burned, and the city government began a long tradition of legal harassment of the Chinese, passing ordinances designed to encourage Chinese removal.[14]

When anti-Chinese violence spread throughout the West has been the subject of conjecture. Certainly the greatest amount of anti-Chinese

TABLE 2

Timing Frequency of Anti-Chinese Violence in the American West, 1852-1908

State	1850s	1860s	1870s	1880s	1890s	1900s	Total
Alaska	0	0	0	0	1	0	1
Arizona	0	2	2	7	0	0	11
California	4	0	13	39	7	0	63
Colorado	0	0	4	2	0	0	6
Hawaii	0	0	0	0	1	0	1
Idaho	0	4	1	5	1	0	11
Montana	0	0	1	7	1	0	9
Nevada	1	4	9	0	0	2	16
New Mexico	0	0	0	4	0	0	4
Oregon	0	1	2	8	0	0	11
South Dakota	0	0	1	0	0	0	1
Utah	0	0	0	1	0	0	1
Washington	0	0	0	12	0	0	12
Wyoming	0	0	0	6	0	0	6
Totals	**5**	**11**	**33**	**91**	**11**	**2**	**153**

violence occurred in the 1880s, but its extent and the evolution of anti-Chinese movements over time has not been examined closely. Tables 2 and 3 help shed some light on the temporal dimension of anti-Chinese violence in the West.

Several observations can be made from Tables 2 and 3 that will correct some misunderstandings.[15] Most general American history texts and most texts devoted to the history of the American West or American law that actually discuss anti-Chinese movements — and not all do — begin their discussions with the Rock Springs Massacre of 1885. Yet approximately one-third (54 of 153) of recorded anti-Chinese riots occurred prior to 1885 and the Rock Springs Massacre.

Butte, Montana; Clifton, Arizona; and San Francisco are representative of areas of anti-Chinese activity prior to the Rock Springs Massacre. In Butte in 1881 a "War of the Woods" ensued between whites and Chinese. A contractor had hired ten or twelve Chinese to cut cordwood on contract. According to the employers, whites would not contract for the job at a reasonable price. Nevertheless, Butte residents saw this as further evidence of solidifying a Chinese presence in Montana, and led by attorney Chance L. Harris, a mob of 200 mounted men went off to force the woodchoppers to leave or to fight them. A confrontation occurred in the woods, but before the mob could assert itself the Chinese escaped. It is not known if any Chinese were injured or killed. Back in Butte, the employer was strongly encouraged to hire white labor.[16]

TABLE 3

Timing Frequency of Anti-Chinese Violence in the American West, 1880s

State	1880-84	1885	1886	1887-89	Total
Alaska	0	0	0	0	0
Arizona	2	0	0	5	7
California	0	8	31	0	39
Colorado	2	0	0	0	2
Hawaii	0	0	0	0	0
Idaho	1	1	3	0	5
Montana	1	2	0	4	7
New Mexico	0	2	1	1	4
Oregon	0	0	7	1	8
South Dakota	0	0	0	0	0
Utah	0	0	0	1	1
Washington	0	11	1	0	12
Wyoming	0	6	0	0	6
Totals	**6**	**30**	**43**	**12**	**91**

Unlike their counterparts in Butte, the citizens of Clifton, Arizona did not react violently when Chinese labor entered their community. Chinese helped build a railroad to the copper smelting works, and they gathered and burned the mesquite used for charcoal in the copper-reduction process. However, in 1879 when the mining company hired Chinese to work in the underground shafts, labor would not stand for it. White miners rebelled and forced the Chinese to withdraw from the mines.[17]

The anti-Chinese violence in Clifton and Butte was not as extensive as that in San Francisco during the 1870s. Previously, the first Chinese residents of the Bay Area had met mob action, but during the 1860s a calmer atmosphere had replaced the earlier hysteria. By 1877, however, agitation to force the Chinese to leave had once again become strong.[18] On the evening of 23 July, anti-Chinese politicos began the first of three nights filled with militant speeches. The speakers demanded mass riots against the Chinese in order to force them from San Francisco. Twenty-five laundries were destroyed after anti-Chinese riots, and an estimated $1 million worth of damage was done to Chinese businesses. The governor called in the United States Army and Navy and the California militia to restore order in the city.[19] Thus, San Francisco launderers, along with Idaho woodchoppers, Arizona copper miners, and many others in the American West, were targets of anti-Chinese violence before 1885.

Most texts also portray the anti-Chinese movement as a temporary happening in 1885 with a spillover effect in 1886. It is true that seventy-three riots, or approximately 48 percent of all outbreaks, did occur in these two years, but twenty-five upheavals occurred later, including several with extreme forms of physical violence (such as the Snake River Massacre in Oregon in 1887; in Bonners Ferry, Idaho, in 1892; and in Tonopah, Nevada in 1903).

The time framework of anti-Chinese riots is also important to understanding these events. Several historians have offered observations about the timing of the anti-Chinese riots that have proved useful. These generalizations were based on very specific considerations. Sucheng Chan, in *This Bittersweet Soil*, delineates three time phases for anti-Chinese activities in rural agricultural California. They occurred in 1876-79, 1886, and 1893-94.[20] Separating the California data from the information for the entire West confirms this. There were twelve outbreaks of anti-Chinese violence in California in 1876-79, thirty-one in 1886, and seven in 1893-94 — a total of fifty of the sixty-two outbreaks in California during the entire period.

Roger Daniels, in his recently published text, *Asian America: Chinese and Japanese in the United States since 1850*,[21] surveyed anti-Chinese violence. He confines his specific discussion to the "worst outrages," the urban anti-Chinese riots, while recognizing that there were significant rural movements. Daniels observes that the initial center for anti-Chinese activity was California, but this shifted in the 1880s to the Pacific Northwest.[22] This is for the most part an accurate generalization. Table 2 shows that prior to the 1880s most of the anti-Chinese violence occurred in California (seventeen outbreaks), but Nevada was also a very significant anti-Chinese center (fourteen outbreaks).

In fact Nevada, more than any other state, embraced the anti-Chinese movement throughout the six decades. Anti-Chinese activities in Virginia City are particularly representative. They spread from 1865 to 1877. In 1869, 300 Chinese were working for the Virginia and Truckee Railroad in its mines near Virginia City. On 3 August a convention was convened at the Storey County Courthouse of the Miner's Unions of Virginia City, Gold Hill, Humboldt, and White Pine. Other labor unions sent sympathetic representatives. They issued a statement decrying Chinese labor and offered a plan to drive the Chinese from Nevada. On 29 September a mob of nearly 400 miners from Virginia City marched on the Chinese. They overwhelmed the sheriff, who gamely tried to prevent violence, and destroyed all of the Chinese shanties and their property. William Sharon, a railroad official, came to a far-reaching agreement with the mob, promising not to hire any more Chinese miners. They were allowed to work briefly on railroad construction, but they were never again allowed to work in company mines or even to ride on the railroad once it was completed. Their only solace was that no Chinese were injured that fateful day.[23]

Table 3 shows the shift of anti-Chinese activity to the Pacific Northwest in the 1880s. In fact, in 1885 the primary anti-Chinese outbreaks occurred in Wyoming and Washington, anchored by the Rock Springs and Seattle-Tacoma upheavals. Five days after the Rock Springs Massacre anti-Chinese violence came to Washington. In the Squak Valley near Issaquah, a mob of five whites and two Native Americans attacked a camp of Chinese hop pickers as they slept. Three Chinese were murdered and three or four were wounded; twenty-eight others escaped into the woods. The surviving Chinese left the valley the next day.[24] This led to active anti-Chinese movements throughout the Puget Sound region.

In 1886, Oregon and California were very active, with the Willamette Valley area in flames. Leaders of the International Working People's Association arrived in Portland from San Francisco shortly after the Tacoma riots. Portland's business leaders were upset at the prospect of violence and supported the mayor, who increased the police force in anticipation. On 27 February a large, anti-Chinese protest march was held in Portland. It ended up in nearby Oregon City where thirty-nine Chinese working at the Jacob Woolen Mills were kidnapped and taken to the center of Portland. The next day a group of masked men drove 180 Chinese woodcutters from rural areas to Portland. Then on 4 March a similar mob forced 125 Chinese from Mount Tabor. Eight days later whites attacked Chinese vegetable farmers, and a Chinese laundry in downtown Portland was almost blown up. Sporadic violence occurred against the Chinese throughout Portland with many Chinese leaving.[25]

After 1886, anti-Chinese activities picked up in Montana in the Northwest and Arizona in the Southwest. There were outbreaks of violence in Helena, Butte and Missoula in Montana, and in Flagstaff, Bisbee, Kingman, Nogales, Tombstone and Yuma in the Arizona Territory. These were on a smaller scale than previous outbreaks, and no murders were recorded.

Thus, certain trends are discernable about anti-Chinese violence by looking at the numbers of anti-Chinese riots over time. Anti-Chinese movements appear to cover the entire six-decade period, but the primary time of violence is the 1880s. Most of the outbreaks are recorded in 1885 and 1886, but they are not isolated incidents in time or geography — anti-Chinese violence proved to be long standing in the American West.

THE VICTIMS

Chong Bing Long, Sing Lee, and Chung Sun never knew each other, but they had a great deal in common. All three came to Gold Mountain, the United States, from China during the 1860s or early 1870s. There were reasons for this migration, some personal and unrecorded, others economic. Chong Bing Long and Sing Lee most certainly did not have much and came to the United States seeking to improve their station in life. Towards that end both became laundry workers, perhaps having been miners or railroad workers before turning to a traditional occupation among Chinese immigrants. Chung Sun was better off, arriving with $600, an ability to speak English, and a desire to establish a tea plantation in southern California.[26]

All three were victims of anti- Chinese violence. Chung Sun arrived in Los Angeles in 1871 at an unfortunate time. He moved into Chinatown on what whites of Los Angeles called "Nigger Alley." Los Angeles's Chinatown was not very large, holding several hundred Chinese; certainly it was quite small when compared to that of San Francisco and other northern California cities. Most of the Chinese in Los Angeles held positions as gardeners, laundry operators, or domestic help.

Los Angeles was known as a rowdy town. Law enforcement was relatively undeveloped, and some prostitution and opium dens were located in Chinatown. During the late 1850s gold miners and failed businessmen migrated to Los Angeles from northern California, and the racial climate of the city changed. Anti-Chinese agitation began. In 1857 meetings were held concerning Chinese "coolieism." Periodic hate gatherings were held throughout the 1860s; those attending expressed concern about increased Chinese immigration and potential American citizenship for the Chinese.

On the evening of 24 October 1871, Chung Sun was in Chinatown. Suddenly he was attacked by some of a huge mob, estimated by those present at over 500 whites and Hispanics. The riot started ostensibly from a police action. Supposedly a feud had erupted among several Chinese over a Chinese woman. Los Angeles police arrested the participants, booked them, and then released them on bail. Upon bail, the Chinese resumed fighting, the police intervened, and two officers were wounded with one white civilian killed. The riot then began, with some police encouraging the violence by offering bribes to the rioters.

When the riot was over Chung Sun was near death, having been seriously beaten and robbed. According to him, he was saved only because he could speak English. He later migrated to the Monterey Bay area in northern California. Nineteen other Chinese were not as fortunate. They were murdered, fifteen being hung from hastily constructed gallows. At least $30,000 in cash and personal property was stolen.

Los Angeles continued to be a hotbed for anti-Chinese rhetoric. In 1873 meetings were held and a chapter of an Anti-Coolie Club was formed. Four years later, after riots in San Francisco, Los Angeles laborers demanded the eradication of the Chinese. They could not accomplish this with violence, so they turned to political action and formed the Workingmen's Club No. 1. Through this political organization, and the Workingmen's Party, anti-Chinese elements were successful in taking over the Los Angeles city government, electing the mayor and twelve out of fifteen city council members in 1880. The new council passed anti-Chinese ordinances authorizing special taxes on Chinese and land-use restrictions in Chinatown. In the early 1880s many Chinese left Los Angeles for Arizona, to work on railroads.[27]

Chung Sun was bitter over his treatment but at least he survived. He became a laborer digging ditches in Watsonville for $1.50 per day. At this job, he became friends with C.O. Cummings, the publisher of the *Watsonville Pajaronian*. Cummings printed letters by Chung Sun who explained his reactions to the riot and the impact it had had on his life. Chung wrote:

> Unlearned as you may think us to be, we are not wholly ignorant of your history ... we [Chinese] are taught to believe that the sublime teachings of our own Confucius and other sages of the East are [in the United States] reduced to a practical philosophy, regulating, governing, and harmonizing all your civil and political conduct; ... that your government is founded and conducted upon principles of pure justice and that all of every clime, race, and creed are here surely protected in person, liberty and property.[28]

Chung Sun had left China, as he explained, because he sought in the United States

> freedom and security which I could never hope to realize in my own [country], and now after some months' residence in your great country, with the experience of travel, study and observation, I hope you will pardon me for expressing a painful disappointment. The ill treatment of [my] own countrymen may perhaps be excused on the grounds of race, color, language and religion, but such prejudice can only prevail among the ignorant...[29]

Chung Sun reflected on his lot:

> being a man of education and culture I am capable of other work than digging in the streets, but my philosophy teaches me, any *useful* work is more honorable than idleness. I shall therefore, with patience and resignation, continue to dig with an abiding hope for something better...

Chung Sun wrote to the editor for a reason:

> I shall try to be charitable as well as just to all mankind, but as a people will hardly correct their faults without knowing them, I write this in a spirit of kindness, notwithstanding my ill treatment, and ask you to publish it...[30]

Another letter from Chung Sun, describing the United States to a friend in China, was published on 16 November 1871. He concluded by observing that "in civility, complaisance, and polite manners [Americans] are wholly wanting and are very properly styled barbarians."[31] His journey proved to be a bitter one. Shortly thereafter Chung Sun went home to China, never to return to Gold Mountain.

The circumstances for Sing Lee and Chong Bing Long did not allow them to return to China alive. Sing Lee was a victim of the Denver riot of 1880, nine years after the assault on Chung Sun in Los Angeles. At least 600 Chinese lived in Denver by 1880. Many originally came to Colorado to work in the mines, and those who settled in Denver were primarily merchants or workers in restaurants, vegetable and fruit stands, and laundries.[32] Sing Lee worked in a laundry where life was difficult. Socially, the Chinese were isolated. Work was tedious, dangerous, and physically demanding. Laundries were also a special target of mobs — usually the first Chinese to be attacked were those working in the laundries and the laundry building was the first structure to be destroyed. The laundrymen endured physical persecution; some were stoned or had laundry baskets upset, others were assaulted and murdered.[33]

In Denver, the *Rocky Mountain News* led a campaign to force the Chinese from the city. It trumpeted anti-Chinese rhetoric during the political campaign in the fall of 1880. On the evening of 30 October, a political rally was held in Denver, and a particularly hostile, ugly anti-Chinese procession concluded the rally. The next day in a Chinatown tavern two Chinese men and a white man were playing pool. Three or four other whites attacked the three, and news of a potential riot engulfed the city. By 2:00 P.M. a crowd of 3,000, mostly Irish laborers with some other whites and African Americans, gathered and demanded Chinese blood. Amazingly, Denver's police force chose to do nothing, perhaps because the force numbered only fifteen and no chief had been appointed to fill the recent vacancy. The mayor attempted to disperse the crowd, and upon his failure he called out the fire department. The Denver firemen drenched the mob, whereupon the crowd broke loose and burst into Chinatown.[34]

The mob first attacked the laundries, in one of which they found Sing Lee. Sing was assaulted and dragged into the street, where a rope was placed around his neck and he was lynched. Every laundry in the city was destroyed, and all but two houses owned by Chinese were significantly damaged. To protect the Chinese the Colorado governor ordered the militia to Denver to restore order. The Chinese were rounded up and placed under protective custody in the jails; up to 400 were housed in Denver's prison facilities.

Once order was restored the Chinese were allowed to return to their Chinatown in Hop Alley. There they found over $50,000 worth of damage to their property. Some Chinese left, but many stayed and rebuilt; none were reimbursed for their losses, and the rioters tried for the murder of Sing Lee were acquitted.[35]

Like Sing Lee, Chong Bing Long worked in a laundry. He lived in Tonopah, in south-central Nevada. The turn of the century brought silver strikes in the region and precipitated one of the last mining rushes. Chinese were not allowed to work in the mines, a kind of discrimination which had dogged them throughout the mining frontier. Nevertheless a number of Chinese moved to Tonopah to work the tailings and worn-out claims, and a small Chinatown was established.[36]

On 15 September 1903, a large mob of white laborers, most out of jobs, attacked the homes and businesses of Tonopah's Chinese. Over 100 Chinese establishments were burnt, and sixty-six-year-old Chong Bing Long, a longtime resident, was murdered. Fifteen whites were arrested, nine were released, and six were acquitted of all charges. Many Chinese left Tonopah after the riot, but those who escaped to Reno were not safe. Five years later, Reno city officials ordered all buildings in its Chinatown destroyed. In an early example of "urban renewal," many older Chinese were left homeless. These actions in Reno and Tonopah marked the end of the anti-Chinese riots as the West knew them.[37]

The victims of anti-Chinese riots were many throughout the West. Few have left their views, such as Chung Sun, or could have stated how they felt, such as the murdered Chong Bing Long and Sing Lee. Little work has been accomplished by historians identifying an economic and social profile of just who these victims were. Sucheng Chan, in her study of anti-Chinese movements in rural California, has posited the idea that Chinese moving into traditional non-Chinese merchant activities caused greater racial stress than previously thought. Class, therefore, has much to say for it as a causal dimension.[38] This remains to be determined, but what can be said at present is that Chinese victims of anti-Chinese violence ranged throughout the economic spectrum, from the wealthy entrepreneur Chung Sun to the penniless launderer or miner. Thousands of Chinese were assaulted and displaced, hundreds more were lynched and robbed during the five-decade period of anti-Chinese violence.

CONCLUSION

Much remains to be uncovered about anti-Chinese violence in the American West. All of the previously discussed questions require further amplification, and more information needs to be distilled regarding the role and composition of the perpetrators of the violence, the response of the legal system, including local police and lower court justices and attorneys, and the primary causal factors behind the violence.

This essay has also examined another important area of anti-Chinese violence — the reaction of its victims to their mistreatment. This, too, is a topic which demands further research. It was not only individuals, such as Chung Sun, who gave vent to their frustration and profound sense of injustice at the violence that was directed towards them. The Chinese community at large reacted not only by organizing for self-help and appealing to the law for protection, but also by engaging in subtle acts of cultural resistance. An interesting example which demonstrates this phenomenon, as well as white society's ignorance of and insensitivity to the Chinese experience in America, is the derivation of the word "hoodlum."

In all of the literature on anti-Chinese violence, those attacking the Chinese are referred to as hoodlums. This term has come to mean a tough, dangerous youth who spends much time on the streets of towns and cities and causes a great deal of trouble. The most recent edition of the *Oxford English Dictionary* notes that "hoodlum" originated as slang in San Francisco about 1870-72 and caught on in American usage by 1877. American newspapers attributed its origins to a lawless group of youths in that city.[39]

Most of the Chinese who moved to San Francisco in the 1850s and 1860s spoke Cantonese Chinese. In the 1830s they had witnessed white persons for the first time in China, and called them "hueilum." This was a term meaning "devil" in the Cantonese dialect. When this word emerged cannot be specifically ascertained, but probably it was used no later than the 1830s. For the Chinese, the physical appearance of whites was too strange to be accepted — blue eyes, high noses, yellow or red hair. At first "hueilum" would not necessarily have been derogatory, but with the defeat of the Qing government in the Opium Wars in the 1840s, anti-foreign sentiment in China was strong. By then "hueilum" was used not only by Cantonese but by other Chinese to describe the dreaded westerners. The gold rush brought the first Cantonese to San Francisco and it also brought the term to Chinatown. Even today this word can still be heard in San Francisco's Chinatown, and it is no doubt the source of the term "hoodlum."

In reality the word derives from Chinese discourse and reflects the immigrants' rueful characterization of their detractors. The confusion over the derivation of the word "hoodlum" serves as a symbolic reminder of the ignorance still to be found in the literature surrounding the historical role of the Chinese in the American West.

NOTES

1. Marlon K. Hom, *Songs of Gold Mountain: Cantonese Rhymes from San Francisco Chinatown* (Berkeley: University of California Press, 1987), 48.

2. Individual violence by non-Chinese against Chinese occurred. One can only estimate that it was significant activity, because very little historical work or analysis has been accomplished by historians or others on this subject.

3. Strangely, one author wrote in 1982 that too much had been written about anti-Chinese violence. Randall E. Rohe, in his essay "After the Gold Rush: Chinese Mining in Far West, 1850-1890," *Montana, Magazine of Western History* 32 (Autumn 1982): 2-19, argues "Hopefully researchers will move away from the overworked theme of anti-Chinese discrimination and investigate other aspects of the Chinese experience on the western mining frontier" (p. 19). This is not an accurate portrayal of the state of legal historical writing on the anti-Chinese movements. For example, in the heralded book on the history of violence in America by Hugh Davis Graham and Ted Robert Gurr, *Violence in America: Historical and Comparative Perspectives* (New York: Bantam, 1969), anti-Chinese violence is simply ignored.

   Roger Daniels, in *Asian America: Chinese and Japanese in the United States since 1850* (Seattle: University of Washington Press, 1988), correctly concludes that "Historians have ignored much of the anti-Chinese and anti-Asian violence" (p. 59, note 66). Richard Maxwell Brown, in "Historiography of Violence in the American West," in Michael P. Malone, ed., *Historians of the American West* (Lincoln: University of Nebraska Press, 1983), 234-69, has only two sketchy paragraphs on anti-Chinese violence (pp. 250-51). This is simply because historians have not come to this topic with the same vigor they have approached other kinds of racial violence.

   Patricia Nelson Limerick, in her path-breaking book, *The Legacy of Conquest: The Unbroken Past of the American West* (New York: Norton, 1987), has difficulty identifying specific examples of anti-Chinese violence, specific Chinese participants, and getting beyond the works of Alexander Saxton and Stuart Miller and the state of California. Future editions will hopefully be able to correct this vacuum.

4. Sucheng Chan, "Introduction," in Jeff Gillenkirk and James Motlow, *Bitter Melon: Stories from the Last Rural Chinese Town in America* (Seattle: University of Washington Press, 1987), 25.

5. Shih-Shan Henry Tsai, *The Chinese Experience in America* (Bloomington: Indiana University Press, 1986), 68.

6. It is important to stress that this compilation is by no means definitive. Much rural Chinese violence needs to be identified and explored. Only one state, California, in Sucheng Chan's outstanding book, *This Bittersweet Soil: The Chinese in California Agriculture, 1860-1890* (Berkeley: University of California Press, 1986), has had its rural areas treated with anything approaching thoroughness, and that treatment is limited in terms of time and scope. Anti-Chinese violence in mining areas has not been discussed in detail. Urban violence has also been ignored. No complete treatment of anti-Chinese violence exists, for example, for San Francisco. Anti-Chinese riots in Los Angeles, Seattle, Tacoma, and Denver have been covered in article form without a comprehensive exploration of either the victims or the perpetrators of the violence.

7. See Appendix to this essay for a specific listing of each anti-Chinese outbreak of violence and its source.

8. Christopher H. Edson, *The Chinese in Eastern Oregon, 1860-1890* (San Francisco: R and E Research Associates, 1974), 51; David H. Stratton, "The Snake River Massacre of Chinese Miners, 1887," in Duane A. Smith, ed., *A Taste of the West: Essays in Honor of Robert G. Athearn* (Boulder, CO: Pruett Publishing Co., 1983), 124-25.

9. Murray L. Carroll, "Governor Francis E. Warren, the United States Army and the Chinese Massacre at Rock Springs," *Annals of Wyoming* 59 (Fall 1987): 17-24; Paul Crane and Alfred Larson, "The Chinese Massacre," *Annals of Wyoming* 12 (Fall 1940): 47-55, 153-60. See also Virginia Huidekoper, "Mosaic of a Massacre: The Chinese Experience in Wyoming, 1879-1890," unpublished manuscript prepared for the Wyoming Council for the Humanities.

10. B.P. Wilcox, "Anti-Chinese Riots in Washington," *Washington Historical Quarterly* 20 (1929): 206-11; Jules Alexander Karlin, "The Anti-Chinese Outbreak in Tacoma, 1885," *Pacific Historical Review* 23 (August 1954): 271-83; John R. Wunder, "The Chinese and the Courts in the Pacific Northwest: Justice Denied?" *Pacific Historical Review* 52 (May 1983): 191-211; and Jules Alexander Karlin, "Anti-Chinese Violence in Seattle," *Pacific Northwest Quarterly* 39 (Spring 1948): 103-29.

11. Elmer Clarence Sandmeyer, *The Anti-Chinese Movement in California* (Urbana: University of Illinois Press, 1973), 48; Susan W. Book, *The Chinese in Butte County, California, 1860-1920* (San Francisco: R and E Research Associates, 1976), 49-57; Sucheng Chan, *This Bittersweet Soil*, 371-74.

12. Lynwood Carranco, "Chinese Expulsion from Humboldt County," *Pacific Historical Review* 30 (November 1961): 329-40.

13. M. Alfreda Elsensohn, *Idaho Chinese Lore* (Cottonwood, ID: Idaho Corporation of Benedictine Sisters, 1971), 116-17.

14. Sandmeyer, *Anti-Chinese Movement*, 42; Robert Seager II, "Some Denominational Reactions to Chinese Immigration to California, 1856-1892," *Pacific Historical Review* 28 (February 1959): 49.

15. See Appendix.

16. Larry D. Quinn, "'Chink Chink Chinaman': The Beginning of Nativism in Montana," *Pacific Northwest Quarterly* 58 (April 1967): 84.

17. Lawrence Michael Fong, "Sojourners and Settlers: The Chinese Experience in Arizona," *Journal of Arizona History* 21 (Autumn, 1980): 232.

18. For a discussion of San Francisco politics and labor union attitudes of this era see Gunther Barth, *Bitter Strength: A History of the Chinese in the United States 1850-1870* (Cambridge, MA: Harvard University Press, 1964); Stuart Creighton Miller, *The Unwelcome Immigrant: The American Image of the Chinese, 1785-1882* (Berkeley: University of California Press, 1969); and Alexander Saxton, *The Indispensable Enemy: Labor and Anti-Chinese Movement in California* (Berkeley: University of California Press, 1971).

19. Sandmeyer, *Anti-Chinese Movement*, 48; William J. Courtney, *San Francisco Anti-Chinese Ordinances, 1850-1900* (San Francisco: R and E Research Associates, 1974), 65.

20. Sucheng Chan, *This Bittersweet Soil*, 370.

21. Roger Daniels, *Asian America*.

22. Ibid., 59.

23. Russell M. Magnaghi, "Virginia City's Chinese Community, 1860-1880," *Nevada Historical Society Quarterly* 24 (Summer 1981): 149-54; Loren B. Chan, "The Chinese in Nevada: An Historical Survey, 1856-1970," *Nevada Historical Society Quarterly* 18 (Winter 1975): 279-98.

24. Wilcox, "Anti-Chinese Riots in Washington," 205.

25. Ralph James Mooney, "Matthew Deady and the Federal Judicial Response to Racism in the Early West," *Oregon Law Review* 63, no. 4 (1984): 574.

26. Loren Chan, "Chinese in Nevada," 295; Patricia K. Ourada, "The Chinese in Colorado," *Colorado Magazine* 29 (Winter 1952): 282-83; Roy T. Wortman, "Denver's Anti-Chinese Riot, 1880," *Colorado Magazine* 42 (Fall 1965): 275-91; William R. Locklear, "The Celestials and the Angels: A Study of the Anti-Chinese Movement in Los Angeles to 1882," in Roger Daniels, ed., *Anti-Chinese Violence in North America* (New York: Arno Press, 1978), 239-56; and Sandy Lydon, *Chinese Gold: The Chinese in the Monterey Bay Region* (Capitola, CA: Capitola Book Company, 1985), 134-35. There is some confusion over the identity of Sing Lee. Ourada says the sole victim of the Denver riot of 1880 was Look Young, while Wortman, describes the person as Sing Lee. Because Wortman published his essay thirteen years after Ourada's article appeared in print and other discrepancies, Wortman corrects of Ourada, it seems reasonable to conclude that the accurate identity of the casualty of the Denver riot is Sing Lee.

27. Locklear, "Celestials and the Angels," 241-55.

28. *Watsonville Pajaronian*, 9 November 1871, quoted in Lydon, *Chinese Gold*, 134.

29. Ibid.

30. Ibid., 134-35.

31. Ibid., 16 November 1871, quoted in Lydon, *Chinese Gold*, 135.

32. Ourada, "Chinese in Colorado," 278-83; Wortman, "Denver's Anti-Chinese Riot," 275-80.

33. William Hoy, "Tales of the California Chinese," unpublished radio talk, San Francisco, 16 September 1940, as quoted in Paul C.P. Siu, *The Chinese Laundryman: A Study of Social Isolation* (New York: New York University Press, 1987), 50-54.

34. Wortman, "Denver's Anti-Chinese Riot," 285-91. The Denver *Rocky Mountain News* published the preposterous story that the riot was caused by the Chinese. According to the *News*, a Chinese laundry owner demanded ten cents more from a white customer who refused to pay. The Chinese launderer then purportedly slashed the face of the

white man. After a crowd gathered, the Chinese laundry owner fired a gun at the crowd, and this precipitated the riot. Subsequent investigation by historians have prove this explanation a fabrication.

35. Ibid., 287-90; Ourada, "Chinese in Colorado," 278-83.

36. Loren Chan, "Chinese in Nevada," 295.

37. Ibid., 295-97, 304. See also Gary P. Be Dunnah, *History of the Chinese in Nevada, 1855-1904* (San Francisco: R and E Research Associates, 1973); Gregg Lee Carter, "Social Demography of the Chinese in Nevada: 1870-1880," *Nevada Historical Society Quarterly* 18 (Summer 1975); and Magnaghi, "Virginia City's Chinese Community."

38. Sucheng Chan, "Anti-Chinese Activities in Rural California in the Late Nineteenth Century," paper presented to the 100th meeting of the American Historical Association, New York, 27-30 December 1985. Revised versions of this paper were incorporated into Chan's Book, *This Bittersweet Soil.*

39. *The Oxford English Dictionary*, 2nd ed., (Oxford: Clarendon Press, 1989), vol. 7, 362. According to Quinn, "'Chink Chink Chinaman'," 84 (note 11), "the word 'hoodlum' was first used in San Francisco and referred to gangs of toughs employed to beat up the Chinese."

APPENDIX
Anti-Chinese Violence in the American West, 1852-1908

Alaska: Juneau (1893)[1]

Arizona: Prescott (1869)[2] Tubac (1873)[3] Clifton (1879)[4] Tucson (1880)[5] Safford (1884)[6] Bisbee (1888)[7] Kingman (1888)[8] Nogales (1888)[9] Tombstone (1888)[10] Yuma (1888)[11] Flagstaff (1889)[12]

California: San Francisco (1852, 1859, 1877)[13] Mariposa (1856)[14] Shasta (1859)[15] Los Angeles (1871)[16] Sacramento (1876)[17] Truckee (1876)[18] Chico (1877)[19] Colusa (1877)[20] Grass Valley (1877)[21] Lava Beds (1877)[22] Rocklin (1877)[23] Roseville (1877)[24] Santa Cruz (1877)[25] Antioch (1878)[26] Linden (1878)[27] Arcata (1885)[28] Crescent City (1885)[29] Eureka (1885)[30] Ferndale (1885)[31] Fresno (1885)[32] Merced (1885)[33] Modesto (1885)[34] Stockton (1885)[35] Anderson (1886)[36] Auburn (1886)[37] Calistoga (1886)[38] Carson (1886)[39] Cloverdale (1886)[40] Dixon (1886)[41] Gold Run (1886)[42] Healdsburg (1886)[43] Hollister (1886)[44] Lincoln (1886)[45] Martinez (1886)[46] Napa (1886)[47] Nevada City (1886)[48] Nicolaus (1886)[49] Oakland (1886)[50] Pasadena (1886)[51] Petaluma (1886)[52] Placerville (1886)[53] Red Bluff (1886)[54] Redding (1886)[55] Saint Helena (1886)[56] San Buenaventura (1886)[57] San Jose (1886)[58] Santa Barbara (1886)[59] Santa Rosa (1886)[60] Siskiyou (1886)[61] Sonoma (1886)[62] Vallejo (1886)[63] Ventura (1886)[64] Wheatland (1886)[65] Yuba City (1886)[66] Compton (1893)[67] Panamint City (1893)[68] Redlands (1893)[69] Tulare (1893)[70] Ukiah (1893)[71] Vaca Valley (1893)[72] Visalia (1893)[73]

Colorado: Caribou (1874, 1879)[74] Central City (1874)[75] Leadville (1879)[76] Denver (1880)[77] Grand Junction (1883)[78]

Hawaii: Honolulu (1892)[79]

Idaho: Lewiston (1865, 1883)[80] Orofino (1867)[81] Salmon City (1868)[82] Boise (1869, 1886)[83] Loon Creek (1872)[84] Pierce City (1885)[85] Broadford (1886)[86] Hailey (1886)[87] Bonners Ferry (1892)[88]

Montana: Cedar Creek (1870)[89] Butte (1881, 1885, 1888)[90] Anaconda (1885)[91] Helena (1887)[92] Great Falls (1888)[93] Havre (1888)[94] Missoula (1892)[95]

Nevada: Gold Hill (1859)[96] Virginia City (1865, 1869, 1875, 1876)[97] Carson City (1867, 1870)[98] Unionville (1869)[99] Eureka (1872, 1876)[100] Elko (1876)[101] Pioche (1877)[102] Tuscarora (1878)[103] Reno (1878, 1908)[104] Tonopah (1903)[105]

New Mexico: Raton (1885)[106] Silver City (1885, 1886)[107] Deming (1888)[108]

Oregon: Oswego (1867)[109] Baker City (1872)[110] Portland (1873, 1886)[111] Oregon City (1886)[112] Aurora (1886)[113] Mount Tabor (1886)[114] LeGrande (1886)[115] Newberg (1886)[116] Jacksonville (1886)[117] Enterprise (1887)[118]

South Dakota: Deadwood (1878)[119]

Utah: Carbon County (1888)[120]

Washington: Coal Creek (1885)[121]

Issaquah (1885 [2])[122] Auburn (1885)[123] Tacoma (1885)[124] Puyallup (1885)[125] Port Townsend (1885)[126] Everett (1885)[127] Anacortes (1885)[128] Bellingham (1885)[129] Olympia (1885)[130] Seattle (1886)[131]

Wyoming: Rock Springs (1885)[132] Almy (1885)[133] Evanston (1885)[134] Cheyenne (1885)[135] Green River (1885)[136] Carbon (1885)[137]

1. Shih-Shan Henry Tsai, *The Chinese Experience in America* (Bloomington: Indiana University Press, 1986), 68.

2. Lawrence Michael Fong, "Sojourners and Settlers: The Chinese Experience in Arizona," *Journal of Arizona History* 21 (Autumn 1980): 232.

3. Ibid., 233.

4. Ibid., 241.

5. John R. Wunder, "Law and the Chinese on the Southwest Frontier, 1850s-1902," *Western Legal History* 2 (Summer/Fall 1989): 141.

6. Ibid.

7. Sucheng Chan, "Introduction," in *Bitter Melon: Stories from the Last Rural Chinese Town in America* (Seattle: University of Washington Press, 1987), 25.

8. Ibid.

9. Ibid.

10. Ibid.

11. Ibid.

12. Wunder, "Chinese on the Southwest Frontier," 141.

13. Elmer Clarence Sandmeyer, *The Anti-Chinese Movement in California* (Urbana: University of Illinois Press, 1973), 42; Robert Seager II, "Some Denominational Reactions to Chinese Immigration to California, 1856-1892," *Pacific Historical Review* 28 (February 1959): 49; William J. Courtney, *San Francisco Anti-Chinese Ordinances, 1850-1900* (San Francisco: R and E Research Associates, 1974), 65; Alexander Saxton, *The Indispensable Enemy: Labor and the Anti-Chinese Movement in California* (Berkeley: University of California Press, 1971), 72-75.

14. Pauline Minke, *Chinese in the Mother Lode, 1850-1870* (San Francisco: R and E Research Associates, 1974), 43-44.

15. Ibid., 45-46.

16. William R. Locklear, "The Celestials and the Angels: A Study of the Anti-Chinese Movement in Los Angeles to 1882," in Roger Daniels, ed., *Anti-Chinese Violence in North America* (New York: Arno Press, 1978), 239-50.

17. Sylvia Sun Minnick, *Samfow: The San Joaquin Chinese Legacy* (Fresno, CA: Panorama West Publishing, 1988), 128-29.

18. Sandmeyer, *The Anti-Chinese Movement in California*, 97-98; Sucheng Chan, *This*

Bittersweet Soil: The Chinese in California Agriculture, 1860-1890 (Berkeley: University of California Press, 1986), 370-81.

19. Sucheng Chan, *Bittersweet Soil*, 371-74; Susan W. Book, *The Chinese in Butte County, California, 1860-1920* (San Francisco: R and E Research Associates, 1976), 49-57.

20. Sucheng Chan, *Bittersweet Soil*, 374.

21. Ibid.

22. Ibid.

23. Ibid.

24. Ibid.

25. Sandy Lydon, *Chinese Gold: The Chinese in the Monterey Bay Region* (Capitola, CA: Capitola Book Company, 1985), 119-33.

26. Minnick, *Samfow*, 129.

27. Ibid.

28. Lynwood Carranco, "Chinese Expulsion from Humboldt County," *Pacific Historical Review* 30 (November 1961): 329-40.

29. Ibid.

30. Ibid.

31. Ibid.

32. Sucheng Chan, *Bittersweet Soil*, 378-79.

33. Sandmeyer, *The Anti-Chinese Movement in California*, 97-98.

34. Sucheng Chan, "Introduction," 25.

35. Minnick, *Samfow*, 135-62.

36. Sandmeyer, *The Anti-Chinese Movement in California*, 97-98.

37. Ibid.

38. Sucheng Chan, "Introduction," 25.

39. Sandmeyer, *The Anti-Chinese Movement in California*, 97-98.

40. Ibid.

41. Ibid.

42. Ibid.

43. Ibid.

44. Ibid.

45. Ibid.

46. Sucheng Chan, "Introduction," 25.

47. Sandmeyer, *The Anti-Chinese Movement in California*, 97-98.

48. Ibid.

49. Sucheng Chan, *Bittersweet Soil*, 374-75.

50. Sandmeyer, *The Anti-Chinese Movement in California*, 97-98.

51. Ibid.

52. Ibid.

53. Ibid.

54. Ibid.

55. Ibid.
56. Sucheng Chan, "Introduction," 25.
57. Sandmeyer, *The Anti-Chinese Movement in California*, 97-98.
58. Ibid.
59. Ibid.
60. Ibid.
61. Sucheng Chan, "Introduction," 25.
62. Sandmeyer, *The Anti-Chinese Movement in California*, 97-98.
63. Ibid.
64. Sucheng Chan, "Introduction," 25.
65. Sandmeyer, *The Anti-Chinese Movement in California*, 97-98; Sucheng Chan, *Bittersweet Soil*, 374-75.
66. Sandmeyer, *The Anti-Chinese Movement in California*, 97-98.
67. Sucheng Chan, *Bittersweet Soil*, 278-79.
68. Sucheng Chan, "Introduction," 25.
69. Sucheng Chan, *Bittersweet Soil*, 278-79.
70. Ibid.
71. Ibid.
72. Ibid.
73. Ibid.
74. Patricia K. Ourada, "The Chinese in Colorado," *Colorado Magazine* 29 (Winter 1952): 278-79.
75. Ibid., 279.
76. Ibid., 278.
77. Ibid., 282-83; Roy T. Wortman, "Denver's Anti-Chinese Riot, 1880," *Colorado Magazine* 42 (Fall 1965): 275-91.
78. Christian J. Buys, "Chinese in Early Grand Junction," *Journal of the Western Slope* 2 (Spring 1987): 69-70.
79. Tsai, *The Chinese Experience in America*, 68.
80. M. Alfreda Elsensohn, *Idaho Chinese Lore* (Cottonwood, ID: Idaho Corporation of Benedictine Sisters, 1971), 16; John R. Wunder, "The Courts and the Chinese in Frontier Idaho," *Idaho Yesterdays* 25 (Spring 1981): 23.
81. Elsensohn, *Idaho Chinese Lore*, 28.
82. Sucheng Chan, "Introduction," 25.
83. Elsensohn, *Idaho Chinese Lore*, 90-91.
84. Ibid., 103.
85. Ibid., 29-30; Kenneth Owens, "Pierce City Incident," *Idaho Yesterdays* 3 (Spring 1959): 8-13.
86. Sucheng Chan, "Introduction," 25.
87. Elsensohn, *Idaho Chinese Lore*, 113.
88. Ibid., 116-117.
89. Larry D. Quinn, "'Chink Chink Chinaman': The Beginning of Nativism in Montana," *Pacific Northwest Quarterly* 58 (April 1967): 86.

90. Ibid., 84-85, 88.

91. Ibid., 88.

92. John R. Wunder, "Law and Chinese in Frontier Montana," *Montana, Magazine of Western History* 30 (Summer 1980): 20.

93. Sucheng Chan, "Introduction," 25.

94. Ibid.

95. Quinn, "'Chink Chink Chinaman'," 85.

96. Gregg Carter, "Social Demography of the Chinese in Nevada: 1870-1880," *Nevada Historical Society Quarterly* 18 (Summer 1975): 77.

97. Russell M. Magnaghi, "Virginia City's Chinese Community, 1860-1880," *Nevada Historical Society Quarterly* 24 (Summer 1981): 132, 149-54; Loren B. Chan, "The Chinese in Nevada: An Historical Survey, 1856-1970," *Nevada Historical Society Quarterly* 18 (Winter 1975): 297-98.

98. Carter, "Social Demography," 77; Magnaghi, "Virginia City's Chinese Community," 152; Loren Chan, "The Chinese in Nevada," 270.

99. Loren Chan, "The Chinese in Nevada," 284-85.

100. Ibid., 284; Carter, "Social Demography," 77.

101. Loren Chan, "The Chinese in Nevada," 278.

102. Ibid., 289.

103. Ibid., 280.

104. Ibid., 304; Gary P. Be Dunnah, *History of the Chinese in Nevada, 1855-1904* (San Francisco: R and E Research Associates, 1973), 22.

105. Loren Chan, "The Chinese in Nevada," 295.

106. John R. Wunder, "*Territory of New Mexico v. Yee Shun*: A Turning Point in Chinese Legal Relationships in the Trans-Mississippi West," *New Mexico Historical Review* 65 (July 1990): 308.

107. Ibid.; John R. Wunder, "Chinese in Trouble: Criminal Law and Race on the Trans-Mississippi West Frontier," *Western Historical Quarterly* 17 (January 1986): 25-27.

108. Wunder, "*New Mexico v. Yee Shun*," 307-08.

109. Ralph James Mooney, "Matthew Deady and the Federal Judicial Response to Racism in the Early West," *Oregon Law Review* 63, no. 4 (1984): 574.

110. Christopher H. Edson, *The Chinese in Eastern Oregon, 1860-1890* (San Francisco: R and E Research Associates, 1974), 43-44.

111. Mooney, "Matthew Deady," 574-75.

112. Ibid., 575.

113. Ibid.

114. Ibid.

115. Sucheng Chan, "Introduction," 25.

116. Ibid.

117. Ibid.

118. Edson, *The Chinese in Eastern Oregon*, 51; David H. Stratton, "The Snake River Massacre of Chinese Miners, 1887," in Duane A. Smith, ed., *A Taste of the West: Essays in Honor of Robert G. Athearn* (Boulder, CO: Pruett Publishing Co., 1983), 124-25.

119. Watson Parker, *Deadwood: The Golden Years* (Lincoln: University of Nebraska Press, 1981), 147-48.

120. Don C. Conley, "The Pioneer Chinese of Utah," in Helen Z. Papanikolas, ed., *The Peoples of Utah* (Salt Lake City: Utah State Historical Society, 1976), 270-71.

121. Virginia Huidekoper, "Mosaic of a Massacre: The Chinese Experience in Wyoming, 1870-1890" (unpublished manuscript prepared for Wyoming Council for the Humanities), 94.

122. B.P. Wilcox, "Anti-Chinese Riots in Washington," *Washington Historical Quarterly* 20 (1929): 205; Jules Alexander Karlin, "The Anti-Chinese Outbreak in Tacoma, 1885," *Pacific Historical Review* 23 (August 1954): 271-83; John R. Wunder, "The Chinese and the Courts in the Pacific Northwest: Justice Denied?," *Pacific Historical Review* 52 (May 1983): 191-211.

123. Wilcox, "Anti-Chinese Riots in Washington," 205.

124. Karlin, "Outbreak in Tacoma," 271-83.

125. Ibid., Karlin, "Outbreak in Tacoma," 207; Wunder, "Chinese in Pacific Northwest," 191-211.

126. Ibid.

127. Ibid.

128. Ibid.

129. Ibid.

130. Ibid.

131. Wilcox, "Anti-Chinese Riots in Washington," 208-11; Jules Alexander Karlin, "Anti-Chinese Violence in Seattle," *Pacific Northwest Quarterly* 39 (Spring 1948): 103-29.

132. Murray L. Carroll, "Governor Francis E. Warren, the United States Army and the Chinese Massacre at Rock Springs," *Annals of Wyoming* 59 (Fall 1987): 17-24; Paul Crane and Alfred Larson, "The Chinese Massacre," *Annals of Wyoming* 12 (Fall 1940): 47-55, 153-60; Huidekoper, "Mosaic of a Massacre."

133. Carroll, "Governor Francis E. Warren," 18.

134. Ibid., 18-19.

135. Ibid., 21.

136. Ibid., 21-22.

137. Ibid., 22.

The Early British Columbia Judges, the Rule of Law and the "Chinese Question": The California and Oregon Connection

John McLaren

INTRODUCTION

In five reported cases between 1878 and 1886, members of the British Columbia Supreme Court struck down anti-Chinese provincial statutes or municipal bylaws as unconstitutional.[1] In each case the judges went beyond deciding the straight constitutional issue and both examined and criticized the discriminatory character of the enactment before them. In the process they voiced disapproval of at least some aspects of the racist policies embodied in the legislation. The decisions clearly ran against the political grain in the province and assisted in generating public displeasure at the role of the courts.[2] None of this seems to have deflected the judges from doing what they thought was right — to afford equal protection of and equal treatment by the law to all who resided in British Columbia.

An intriguing feature of the judgments of the British Columbia courts in four of the five cases is that the judges drew their constitutional and public policy inspirations from decisions of the Supreme Court of California and of the federal Circuit Court for the Districts of California and Oregon.[3] This essay focuses on two issues: first, why the British Columbia judges were attracted to these American decisions in interpreting the division of powers in a constitution which was the reverse image of that of the United States; and second, whether the Supreme Court judges in British Columbia and their counterparts in the federal courts in California and Oregon shared a similar political and social philosophy, and a common ideology of law and its function which would explain the parity of views identified.

THE ANTI-CHINESE DISCRIMINATION DECISIONS OF THE BRITISH COLUMBIA COURTS, 1878-1888

British Columbia shared with California and Oregon a white settler community living alongside a population of Chinese immigrants, the members of both groups having come to the region with improvement of their economic lot firmly in mind.[4] After a short period of sufferance of the Chinese, who were initially thought to be temporary sojourners, strong antipathy grew within the white community towards those who appeared to be settling in. They were viewed as unfair competitors in the market and workplace (in the evocative rhetoric of the period a new "slave" population), and as possessing vicious customs and habits which, it was feared, would corrupt both the bodies and minds of the European population.[5] These negative attitudes were strengthened by the alarmist rhetoric of local politicians and populist opinion makers (most notably newspaper editors) who saw in the "Chinese question" an increasingly powerful catalyst for fostering white communal identity and thereby achieving personal political success.[6]

Soon this racist sentiment translated into pressure for legislation designed to prevent further immigration of Chinese and to make life intolerable for those already resident. A motion favoring the imposition of a head tax was heard as early as 1860 in Victoria.[7] However, by contrast with the West Coast states, discriminatory legislation was slow in coming in British Columbia. First, the frostiness of the colonial administration, represented by Governor James Douglas and Justice Matthew Baillie Begbie, towards discrimination against non-whites,[8] and later constitutional scruple about infringing on dominion jurisdiction subverted attempts by British Columbia legislators to exclude or dislodge Chinese immigrants.[9] By 1878, however, a dramatic increase in the number of Chinese disembarking in the province and fears of a new influx associated with rumors of exclusion legislation in the United States induced the legislature to move. It enacted the Chinese Taxation Act, inspired, it seems, by recent legislation in the Australian colony of Queensland.[10] The statute, which claimed in its preamble to be dedicated to forcing the Chinese to pay their allotted share of existing taxes, in actuality applied a new and discriminatory tax to them. The latter was to be payable every quarter by each Chinese resident of the province over the age of twelve years. The penalties for infringement were harsh, including a heavy fine, seizure of property and even imprisonment.[11] The enactment was challenged by a number of Chinese merchants in Victoria whose goods had been seized under its provisions.

In *Tai Sing v. Maguire*[12] Justice John Hamilton Gray struck down the legislation. He concluded that it trenched upon the jurisdiction of the dominion Parliament over aliens and trade and commerce under section 91 of the British North America Act, and interfered with Canada's ability to carry out the terms of imperial treaties. In his judgment he referred with approval to the decision of the California Supreme Court in *Lin Sing v. Washburn*[13] in which similar legislation of that state had been found to be unconstitutional for infringing the trade and commerce power which resided in Washington. Indeed, Justice Gray found great solace in this decision because it had been rendered in a constitutional system which, unlike Canada's, reposed the residual power in the states.[14] If the conclusion in favor of the central government, he reasoned, was called for in the United States under its Constitution then *a fortiori* it must be in Canada. In praising California decisions which had quashed discriminatory legislation against Chinese he remarked:

> There, almost every argument that legal ingenuity could suggest has been used to take from the General and vest in the Local Government the power of expulsive or prohibitory legislation as against this particular class of foreigners; and though mobs may there occasionally exhibit a somewhat rude exhuberance of license, few countries can be found where, in considering their cases, more correct views of law are laid down than in the higher courts of that State.[15]

In his judgment in *Tai Sing*, Gray had suggested that if exceptional legislation was needed to deal with Chinese immigration then it must be sought through "the proper channel, that is by action of the Dominion Parliament."[16] For the next six years British Columbia politicians followed his advice, and buoyed by the enactment of exclusionary or restrictive legislation in both the United States and the Australian colonies, pressured Ottawa to prevent further Chinese immigration to Canada. When the dominion government made it clear that it put the completion of the Canadian Pacific Railway (to which Chinese labor was crucial) before local sentiment in the country's westernmost province, the British Columbia legislature again took matters into its own hands.[17] In 1884 it passed a package of acts designed to bar further immigration of Chinese to British Columbia and to force existing immigrants to return to their homeland. Among these statutes was the Chinese Regulation Act.[18] This enactment, which contained a scurrilous preamble in which the "sins" of the Chinese population of the province were publicly pronounced, provided, *inter alia*, for the imposition of an annual tax on all Chinese residents of British Columbia.

The act was challenged by a Chinese resident of Victoria, who had been fined by a magistrate for being without the license required under it.[19] In *R. v. Wing Chong*[20] Justice Henry Pellew Crease, following Gray's earlier decision, found that the legislation infringed federal authority over trade and commerce and aliens, imposed indirect and discriminatory taxation which was outside provincial jurisdiction, and undermined imperial treaties with China which provided for reciprocal and free access of British subjects and Chinese citizens to China and the British Empire respectively. Despite the fact that in the intervening period the Privy Council had in two opinions rejected the notion that the provinces were mere delegates of the British Parliament, and recognized that both the dominion Parliament and provincial legislatures might legislate on the same matter within their own separate domains of national and local interest,[21] Crease saw clear conflict here between the discriminatory license and the trade and commerce power. Like Gray, he found his inspiration in *Lin Sing v. Washburn*, which he felt was directly relevant because it reflected a constitutional arrangement which in common with Canada's had reposed the power over trade and commerce in the national government. In that case the court had concluded that a discriminatory tax imposed on Chinese residents by the state of California was by its nature an interference with commercial intercourse and therefore designed to "defeat the commercial policy of the nation."[22] The concurrence of the two constitutions on where power over trade and commerce and naturalization and aliens reposed, said Crease, made "the analogy [with *Lin Sing*] so close as to become almost a direct authority."[23] The judge also found guidance in a California decision in refuting the argument of the province's attorney general that the purpose of the British Columbia act was in actuality that of direct taxation to raise revenue for provincial purposes. The decision in *In re Tiburcio Parrott*[24] was, he suggested, instructive in pointing out that a legislature could not successfully counter a constitutional challenge to a statute, the purpose of which was patently discriminatory and thus unlawful, by dressing it up in some other, ostensibly acceptable, garb.[25] Following Gray's lead, Crease also made general reference to the value of California precedents on anti-Chinese legislation because they reflected longer experience with such litigation. "[T]here is no country," he asserted, "which has such experience generally in constitutional law as applicable to a federation of states."[26]

Although Crease's judgment may be read as striking down the Chinese Regulation Act as a whole, it apparently was not viewed by the provincial government in that light, for the latter continued to rely on another discriminatory provision in the same statute, which applied a special license fee to Chinese seeking a "free miners' certificate"[27] — the fee was three times that charged to applicants of other races. When this section was challenged by a Chinese anxious to set up business in a mining region of the province, the divisional court composed of Chief Justice Begbie and Justices Crease, Gray and McCreight disallowed the provision as *ultra vires* the provincial legislature.[28] In a short judgment rendered by Justice John Foster McCreight the court, following the decisions in *Tai Sing* and *Wing Chong*, found that the section imposed a discriminatory form of taxation and thus interfered with the right of Chinese residents to carry on business. McCreight rejected arguments of the provincial attorney general based on the dissenting opinion of Justice Stephen J. Field in the *Lin Sing* case, which had stressed the origin of the taxing power in the individual states. These, he suggested, whatever their force in the context of the United States constitutional division of powers, were not relevant in Canada. He added that the preference of the divisional court was for the majority opinion in *Lin Sing*.

Although only vestiges of the British Columbia anti-Chinese legislation of 1884 survived disallowance and court challenge, it clearly did have the desired effect of shaming Ottawa into action on the "Chinese question." In 1885, with the Canadian Pacific Railway complete, the dominion government finally responded positively to settle racist sentiment on the West Coast. Following the recommendations of the Royal Commission on Chinese Immigration (on which Gray sat as one of two commissioners), the dominion Parliament passed the Chinese Immigration Act. The statute restricted further Chinese entry by the combination of a head tax and limits on the number of Chinese who might be carried on inbound vessels.[29] By and large the federal legislation seems to have placated for the moment the racist concerns of white British Columbians about Chinese immigration. It did not, however, mean an end to attempts by both the provincial legislature and municipalities to increase pressure on the existing immigrant population to move out.

In 1886 Chief Justice Begbie sat on a case in which a constitutional challenge was directed at a city of Victoria bylaw made under the Municipal Act of the province. The latter enactment had been amended in 1885 to extend the powers of municipalities to include "licensing and regulating wash-houses and laundries" and to impose a license fee on the operators of such establishments of up to $75 every six months.[30] This flimsy attempt at providing local communities with the power to close down a form of business which was almost exclusively Chinese was eagerly pursued by the city of Victoria, which passed a bylaw to that effect. In *R. v. Mee Wah*[31] a conviction under the bylaw was challenged by a Chinese laundry operator before Begbie sitting in the county court. The latter allowed the appeal, finding that the section of the Municipal Act empowering the city to charge a differential license fee was probably outside the limits of the province's jurisdiction to exact indirect taxation, but more importantly that it was unconstitutional because it was designed to discriminate against a particular class of persons.

Like his brethren Begbie expressed enthusiasm for the guidance afforded by American decisions, noting their longer experience in dealing with discrimination issues and the analogous nature of their institutions. Their opinions and reasoning, which he felt were based on international law, equity and common sense, were "entitled to great weight beyond the limits of their own jurisdiction."[32] In framing his judgment Begbie cited no less than four decisions of the Circuit Court for the Districts of California and Oregon which, he suggested, supported the proposition "that a State, or provincial law imposing special disabilities on Chinamen is unconstitutional and void."[33] He gave short shrift to attempts by the province to argue that this was general legislation which had no discriminatory intent. In doing so he quoted directly from Justice Stephen J. Field in the so-called *Queue Case*, in which the latter had struck down a San Francisco bylaw providing for the clipping of hair of prisoners in the county jail, because it was designed not to preserve public health but in the most outrageous fashion to insult and humiliate Chinese prisoners. Many Chinese wore their hair braided, believing that to cut the queue adversely effected their chances in the afterlife. Field stated:

> When we take our seats on the Bench, we are not struck with blindness and forbidden to know as judges what we see as men; and when an ordinance, though general in its terms, only operates against a special race, sect or class, it being universally understood that it is to be enforced only against that race, sect or class, we may justly conclude that it was the intention of the body adopting it that it should only have such operation and treat it accordingly.[34]

Applying that expression of sentiment Begbie concluded that the laundry bylaw had no other purpose than "to compel [the Chinese] to remove certain industries from the city or themselves from the Province."[35] To uphold an indirect attempt to discriminate against a group, when a direct attempt would be struck down, said the chief justice (again quoting from Field), would mean that "no kind of oppression can be named against which the framers of [the British North America Act] intended to guard which may not be effected."[36]

THE ATTRACTION OF UNITED STATES JURISPRUDENCE

The Lack of Existing Precedent

The simple, pragmatic reason for the British Columbia Supreme Court justices appealing to California and Oregon authority in the anti-Chinese discrimination cases was the absence of any guidance on how to deal with the issue in English or Canadian jurisprudence. With the exception of several celebrated decisions on slavery, English courts had had little or no experience in dealing with the domestic legal disabilities of non-white racial groups.[37] Moreover, the English judges operated in a unitary legal system and had not had to address this type of issue in the context of a federal state with a division of powers.

Canada had been a federation only since 1867 (the first in the British Empire) and it naturally took time before the courts there and the Privy Council in London could develop anything approaching a discernible theory of constitutional interpretation.[38] By contrast there was a rich body of constitutional doctrine in the United States, the product of judicial thinking and intellectual refinement covering many decades. The California courts — state and later federal — had been dealing with discriminatory laws and bylaws against the Chinese since the 1850s. From the late 1860s, assisted by the passage of the Fourteenth Amendment, they had developed what looked like a firm and consistent theoretical basis for deciding those cases, in a constitutional context which could be identified to some extent with Canada's.[39] For Canadian judges starting from scratch the American decisions were a natural point of reference. The fact that the constitutional issues raised in the anti-Chinese discrimination cases involved trade and commerce, immigration, aliens, naturalization and treaty making, which in both constitutions were activities or functions exclusively or predominantly within the federal domain, helped to underline the relevance and utility of United States West Coast jurisprudence for the British Columbia superior courts.

Because of the lack of a developed constitutional jurisprudence in Canada during the 1870s and 1880s the British Columbia judges felt largely unconstrained in their handling of these cases. True their role was to determine where the matter at hand fell within the division of powers established by sections 91 and 92 of the British North America Act.[40] However, the absence of well-defined limits on the interpretative process meant that they felt free to go behind the impugned legislation, its purpose and motivations and to indulge their own creative views on constitutional theory.[41] As judges who were faced with the adjudication of issues on both the geographic and politico-legal frontier, they undoubtedly felt a close affinity with American counterparts operating in similar conditions. They were clearly impressed by the stature of the judges who penned the California and Oregon decisions, in particular of Justice Stephen J. Field, already on his way to establishing a reputation as the major exponent of judicial activism in *postbellum* America. As the comments of Gray, Crease and Begbie on the value of American guidance in these cases show, this was not mere slavish copying of American precedent. They were well aware of and at pains to point out the fundamental difference in the balance of power between the center and the parts in the two constitutions. However, it was that cardinal distinction which made the United States decisions particularly attractive because, despite the greater power vested in the states in that constitutional system, they recognized a strong federal claim to exclusive jurisdiction in the areas of social and economic activity in question.

An Ideological Identity

The vacuum of authority and theory, while it shows why the British Columbia judges would look to decisions in California and Oregon as the only relevant authority available and therefore worthy of serious consideration, does not necessarily explain why they chose to follow them. American decisions had no claim to binding authority in Canada and it would have been perfectly possible for the members of the British Columbia Supreme Court to have developed an authentic and indigenous approach to constitutional interpretation which gave more consideration to the priorities and sensibilities of the provincial government and legislature. Some of the earlier California decisions revealed a strong bias towards the primacy of local jurisdiction.[42] In Canada itself in due course, under the tutelage of the Judicial Committee of the Privy Council in London, there was a significant shift to a more province-oriented theory of constitutional interpretation.[43] My thesis is that above and beyond the formal attractions of using California and Oregon authority, those decisions were compelling because there were ideological similarities in the way in which the two groups of judges viewed the role of the courts in the constitutional process. These similarities, I would argue, reflected an overlapping set of political, social and economic values which they held. Indeed, the more closely one compares the judicial records of these men on the anti-Chinese discrimination cases in the context of their more general approach to law and constitutional theory, the more one is struck by the commonality of belief and perception. Given that the two political and social cultures diverged in terms of the character and duration of the colonial experience, the timing and pace of democratic changes and perceptions of the nature of the relationship between the individual and the state, what explains these similarities in thought?

A Spirit of Judicial Activism

There is evidence that both groups of judges were inspired by the belief that the courts had a dominant role to play in the constitutional system of which they were a part. American scholars have shown that the California federal judges, while their impulses and objectives may have differed, were committed to an activist stance in interpreting the Constitution and in particular the Fourteenth Amendment. Charles McCurdy describes Stephen J. Field, who served on the United States Supreme Court from 1862 to 1897, as "arguably the Court's self conscious 'activist' and ... certainly the first justice to describe the judicial protection of substantive rights as a democratic endeavor."[44] Through creative use of the Fourteenth Amendment and the development of the notion of "substantive due process" Field was to chart the legal relationship between government and business enterprise in the last decades of the nineteenth century, a period of great economic expansion and capital accumulation in America. He did so in a way which would confine within relatively narrow compass the areas of the economy which government could legitimately regulate, leaving large segments of industrial and commercial activity effectively immune from legislative scrutiny.[45] By combining a commitment to formal legal equality and a belief in the right of individuals to apply their skills and property to economic pursuits as they wished, he also found in the Fourteenth Amendment the inspiration for the doctrine of "invidious discrimination." This was the doctrine which he and his colleagues on the United States Supreme Court and among the California and Oregon judiciary employed as a weapon against state legislation adversely affecting the civil rights of the Chinese.[46] It reflected a shared conviction that, while racial discrimination in terms of access to the political process and social status was justified and embedded in the constitutional order, selective denial of justice and of the protection of the law was offensive to that order and would not be countenanced.

Justice Lorenzo Sawyer, who was Field's colleague as member of the United States Circuit Court for the Ninth Judicial Circuit, had strong Republican party connections. Linda Przybyszewski notes that Sawyer was firmly of the belief that the victory of the North in the Civil War spelled the death knell of states' rights thinking and the victory of nationalism[47]:

> As a judicial representative of the national government, Sawyer felt authorized to oversee the legislation of the now subordinated state governments.[48]

On the issue of race as it emerged on the West Coast — the relentless campaign to exclude and dislodge Chinese immigrants — Sawyer acted consciously in what he considered to be the national interest in protecting the civil rights of minorities from the narrow-minded localism of state and municipal governments and in upholding the treaty obligations of the United States to China.

Justice Matthew Deady from Oregon who, James Mooney indicates, started political life as a Democrat with distinctly racist tendencies, grew into an active supporter of the federal cause as a judge.[49] Appointed by President Buchanan to the federal bench as district judge for Oregon in 1859, he changed parties in 1862. In the wake of this conversion Deady expressed himself as having greater affinity with Alexander Hamilton and George Washington than with Thomas Jefferson.[50] On the Chinese question, as on other issues, the rule and reason of law administered fearlessly by the courts was for the Oregon judge the necessary condition of an enlightened civilization.[51]

In common with his colleagues he attached the greatest weight to the treaty obligations of the United States as the supreme national law. The commitment of the California and Oregon judges to judicial activism reflected a belief that in the post-Civil War period the federal courts provided the only forum in government which could dispense the reasoned and intelligent guidance needed.[52]

A belief in judicial activism similarly motivated the British Columbia judges. For them, like Sawyer and Deady, this stance was needed to control provincial legislatures and governments. However, unlike their American counterparts who saw themselves in one way or another as part of a new politico-legal order, the impetus to judicial activism in constitutional matters in British Columbia was largely a product of nostalgia for the past. Two of the judges, Chief Justice Begbie and Justice Crease, had been part of the pre-Confederation colonial establishment. Begbie, a former Chancery barrister appointed from England as the first professional judge on the British Pacific Coast in 1858, had enjoyed superior status and power both in that position and as the legal adviser to and confidant of James Douglas, the governor of the twin colonies of Vancouver Island and British Columbia.[53] From 1858 to 1864 Douglas and Begbie between them effectively ran government and justice on the mainland.[54] Begbie, as the only superior court justice and initially the only qualified lawyer, had been the "originator" of much of the colony's law, both through his judicial decisions and the legislation which he drafted.[55]

Crease, who had also been trained and had worked as a lawyer in England, spent some time in Upper Canada before arriving in British Columbia in 1860. He very soon became part of the political and legal elite of the colony, receiving an appointment as attorney general of the mainland colony in 1863 and of the integrated colony of British Columbia in 1866. He held the latter position until British Columbia became a province in 1871.[56]

Both men doubted the wisdom of British Columbia joining Confederation. Begbie worried about a diminution in the power of the judges in a constitutional structure which reduced the colonial Supreme Court to provincial status, and Crease fretted over his future in a governmental system in which local interests predominated.[57] Although both came to terms with the immediate reality, their egos satisfied by appointment as chief justice and puisne justice respectively, neither seems to have been comfortable with the new constitutional and political order. As might have been expected, they believed that the power vacuum left by the ending of colonial status had been filled in constitutional terms by the dominion government and Parliament. They were accordingly vigorous supporters of the federal cause in constitutional litigation and became jaded at the apparent unconcern in Ottawa about their court's difficulties with the government in Victoria.[58] As Hamar Foster has demonstrated, this was nowhere more evident than in cases in which their own convenience and traditional prerogatives — for example the determination of court circuits and control of the rules of courts — were challenged by the provincial authorities.[59]

Begbie and Crease's brand of federalism was shared by Justice John Hamilton Gray. Gray was of American loyalist stock and had been one of the "Fathers of Confederation" from New Brunswick. He had served as a Conservative member of Parliament in Ottawa from that maritime province before migrating to British Columbia in 1872 with an appointment to the bench engineered by Prime Minister Sir John A. Macdonald.[60] Politically he was wedded to the idea of a strong central government.

The commitment of the British Columbia judges to a constitution with the dominant power in federal hands was not purely opportunistic. They seem genuinely, if idealistically, to have believed that there were within the Canadian constitutional order elements of fundamental law which operated as a legitimate curb on the excesses of provincial legislatures. This position took its formal inspiration from Diceyan notions of the "rule of law" and the long-standing belief of Whig constitutionalists that there existed a body of fundamental legal principles against which positive law could and should be judged, and discarded, if found wanting.[61] The division of powers established by the British North

America Act which, in their opinion, consciously shielded important civil rights issues from local interference reflected this normative structure. The British Columbia judges believed they were the guardians of this order. Conscious of the fact that they were operating in a legal culture which was influenced by North American as well as British values, and lacking guidance from British sources, they drew upon United States experience and norms to provide the substantive content of the principles underlying the Canadian Constitution. What resulted was a peculiar and, as it turned out shortlived, hybrid constitutional order which sought to repose significant power in the hands of the judges.[62]

Political and Social Conservatism

The penchant for judicial activism among both groups of judges was in part a reflection of a shared political and social conservatism and suspicion of popular democracy. Justice Field, for all his appeal to "democratic rights" and "equality," was one who distrusted the peoples' representatives in both Congress and the state legislatures. This was especially true in cases in which he felt that legislative bodies were unduly influenced by sectional interests which led them to interfere with private-property rights. Despite the fact that in the era of economic expansion which followed the Civil War there were greater concentrations of wealth than earlier, Field and those who thought like him saw the welfare of the nation as dependent on the commitment, initiative and wisdom of the business sector, including the great entrepreneurs.[63] This lack of confidence in the motives of legislators seems also to have encouraged his intervention in the discrimination cases. Although Justice Field's commitment to protection of the Chinese from the abrogation and limitation of their civil rights was less consistent after 1880,[64] there is evidence that earlier he did experience acute embarrassment at the "red neck" antics of California legislators and civic politicians and felt impelled to take a stand against them:

> [N]othing can be accomplished. ... by hostile and spiteful legislation on the part of the state, or of its municipal bodies, like the ordinance in question — legislation which is unworthy of a brave and manly people. Against such legislation it will always be the duty of the judiciary to declare and enforce the paramount law of the nation.[65]

Both Sawyer and Deady made no pretense of their distaste for the openly racist policies and the demagoguery which supported discriminatory legislation and administrative activity against the Chinese. In his decision in the case of *Tiburcio Parrot* in which the circuit court struck down both Article 19(2) of the California Constitution and a provision in the state's penal code which made it a criminal offense for a corporation to employ "Chinese or Mongolians,"[66] Sawyer, with thinly veiled anger, warned the government and citizens of California against what he felt were attempts to legalize mob sentiment.[67] The legislation he likened to "incipient rebellion." Moreover, he characterized a campaign of white intimidation in San Francisco "in anticipation of the statute now in question" as likely to lead to violence equivalent to the "riotous attack" by Chinese against Christian missionaries stationed at Tien-tsin in 1870.[68] He noted that the government of China had been pressured into making amends for the unwarranted and unprovoked action of its citizens in that instance. Having cited the elements of federal law designed to enforce the Fourteenth Amendment he added:

> These provisions of the United States statutes — the supreme law of the land — are commended to the consideration of all persons who are disposed to go from place to place, and by means of threats and intimidation, endeavor to compel employers to discharge peaceable and industrious Chinamen engaged in their service.[69]

Matthew Deady was similarly incensed by "sand-lot politics" and the "communistic mob" which he associated with victimization of the Chinese.[70] Like Sawyer he went as far as to suggest that state anti-Chinese legislation bordered on the treasonous. "Between this and 'firing on Fort Sumter' by South Carolina," he asserted, "there is the difference of the direct and indirect nothing more."[71] He was no more charitable towards Congress. In a decision involving interpretation of the Chinese Exclusion Act of 1888,[72] which was designed to prevent the return of previously resident Chinese laborers to the United States, he referred bitterly to the politics of popular whim:

> So harsh and unjust a measure as this concerning the intercourse between friendly nations maintaining diplomatic relations is something unprecedented in this age of the world, and can only be accounted for by the fact that a presidential election is pending, in which each political party is trying to outbid the other for the "sandlot" vote of the Pacific coast, and particularly for that of San Francisco.[73]

Mooney suggests that "[t]hroughout his adult life Deady held essentially elitist political views" and that his "social views were similarly aristocratic."[74]

"Aristocratic" or "patrician" would be apt words to describe the political and social values of the British Columbia judges, especially Begbie and Crease. They also chaffed at the power exercised by a legislature, the membership of which was voted in by adult, white male electors, many of whom they viewed as ignorant and fickle. On the "Chinese question" these judges were clearly out to trim the wings of the local politicians because of the tendency of the latter to cater to popular cant and extremism. Gray, in later explaining his decision in *Tai Sing* and his striking down of the Chinese Taxation Act in the report of the Royal Commission on Chinese Immigration of 1885, admitted as much:

> Such legislation would hardly be tolerated anywhere among a free people, nor in any country in which fanaticism had not usurped the place of reason. It was that Act which led to the Chinese strike in Victoria, in 1878, and was disallowed by the Dominion Government as soon as attention was by this judgement called to its provisions.[75]

Criticism of provincial legislators and their "appeal to gallery" was also evident in the opinions submitted to the royal commission by Begbie and Crease. The latter was characteristically direct and acerbic:

> The outcry against the Chinese takes its rise in great measure in the efforts of persons, who, for political motives, are desirous of posing themselves as the friends of the working classes, through their sweet votes to gain political power and influence. All political parties, the "ins" as well as the "outs" aim at this: and through the press and orations, and even no little misrepresentation, exaggerate.[76]

The chief justice contented himself with elaborating what he considered to be the constitutional hallmarks of a popular assembly and how they explained the legislative treatment meted out to the Chinese. He noted that in "a constitutional state" the members of the legislature "are in duty bound to take the views of their constituencies as expressed at the polls; and to support such measures as please their constituents."[77] In turn a "constitutional ministry" is bound by a majority of votes in the house, acting as "a sort of managing committee to carry into effect the wishes of that majority." As the provincial franchise extended to adult male Europeans, many of whom harbored an inbred antipathy to a racially distinct group who they feared as competitors in the labor market and who they believed were draining the local economy of wealth, it was in Begbie's mind no surprise that the outcome would be discriminatory legislation.[78]

Although I have no direct evidence of the connection, it is likely that the political and social views of the British Columbia judges were influenced by the vigorous debate on the advisability of extending the franchise going on in Britain during these decades. In that dialectic the exponents of representative government led by John Stuart Mill were ranged against those still attracted to whiggish notions of government by the well-bred and wise, for whom James Fitzjames Stephen was a leading spokesman.[79] By background and experience men of the ilk of Begbie, Crease and Gray would have been drawn instinctively to the latter position.

A Commitment to Economic Liberalism

Beyond the overlapping of views of the two groups of judges on political and social relationships, there was also a degree of commonality of opinion on economics. What we know of the economic philosophy of the American judges suggests that in varying degrees it proceeded from a strong belief in the virtues of the free market and competition, reflecting a more general commitment to preventing the law from discouraging individual initiative. As pragmatists rather than theoreticians, their acceptance of the "unseen hand" as a basic verity did not induce them to take a stand antithetical to big business. For them, the great captains of industry and commerce were prime examples of the intelligent application of wealth and capital. As a consequence they were able to accommodate the control of segments of the market by virtually monopolistic forces, while preaching the gospel of competition in areas of economic activity in which big business was not a player. Sensitivity to both the economic imperatives of big business and the ideal of competition featured in the judges' attitudes towards anti-Chinese discrimination.

As I have already noted, Stephen J. Field was in many ways the architect of the supportive legal framework in which business enterprise operated in the decades after the Civil War. A strong commitment to the protection of private-property rights, combined with an appreciation of the dynamic economic forces at work in the country, induced him to select a boundary line between the domains of public and private enterprise which left large areas of business and industry outside the reach of the law, except for limited controls justified by the exercise of the police power.[80] Although not devoid of more human sentiments, his tendency in working out his rationalist scheme of law was to accord greater significance to materialist values and interests.[81]

Questions arise concerning Justice Field's motives in anti-Chinese discrimination litigation because of his clear bias in favor of "enterprise jurisprudence." The earliest group of decisions which he wrote do hint at some degree of empathy with the Chinese and the difficult circumstances in which they were forced to live.[82] Moreover, as his decision in *In re Quong Woo*[83] in which he struck down a San Francisco ordinance effectively excluding Chinese from running laundries demonstrates, he understood the relationship between the United States and China to require that Chinese residents be free to apply their labor as they wished. They were, he said, "entitled to follow any of the lawful ordinary trade and pursuits of life, without let or hindrance from the state, or any of its subordinate   municipal   bodies."[84]   However,   his   more   general commitment to protecting industry and business, and his friendship with railway moguls such as Leland Stanford and Collis P. Huntington, raise the question of whether his motivation was a willingness to contemplate free competition by the Chinese or flowed rather from a recognition of their value as cheap labor — a reserve industrial army — to big business.[85] The fact that he was on record as regretting the presence of the Chinese and opposing further immigration suggests that at best he viewed them as an economically necessary, but temporary, evil.[86]

Mooney has speculated that similar thinking may in part explain Matthew   Deady's   favorable   disposition   to   the   Chinese   in   the discrimination cases on which he sat. Indeed, he suggests that if Deady viewed the value of the Chinese in America as providing a pool of cheap labor, a new "servile class," then there may well have been a degree of continuity with his much earlier position in support of slavery in Oregon.[87] Moreover, insofar as the judge may have believed that reliance on this immigrant population for a workforce allowed business to keep working-class whites "in line," it would tie in well with his aristocratic biases and his antagonism to what he described as demagoguery and "sand-lot politics."[88]

Przybyszewski admits to difficulty in determining the extent to which Sawyer may have been affected in his view of anti-Chinese legislation by the economic significance of this population to large entrepreneurs, especially the railroad owners.[89] The available evidence suggests that he was not as beguiled as Field was and Deady may have been. On the one hand Sawyer had connections with Leland Stanford, whose Central Pacific Railroad had employed large numbers of Chinese laborers, and was well disposed towards that "great enterprise."[90] On the other, he did express during his career a more general respect for the Chinese and their economic ambition. In his judgment in *Tiburcio Parrott*, while his colleague Ogden Hoffman, who believed Chinese immigration to have been a mistake, saw the issue as one of the frustrating of corporate enterprise,[91] Sawyer placed the emphasis on the interference with "the right of the Chinese residents to labour" thereby depriving them of the means of living.[92] When it came, as it did in *In re Wo Lee*,[93] to another attempt by the board of supervisors of San Francisco to force Chinese laundries out of business, Sawyer had no doubts that what was at stake was the preservation of small business and Chinese access to it:

> The necessary tendency, if not the specific purpose, of this ordinance, and of enforcing it in the manner indicated in the record, is to drive out of business all the numerous small laundries, especially those owned by Chinese, and give a monopoly of business to the large institutions established and carried on by means of large associated Caucasian capital.[94]

There is some sense with Sawyer, as Przybyszewski suggests, that a commitment to "economic evenhandedness or simple indignation at injustice" may have acted as a counterbalance to the warmth he felt towards big business and its imperatives.[95]

The comments of Begbie, Crease and Gray in connection with the royal commission in 1885 reveal that their economic views fit into a similar pattern. These judges believed strongly that the presence of the Chinese had been a considerable benefit to the economy of the province and that, in the absence of adequate and reliable pools of white labor, they served a continuing need. It was natural, in their minds, that the immigrants should be hired by employers who were the risk takers responsible for opening up the economic potential of British Columbia at wages lower than those which white labor might demand. By the same token the judges, betraying their strong class bias, were critical of the attitude of white workers who, they claimed, had made unrealistic financial demands on employers and, when they were rebuffed, proved entirely opportunistic in seeking employment in the United States. By contrast with the white working class, the judges considered the Chinese to be industrious, thrifty and sober. As Begbie remarked: "Their ceaseless toil is like nothing but an ant hill."[96]

Crease pointed to the significant contribution made by the Chinese in household service, railway construction, mining and the fish canneries. He was quick to attribute the blame for anti-Chinese sentiment to white labor. In apocalyptic terms he described the crippling effect the exclusion of the Asian immigrants would have on the life and economy of the province:

> [It] would necessarily be to create the worst of all monopolies, next to that of capital: the tyranny of labour under whose withering blight mines, fisheries, manufacture, arts and improvements of all kinds would speedily languish or die.[97]

Begbie, who according to David Williams counted amongst his friends the wealthiest man in British Columbia, mine owner Robert Dunsmuir, was, not surprisingly, well disposed to capital.[98] In his comments to the royal commission the chief justice openly articulated a market theory of labor to justify employers paying the wages they felt the market would bear. Workers had to realize that the goods produced with their labor must be worth more than the wages they received:

> The lowest limit of wages is the money which will buy the necessaries of life for the laborer. The highest limit is the whole of the augmented value which his labor confers on the material operated on. If the laborer accepts less than the first, he will die of want. If the employer give the whole of the second he will leave himself nothing to live upon, and will speedily die of want in his turn...[99]

Between these two outer limits, Begbie added, "the rate of wages oscillates according to supply and demand."[100]

In his report as commissioner, Gray came close to suggesting that the Chinese occupied the role of a serf class in British Columbia. They did not, in his view, constitute realistic competition for white workers. Indeed, he suggested that the attraction of the Chinese to hard bodily exertion relieved the white worker from toil and slavery "in grovelling work, which wears out the body without elevating the mind."[101] He likened them to machines but with the added benefit that they were both creators and consumers of wealth and trade. It was, said Gray, the availability of cheap Chinese labor which made the investment of capital in the province attractive.[102]

The comments of the British Columbia judges, both from the bench and off, suggest that their affection for big business was balanced by a concern not to place barriers in the way of small entrepreneurs competing among themselves. As one might have expected of Begbie and Crease, whose formative years as young lawyers tracked closely the rise of *laissez-faire* economic thinking in Britain, they recognized the value of competition in the marketplace and the right of anyone, including the Chinese, to make a mark in a trade or business. In three of the five reported cases in which they dealt with anti-Chinese legislation or administrative action, the British Columbia Superior Court justices were faced with attempts to exclude the immigrants from specific business activities.[103] In each instance they struck down the legislation or impugned the action in question because it impinged on the right of the Chinese to apply their labor as they wished. Chief Justice Begbie's decision in R. v. Corporation of Victoria provides the clearest illustration.[104] In that case the city had refused to renew pawnbroking licenses to Chinese residents. Begbie decried the use of discretionary administrative power to encourage monopoly. *"Prima facie,"* he asserted, "every person living under the protection of British law has a right at once to exercise his industry and ability in any trade or calling he may elect."[105]

The view that it should be open to all individuals in society to better themselves by independent productive endeavor also appealed to Gray. He made it explicit in his report as commissioner:

> The gradations of labour are simply the dispensations of Providence, by which the highest good can be obtained for mankind, and he who commences on the lowest rung of the ladder frequently attains the highest.[106]

While no doubt Gray, like his colleagues, would have had difficulty in accepting the Chinese as political or social equals, he was willing to accept that they should have some degree of mobility within the economy.

A Limited Theory of Rights

Both the American and British Columbia judges were clearly wedded to a particular juristic theory of rights which is evident in their judgments and other public pronouncements on the subject of discrimination against the Chinese. The latter were entitled, in their view, to equal access to the regular processes of the law, were shielded from the discriminatory exercise of administrative discretion and were afforded protection from legislation or administrative action which applied differential penalties to them, created racially specific offenses for them and interfered with their right to earn a living. My thesis is that this limited conception of rights was molded by the judges' political and social conservatism, economic determinism, and also by how they felt at a more personal level about the "Chinese fact" and the place of the Chinese within their respective societies. It is also my contention that to an extent it represented an independent, intellectual and moral exercise which derived from the judges' perception of the judicial role in the common-law tradition, and the demands which that made on the mind and conscience of each of them.

McCurdy has explained how Stephen J. Field and his colleagues on the United States Supreme Court, in working out the implications of the Fourteenth Amendment in the context of race, developed a distinction between on the one hand a narrow band of "civil rights" which were open to constitutional protection and on the other a much wider band of "political and social rights"[107] which were not:

> The only rights Congress intended to protect with the Fourteenth

Amendment, [Field] contended in dissent, were ... to own property, to make and enforce contracts, to sue and give evidence in one's own behalf, and to enjoy "the full and equal benefit of all laws for the security of persons and property."[108]

By contrast, McCurdy suggests, Field believed that no protection was meant to be afforded to political rights, for example the franchise or jury service. Social rights such as "marriage and access to public goods such as transport facilities, tax-supported libraries, public schools and the like" were, to his mind, also beyond the reach of the Constitution.[109] The rationale was straightforward: both political and social rights had always been regulated by law on the basis of age, sex, race and citizenship. The Fourteenth Amendment had not changed that. All that it required in these contexts was that equality exist within the relevant, preestablished classification.

McCurdy's thesis is that the distinction accommodated Field's confessed racism. Moreover, he argues, it reconciles the justice's decisions involving blacks and Chinese in which he seems to have favored the latter at the expense of the former. An analysis of the jurisprudence shows that the two groups were in fact seeking different types of rights. Unlike the blacks who came to court to challenge political and social discrimination as well as the abrogation of their civil rights, the interest of the Chinese was confined to ensuring their equal treatment by the process of law and their rights to use their property and earn a living, in other words "civil rights."[110]

To what extent does this explanation of the motives and sentiments of Stephen J. Field fit our knowledge of his colleagues on the California and Oregon courts and his counterparts in British Columbia? Field never made any secret of his opinion that the Chinese had no place in the American polity. Even in *Ho Ah Kow*,[111] in which he took such a strong position against discriminatory lawmaking by states and municipalities he recognized the strength of anti-Chinese sentiment in California, pointed to the unassimilability of its oriental population and hinted that he was in favor of ending immigration from China:

And thoughtful persons, looking at the millions which crowd the opposite shores of the Pacific, and the possibility at no distant day of their pouring over in vast hordes among us giving rise to fierce antagonisms of race, hope that some way may be devised to prevent their further immigration.[112]

In a later decision in the United States Supreme Court in interpreting the Chinese Exclusion Act of 1888, he expressed his approval of the steps taken by Congress to stem the tide, suggesting that whatever the original value of the Chinese to the economy of California, they had outlived their welcome.[113]

Field's views on race ironically coincided with those of Justice Ogden Hoffman, the judge for the northern district of California with whom the senior judge had permanently strained relations. Hoffman considered the Chinese as a group a menace to the present and future welfare of the state and favored the termination of immigration.[114]

Sawyer, who could be at times quite generous in his comments about the Chinese, and employed interpretations of the law designed to afford them protection, was capable of the same negative sentiment about their presence as Field and Hoffman. His earliest opinion, developed as he traveled on the Overland Trail to the West Coast in 1850, was that the Chinese were the most impressive of the various racial and ethnic groups he had come across:

> [He] noted with approval "their industriousness" and their "grave and dignified" deportment, and how the Chinese took "a greater interest in our institutions than any other people."[115]

These views were incorporated into his judgments on the circuit court in which he went out of his way to point to the contribution made by the Chinese to the community. Przybyszewski asserts that Sawyer "never viewed the Chinese as an economic blight" and suggests that he would not have been averse to some recognition of social rights, for example those relating to education, in their case.[116] She points out, furthermore, that in the decisions in which he sought to mitigate the effects of the progressively more restrictive Chinese Exclusion Acts in the 1880s he came more and more into conflict with his senior judge, Field, who had undergone a conversion to a policy of strict construction in the matter of Chinese immigration.[117] Sawyer took some pride in this stand, even though it brought him and his colleagues into increasing professional and public odium.[118]

However, even while interpreting the acts in a way which he felt was faithful to the important treaty obligations of the United States, and thereby affording protection to individual Chinese litigants, Sawyer expressed opinions on Chinese immigration in general which were similar to those of Field and Hoffman and betrayed an underlying racism. In an interview with the historian H.H. Bancroft in 1886, the judge suggested that the only value of the immigrants was as machines who should be discarded when no longer productive.[119] He further remarked that he objected to those Chinese who left "offspring" behind them, a comment which Przybyszewski suggests reflects an apprehension that Chinese demands might before long blossom into claims of citizenship.[120]

Deady very clearly saw himself as a protector of the Chinese. There are references in his judgments to their engagement in "lawful labour for an honest living,"[121] as well as the breach of faith involved in the white community inviting the immigrants to become permanent residents, only to prevent them from earning a livelihood upon their arrival.[122] In his diary he expressed concern for the victimization to which they were subject at the hands of both organized groups and mobs of whites.[123] The threat to white society said to arise from the use of opium by the Chinese, Deady described as hypocrisy. The abuse of tobacco and whiskey in the white community he considered to be of "much greater injury to the health, peace and morals of society than the present use of opium."[124]

Deady seems to have maintained his concern about the mean treatment accorded to the Chinese until his death. Indeed, Mooney notes that both Deady's diary and his correspondence reveal that as he grew older he became "markedly more tolerant and humane."[125] However, his interpretation of Deady's motives, manifest particularly in the latter's acerbic references to white labor, was that they were aristocratic, paternalistic and pro-business.[126] On this view there is at least doubt about whether Deady would have disagreed with Field, Hoffman and Sawyer that the effective boundary of legitimate claims to rights by the Chinese were the outer limits of "civil" rights articulated by the United States Supreme Court.[127]

The ambivalence evident among the California and Oregon judges about the Chinese, the limited role which they saw them as occupying in West Coast society, and the belief that protection which the law afforded to them was confined to civil and some economic rights is replicated to one degree or another among their British Columbia counterparts. Perhaps because of the slower pace of European settlement and economic development in British Columbia, statements of regret about Chinese immigration are difficult to find. Indeed, their presence seems rather to have been applauded. Moreover, there was no attempt by these judges to develop an express theory or classification of rights similar to Field's. As a result one is forced to look for hints rather than express statements of a circumscribed body of rights to which the judges felt the Chinese had a legitimate claim.

There was a strong feeling among these men that the Chinese were the victims of stereotyping which distorted the white community's view of their way of life, and consequently got in the way of an appreciation of the valuable contribution they had made and were making to the British Columbia economy. Gray, in particular in the report on Chinese immigration, warned against this practice and suggested that it revealed more about the biased motives of their detractors than it did about the customs and beliefs of the immigrants.[128] Like Deady, the British Columbia judges were unimpressed with the arguments of the Sinophobes that the Chinese were more immoral than whites. Both Begbie and Crease noted that their vices, such as opium smoking, gambling and prostitution, were conducted in private, unlike those of their white counterparts.[129] The chief justice indicated in his response to the royal commission that Chinese vices were less debilitating. The problems associated with opium, he asserted, paled into insignificance in comparison with those attributable to whiskey drinking among whites.[130] Crease in true form gave graphic meaning to the term "white vices" by equating the scenes in towns on the mainland on payday with conditions in Sodom and Gomorrah.[131] For his part Gray pointed to the "irony" of white society complaining of the "vicious habits" of the Chinese in using opium against the background of British policy in the Opium Wars. By those conflicts, he noted, importation of the product from India had been forced at gunpoint on China by the British. The criticism of the Chinese was also, he suggested, hypocritical when one considered that opium was a perfectly legitimate item of trade in Canada and was being used by "the higher and cultivated members of English, European and American society."[132]

The judges rejected the widespread contention in the white community that the Chinese were a potential source of leprosy.[133] They did, however, differ on whether they constituted a more general threat to public health. Begbie considered their living quarters no worse than those in which whites resided in close proximity.[134] Crease noted the ghettoization of the Chinese but attributed it to the hostility shown to them by the white population and their exploitation at the hands of white landlords.[135] Gray for his part was inclined to believe that the Chinese did present a health threat, but added that it was one which could be dealt with satisfactorily by the proper public health regulations and vigorous enforcement.[136]

That Gray was not beyond applying the stereotypes which he distrusted is evident in his accusation that the Chinese did not understand the British system of government, exhibited suspicion towards the exercise of authority, and communally evaded their legal responsibilities.[137] They had, he charged, scant respect for the truth, especially in criminal cases.[138] He did reduce the sting of his comments somewhat by suggesting that the problems with commitment and probity among the Chinese population might be alleviated by giving them more responsibility for administration of the law in their community.[139] Crease agreed that the immigrants were untrustworthy when it came to criminal trials, but explained the problem not as a natural proclivity of the race but as a result of language difficulties and misunderstanding as to the significance of the oath.[140] The chief justice indicated that his experience was different. He described the Chinese as generally law abiding. Far from lacking respect for the law, "they place perfect confidence in the administration of justice by our officials; and they testify their submission to and acquiescence in the judgements of our courts by every means apparently in their power."[141]

Little was said about the judges' perception of how the Chinese fit into British Columbia society and what the future might hold. All three saw their continuing presence as necessary to the economic welfare of the province. Gray, no doubt because he was involved in a process of providing the dominion government with a basis for responding to racist sentiment on the coast by limiting further immigration, concluded that restrictive legislation was necessary.[142] Assimilation was only briefly discussed. Crease alone was moved to comment. He remarked pessimistically that the Chinese would never assimilate, because of their lifestyle, lowly status and lack of emotional commitment to British Columbia. He evidently hoped that some at least would return to their homeland as he felt that they were not the stock from which the citizens of "a free and progressive country" would spring.[143] Furthermore, he opined, "miscegenation with the race is on any scale impossible."[144]

Only oblique reference was made to the political disabilities under which the Chinese population labored. Begbie in his evidence before the royal commission noted that the Chinese had been denied the franchise after British Columbia joined Confederation in 1871.[145] His comments suggest that he felt this was the sort of stratagem to be expected in a democratic society in which the presence of a minority, alien community was vigorously opposed. It certainly had not been done with any analysis of whether the Chinese were or were not more prone to bribery than "the ordinary white voter."[146] Although this might be taken as suggesting that Begbie favored the Chinese enjoying the franchise, it could just as well be interpreted as reflecting the feeling that the extension of the vote to any laboring class, whatever its race, was a mistake. Gray, who suggested in his report that the Chinese were dangerous because of a proclivity towards forming secret societies, associated this with their exclusion from the mainstream of life of the dominant community.[147] This insight did not lead him, however, to advocate access by the immigrants to full political rights. Instead he expressed great interest in the devolution of some aspects of government, administration and judicial activity to the Chinese community, as had been done effectively in Manila, and in the system of conjoint policing tried with success in Canton during its occupation by British and French forces.[148]

Given what we know of the British Columbia judges, their values and impulses, it seems likely that they, like their American counterparts, saw the ambit of Chinese "rights" as limited. Their attitude towards this subject population was basically paternalistic. They did not consider the Chinese to be their political or social equals but as a group of outsiders of which they, the judges, were the special, if not the only, protectors. Considerations of class, combined with those of race, would have suggested to them that the Chinese had no natural claim to political and at best a limited claim to social rights, although they were entitled to be free from discrimination within the normal processes of the law and to make a living.

Although both groups of judges contained men who were racist to one degree or another, the fact that they were willing even in a limited sphere to see their personal attitudes transcended by what they perceived to be the rule of law is significant. It was this ideology which provided the strongest common link between them. True they shared an elitist view of law, politics and society and a belief in the virtues of capital, each or both of which might have explained their iconoclastic stand against discrimination. However, my belief is that what set them apart was that they believed that to be a judge in and of itself meant at least some capacity for taking a detached position and ignoring sectional interests, including those with which they had some personal sympathy. That this was not a particular form of sectionalism parading as judicial neutrality is evident in the fact that even judges such as Ogden Hoffman, who was openly ill-disposed towards Chinese immigration and their presence in North America, and Gray, who for political reasons persuaded himself of the need for restrictions, felt a strong obligation to afford existing or returning residents all the available protections which the law provided.[149] This was so in the face of legislation which had made it clear that national policy was set on the course of exclusion or drastic restriction. This is not to suggest that individual judges were entirely consistent in adhering to a transcendental position. As Field's later decisions and Gray's report demonstrate, political considerations could and did intrude. However, overall the impression is strong that both groups of judges saw the anti-Chinese discrimination cases as raising a significant challenge to the independence and integrity of the judicial role which needed to be dealt with directly and firmly.

Although further investigation is called for, there is already scattered evidence that the judges in question were, and prided themselves that they were, more worldly than many of their contemporaries. To one degree or another they were beneficiaries of a nineteenth-century liberal education and the stimulus which it provided for ongoing study and speculation. Field had received his formal higher education at Williams College and traveled in the Near East by his late teens.[150] He seems to have been influenced at a less formal level by his association with Theodore Sedgewick, the celebrated political economist who lived in his hometown of Stockbridge, Massachusetts.[151] Intellectual stimulation had also been the experience of Ogden Hoffman. The scion of a well-placed Whig family from New York City with literary connections, he was educated at Columbia and then the Harvard Law School and traveled in Europe before settling down to work as a lawyer.[152] Matthew Deady, who had received a rather minimal education as a boy, benefited culturally as a young man from his friendship in Barnesville, Ohio, with William Meek, a bastion of the local Democratic party.[153] In the process of self-education Deady developed a voracious appetite for reading and was respected in Oregon for his erudition.[154] Begbie and Crease were both graduates of Cambridge University.[155] They went on to practice law for a time in London during a period of great political, social, philosophical and religious debate conducted in the press, especially the literary journals, and in discussion circles of all sorts.[156] Begbie had traveled widely in Europe and the Middle East before his translation to British Columbia.[157]

Training in the virtues of intellectual curiosity combined in these judges with a keen sense of the importance of their looking beyond local considerations and interests. The latter, they believed, were the product of narrow minds all too often ignorant of history and political and philosophical thought, and the lessons which that learning provided. Each man, it seems, considered his role as one of applying a cultured mind to the problems which presented themselves in court or in other public forums. As biographical work done on Field, Deady and Begbie shows, they took seriously the challenge of informing themselves.[158] Their pronouncements as judges make it clear that this was not arid learning. Into their decisions and other statements on the "Chinese question," as on other issues, are woven unmistakably the wisdom, as they saw it, of historians, and political, economic and philosophical thinkers.[159] Although they erred on the side of enthusiasm rather than discrimination in assimilating what they read, and tended to pragmatism and eclecticism as they sought plausible and feasible solutions to concrete problems, their views on the issue of race and its legal implications demonstrated considerably more understanding and principle than most of their contemporaries.

The parity of views of the two groups of judges in dealing with anti-Chinese measures is so close that one is left wondering whether it was simply a product of a conjunction of ideology and of formal borrowing by the British Columbia judiciary from the decisions of their California and Oregon counterparts. The similarity of reasoning and sentiment raises the question of whether they discussed these issues in person or corresponded with each other. At least one of the American judges, Matthew Deady, met with and was entertained by Begbie, Crease and Gray. Deady in his diary describes a visit to Victoria in 1880 during which he spent time with all of them, including a visit to the courthouse with the chief justice.[160] While the pages of the diary reveal little about the subject of their conversations, it is certainly not beyond the bounds of possibility that the problem of the Chinese was discussed.[161] There is also extant one letter which suggests that correspondence on the Chinese issue took place between some members of the two groups. In February 1886, shortly after his decision in the *Mee Wah* case, Begbie wrote to Deady enclosing a newspaper from which, he suggested, the American judge might "see that I have been following your example (and indeed citing your authority) for quashing by-laws [*sic*] against Chinamen." He also expressed satisfaction at being able to quote from Justice Field in striking down the Victoria laundry bylaw. The chief justice went on to note the recent anti-Chinese riots in Seattle and commented on the report that the authorities intended to use "military courts" to try the culprits. He expressed his approval, asserting that in such matters trial by jury was an impediment to justice:

> The writ of *habeas corpus*, free press, trial by jury, representative institutions even, fine things as they are in many cases are very inappropriate in others. A man who has a favourite horse would show little kindness to him in feeding him on champagne and pate de foie gras, or even on roast mutton, claret and potatoes.[162]

Although there is no record of Deady's response, it would not be idle speculation to suggest that his views on the desirability of "special" justice would have accorded with those of Begbie and that there was a process of mutual reinforcement at work here.

CONCLUSION

The explanation of why the members of the British Columbia court found the decisions of the California and Oregon courts in the matter of anti-Chinese legislation so compelling is twofold. First, they constituted the only juristic guidance available. Second, they were the product of a judicial frame of mind and of a cluster of political, social and economic beliefs which were shared in large part by the British Columbia judges. In both jurisdictions the prevailing judicial ideology was elitist, reflecting the strongly held view that neither government, economic policy nor law, particularly at a local level, could safely be left to the politicians and bureaucrats and that the judges occupied a special and rightful place as the guardians of constitutionalism. The latter embodied a set of values and norms which were believed to transcend the sectional, self-serving and chauvinistic interests and fads represented in legislative assemblies and municipalities.

The juncture of judicial ideology at this particular period in these two different places is explained by a common fear of popular democracy. In the United States the catalyst was in part reaction to the perceived excesses of the Jacksonian era and in part a response to the dual challenges of encouraging and managing the industrial and commercial energies released in the country after the Civil War.[163] By contrast in British Columbia, where responsible government and the extension of the franchise were recent phenomena, it was inspired by nostalgia for the colonial era which had put a premium on order and place. It is likely that this sentiment among Begbie and his colleagues was strengthened both by intellectual opposition to the further democratization of the franchise from the 1860s to 1880s in Britain, and by the evolution of a more aggressive imperial policy of colonization which condoned white settlement but at the same time stressed "trusteeship" of the lesser races.[164]

The fact that these judges were by and large as a group willing to transcend both widespread and virulent popular ethnocentrism and their own biases against members of another race suggests that judicial ideology is not simply and invariably the mirror image of prevailing political and social ideology, but is capable of creating its own moral and normative order. The extent to which Canadian and American courts have subscribed to or diverged from this position, and what that may tell us about the similarities and differences in how the relationship between law and politics is viewed in the two countries, is to date a largely ignored facet of North American legal culture. It stands as a significant challenge to legal historians.

NOTES

1. *Tai Sing v. Maguire* (1878), 1 B.C.R. Pt.II 101 (S.C.); *R. v. Wing Chong* (1885), 1 B.C.R. Pt.II 150 (S.C.); *R. v. Mee Wah* (1886), 3 B.C.R. 403 (Cty. Ct.); *R. v. Gold Commissioner of Victoria District* (1886), 1 B.C.R. Pt.II 260 (S.C., Full Ct.); *R. v. Corporation of Victoria* (1888), 1 B.C.R. Pt.II 331 (Div. Ct.).

2. Three of the judges, Chief Justice Begbie and Justices Crease and Gray, came in for particular criticism in 1885 because they had expressed, in public, favorable comments about the Chinese in connection with the Royal Commission on Chinese Immigration, 1885 (the former two as witnesses, the latter as commissioner). See *Victoria Daily Times*, 22 May 1885, 1 (Chief Justice denounced "in scathing terms" at public meeting); ibid., 23 May 1885, 2 (resolution at public meeting "fastening the blame of future bloodshed on the heads of our ... judicial rulers"); *Victoria Daily Colonist*, 4 August 1885, 3 (local M.P. inveighs against royal commission for failing to listen to local sentiment and not excluding the Chinese "hordes" altogether).

3. The cases which were cited with approval were *Lin Sing v. Washburn*, 20 Cal. Rep. 534 (S.C., 1862); *Ho Ah Kow v. Nunan*, 12 Fed. Cas. 252 (Circ. Ct., D. Cal., 1879); *Baker v. Portland*, 2 Fed. Cas. 472 (Circ. Ct., D. Oreg., 1879); *In re Tiburcio Parrott*, 1 Fed. Rep. 481 (Circ. Ct, D. Cal., 1880).

4. On the arrival of the Chinese to pan for gold, see P. Ward, *White Canada Forever: Popular Attitudes and Public Policy Towards Orientals in British Columbia*, 2nd ed. (Montreal/Kingston: McGill-Queen's University Press, 1990), 22-27; P. Roy, *A White Man's Province: British Columbia Politicians and Chinese and Japanese Immigrants 1858-1914* (Vancouver: University of British Columbia Press, 1989), 3-6.

5. Ibid., 27-31; 6-11. See also M. Zaffroni, "The Great Chain of Being: Racism and Imperialism in Colonial Victoria, 1858-1871" (M.A. thesis, University of Victoria, 1987), 26-66. For accounts of the U.S. experience, see S. Miller, *The Unwelcome Immigrant: The American Image of the Chinese, 1785-1882* (Berkeley: University of California Press, 1969); A. Saxton, *The Indispensable Enemy: Labour and the Anti-Chinese Movement in California* (Berkeley: University of California Press, 1971).

6. A prime example in British Columbia was Amor De Cosmos, newspaper editor, member of the Legislative Assembly, premier and later member of Parliament — G. Woodcock, *Amor De Cosmos: Journalist and Reformer* (Toronto: Oxford University Press, 1975). On the conversion of De Cosmos to the anti-Chinese cause, see Ward, *White Canada Forever*, 27-28. The importance of the press as opinion formers in colonial frontier societies is discussed in R. Evans, K. Saunders and K. Cronyn, *Exclusion, Exploitation and Extermination: Race Relations in Colonial Queensland* (Sydney: Australia and New Zealand Books, 1976), 15-16.

7. *Victoria Daily Colonist*, 6 March 1860 (report of public meeting).

8. On the position of Douglas and Begbie and their commitment to implanting British conceptions of law and justice on the frontier, see B. Gough, "Keeping British Columbia British: The Law and Order Question on a Gold Mining Frontier," *Huntington Library Quarterly* 38 (1975): 269.

9. Unsuccessful attempts to introduce a head tax were made on three occasions in 1871 — J. Hendrickson, ed., *Journals of the Legislatures of the Colonies of Vancouver Island and British Columbia, 1851-1871*, vol. 5 (Victoria: Public Archives of British Columbia, 1880), 400 (26 January 1871); British Columbia, *Journals of the Legislative Assembly*, vol. 1, 1872, 15-16. These scruples were not, however, seen as preventing the denial of the franchise

to the Chinese — see Act to Make Better Provisions for the Qualification of Voters, S.B.C. 1874, c. 12, s. 2.

10. Act to provide for the better collection of Provincial Taxes from the Chinese, S.B.C. 1878, c. 35. The Queensland statutes were: Act to regulate the Immigration of Chinese and to make provision against their becoming a charge upon the Colony, Stat. Q'ld., 1877, no. 8; Act to amend "The Gold Fields Act, 1874" so far as relates to Asiatic and African aliens and in Other Respects, Stat. Q'ld., 1877, no. 12.

11. Ibid., ss. 2, 8.

12. *Tai Sing v. Maguire* (1878), 1 B.C.R. Pt 1 101 (S.C.).

13. *Ling Sing v. Washburn*, 20 Cal. Rep. 534 (S.C., 1862).

14. *Tai Sing*, 104-05. Gray quoted from his own work, *Gray on Confederation* (Toronto: Copp, Clark, 1872), 55-56 to contrast the U.S. constitution in which the states had conferred powers on the federal government, retaining those not so granted for themselves, with the British North America Act under which the British Parliament had bestowed specific powers on the provinces, vesting any residual general power in the dominion Parliament. In the U.S. constitution, he suggested, power flowed upwards from the individual states, while in Canada it flowed down from a superior sovereign authority, Parliament in London.

    With regard to treaty-making power, Gray was well aware that the United States was the sovereign authority. The relationship of California to the United States was, he said, equivalent to that of Canada to Great Britain.

15. Ibid., 106.

16. Ibid., 113.

17. On dominion government policy on the railway and the "Chinese question," see P. Roy, "A Choice Between Evils: The Chinese and the Construction of the Canadian Pacific Railway in British Columbia," in H. Dempsey, ed., *The CPR West: The Iron Road and the Making of a Nation* (Vancouver: Douglas and MacIntyre, 1984), 13.

18. Act to Regulate the Chinese Population of British Columbia, S.B.C. 1884, c. 4. The companion enactments were an Act to prevent the Immigration of Chinese, S.B.C. 1884, c. 3, the purpose of which was to stem further immigration of Chinese to B.C., and the Act to prevent Chinese from Acquiring Crown Lands, S.B.C. 1884, c. 2, the title of which is self-explanatory.

19. Unlike the Chinese Immigration Act which was disallowed on the advice of the dominion government, the Chinese Regulation Act was allowed to stand by Ottawa. Minister of Justice Alexander Campbell expressed the view that its constitutional validity should be left to the courts to decide — W. Hodgins, *Correspondence, Reports of the Ministers of Justice and Orders-in-Council, 1867-1895* (Ottawa: Government Printing Bureau, 1896), 1060-65.

20. *R. v. Wing Chong* (1885), 1 B.C.R. Pt.II 150 (S.C.).

21. *Russell v. The Queen* (1881), 7 App. Cas. 829 (P.C., Can.); *Hodge v. The Queen* (1883), 9 App. Cas. 117 (P.C., Can.).

22. *Wing Chong*, 159.

23. Ibid., 160.

24. *In re Tiburcio Parrott*, 1 Fed. Rep. 481 (Circ. Ct., D. Cal., 1880).

25. *Wing Chong*, 160.

26. Ibid., 159-160.

27. Act to Regulate the Chinese Population of British Columbia, S.B.C. 1884, c. 4, s. 14.

28. *R. v. Gold Commissioner of Victoria District* (1886), 1 B.C.R. Pt.II 260 (Div. Ct.).

29. Act to restrict and regulate Chinese immigration into Canada, S.C. 1885, c. 71. The act drew inspiration from earlier Queensland legislation (see note 10) and a recent enactment of the New South Wales legislature — Act to restrict the influx of Chinese into New South Wales, Stat. N.S.W., 1881, No. II.

30. Act to amend the "Municipality Act," 1885 S.B.C., c. 21., ss. 10, 11.

31. *R. v. Mee Wah* (1886), 3 B.C.R. 403 (Cty. Ct.).

32. Ibid., 410.

33. The cases were *Lee* [sic] *Sing v. Washburn*, 20 Cal. Rep. 534 (S.C., 1862); *Baker v. Portland* 5 Law 750 (1879); *In re Teburcio Parrott*, 1 Fed. Rep. 481 (Circ. Ct., D. Cal., 1880); and *Ho Ah Kow v. Nunan*, 12 Fed. Cas. 252 (Circ. Ct., D. Cal., 1879) (the "Queue case").

34. *Mee Wah*, 412, quoting from *Ho Ah Kow v. Nunan*, 12 Fed. Cas. 252 (Circ. Ct., D. Cal., 1879), 255.

35. Ibid., 412.

36. Ibid., 412, quoting from the judgment of Justice Field in *Cummings v. Missouri* (1866), 71 U.S. Sup. Ct. Reps. 351, 365 (S.C., 1866).

37. See, for example, *R. v. Knowles, ex parte Sommersett* (1772), 20 State Trials 1.

38. In one of the earliest Canadian cases to reach the Privy Council, *Hodge v. The Queen* (1883), 9 A.C. 117 (P.C., Can.) the board had decided that the dominion Parliament and each provincial legislature had full plenary powers within their relative spheres of jurisdiction under the B.N.A. Act. Moreover, they could legislate on the same subject matter as long as the former related to a head of federal jurisdiction listed under section 91 and the latter to the exercise of local police powers by provinces under section 92.

39. On this development, see C. McClain, "The Chinese Struggle for Civil Rights in Nineteenth Century America: The First Phase, 1850-1870," *California Law Review* 72 (1984): 528.

40. British North America Act (1867), 30 & 31 Vict., c. 3.

41. In his decision in *R. v. Wing Chong* (1885), 1 B.C.R., Pt.II 150 (S.C.), 157-58, Justice Crease found nothing in *Hodge* which precluded an examination of the underlying intention and motives of provincial legislation in order to determine whether it genuinely fell within s. 92 or, by contrast, was an attempt to usurp federal jurisdiction under s. 91.

42. McClain, "The Chinese Struggle," 539-53. See in particular *People v. Naglee*, 1 Cal. Rep. 232 (S.C., 1850-51); *People v. Hall*, 4 Cal. Rep. 399 (S.C., 1854).

43. G. Browne, *The Judicial Committee and the British North America Act* (Toronto: University of Toronto Press, 1967).

44. C. McCurdy, "Stephen J. Field and the American Judicial Tradition," in P. Bergan, O. Fiss and C. McCurdy, *The Fields and the Law* (San Francisco: U.S.D.C. for N.D. of California Historical Society, 1986), 5.

45. Ibid., 10. For a more detailed discussion of *"laissez faire* constitutionalism," see C. McCurdy, "Justice Field and the Jurisprudence of Government-Business Relations: Some Parameters of Laissez Faire Constitutionalism, 1863-1897," in L. Friedman and H. Scheiber eds., *American Law and the Constitutional Order* (Cambridge, MA: Harvard University Press, 1978), 246-65. On the broader dimensions of constitutional interpretation in the the *postbellum* period, see H. Hyman and W. Wiecek, *Equal Justice*

under Law: Constitutional Development, 1835-1875 (New York: Harper and Row, 1982), 386-515; W. Nelson, *The Fourteenth Amendment: From Political Principle to Judicial Doctrine* (Cambridge, MA: Harvard University Press, 1988), 148-96.

46. McCurdy, "Stephen J. Field," 12-17.

47. L. Przybyszewski, "Judge Lorenzo Sawyer and the Chinese: Civil Rights Decisions in the Ninth Circuit," *Western Legal History* 1 (Winter/Spring 1988): 29-31.

48. Ibid., 23.

49. R. Mooney, "Matthew Deady and the Federal Judicial Response to Racism in the Early West," *Oregon Law Review* 63 (1984): 561-63, 577-84.

50. Ibid., 633.

51. R. Mooney, "Formalism and Fairness: Matthew Deady and Federal Public Land Law in the Early West," *Washington Law Review* 63 (1988): 368.

    The judicial activism of the members of the Ninth Judicial Circuit, especially on the "Chinese question," was recognized and disparaged by contemporaries. It was viewed with particularly jaundiced eyes by legal progressives concerned at what they saw as a more general trend towards the federal judges' usurpation of state legislative functions — Przybyszewski, "Judge Lorenzo Sawyer," 45-46.

52. That having been said, it is also important to recognize that they were not necessarily at one in terms of the objective to be attained. Here differences in political affinity intruded, for while Field, the Democrat, was careful to balance his activism with his commitment to a states' rights philosophy, Sawyer and Deady, both of whom possessed Republican sympathies, seem to have accepted as an article of faith that the national government was the predominant force within the Constitution. McCurdy, "Stephen J. Field"; Przybyszewski, "Judge Lorenzo Sawyer," 29-34; Mooney, "Deady and Racism," 633-34.

53. D. Williams, *The Man for A New Country: Sir Matthew Baillie Begbie* (Victoria: Sono Nis, 1977), 16-99.

54. Gough, "Keeping British Columbia British," 269.

55. Williams, *Man for a New Country*, 148-56.

56. D. Verchere, *A Progression of Judges: A History of the Supreme Court of British Columbia* (Vancouver: University of British Columbia Press, 1988), 42-46.

57. Williams, *Man for a New Country*, 159-62, 167; H. Foster, "The Struggle for the Supreme Court: Law and Politics in British Columbia, 1871-1885," in L. Knafla, ed., *Law and Justice in a New Land: Essays in Western Canadian Legal History* (Calgary: Carswell Ltd., 1986), 168-70.

58. Williams, *Man for a New Country*, 164; H. Foster, "The Kamloops Outlaws and Commissions of Assize in Nineteenth Century British Columbia," in D. Flaherty, ed., *Essays in the History of Canadian Law*, vol. 2 (Toronto: Osgoode Society, 1983), 310.

59. Foster, "Struggle."

60. C. Wallace, "John Hamilton Gray," *Dictionary of Canadian Biography*, vol 11, (Toronto: University of Toronto Press, 1982), 372-76.

61. On the "rule of law" ideology in British and Canadian legal thinking in the nineteenth century, see P. Romney, "Very Late Loyalist Fantasies: Nostalgic Tory History and the Rule of Law in Upper Canada," in W. Pue and B. Wright, *Canadian Perspectives on Law and Society: Issues in Legal History* (Ottawa: Carleton University Press, 1988), 119; P. Romney, "From the Rule of Law to Responsible Government: Ontario Political Culture

and the Roots of Canadian Statism" *Canadian Historical Association Papers* (1989): 86. Ironically Romney sees the last vestiges of Whig constitutionalism being played out in Canada in the notion of the protection of provincial rights.

62. As Hamar Foster has noted, the B.C. judges were even capable of rhetorical flourishes which challenged parliamentary sovereignty. Begbie in a memorandum to Premier George Walkem on the issue of where the power to make and change the rules of court lay invoked *Bonham's Case* (1610), 8 Co. Rep. 114a as authority for the proposition that by immemorial custom it was unconstitutional for Parliament to take this power from the judges — Foster, "Struggle," 200.

63. On the general trend to judicial support of business enterprise and initiative after the Civil War, see J. Lurie, *Law and Nation, 1865-1912* (New York: Alfred Knopf, 1983), 27-42. R. McCloskey, *American Conservatism in the Age of Enterprise* (Cambridge, MA: Harvard University Press, 1951), 72-126 interpreted the Field record on the Supreme Court as reflecting an unrelenting commitment to free enterprise jurisprudence. For a fuller and more balanced approach, see McCurdy, "Justice Field."

64. McCloskey, *American Conservatism*, 121-22, attributes this change to what he described as a "vicious campaign of vilification" against Field for his stand against harassment of the Chinese, and hints that it might have been assisted by Field's unsuccessful bid to secure the backing of California's Democratic Convention for his presidential candidacy in 1884. In fact Field continued to side with the Chinese in the most obvious cases of harassment — see *Baldwin v. Franks*, 120 U.S. 679 (1887). The latter case and its legal significance is analyzed in full in C. McClain, "The Chinese Struggle for Civil Rights in 19th. Century America: The Unusual Case of *Baldwin v. Franks*," *Law and History Review* 3 (1985): 349.

65. *How Ah Kow v. Nunan*, 12 Fed. Cas. 252 (Circ. Ct., D. Cal., 1879).

66. *In re Tiburcio Parrott*, 1 Fed. Rep. 481 (Circ. Ct., D. Cal., 1880).

67. Ibid., 518-19.

68. Ibid., 519.

69. Ibid., 521.

70. Mooney, "Deady and Racism," 633-34.

71. *Baker v. City of Portland*, 2 Fed. Cas. 472, 475 (Circ. Ct., D. Ore., 1879).

72. Chinese Exclusion Act, 25 Stat. U.S. 504 (1888).

73. *In re Yung Sing Hee*, 36 F. 437, 439 (Circ. Ct., D. Ore., 1888).

74. Mooney, "Deady and Racism," 633-34.

75. Royal Commission on Chinese Immigration, *Report and Evidence* (Ottawa: Queen's Printer, 1885) (Report of Justice John H. Gray, Commissioner), lxxii.

76. Ibid., *Minutes of Evidence* (Crease), 143.

77. Ibid., (Begbie), 73.

78. In his evidence Begbie expatiated at some length on the human characteristic of suspicion of, and hostility towards, those of different race or ethnic background especially when they were perceived to be seeking or exploiting an economic advantage. In particular he drew parallels between the treatment accorded to the "Jews of Europe" and the Chinese in North America as the "scapegoats" of envy, insecurity and ignorance of the dominant community — ibid., 72.

79. K. Smith, *James Fitzjames Stephen: Portrait of a Victorian Rationalist* (Cambridge: Cambridge University Press, 1988), 190-96.

80. McCurdy, "Stephen J. Field," 6-12.

81. For evidence of Field's concern about the need to protect social interests, see McCurdy, "Justice Field," 250-51.

82. See especially *Ho Ah Kow v. Nunan*, 12 Fed. Cas. 252 (Circ. Ct., D. Cal., 1879); McCloskey, *American Conservatism*, 109-11.

83. *In re Quong Woo*, 13 Fed. Rep. 229 (Circ. Ct., D. Cal., 1882).

84. Ibid., 233.

85. On his connections with Stanford and Huntington, see C. Swisher, *Stephen J. Field: Craftsman of the Law* (Hamden, CN: Archon Books, 1963), 240-67.

86. Ibid.

87. Mooney, "Deady and Racism," 634-36.

88. Ibid., 635-36.

89. Przybyszewski, "Judge Lorenzo Sawyer," 53.

90. Ibid.

91. *In re Tiburcio Parrott*, 1 Fed. Rep. 481, 497-99 (Circ. Ct., D. Cal., 1880). On the career of Ogden Hoffman and his approach to the "Chinese question" see C. Fritz, "Judge Ogden Hoffman and Northern District of California," *Western Legal History* 1 (1988): 107-10; C. Fritz, *Federal Justice: The California Court of Ogden Hoffman 1851-1891* (Lincoln: University of Nebraska Press), 210-49.

92. Ibid., 509-10, 516.

93. *In re Wo Lee*, 26 Fed. Rep. 471 (Circ. Ct., D. Cal., 1886).

94. Ibid., 474.

95. Przybyszewski, "Judge Lorenzo Sawyer," 53.

96. Royal Commission, *Minutes of Evidence* (Begbie), 71. The Chief Justice went on to suggest that this facility for hard work was the cause of the unpopularity of the Chinese.

97. Royal Commission, *Minutes of Evidence* (Crease), 143.

98. Williams, *Man for a New Country*, 200.

99. Royal Commission, *Minutes of Evidence* (Begbie), 77.

100. Ibid.

101. Ibid., *Report* (Gray), lxviii-lxix.

102. Ibid., lxix.

103. *R. v. Mee Wah* (1886), 3 B.C.R. 403 (B.C. Cty. Ct.) (laundry); *R. v. Gold Commissioner of Victoria District* (1886), 1 B.C.R. Pt.II 260 (S.C., Full Ct.) (business in mining community); *R. v. Corporation of Victoria* (1888), 1 B.C.R. Pt.II 331 (Div. Ct.) (pawnbroking).

104. *R. v. Corporation of Victoria* (1888), 1 B.C.R. Pt.II 331 (Div. Ct.).

105. Ibid., 332.

106. Royal Commission, *Report* (Gray), lxxiii.

107. McCurdy, "Stephen J. Field," 13-17. A useful graphic representation of this rights theory is found in Hyman and Wiecek, *Equal Justice Under Law*, 396.

108. Ibid., 13-14.

100. Ibid., 14.

110. Ibid., 17. The Chinese were denied access to citizenship during this period, see E.

Sandmeyer, *The Anti-Chinese Movement in California* (Urbana, IL: University of Illinois Press, 1939), 46-47.

111. *Ho Ah Kow v. Nunan*, 12 Fed. Cas. 252 (Circ. Ct., D. Cal., 1879).

112. Ibid., 256. He had made the same point in an earlier decision, *In re Ah Fong*, I Fed. Cas. 213 (Circ. Ct., D. Cal., 1874), 217.

113. *Chae Chang Ping v. United States*, 130 U.S. 1068, 1071-1073 (S.C., 1888).

114. Fritz, "Judge Ogden Hoffman," 108.

115. Przybyszewski, "Judge Lorenzo Sawyer," 25.

116. Ibid., 43.

117. Ibid., 41.

118. Ibid., 44-45.

119. Ibid., 55. The author actually records the year as 1890. Professor Fritz has indicated that that is incorrect and that the statement was made by Sawyer in 1886 in the midst of the *habeas corpus* cases handled by him and Hoffman (Correspondence from C. Fritz, 15 April 1991).

120. Ibid., 55, n. 125. "Sawyer's notions of acceptable roles for the Chinese seem to me the necessary forerunner of the peculiar division of rights that McCurdy ... finds Field indulging in. Once a truly equal position is threatened from one side and rejected from the other, legislators and then judges must construct a range of types of rights to counter the variety of demands that the struggle for full equality rights might engender."

121. *In re Impaneling and Instructing the Grand Jury*, 26 Fed. Cas. 749 (Dist. Ct., Ore., 1886).

122. *Baker v. City of Portland*, 2 Fed. Cas. 472, 474 (Circ. Ct, D. Ore., 1879).

123. M. Clark, ed., *The Diary of Judge Matthew P. Deady 1871-1892: Pharisee Among the Philistines* (Portland, OR: Oregon Historical Society, 1975), vol. 1, 104. In describing the attempts to deal with a fire in Portland in 1872, Deady noted: 'The poor Chinamen were cruelly used by the Fenian Guards [Emmet Guard, Company B, 2nd. Brigade, Oregon Militia] and the street Arabs upon pretense of making them work the engines."

124. *Ex parte Ah Lit*, 26 F. 512, 513 (Dist. Ct., Ore., 1886).

125. Mooney, "Deady and Racism," 637.

126. Ibid., 635-36.

127. Deady was a friend and confidant of Stephen J. Field, and is said to have "agreed, with some mutual reservations, on most of the larger legal questions of the day" with his senior colleague — M. Clark, ed., "My Dear Judge — Excerpts from the Letters of Justice Stephen J. Field to Judge Matthew P. Deady," *Western Legal History* 1 (1988): 81.

128. Royal Commission, *Report*, (Gray), lv. After describing the false description on a statue of George III commissioned by his son, George IV, which read *"Pius filius optimo Patri"* Gray observed "it ... clearly indicates one suggestion that to arrive at truth, we must examine the characters of those who give characters to themselves or others, as well as the characters of those to whom the characters are given."

129. Royal Commission, *Minutes of Evidence*, (Begbie), 80; (Crease), 143-44.

130. Ibid., (Begbie), 74-75.

131. Ibid., (Crease), 144.

132. *Report*, lvi-lix.

133. Ibid., lxv-lxvi; *Minutes of Evidence*, (Begbie), 74, 80; (Crease), 148.

134. *Minutes of Evidence*, (Begbie), 73-74.

135. Ibid., (Crease), 143-44.

136. *Report*, lxiii-lxvi. Gray did agree with his colleagues that the Chinese showed probity and honesty in their business dealings.

137. Ibid., lx-lxi.

138. Ibid., lxi-lxii. "[A]n adherence to truth ... is simply an admission of weakness... Duplicity and capacity to deceive are of higher value than truth."

139. Ibid., lxii-lxiii.

140. *Minutes of Evidence*, (Crease), 146.

141. Ibid., (Begbie), 82.

142. *Report*, lxxxvi-lxxxvii.

143. *Minutes of Evidence*, (Crease), 145.

144. Ibid., (Crease), 146.

145. Ibid., (Begbie), 73.

146. Ibid.

147. *Report*, lx-lxi.

148. Ibid., lxii-lxiii. These precedents led Gray to recommend in his report a joint judicial and administrative tribunal in British Columbia to settle all civil disputes involving Chinese and to administer the tax and inheritance laws and public health regulations as they applied to the Chinese population — lxxxvi-lxxxix.

149. Hoffman's record in upholding the rights of Chinese laborers in the face of the Exclusion Acts of the 1880s and running what he and Sawyer described as a "habeas corpus" mill is examined in C. Fritz, "A Nineteenth Century 'Habeas Corpus Mill': The Chinese Before the Federal Courts in California," *American Journal of Legal History* 32 (1888): 345. Fritz (at p. 372) suggests that, despite Hoffman's own anti-Chinese proclivities and desire not to engage in this form of adjudication, the judge "could not avoid that obligation without repudiating his concept of judicial review, duty and common law tradition. This Hoffman was not prepared to do." After 1885 when Gray submitted his report he continued to favor protecting the rights of Chinese already resident in British Columbia.

150. Clark, "My Dear Judge," 79.

151. McCurdy, "Stephen J. Field," 6-7.

152. Fritz, *Federal Justice*, 1-10.

153. Clark, *The Diary of Judge Matthew Deady*, vol.1, xxxii-xxxiii.

154. Clark, "My Dear Judge," 80.

155. Williams, *Man for a New Country*, 9-14; Verchere, *A Progression of Judges*, 42-43. Begbie read mathematics and classics at Cambridge.

156. Williams, *Man for a New Country*, 16-25.

157. Although we know less about Gray's education and extracurricular life, he did receive a "classical education," graduating from King's College, Windsor, Nova Scotia with a B.A. — Wallace, "John Hamilton Gray," 372.

158. McCurdy, "Stephen J. Field," 5; Mooney, "Matthew Deady," 561; Williams, *Man for a New Country*, 216-17. Deady's diary is full of references to books which he had just read or was in the process of reading. Williams's biography of Begbie portrays an

individual with a wide range of interests including languages, meteorology, mathematics, classical literature, sketching and cartography.

159. On the Chinese question, as their decisions indicate, both sets of judges had a clear understanding of recent Chinese history and the involvement of both the European powers and the United States in the affairs of that country. In the Royal Commission Report of Gray and the evidence before the commission of Begbie there are direct quotations from contemporary authors on China and in the case of the chief justice on the historical experience of other rejected peoples, notable the Jews. Begbie and Crease in their evidence give the impression that they were aware of the writing of *laissez-faire* economists. Begbie also seems to have been tuned into the critiques of an extended franchise current in Britain at that time.

160. Clark, *The Diary of Judge Matthew Deady*, vol. 1, 313-15. This visit post-dates the first of the B.C. decisions, *Tai Sing*, and pre-dates the other four. It was only the previous year that Deady had rendered his first and celebrated judgment in *Baker v. City of Portland*.

161. This is a question which warrants further examination.

162. Oregon Historical Society Archives, Deady Papers, MSS. 48, Box 2, B274. Letter, Begbie to Deady, 18 February 1886.

163. McCurdy, "Justice Field."

164. On the development of this sentiment, see J. Manning Ward, *Colonial Self-Government* (Toronto: University of Toronto Press, 1976), 233-46.

Water Law of the Canadian West: Influences from the Western States

David R. Percy

INTRODUCTION

The development of Canadian private law has been much more heavily influenced by the English common law than its American counterpart. Even to the present day, the Canadian law of property, torts and contracts bears distinct, though diminishing, signs of its English roots. However, for well over a century the concepts of private law that were applied to Canada's natural resources have assumed a distinctly American appearance, in demonstration of the principle that resources law is shaped more by climatic and geographical imperatives than by legal tradition.

Nowhere is this trend more evident than in the development of western Canadian water law, which has been heavily influenced by American concepts since the earliest days of European settlement. As a result, the water law of the provinces of western Canada bears far more similarity to the regimes found in the western United States than to the common-law based systems of Ontario or Atlantic Canada. The water-law systems of those regions in turn are closely related to those of the central and eastern United States.[1]

The mere observation that regional similarities exist in North American water law provides little justification for even the present tentative historical exploration. There are, however, three more important reasons for this essay. First, although the historical connection with the United States was so obvious and so important in the earliest days of Canadian water law, this relationship was quickly forgotten. From a common starting point, Canadian and American water law has subsequently developed along largely separate lines. Second, although the amateur legal historian must be very conscious of the simplistic approach to drawing lessons from history, much can be learned in Canada from subsequent developments in western American water law. Because of climate and because intensive economic development generally occurred at an earlier date, the common central concepts of water law were first subjected to stress in the United States. It is thus possible to predict which portions of Canadian water law will require change as the demands on the available supply increase, and to canvass some of the options for reform that have been applied in the United States. Indeed, the American experience provides Canadian provinces the opportunity to avoid costly legal disputes in the future by recognizing some glaring defects in their water law and addressing those defects before a crisis occurs. Third, an examination of the history of western water law in both countries reveals an unexpected Australian connection. This connection allows an examination of how a water-law regime that was based on similar principles has developed in a very different context and of solutions to common problems that were adopted in Australia.

In order to address these issues, there will be a discussion in the second section of the essay of the reception in western North America of the common-law doctrine of riparian rights. In the third and fourth sections the development of water law in British Columbia and in the prairie provinces respectively will be described. Finally, the fifth section will evaluate the type of challenges that Canadian water law will inevitably have to meet in the future in order to resolve the problems already faced by American states with similar water-law regimes.

RECEPTION OF RIPARIAN RIGHTS IN WESTERN JURISDICTIONS

European settlers in western North America did not approach water-law problems with a clean legal slate. In the early years of settlement, the English common-law doctrine of riparian rights would ordinarily have applied to resolve conflicts in water use. Under the doctrine of riparian rights in the form which it had assumed by the mid-nineteenth century, water rights were restricted to those who owned property adjoining a watercourse. Riparian owners were entitled to receive the flow of water to their property undiminished in quantity and unimpaired in quality, subject only to the right of upstream riparians to take sufficient water for their domestic purposes. In addition, upstream riparians were entitled to use water for nondomestic purposes, provided that they did not perceptibly diminish the flow of the stream and thereby interfere with the rights of other riparians.[2]

The doctrine of riparian rights bore clear signs of its development in a country that enjoyed abundant natural water supplies. When its possible transplantation to more arid jurisdictions was considered, it became clear that the doctrine suffered from at least three serious defects. First, the restriction of the right to use water to riparian owners, who were entitled to use the water only on riparian lands, inhibited the development of land that was distant from a good source of water. Second, even riparian owners could not use water intensively, for they were not entitled to substantially diminish the flow of water in the watercourse.[3] Third, in times of shortage when there was insufficient water to meet the needs of all riparian owners, there was no system of priorities to allocate water to its most important uses. All riparian owners had equal claims to the resource and in practice the ability to obtain water was determined by the location of the riparian owner. Those who had settled upstream had a greater chance of fulfilling their entitlement to water by intercepting the stream flow before it reached downstream neighbors.[4]

All jurisdictions in western North America discovered that these defects made the riparian doctrine an entirely unsuitable method of allocating water rights and determining priorities in water use. It was never applied for more than a brief period in any of the water-short regions of western North America or in the more arid states of Australia. However, the method by which riparian rights were abolished or curtailed demonstrates some significant differences in legal culture. In the United States, the doctrine of riparian rights was first modified by practical necessity in the mining camps of the California gold rush.[5] As settlement spread across the Great Plains and Rocky Mountain states, the doctrine was most frequently abolished by bold acts of judicial legislation. In a classic judgment in 1882, the Colorado Supreme Court concluded that the riparian doctrine was inapplicable in an arid region and that "imperative necessity, unknown to the countries which gave it birth, compels the recognition of another doctrine in conflict therewith."[6] In western Canada, on the contrary, all inroads on the riparian doctrine occurred through the legislative process, which began as early as 1858 in British Columbia.[7] In the prairie provinces, riparian rights became the object of a political outcry before alternative water-law regimes were studied by a government commission and legislation was introduced in 1894.[8] In the Australian state of Victoria, after a limited statute was passed in 1883, a royal commission in 1884 led to a significant curtailment of riparian rights in the Irrigation Act of 1886.[9]

The contrast in the approaches to replacing the doctrine of riparian rights is partly explained by the differing views on the role of the courts in reforming unsuitable laws that were held in the United States on the one hand and in Canada and Australia on the other. The characteristically bold innovations exhibited by the American courts can be readily contrasted with the "judicial philosophy of passivity"[10] that prevailed in systems based on English law. However, it is equally important not to exaggerate the effects of this difference in philosophy because, in other areas of water law, Canadian courts exhibited a surprising degree of activism.[11] In reality, the careful approach taken to legislative change in Canada appears to have been the result of both a difference in legal culture and a conscious policy choice. The main architect of the legislation that was applied to the Canadian Prairies introduced many of the judicially developed concepts of American law in order to curtail riparian rights. However, he urged a system based on strong government control in order to avoid the litigiousness of the American approach, which he considered might be profitable for lawyers but contrary to the interests of agriculture.[12]

Although it was reformed by different methods, the common-law doctrine was found universally wanting in the face of hostile geographical conditions. The main focus of this essay is to trace the sources of the law that replaced it in western Canada.

DEVELOPMENT OF BRITISH COLUMBIA WATER LAW

The demise of the doctrine of riparian rights in the western United States, and its replacement by a principle which protected the rights of those who first put water to productive use, was influenced by a number of factors. There were indications of more extensive applications of water than the riparian doctrine would allow in both the practices of the early aboriginal inhabitants[13] and the law and institutions of the Spanish colonists in the area of the continent that now constitutes the American Southwest.[14] The early Mormon settlers who colonized Utah adopted a system of water titles that was certainly inconsistent with the principles of riparian rights and ultimately had an influence on the Canadian Prairies.[15] There is little evidence that any of these sources produced more than the seeds of prior appropriation, which was soon to replace riparian rights throughout the American West, but they undoubtedly involved uses of water not permitted by the common law. The most important impetus for a new legal regime came from the practices of the mining camps established during the California gold rush in 1848 and 1849.[16] Gold mining is a water-intensive business and, in order to allow the acquisition of secure water rights, the miners adapted the principle of staking which they had employed in order to acquire the right to mine in the first place. In acquiring rights to water, their practice generally required posting and recording of an intention to divert a specified quantity of water, actual diversion, putting the water to beneficial use with reasonable diligence, and the continued exercise of the right. In addition, the right to use water was subject to forfeiture if the rules were not complied with and priorities in water use were determined according to the date at which the "claim" to water was posted or staked.[17]

The practice of the mining camps was ultimately codified in California water law[18] and it contained all the elements of the developed doctrine of prior appropriation. The right to water did not depend on the ownership of riparian land but was gained by the person who first put water to beneficial use. The quantity of water was not limited by the rights of downstream users, but only by the amount required for the purpose of the appropriator. In times of shortage, water was allocated according to seniority, so that the first appropriators were permitted to receive their total entitlement before a junior appropriator could take any water at all.

The influence of the California gold rush on the development of the central concepts of western American water law is beyond doubt. Its influence on British Columbia water law is more indirect.

The riparian system that British Columbia would ordinarily have inherited did not disappear as swiftly as it did in the western United States. Instead, as an early commentator noted, it was gradually "whittled" away by a series of legislative enactments.[19] This process began with the British Columbia gold rush of 1858, which inevitably required the curtailment of riparian rights, unless placer mining was to be conducted without any regard for existing law. It was clear from a variety of enactments that Governor Douglas was determined to avoid legal disorder during the gold rush[20] and his early regulation of gold mining had an important incidental effect on water law.

As might be expected, the legislation was shaped both by the responses of those jurisdictions which had experienced earlier gold rushes and the practices of those who had participated in them. Many of the miners were veterans of the New Zealand and California gold rushes and, as Lou Knafla has observed, "they brought with them well-established systems of law and government"[21] and, in some camps, imported their law directly from California. The drafting of the early legislation was entrusted to Sir Matthew Begbie who, as David Williams has pointed out, drew heavily on New Zealand and Australian sources, at least for those sections that dealt purely with mining.[22] A proclamation of Governor Douglas in 1859, commonly known as the Gold Fields Act, was clearly intended to allow miners to obtain some type of water privilege, but despite Begbie's drafting skills it is difficult to state the effect of the proclamation with any precision. Its effect was not limited to gold-mining districts or to miners, for it allowed any person to register a "ditch or water privilege" with the gold commissioner. In case of dispute over mining claims or ditches and water privileges, the matter was to be resolved in the first instance by the relevant gold commissioner, who was required to determine priorities according to the date of registration of the claim, ditch or water privilege in question.[23] Regulations required a description of the proposed ditch head and the quantity of water required, and water rights were granted for a term not exceeding five years.[24]

Beyond this very basic description, the legislation does not describe in any detail the effect of the water rights granted to an applicant. By inference, it recognizes that a water right might be acquired even if the applicant did not own riparian land and it appears to have been intended to apply only to miners, although no such limitation appears in the legislation. A land proclamation of the same year makes an oblique reference to the possibility of any holder of Crown lands obtaining a ditch privilege,[25] but it did not become clear until 1870 that all those entitled to hold a right of preemption to Crown land and "lawfully occupying and bona fide cultivating [Crown] land" were entitled to divert any unrecorded or unappropriated water for agricultural or other purposes.[26] At that time, a district commissioner was authorized to record diversions of this nature, which received priority according to the date of the record.[27] The 1870 legislation still bore traces of the riparian doctrine, for it authorized the grant of water records only in respect of watercourses adjacent to or passing through Crown land held by the applicant. However, for the first time, an express limitation on riparian rights was imposed by a declaration that riparian owners had no exclusive right to take water unless a water record was first obtained.[28] The effect of this provision does not appear to have been general, for the 1870 legislation applied only to water that flowed on or adjacent to Crown lands.

The water rights of holders of public lands were better defined in an 1875 codification of Crown lands legislation. As of that date, the restriction of water rights to those who held a right of preemption had been removed and water rights accrued to all those who were "lawfully entitled to hold" Crown lands and who were lawfully occupying and *bona fide* cultivating such lands.[29] The characteristics of water rights were better defined, as the holder was allowed only such quantity of water as was "reasonably necessary" for agricultural and other purposes.[30] A water right was not perfected until the necessary ditches had been constructed and the extent of the right was limited by the capacity of the ditch.[31] The holders of water rights were given additional flexibility by a provision that allowed them to obtain a right of entry upon land owned by another for the conveyance of water, upon payment of compensation which could be fixed by the commissioner if it was not agreed by the parties.[32] At the same time, the principle was clearly established that priority in water rights was dependent on the date that the right was recorded, although the right of water users to enforce priorities in water use by resort to self-help was strictly limited.[33] This embryonic code of water rights also included a general prohibition against waste.[34]

The water rights of holders of Crown lands were further consolidated in 1884,[35] but remained substantially unchanged until 1897. Although all the early legislation demonstrated the Crown's ability to assert control over water, the basis of Crown power was made explicit by a declaration in the Water Privileges Act of 1892, which vested in the provincial Crown the right to the use of all water in any watercourse in the province, unless it was within federal jurisdiction.[36] As will be shown later, this legislative formula was very similar to that which had been used in 1886 in the Australian state of Victoria and which would later be adopted on the Canadian Prairies in 1894.[37]

At this stage, when the development of water law on the Canadian Prairies was in its early stages, British Columbia water law was drawn from three sources. Water rights on Crown lands were dealt with under public-lands legislation, water rights for mining purposes were granted under the Mining Acts,[38] although they could also be granted under public-lands legislation,[39] and the Water Privileges Act regulated other types of water rights. Only in 1897 were the separate strands of legislation drawn together in the Water Clauses Consolidation Act, which was intended to constitute "an exclusive and comprehensive law governing the granting of water-rights and privileges."[40]

The early British Columbia legislation thus adopted a number of concepts from western American water law, particularly in the determination of priorities between water rights. However, it did so by means of detailed statutory schemes of which the cornerstone was the declaration that the right to use all water was vested in the Crown. The 1897 act was more than a mere consolidation of existing water legislation. It set out a statutory code that permitted the Crown to grant rights in the water which was vested in it for agricultural, domestic, mechanical, industrial, mining and related purposes.[41] The system that it established should be described as one of prior allocation rather than prior appropriation, for in order to obtain a water right it was necessary not simply to put the water to beneficial use, as the doctrine of prior appropriation required, but to make an application to the relevant representative of the commissioner of Lands and Works or of the gold commissioner.[42] Once granted, however, British Columbia water rights were similar to those granted under the American doctrine of prior appropriation. The rights were generally granted without term and their exercise was limited only by the principle of reasonable use and prohibitions against waste.[43] Disputes between holders of water rights and allocations in time of shortage were governed by the principle of priority in time which, under the British Columbia legislation, ordinarily depended upon the date that the water right was recorded.[44] In order to obtain a water right, the applicant was required by section 11 of the act to provide notice of an intention to apply for a record. In the interim, before the record was granted, priorities were determined according to the date of the applicant's notice.[45]

As a result, by 1897 British Columbia possessed a comprehensive and detailed code of water rights. The code had its origins in the American doctrine of prior appropriation, but some of its legislative roots were found in the state of Victoria. In the same era, major water legislation was also being developed in the prairie provinces and this will be considered in the following section of this essay.

DEVELOPMENT OF WATER LAW ON THE CANADIAN PRAIRIES

On the Canadian Prairies it was irrigation rather than mining that exposed the shortcomings of the riparian doctrine. As agricultural settlement followed in the wake of the Canadian Pacific Railway, the need for irrigation was not immediately apparent because unusually heavy precipitation in the southern Prairies ensured good growing conditions until 1887. The onset of a lengthy drought in that year both created an obvious need for irrigated agriculture and began to emphasize the incompatibility of irrigation and riparian rights.[46]

The defects in the riparian-rights doctrine that first emerged through mining activities in British Columbia also threatened to hamper agricultural development on the Prairies. In particular, the restriction of water rights to riparian land posed an almost insurmountable obstacle to the development of farms that were distant from good sources of water. This problem was exacerbated by the tendency of early settlers to claim land close to watercourses and to fence them off, thus depriving range cattle of access to water.[47] A number of minor irrigation projects were begun despite the prevailing law of riparian rights, but a major impetus for reform was provided by Mormon settlers in southwestern Alberta. They brought considerable knowledge and experience of irrigation farming from Utah, together with, no doubt, a familiarity with Mormon systems for the allocation of water rights. The Mormon elder, Charles Card, became a strong advocate of the enactment of a new model of water law that would allow the guaranteed supply of water to irrigation.[48] Card found an influential supporter in William Pearce who, as superintendent of Mines for the Department of the Interior stationed in Calgary, saw at first hand the difficulty of carrying on agriculture in an arid region.

Pearce became an enthusiastic convert to irrigation and vigorously promoted the need for new legislation. In 1892 he was recalled to Ottawa to begin work on legislation, while in 1893 and 1894, J.S. Dennis, chief inspector of Surveys for the Department of the Interior, was sent to examine irrigation systems and laws in operation in Washington, California, Utah and Colorado.[49] Their joint work led to the introduction in 1893 of a bill for the purposes of discussion and ultimately to the Northwest Irrigation Act of 1894.[50] Although the sources of British Columbia water law emerged generally as a matter of inference, the legal roots of the Northwest Irrigation Act are well documented. As in British Columbia, the core of the legislation involved the restriction of riparian rights and the vesting in the Crown of the right to use all surface water. It was acknowledged by the framers of the act that the formula for this was taken directly from the Victoria Irrigation Act of 1886.[51] The principle of prior appropriation to govern the allocation of water supply during times of shortage was borrowed from American law and some sections of the act are almost a codification of American prior-appropriation law as it stood in the last decade of the nineteenth century.[52] Pearce's own files emphasize the influence on the new Canadian legislation of Australian and American law, for they contain a summary of the Victoria Irrigation Act as well as detailed analyses of the laws of some western states.[53]

Although it is reported that the effect of the act on riparian rights was contentious, it was passed after only two days of debate, in contrast to the twenty-six days that had been required for similar legislation in New South Wales.[54] Its easy passage was fostered by political pressure from an irrigation convention held in Calgary in March 1894, which Pearce himself encouraged as a means of strengthening the government's resolve,[55] and also by weather conditions on the second day of debate, which were described as "sweltering."[56] As a result of this process, the bulk of the territory that now comprises the provinces of Manitoba, Saskatchewan and Alberta became governed by a law in which water rights were vested in the Crown and the Crown allocated those water rights by way of license on a first come, first served basis. Conflicts in water use were decided according to a priority that was determined by the date upon which the application for a license was first submitted.[57]

There is thus a great deal of similarity between the water law that applied on the Prairies from 1894 and that which applied in British Columbia after 1897. This fundamental similarity might be thought to have resulted from cooperation between resource managers in the federal and British Columbia governments, or at least from a cross-fertilization of ideas from the two pieces of legislation. Certainly, a superficial analysis of the legislation suggests that this might have occurred. British Columbia had adopted a formula vesting water in the Crown in 1892 that was substantially similar to that contained in the Irrigation Act of 1894[58] and both acts incorporated the central concepts of prior appropriation. However, an examination of the available documentation of the legislative history and of the texts of the acts suggests that they were both derived from common external sources and that they had little, if any, influence on each other.

British Columbia's vesting formula and statutory adoption of the principle of prior allocation both existed by 1892 and would have afforded a ready model for the architects of the Irrigation Act. Perhaps their influence was limited because of the fragmentary state of British Columbia legislation at that time, but in any event they do not appear to have come to the attention of Pearce or Dennis. In his own account of the development of the Northwest Irrigation Act, Dennis stated that it was based on "a careful examination of existing laws in the different states and territories of the United States, in Australia and elsewhere where irrigation was practised."[59] His own investigation concentrated on the western United States and his assessment of British Columbia legislation and practices suggested that they were discarded as a possible model. Although Dennis acknowledges the development of irrigation in central British Columbia, he notes that it was limited in scope and governed by the Land Act. In his opinion, the provisions of the Land Act were "as far as they go clear and definite" but they were "of a very incomplete character and will require considerable additions and amendments as soon as the principle of irrigation comes into more common use."[60] It will be recalled that the water-rights provisions of the Land Act were indeed rudimentary at this stage,[61] and Dennis's criticisms of them were certainly justified, but he does not seem to have been aware of the existence of the Water Privileges Act of 1892. The parliamentary Debates at the time the Northwest Irrigation Act received first reading provide some further evidence for this position, for the minister assured the House of Commons that American law, especially that of California, Idaho, Montana and Wyoming, as well as Australian law, had been fully considered in drafting the legislation. He made no mention of the influence of British Columbia law.[62]

The texts of the relevant statutes also suggest that the legislative incorporation of the principles of prior appropriation in British Columbia had no effect on the drafting of the Northwest Irrigation Act and that the Water Clauses Consolidation Act of 1897 in British Columbia was drafted with no regard to the Irrigation Act. Sections establishing the priority of water rights in British Columbia had existed since the Gold Fields Act of 1859.[63] By 1870 the land ordinance expressed the prevailing rule by the words "[p]riority of right to any ... water privilege, in case of dispute, shall depend on priority of record."[64] Similar language was used in the water-rights provisions of mining legislation and was carried forward to the Water Clauses Consolidation Act of 1897.[65] In contrast, the Northwest Irrigation Act incorporated the same principle in totally different and much more wordy phraseology. The relevant section of the Northwest Irrigation Act constituted in effect a twenty-three-line paraphrase of the judicially developed American law of prior appropriation.[66]

There are many other differences in the style of the federal and British Columbia legislation that suggest that neither was influenced by the other. The British Columbia Act was far longer and more comprehensive and dealt in detail with matters such as the exercise of the commissioner's discretion to grant a water record, and the principle of reasonable use,[67] as well as contentious issues such as providing water rights to Indian reserves and tying water rights to the land in respect of which they were issued.[68] In contrast, the Northwest Irrigation Act failed to deal with any of these items, except for procedures to be observed in getting a license, for which it set out merely a few formalities.

Despite the similarity of the underlying principles, it appears likely that British Columbia and the prairie provinces arrived at their similar basic water law by separate routes. This hypothesis is hardly surprising, for British Columbia would no doubt have been interested in the experience of jurisdictions which had modified water law in order to accommodate mining, while irrigation was by far the greatest concern on the Prairies. Research for either purpose would have resulted in the recognition from American experience that the principle of prior appropriation provided an expedient solution to the immediate problems of each jurisdiction. The Victoria vesting formula provided a convenient basis for the implementation of this principle in colonial jurisdictions and it is quite possible that British Columbia and the federal government decided independently to adopt the formula. The framers of the

Northwest Irrigation Act acknowledged their Australian source directly and British Columbia legislation had been influenced by the Victoria experience since the earliest days.[69] It would have been relatively easy in the early years for British Columbia to remain current with legal developments in Victoria through the Colonial Office. The connection may also have been preserved through personal contact, as Alfred Deakin, commissioner for Water Supply for the state of Victoria (and subsequently prime minister of Australia) is recorded as having visited the western United States in 1885 in his capacity as chairman of a royal commission that ultimately recommended the passage of the Victoria Irrigation Act of 1886.[70]

HISTORICAL ANTECEDENTS AND PREDICTABLE PROBLEMS

After the foundations of its modern water law were laid, British Columbia became preoccupied with detailed administrative questions that arose out of the chaotic state of water records in the province.[71] The Water Act of 1909 created a board of investigation that was charged with adjudicating all claims to water rights, updating valid records and canceling others.[72] Its proceedings were complicated by the jurisdictional dispute with the federal government over water rights in the Railway Belt[73] and it remained very active over a decade in which it rendered approximately 8,000 decisions.[74]

Prairie water law remained at an earlier stage of evolution and at first its administrators continued to be well informed on developments in American water law. William Pearce maintained an active correspondence with Elwood Mead, the territorial engineer for Wyoming, who was a leading figure in American water law and instrumental in incorporating a model water law into the Wyoming Constitution of 1890.[75] Water rights remained within federal jurisdiction when the provinces of Alberta and Saskatchewan were created in 1905, and their administration was not transferred to the provinces until 1930.[76] The first Alberta Water Resources Act provided the last clear example of the specific incorporation of an American concept into Canadian water law, when it specified that water rights were "appurtenant to the land or the undertaking specified in the licence and ... inseparable therefrom."[77] A restriction of this type was first enacted in the United States through Wyoming legislation in 1909 and it became a feature of the water law of several western states.[78]

The disappearance of the interest in, and influence of, American water law was probably inevitable after the initial necessity of finding an appropriate model for water law in a newly settled land had been overcome. The decline of interest in legal developments was encouraged by the fact that water rights in western Canada quickly became less controversial. Once the law permitted the large-scale use of water on all lands, whether riparian or otherwise, there were no longer pressing legal issues to attract immediate attention. Water supply was generally adequate to supply the needs of major users both in British Columbia and on the Prairies and there were few disputes over priorities and allocations. At the same time, the administration of water-rights law in western Canada gradually became the preserve of the engineering profession, which was perhaps less interested in legal issues.[79]

The absence of immediate disputes disguised several latent defects in the water-law system that was adopted in the provinces of western Canada. However, the jurisdictions from which the fundamental legal principles of those systems were borrowed tended to have much less abundant water supplies, and to experience intensive economic development at an earlier stage than western Canada. It became clear in virtually every jurisdiction upon which the Canadian provinces relied in establishing their water law that a system based on prior appropriation was adequate to secure an initial allocation of water rights but that it suffered from serious weaknesses once the available flow of water became fully allocated and serious competition for water supplies arose.

It is not appropriate in this essay to describe in detail the defects that have emerged in jurisdictions whose systems are similar in principle to those of western Canada, but three major shortcomings can be briefly described. First, it has become clear that prior-appropriation or prior-allocation models favor the consumptive use of water, for they were initially designed for that purpose. The grant of water rights by allocation or appropriation can result in the exhaustion of the entire flow of a stream by existing users, without leaving any instream flow to protect the natural functioning of the stream and to safeguard environmental values.[80] It is equally clear that the longer governments wait to impose inflow stream requirements, the more difficult it becomes, because more conflicts will be created with consumptive rights that have been vested under the allocation system.[81]

Second, there is no doubt that systems such as those adopted in western Canada fulfilled their initial objective of allocating water rights so as to encourage economic development. However, once that objective was attained it became difficult to accommodate new users of water.[82] The difficulty amounted to a virtual impossibility where, as in the case of the prairie provinces, a general prohibition against the transfer of water rights was imposed on a prior-allocation system. In effect, the combination of prior allocation and restrictions on transfer has frozen water use in a pattern that is dictated only by historical accident and has converted an expansionary water-rights system into an impediment to economic development.

Third, when prior-appropriation or prior-allocation systems are accompanied by restrictions on the transfer of water rights, they create no incentive in existing rights holders to use less water. A reduction in consumption does not provide any economic benefit to the user and usually results in additional costs, such as those incurred by the installation of modern irrigation equipment. In effect, by ignoring the marginal value of water, western Canadian water law tends to encourage licensees to consume as much water as possible and not to "save" any water for new uses or for environmental purposes in the same way as its American predecessors.

Despite the dangers of drawing simplistic lessons from history, it can be safely concluded that intensive pressure on water supplies in the jurisdictions from which the western provinces borrowed their original water law has revealed problems of this nature which will inevitably arise in Canada. Indeed, the severe droughts that have been experienced periodically since the mid-1970s have already inspired thoughts of reform in each province in western Canada. Once the relationship between provincial water-law systems and their American and Australian counterparts is recognized, it is possible both to pinpoint the source of the problem and to canvass the range of solutions to those problems that have already been adopted elsewhere.

NOTES

The author acknowledges with gratitude the valuable research assistance of Sandra Petersson in the preparation of this paper.

1. For the development of water law on a regional basis, see David R. Percy, *The Framework of Water Rights Legislation in Canada* (Calgary: Canadian Institute of Resources Law, 1988), 72-73.

2. This account is adapted from David R. Percy, "Water Rights in Alberta," *Alberta Law Review* 15 (1977): 143-44.

3. The extent of the riparian's right to interfere with the flow of water depended upon which version of the riparian doctrine was adopted in a particular jurisdiction. One version of the doctrine incorporated the "natural flow" theory, which entitled the downstream riparian owner to receive water "in its natural state, in flow, quantity and quality" (*Chasemore v. Richards* (1859), 7 H.L.C. 349, 382). In contrast the competing "reasonable use" version of the theory allowed more scope to upstream riparians, who were allowed to use water for non-domestic purposes, provided that they did not

unreasonably interfere with the legitimate uses of other riparians — see Gerald V. LaForest, *Water Law in Canada — The Atlantic Provinces* (Ottawa: Department of Regional Economic Expansion, 1973), 208-10. The relationship between the two versions is discussed in Percy, *Framework,* 3-4.

4. For a discussion of the inability of the riparian system to maximize the economic potential of water, see Mason Gaffney, "Economic Aspects of Water Resource Policy," *American Journal of Economics and Sociology* 28 (1969): 137-39.

5. See Wells A. Hutchins, *Water Rights Laws in the Nineteen Western States*, vol. 1 (Washington, DC: Natural Resource Economics Division, United States Department of Agriculture, 1971), 164-65.

6. *Coffin v. Left Hand Ditch Co.*, 6 Colo 443 (Colo. S.C., 1882).

7. See pages 277-81, this essay.

8. See pages 281-83, this essay.

9. Victoria (Australia), Department of Water Resources, *Report No. 1: Water Law Review*, 1986, p. 5. For a discussion of the Victoria Royal Commission, see Sandford D. Clark and Ian A. Renard, "The Riparian Doctrine and Australian Legislation," *Melbourne University Law Review* 7 (1970): 486-89.

10. Louis L. Jaffe, *English and American Judges as Lawmakers* (Oxford: Clarendon Press, 1969), 5.

11. For example, an Alberta court rejected the common law of drainage as inapplicable to the geographical conditions of Alberta in *Makowecki v. Yachimyc* (1917), 1 W.W.R. 1279 (Alta. A.D.). Canadian courts also rejected the English distinction between tidal and non-tidal waters insofar as it related to public rights of navigation and to ownership of the bed. See *Leamy v. R.*, [1916] 54 S.C.R. 143 and Bora Laskin, *The British Tradition in Canadian Law* (London, UK: Stevens, 1969), 52.

12. W. Pearce, "Irrigation Legislation: Its Primary Principles," a submission to the Dominion Lands Association, 10 January 1891.

13. See Robert E. Clark, ed., *Waters and Water Rights* (Buffalo, NY: Allan Smith Co., 1967), 33 where the author refers to the early Arizona decision of *Clough v. Wing*, 17 Pac. 453 (Ariz. S.C., 1888), in which the court recognized the practices of ancient and contemporary Indian people who "used the waters of the streams in husbandry and sacredly recognized the rights acquired by long use and no right of a riparian owner is thought of."

14. Hutchins, *Water Rights Laws*, 160, quoting a decision of the Territorial Court of New Mexico, which proclaimed that "the law of prior appropriation existed under the Mexican Republic at the time of the acquisition of New Mexico" and had been adopted in New Mexico. See *U.S. v. Rio Grande Dam & Irrigation Co.*, 51 Pac 674 (N.M.S.C., 1898), revised on other grounds 174 U.S. 690 (1899).

15. Ibid., 162-63. For a discussion of Mormon influence in Canada see pages 277-78, this essay.

16. Clark, *Waters and Water Rights*, 61.

17. The description is taken from Hutchins, *Water Rights Laws*, 164-65.

18. In the California Civil Code, ss. 1410-1422 (1872).

19. H.W. Grunsky, "Water Legislation and Administration in British Columbia," British Columbia *Sessional Papers*, 13th Parliament, 1st Session, 1912, p. D117.

20. See the description of the development of mining legislation during Governor

Douglas's tenure in Robert Edgar Cail, *Land, Man and the Law: The Disposal of Crown Lands in British Columbia, 1871-1913* (Vancouver: University of British Columbia Press, 1974), 70-73.

21. Louis A. Knafla, "From Oral to Written Memory: The Common Law Tradition in Western Canada," in Louis A. Knafla, ed., *Law and Justice in a New Land: Essays in Western Canadian Legal History* (Calgary: Carswell, 1986), 43.

22. David R. Williams, *The Man for a New Country: Sir Matthew Baillie Begbie* (Victoria, B.C.: Sono Nis, 1977), 150-51.

23. Proclamation to make provision for regulating the Law of Gold Mines in British Columbia and for the Administration of Justice therein [hereinafter referred to as the "Gold Fields Act," 1859], 31 August 1859, in *Proclamations of British Columbia* (1858-1864), ss. 6, 7, 15, 16, 26.

24. J.C. MacDonald, "Water Legislation in British Columbia," *American Water Works Association Journal* 40 (1948): 159.

25. Land Proclamation, 14 February 1859, in *Proclamations of British Columbia* (1858-64), s. 8.

26. The Land Ordinance, 1870, R.L.B.C. 1871, no. 144, s. 30. Section 2 of this legislation repealed the Land Proclamation of 1859. MacDonald, "Water Legislation," 160, suggests that the Land Ordinance dates from 1865.

27. Ibid., s. 32.

28. Ibid., s. 30.

29. The Land Act, S.B.C. 1875, no. 5, s. 48.

30. Ibid.

31. Ibid., s. 50.

32. Ibid., s. 52.

33. Ibid., s. 55.

34. Ibid.

35. The Crown Lands Act, S.B.C. 1884, c. 16, s. 54-78.

36. Water Privileges Act, S.B.C. 1892, c. 47, s. 2.

37. See pages 282-85, this essay.

38. See the Placer Mining Act, S.B.C. 1891, c. 26, s. 54, 56-78; and the Mineral Act, S.B.C. 1896, c. 34, s. 59-79.

39. See the Land Act, S.B.C. 1875, no. 5, s. 54.

40. Water Clauses Consolidation Act, S.B.C. 1897, c. 45 preamble.

41. Ibid., c. 45, ss. 8-10.

42. Ibid., s. 13.

43. Ibid., ss. 7, 146.

44. Ibid., s. 17.

45. Ibid., s. 16.

46. "A General Report on Irrigation in the Northwest Territories (1894)," *Annual Report*, Canada Department of the Interior, 1894, p. 6.

47. E. Alyn Mitchner, "William Pearce and Federal Government Activity in the West, 1874-1904," *Canadian Public Administration* 10 (1967): 240.

48. E. Alyn Mitchner, "William Pearce and Federal Government Activity in Western

Canada, 1882-1894" (Ph.D. dissertation, University of Alberta, 1971), 202; *Debates of the House of Commons*, 25 June 1894, p. 4952.

49. Mitchner, "William Pearce and Federal Government Activity in the West," 241.

50. Northwest Irrigation Act, 57-58 Vic., c. 30.

51. C.S. Burchill, "The Origins of Canadian Irrigation Law," *Canadian Historical Review* 29 (1948): 359-60. Burchill expresses the view (p. 357) that the legislative declaration of Crown "ownership" of surface water first emerged in India. See also, *Debates of the House of Commons*, 5 June 1894 and "General Report on Irrigation," 27-28.

52. See, for example, s. 19, which incorporates the prior-allocation principle and the "relation back" doctrine, which grant priority according to the date of filing, provided that the licensee prosecuted the works with "sufficient vigour." This doctrine is found in ss. 8 and 17 and bears a strong resemblance to that found in such celebrated cases as *Ophir Silver Mining Co. v. Carpenter* 4 Nev. 534 (Nev. S.C., 1869).

53. University of Alberta Archives, William Pearce Papers, M.G. 9/2/7/2/1, 2 and 6 contains extracts and analyses of the Victoria Act and the laws of Colorado, Montana, Washington, and New Mexico.

54. Mitchner, "William Pearce and Federal Government Activity in Western Canada," 244.

55. In a letter to A.M. Burgess, deputy minister of the Interior on 23 February 1894, Pearce suggested obtaining from the convention "a strong expression of sentiment favourable to the abolition for the future of riparian rights" in order to strengthen the hand of government.

56. Mitchner, "William Pearce and Federal Government Activity in Western Canada," 239. The reference to the weather conditions is from the *Toronto Globe and Mail*, 26 June 1894.

57. See the discussion of the relation-back doctrine, Victoria Irrigation Act, s. 19.

58. The Water Privileges Act, S.B.C. 1892, c. 47, s. 2; The Northwest Irrigation Act, 57-58 Vic., c. 30, s. 4.

59. "General Report on Irrigation," 27-28.

60. Ibid., 5. A similar neglect of British Columbia was apparently shared by Pearce. In a letter to A.M. Burgess, deputy minister, Department of Interior, on 7 January 1891, he announced that he would provide a report on irrigation in British Columbia, Montana, Washington, New Mexico, and Colorado. However, the substance of his letter dealt only with the American jurisdictions and failed to mention the British Columbia experience.

61. See page 278, this essay.

62. T. Mayne Daly, *Debates of the House of Commons*, 5 June 1894.

63. See page 278, this essay.

64. The Land Ordinance, s. 32.

65. See, for example, the Mineral Act, ss. 63-64 and the Water Clauses Consolidation Act, ss. 16-17.

66. The Northwest Irrigation Act, s. 19.

67. The Water Clauses Consolidation Act, s. 9, ss. 11-15, s. 7.

68. Ibid., s. 35, s. 19.

69. See pages 278-80, this essay.

70. The visit is recorded in Clesson S. Kinney, *A Treatise on the Law of Irrigation and Water*

Rights (San Francisco: Bender-Moss, 1912), 192; and Clark and Renard, "The Riparian Doctrine," 186.

71.   Cail, *Land, Man and the Law*, 115.

72.   The Water Act, S.B.C. 1909, c. 48, s. 9.

73.   As discussed in the case of *Burrard Power v. R.*, [1911] A.C. 87 (P.C.).

74.   MacDonald, "Water Legislation in British Columbia," 163.

75.   University of Alberta Archives, Accession No. 74-169, s. 9/2/7/1 contains correspondence between William Pearce and Elwood Mead, 12 August - 27 October 1898. Further correspondence between Dennis and Mead was also carried out in October and November 1898 which is contained in a file entitled "Miscellaneous Documents: Water Administration: Canada Irrigation Act 1890-1930," on file with the Controller of Water Rights, Alberta Environment, Edmonton, Alberta. In order to complete a complex chapter of historical interrelationships, Mead later spent six years in Australia as chairman of the State Rivers and Water Supply Commission of Victoria.

76.   The British North America Act, 1930, 21 Geo. V, c. 26 (Imp.).

77.   The Water Resources Act, S.A. 1931, c. 71, s. 18.

78.   Charles J. Meyers, *A Functional Analysis of Appropriation Law* (Washington, DC: United States Water Commission, 1971), Legal Study No. 1.

79.   MacDonald, "Water Legislation in British Columbia," 163, comments that the administration of British Columbia water legislation had come "more and more into the hands of engineers," thus greatly easing the rigidity of the act and giving officials more authority and discretion. A similar process occurred in the prairie provinces.

80.   See the discussion of the effect of western appropriation doctrines in *Water Policies for the Future: Final Report of the National Water Commission* (Port Washington, NY: Water Information Center Inc., 1973), 271-72.

81.   Ibid., 272.

82.   Ibid., 260-61.

Constitution Making in the Nineteenth-Century American West

Christian G. Fritz

INTRODUCTION

The best expression of how the process of constitution making had evolved in the western states by the late nineteenth century can be gleaned from two speeches to the North Dakota constitutional convention of 1889. One speech was given by the former governor of the Dakotas and the other by an eminent constitutional-law scholar. Both men addressed the nature of constitutional conventions and how the process the delegates were about to engage in had changed over time. Each also paid homage to the ideal of a brief, pithy constitution while essentially rejecting the possibility of such a model given their perception of the convention's task.

The former governor, Arthur Mellette, described "the original idea and theory of what a constitution should contain" as one that embodied "as little legislation as possible" and "nothing but fundamental principles."[1] While such an approach may have sufficed for the Revolutionary and early national periods of the country's history, the nineteenth century had brought inescapable changes to American politics:

> [A]s the interests of the people have become more and more complex; as our commercial relations have extended and ... our legislation [becomes] more difficult in every direction, the states have adopted the idea of embracing in their fundamental law as much legislation as they can with safety [include].[2]

The second speaker to address the convention was Thomas Cooley, the author of *Constitutional Limitations* and one of the most influential constitutional-law authorities of his day.[3] At the time of the convention Cooley was chairman of the Interstate Commerce Commission. He argued that the "intricacy of constitution-building" has increased "and it becomes necessary to do many things now that were not important" in an earlier period and "that would even have been irrelevant [to the Founding Fathers]."[4] The North Dakota delegates had the advantage of the experience and history of American constitution making, but Cooley advised the convention: "Don't, in your constitution-making, legislate too much." His primary concern was with retaining legislative flexibility to deal with changing problems and issues and avoiding the possibility of radical constitutional experimentation in fundamental law. Yet, by his own admission, the kind of streamlined constitution of Hamilton's and Jefferson's day was impossible in North Dakota in 1889. Delegates would have to deal with many specifics and incorporate legislation but, he hoped, not too much and nothing radical. Although the delegates applauded Cooley's talk, the convention did not take his advice about pithy constitutions to heart. The constitution which the convention produced was extremely long, detailed, and full of constitutional legislation. In those respects, North Dakota's product presented a classic example of late nineteenth-century western constitution making.[5]

The studies of the federal constitutional convention and its context are voluminous when compared with treatment of state constitutional history.[6] The preoccupation with the federal Founding Fathers implicitly assumes that their work reflects not only the essence of American constitutionalism, but also the principal theme after which all other state constructs are merely variations. Even more telling in the historical literature is the inference of a declension in the standards set by the federal Constitution. How unfortunate, in other words, that nineteenth-century state constitutions became bloated with detailed provisions in contrast with the concise generalities and broad principles found in the federal Constitution. This departure in style is variously explained, but never is it suggested, much less asserted, that the process of nineteenth-century state constitution making — that did indeed yield some extensive constitutions by the end of that century — reflects a more authentic expression of America's gift to political science: written constitutions as expressions of fundamental law based on popular sovereignty.

I suspect, but I am not prepared to make the case just yet, that the history of state constitution making in over one hundred different constitutional conventions from American independence through the end of the nineteenth century is as important in understanding the development of ideas about American constitutionalism as is the formation of the federal Constitution.[7] By American constitutionalism, I mean the evolving understanding of the nature of constitutions, their scope, content and purpose, and how they should be drafted and ultimately ratified.[8] In particular, this essay probes what might be considered aspects of ideology concerning state constitutional revision. How late nineteenth-century constitutional convention delegates viewed the process of constitution making forms part of my ongoing study of the broad sweep of state constitution making from the early national period through the turn of the twentieth century.

My purpose in this essay is different, but linked nonetheless to the larger study. While preliminary, an examination of constitution making in the American West reveals several themes suggestive of the general development of American constitutionalism. My definition of the American West is rather broad and includes the far West, the Pacific Northwest, the Rocky Mountain states and even some of the Great Plains states. Most attention has been paid to seven states that held constitutional conventions between 1849 and 1889 and for which reports of the convention debates exist.[9]

THE CONTEXT OF WESTERN CONSTITUTION MAKING[10]

The comments made by both the former governor of the Dakotas and Thomas Cooley in the North Dakota convention of 1889 identified one important aspect of the broad context within which western constitution making occurred during the nineteenth century. Namely, a shared sense of many delegates that their job of creating a constitution or revising an existing one was part of an ongoing process. More specifically, delegates saw the process of constitution making as a progressive enterprise that required a readjustment of past practices to conform to present requirements. That process or science grew and developed over time in ways that made it important to build on earlier concepts and practices so as to create ever more sophisticated governmental structures. Implicit in this understanding was the idea that constitution making in the past — even in the Revolutionary period of American history — was less perfect and, indeed, possibly even crude when compared with "modern" ideas of drafting fundamental law. The Civil War, of course, was a graphic demonstration of the failure of the existing federal Constitution to accommodate the sectional tensions within the union and the issue of slavery. Moreover, even before the war, delegates to state constitutional conventions reflected a sense of superiority about their efforts as constitution makers. Ideas about the progressive nature of constitution making can be detected in early western conventions even as a more elaborate sense of the scientific nature of drafting constitutions came to be expressed by the late nineteenth century.

Western conventions drew on preexisting constitutional provisions as an integral part of drafting fundamental law. This constitutional borrowing, however, was hardly haphazard or accomplished without serious reflection. One of the recurring themes in that borrowing process was the recognition that the present generation of constitution makers should profit from the constitutional experience of other states and incorporate the best ideas from the existing constitutions. Early in California's 1849 convention a delegate expressed this idea when responding to the suggestion that the existence of a provision in many other constitutions established its merits. The sheer number of other constitutional examples provided "no reason why we should adopt the faults of others. We should rather profit by their experience."[11] Occasionally, the very latest constitutions acquired a special reputation "because they have selected and retained from other constitutions pretty much everything that is worth being retained in a constitution."[12]

The Importance of State Constitutional Models

When the first "western" constitution was drafted in California in 1849, convention delegates had the advantage of more than half a century of state constitutional experience. This experience was actively and self-consciously used by the delegates who gathered at Colton Hall in Monterey to fashion a constitution for California. The debates of that convention reveal that the most recent state constitutional conventions — in Iowa and New York (both in 1846) — were fresh in the delegate's minds. Indeed, some delegates had actually served as members of other state constitutional conventions before coming to California. Yet, it would be a mistake to assume that California was unique in drawing on a wide array of other states' constitutional experiences because of a cosmopolitan population drawn to California during the gold rush. The 1849 convention did indeed illustrate a wide geographical distribution of immigrants to California, but even without the physical migration stimulated by gold, other western constitutional conventions demonstrate the widespread and vigorous migration of constitutional ideas.

A close examination of how western delegates went about their task of creating frames of government dispels the notion that they did so in isolation. The identification of concerns that were peculiar to the West — aridity, mineral extraction, and Mormonism, for example — have obscured the extent to which the western conventions were part of a broader, dynamic process of constitutional understanding.[13] Moreover, western delegates were aware not only of the latest innovations in constitution making, but had access to all the existing state constitutions — including those of the "older" states — as models. Conventions in more or less isolated regions such as Idaho and the Dakotas shared this heightened constitutional awareness.

An important contribution to this wider setting for constitution making was a genre of political science literature that has gone largely unnoticed. This literature originated before the federal constitution and consisted of compilations of the texts of all existing state constitutions. After 1787 the federal constitution was routinely included in these books, but the heart of these works were the state constitutions — evidently thought to be a principal source of guidance. This conclusion is supported by the titles of these works, often appearing in multiple editions over the course of the nineteenth century. One of the most popular titles for compilations was *The American's Guide* that first appeared in 1810 and was used by various publishers as late as 1864.[14] The implicit purpose of these compilations was to provide a comparative basis for thinking about state constitutions and their creation. Printed as pocket-sized volumes and occasionally printed in miniature, such compilations were easily transportable even to remote western regions and were handy reference tools for delegates engaged in constitution making. Thus, despite the physical isolation and primitive conditions in which these western conventions sometimes met, they still had access to the accumulated final products of the American experience in drafting written fundamental law.

Delegates to California's 1849 convention demonstrated their specific knowledge of the text of other state constitutions. One delegate reported that the committee responsible for producing provisions to be considered by the entire convention conducted its work "with the Constitution of every State in the Union before it."[15]

State constitutional compilations were also present at Nevada's 1864 convention. Challenging a colleague's description of a provision in the Vermont constitution dealing with suffrage, one Nevada delegate referred to his "published volume of 'American constitutions'."[16]

These compilations affected the course and style of debate. For example, in the debate over whether the duties of justices of the peace ought to be spelled out in the constitution, one delegate invoked other states' constitutional provisions as a compelling argument against such enumeration. He agreed to drop his opposition if proponents could "find one constitution" within the covers of the book of American constitutions that distinctly defined the jurisdiction of justices of the peace.[17]

South Dakota's 1885 constitutional convention also had access to such compilations. When the debate shifted to the language proposed for the Bill of Rights setting out the right of the people to alter or abolish their government, one delegate, disturbed by the implications of the word "abolish," obtained the consent of the convention to speak at extended length on this point. He then proceeded to recite from a copy of *Charters and Constitutions of the United States* and read the comparable provisions in every existing state constitution from Alabama through Wisconsin.[18]

When California called its second constitutional convention in 1878, it initiated the most extensive western debate over constitutional subjects that fully drew upon existing state constitutions. The convention met for over three months and produced a mammoth verbatim transcript of its proceedings. The debates amply document the wealth of materials drawn upon by the delegates. Numerous copies of state constitutional compilations were evidently owned by or available to delegates.[19] Extensive comparative analysis of other state constitutions formed a regular feature of debate. In discussing a provision dealing with the militia, for example, the chairman of the committee that drafted that article began his defense of the provision by a comprehensive overview of comparable state provisions.[20] At one point a delegate exasperated at all the references to other conventions — both in terms of drafted constitutions as well as reported debates of other conventions — suggested a different approach: "[I]f the law library could be locked up and all these books that the members bring here thrown out of sight, we could go to work and build a constitution out of our heads, out of our inner consciences."[21]

Apart from using compilations to borrow constitutional language, delegates frequently consulted treatises on constitutional law. In the heated debate of Idaho's 1889 convention over the wording of a provision authorizing the taking of private property, one delegate invoked Thomas Cooley's famous treatise, *Constitutional Limitations.*[22]

Beyond compilations and secondary literature, nineteenth-century delegates could draw on contemporary constitutional activity. California delegates to the 1849 convention were aware of controversies within earlier conventions, such as Michigan's 1835 convention, and brought with them insights based on memories of recently concluded conventions, such as that of New York in 1846.[23] Oregon's delegates in 1857 looked to recent experience with constitution making in California and Ohio in 1849.[24]

One natural inclination, followed by California in 1878, was for conventions to gravitate toward their existing state constitution when meeting to revise that document. Delegates quickly pointed out that certain issues, such as corporations, the Chinese, and taxation, prompted the present convention, but they were not prepared to redesign the entire constitutional fabric of the state. In fact, as debates over hotly contested political issues became protracted, delegates suggested that the 1849 constitution be incorporated by reference whenever possible, for noncontroversial issues.[25]

In addition, the selection of constitutional models often followed the perceived relevance of other states' experience and situation to the territory or state currently engaged in constitution making. Nevada's delegates, for instance, were heavily influenced by California's 1849 constitution and constitutional history when they drafted a constitution in 1864.[26] Likewise, Idaho delegates, while receptive to a comprehensive comparative analysis of existing constitutional provisions, indicated a desire to place more emphasis on Rocky Mountain states and western states largely because they felt such states better reflected their own circumstances. Given Idaho's concerns over aridity, and mining and land use issues generally, the constitutional experience of Colorado and California carried greater weight than did that of some of the older eastern states.[27]

Beyond an awareness of the constitutional experience of other states obtained from personal observation or through the published product of earlier conventions, some conventions found themselves engaged in constitution making simultaneously with other states or territories. Such coincidence heightened the self-awareness of the process and importance of shared constitution making. At the end of their convention, the Idaho delegates passed and sent a resolution to these other conventions, advising that Idaho "has agreed to forever prohibit bigamy, polygamy, and other crimes of the Mormon theocracy within its borders."[28]

The Manner of Constitutional Borrowing

The relatively widespread access that western conventions had to constitutional compilations resulted in extensive borrowing of existing provisions in nineteenth-century constitutions. Sometimes this borrowing went on without acknowledgement and can only be detected by linguistical comparisons with other constitutions. More often, however, this importation of constitutional language occurred in an open and self-conscious manner. Indeed, the frankness of such borrowing occasionally triggered complaints by some delegates. These complaints implicitly suggested the desirability of creating a constitution in a context without models. Such an expectation, of course, was unrealistic — even the federal constitution had been drafted in the wake of a decade of state constitution making.

Despite extensive borrowing, the process of constitution making revealed that delegates still discussed and wrestled with the constitutional ideas those provisions entailed. Far from being a constraining influence, the multitude of models often presented the challenge of differentiating options and evaluating the merits of the provisions ultimately selected. Nonetheless, inertia or momentum — rather than explicit discussions — did contribute to the final shape of nineteenth-century state constitutions. What is remarkable, however, is that unthinking adoption or mechanical borrowing of constitutional provisions was relatively limited.

In the final analysis extended convention discussions, often based on the different constitutional practices of other states, may well have helped shape a culture of constitutionalism. That shared constitutional understanding may provide a key insight into the wider process and development of American constitutional thought that evolved beyond the narrower perspective of the Revolutionary generation.

An analysis of the constitutional sources of California's first Bill of Rights illustrates the practice of constitutional borrowing.[29] In the debate over the Bill of Rights early in the convention, one delegate chastised his colleagues for "servilely" copying from other constitutions rather than drawing "wisdom from the spirit and meaning" of them.[30] Toward the end of the convention yet another delegate lamented a lack of originality. He wanted the preamble to contain "a few lines at least of our own manufacture."[31] In fact, the debates of the convention demonstrate that delegates understood the constitutional choices and issues and discussed them at considerable length. Some issues provoked less debate than others because of a consensus of opinion, but such consensus hardly meant that constitutional attitudes or constitution making were static, reflecting an unthinking perpetuation of past constitutional practices. Many more innovative ideas and suggestions were debated than were ultimately incorporated into the final product, and their discussion confirms the dynamic process and changing nature of nineteenth-century constitution making of which California's first convention was a part.

The western constitutional conventions that met later in the nineteenth century showed similar tendencies to borrow from prior constitutions, but they engaged in this process in a different manner. Unlike the scattered comments calling for "originality" that found their way into the 1849 California convention, later conventions show little or no concern with this issue. Rather, one can detect an implicit assumption that such a collective and comparative approach to fashioning a state's fundamental law was not only acceptable but preferred.[32] Instead, the concern shifted

to insuring the appropriate basis for constitutional borrowing. A delegate
to Oregon's 1857 convention expressed this different attitude: "If there is
anything in other constitutions suitable to Oregon, let us take it, but let us
not hastily patch it up with contradictory provisions — let the instrument
be well considered and read harmonious in all its parts."[33] As will be
argued later, nineteenth-century constitution makers revealed a strong
strain of progressive ideology that equated with the belief that the science
of government and constitution making was capable of ongoing
improvement.[34] One of the ways such constitutional improvement or
refinement occurred was by building on the latest improvements found
in other state constitutions.

By the time of California's second constitutional convention in 1878,
western conventions began their work convinced that the product of
their labors would be an amalgam of existing constitutions. Far from
facilitating the task of constitution making, the sheer number of models,
increasing over time, created an embarrassment of riches. The 1878
convention in California organized itself by creating twenty-five
committees, each with responsibility for a certain subject matter in the
constitution. One early problem, given the decision to publish all
proposals for constitutional text, was the vast number of suggestions.
Early in the convention one delegate claimed there were "eight or ten or
twenty complete drafts of a constitution."[35] Whether these constitutions
were literally copies of other constitutions or combinations of other
constitutions is unclear, but as a delegate pointed out, all of them, under
the convention's committee system, "must be cut up and presented as
separate propositions, relating to the different articles in the
Constitution."[36]

One aspect of the borrowing nature of nineteenth-century constitution
making that has received insufficient attention is the judicial significance
of taking provisions wholesale from one constitution and incorporating
them into another, later constitution. Each borrowed provision
potentially had a body of interpretation regarding its meaning, a sort of
judicial gloss from state courts that might have interpreted that
provision. Indeed, courts from different states might interpret similarly
worded provisions differently. The possibilities of ambiguity or of a
specific interpretation based on earlier judicial decisions were matters
that western delegates clearly understood.

In this context, the approach to interpreting a nineteenth-century
"patchwork" constitution posed interesting interpretative questions. One
delegate to California's 1878 convention raised this issue by stating what

he called "a cardinal canon of interpretation of constitutions."[37] Namely, "that where a constitutional provision has been incorporated from the constitution of one state into the constitution of another state ... that the courts invariably turn to the decisions in that [first] state to guide them in their interpretation of the provision."[38] If such a rule of interpretation "universally" prevailed in American states, it casts interesting and new light on the historical development of state constitutional law.

The California delegate was not alone in seeing such a connection between borrowed provisions of fundamental law and its interpretation. In the course of Nevada's 1864 convention one argument advanced for modeling that state's constitution on California's 1849 document was that Nevada could then take advantage of fifteen years of constitutional jurisprudence by the California Supreme Court.[39] Such ideas may well have been a natural way to give interpretative guidance to newly created constitutions but it does, nonetheless, suggest that the impact of "borrowing" in nineteenth-century state constitution making went well beyond copying constitutional text.

One delegate to California's second convention gave the best expression of the dangers or weaknesses of the "borrowing" process of constitution making. He accused some of his fellow delegates of having "contracted the fatal habit of browsing through the organic laws of the other states, borrowing enough to show a want of invention and inventing just enough to show a total want of judgment."[40] He then offered his understanding of the proper basis of borrowing constitutional provisions:

> When there can be found in ... the organic law of any other state, a terse, unmistakable expression of a broad, universal principle of government ... it should be presented here for our consideration. But, when the principle of selection is carried to the extent of pressing upon our approval those special exceptional provisions of other organic laws which had their origin and growth in the peculiar circumstances and condition of the community for which they were framed; [they] are wholly unsuited to the political habits, modes of thought, and social wants of our own people.[41]

The California delegate thus reflected an interesting self-perception. Namely, in some ways delegates perceived themselves as members of a broad American constitutional tradition while at the same time they saw themselves as "Californians" or "Idahoans" and thus requiring distinctive constitutional arrangements.[42]

COMMON STRAINS OF WESTERN CONSTITUTIONALISM

In widely disparate circumstances and areas of the West one can identify ideas that formed the backdrop to constitution making. From the mid- to the late nineteenth century, delegates to many conventions struggled over a wide variety of substantive issues and split over political differences. Nonetheless, transcending these very heated disputes were common strains of constitutionalism that suggest the richness of nineteenth-century constitution making and a reconsideration of the content and significance of that process as part of the American political and constitutional inheritance.

Just how the nature of constitutions, constitutional conventions and constitution making had evolved and could be described was the subject of considerable discussion. The thoughts delegates expressed on this subject provide important insights into how they regarded the documents they were fashioning and their role as constitution makers. In addition, their thoughts on these matters show a collective or shared understanding that formed part of the contemporary constitutional culture.

Belief in the Progressive Nature of Constitution Making

A single word figured prominently in the constitutional culture of the nineteenth-century American West: progress. Nineteenth-century delegates consistently remarked on the idea of progress in terms of constitutional developments that either affected their choices or needed to be considered in performing their duties as constitution makers. Frequently in the convention debates a delegate invoked "the progress of the age" as the reason or necessity of incorporating a particular provision. This phrase first appeared in a western convention during the drafting of the Oregon constitution in 1857, when one delegate sang the praises of the new constitution of Indiana as the best model for the Oregon delegates: "It is gold refined; it is up with the progress of the age."[43] What he found particularly appealing about the constitution was its Bill of Rights which acknowledged the many changes "since our fathers first formed constitutions."[44] To its credit, and worthy of emulation,

> Indiana recognizes this progress, and thus ... embodies them in her bill of rights. She nobly reasserts what our fathers said about the natural rights of man to the pursuit of life, liberty and happiness, but she proceeds to assert the civil rights of the citizens as ascertained in those 70 years of progress.[45]

Implicit in the assertion of the changes since the days of the Founding Fathers was the suggestion that what they said and did about constitutions might best be a starting point for delegates later in the nineteenth century. One manifestation of this suggestion consisted of demythologizing the Founding Fathers. Some nineteenth-century delegates hardly shrank from the comparison to the genius of Madison and his colleagues. They felt adequate if not superior to the task of constitution making because they believed that the nature of the enterprise had substantially changed. As one delegate to the 1864 Nevada convention put it:

> I confess that I have not that profound and reverential regard which some profess for the men who assembled in the conventions in the early days of the republic, when the government was yet but an experiment.[46]

He conceded that there were things "worthy of imitation" in the results of their labors, but he did not regard them with "exalted veneration" because it was more relevant to consider the provisions that drafters — "in their wisdom and judgment" — of the most recent state constitutions had incorporated into their fundamental law.[47] Likewise, from the vantage point of a delegate to California's 1878 convention, the 1829 Virginia convention harkened back to "those primitive times."[48] To that delegate, precedents drawn from the Virginia convention "no more serve to illustrate the present machinery of constitutional conventions than the lumbering old family coaches they used to ride to the capitol in, are like the railroad cars and steamers in which the same journeys are now performed."[49]

The principal means of measuring the constitutional progress that separated the country's first constitutions from the present state of constitution making was through substantive constitutional principles or doctrines incorporated into the fundamental law. Self-consciously, many western convention delegates saw the absence of certain provisions in the early state constitutions and their presence in later nineteenth-century constitutions as direct evidence of progress or greater enlightenment. Normally the advancement in constitutional ideas was attributed to the passage of time, although occasionally some advances were specifically noted in trends of "the western states."[50] These provisions and the concepts they embraced spanned a wide range of subject matter.

Toward the end of Oregon's 1857 convention one delegate congratulated his colleagues for embodying a half-century of constitutional experience in several areas and thus "perfecting republican institutions."[51] The constitution, he suggested, by establishing a free school system "starts out in the light of the history of the states which have preceded us [and] in advance of any of the new states of this Union."[52] Moreover, the provisions dealing with corporations and internal improvement were both of "modern origin" and "wise."[53] Experience had suggested the best ways of dealing with the constitutional regulation of the economy and economic forces in the state.

Conflicting Theories of Sovereignty

Yet, constitution-making inherently produced a tension between stability and progress. At the heart of the discussion over the power and nature of conventions lay competing visions of the implications of republicanism and the promise of democracy. From the earliest period, efforts seeking constitutional revision through conventions raised different visceral responses that underlay the crafted arguments developed and refined by delegates in debate. Those who saw change and the capacity for change as positive ends tended to view conventions as an expression of popular sovereignty and as having powers and characteristics that followed from that status. On the other hand, those who ultimately placed greater value on stability and preserving the status quo saw conventions as potentially dangerous and revolutionary bodies. To such delegates and others of a more conservative bent, conventions were limited by the preexisting procedures and, when applicable, constitutional provisions that called them into being.

The incident that raised these far-reaching issues in California's 1878 convention involved the question of restrictions on delegate selection. At issue was the question of whether an elected delegate, also a district court judge, could participate given a provision of the 1849 constitution making such judges "ineligible to any other office than a judicial office during their term."[54] At one level debate entailed the proper interpretation of the word "office" and the applicability of the constitutional provision. The issue, however, also provoked a more fascinating discussion of whether constitutional conventions were, in some sense, revolutionary. In other words, the deeper issue became the relevance, impact and authority of a preexisting constitutional provision on a later constitutional convention. In the course of the debate the question widened to include the inquiry of whether the convention manifested popular sovereignty and was therefore beyond the control of a legislature, an enabling act, or even a preexisting constitution. Or, on the other hand, were constitutional conventions constrained to act in accordance with provisions that triggered its existence.[55]

Since the issue of establishing the credentials of delegates had to be resolved before the convention could begin its substantive labors, this abstract question became the first major issue of the convention. Eventually the delegate in question was seated, although only by a vote of eighty-three to fifty-three. The controversy posed a rare occasion in the course of constitution making when such theoretical questions about the power and role of conventions were raised.

The convention sought to resolve this issue in a time-honored way: it appointed a special committee. The committee rendered a majority report recommending the delegate's seating as well as a minority report that disagreed. These two reports formed the framework within which the extended debate took place. The majority report concluded that the constitutional provision was intended to prevent judges from using their position to advance themselves in the executive or legislative departments. As such, the provision was concerned with the operation of the government created by the 1849 constitution and did not "anticipate what should be done under a succeeding Constitution."[56] Therefore, viewing membership in the present convention as an office would be, argued the majority report, an overly narrow and literal interpretation that should be rejected.

The majority report emphasized the extraordinary nature of a convention, arguing it was a body that worked on a different plane than the "every-day operations" of the executive, legislative or judicial.[57] Rather, a convention

> outranks them all; it is their creator, and fixes limits to their spheres of action, and boundaries to their powers. It is occasional, exceptional, brief, and peculiar; it represents the people in their primary capacity, and forms the organic, fundamental, and paramount law of state. Its members are mere agents or delegates of the people, and they have no power to adopt or create, but, at most, can only propose and present to the people a draft of a constitution for their adoption or rejection.[58]

Therefore, to confuse the process of making "new organic law" with normal governmental operations was like confusing the architect of "a grand edifice with the people who subsequently occupy it."[59]

The authors of the majority report argued that the applicable provision dealing with constitutional revision was sufficiently broad that "the people were left free to select whom they pleased."[60] Likewise, the statute calling the convention had no "limitation or restriction."[61] Indeed, in the final analysis the majority could not "assume for a moment that the Convention which framed the present Constitution intended to trammel the succeeding generation in any such manner in the formation of a new or revised organic law."[62]

The minority report, on the other hand, claimed that the majority embraced a discredited theory of the sovereignty of constitutional conventions, a theory the minority expressly rejected. The minority acknowledged the basis of government to be the people and their right to change that government, but in terms that were loaded with conservative meaning. Constitutional conventions were means of expressing public opinion, but conventions designed to sweep aside constitutions and reduce society "into its individual elements" simply implied "revolution."[63] The minority could not countenance such a convention nor would they accept the implication that "every provision of the present Constitution, regulating the calling and purpose of this Convention, may be ignored at will."[64] Rather, the minority concluded that the present convention was bound by the existing constitution.

One of the arguments employed by delegates stressing the non-revolutionary nature of the 1878 California convention was the fact that California already had a constitution. Implicitly, they argued that the 1849 constitution had already altered the relationship between the people and the convention, namely, that the present convention did not represent the people in "their primary capacity."[65] Moreover, the existing constitution was not "resolved into chaos" simply with the calling of a new convention.[66] The 1849 constitution continued to have validity and yet conventions implicitly operated with a competence greater than the existing constitution or legislature. Accepting both propositions meant accepting the role of constituent assemblies in republican governments as embodying the closest thing to popular sovereignty in practice. In the final analysis, working out the practical implications of the theoretical commitment to popular sovereignty resisted easy answers because it did entail a tension or balance at the most basic level of the American experience with self-government.

A further example of the sensitivity of those who feared the prospect of change emerged during the 1878 California convention's debate over the wording in the state Bill of Rights. The proposed wording called for the right of the people "to alter or reform the [constitution] whenever the public good may require it."[67] One delegate objected that such wording merely encouraged revolution and undermined the authority of the constitution. The "right of revolution is an ultimate right" but the delegate argued it "is not one to be provided for in the organic law, because it is not supposed that we will embody in the constitution the seeds of its own destruction."[68] Similarly, delegates to the South Dakota convention of 1885 suggested that language about the right of the people to "abolish" government might offend Congress. South Dakota in 1885 was still a territory and the document the delegates gathered to draft ultimately required Congressional approval.

Ultimately, delegates to conventions disagreed over what power those conventions possessed. On the one hand, those who argued for the revolutionary nature kept stressing popular sovereignty and the function of the delegates as representatives of this ultimate political power of the state. Their opponents kept emphasizing the preexisting authority of prior constitutions as being the manifestation of that popular sovereignty. They maintained that until the prior constitutions were changed through the procedures spelled out in those documents, conventions were merely making suggestions that required the ultimate ratification of the people. Finally, they denied that delegates representing the people had revolutionary power. It seems likely that the culture of constitutionalism within which nineteenth-century western delegates met to draft fundamental law principally accounted for the constitutional debates over sovereignty rather than anything peculiar to "western" constitution making.

SELF-PERCEPTION REGARDING THE PURPOSE OF WESTERN CONSTITUTIONS

Related to the question of how free delegates felt they were to produce a document that broke from the past was their understanding of the purpose of constitutions. It was agreed that the nature and object of constitutions was to go beyond fundamental principles to what delegates themselves called constitutional legislation. How delegates conceived of themselves as playing an institutional role that clearly supplanted, in some respects, the choices and decisions of the ordinary legislature reveals their understanding of the substance of constitutions. But the underlying purpose of those provisions and the significance assigned to that role by delegates has not yet been explored. There were a number of different possibilities. Conceivably delegates saw constitutions primarily as the means to control and restrict the legislature. On the other hand, they might have understood the fundamental law they were drafting as a restriction imposed by the people — represented by the convention — on themselves. Or possibly, they could have seen the constitution as the repository of moral goals for society. Whatever the case, it forms part of the general context within which western constitution making in the nineteenth century took place and provides further insight into that period's constitutional culture.

The central purpose of constitutions as expressed by nineteenth-century delegates was to restrict or limit the powers of the government and the legislature in particular. This understanding rested on a theory of federalism that equally prevails today, but which in the nineteenth century assumed a content and texture that is hard to recapture given the pervasive presence of national power in virtually every aspect of our twentieth-century lives. For the nineteenth century, what distinguished federal and state governments was that while the federal Constitution created a government "of expressed delegated powers," state governments were created by "a constitution of restrictions."[69] This understanding of the difference between the two types of constitutions emphasized that the federal Constitution was the creature of what the states or the American people had provided, whereas the state governments were understood to exert all power except that which the people chose not to give them.[70] As one delegate put it: "The legislature of the state can do anything, unless it is restrained by its constitution."[71] That virtual omnipotence stemmed from the operation of popular sovereignty at the state level. Popular sovereignty could not exist in the legislature because in the final analysis it was "but the creature of that supreme power — the people" and only "exercises certain specific and well defined powers, limited by the Constitution."[72]

Delegates did indeed express a concern about what they perceived as excessive legislating in the constitution, but that response was tempered or checked by a belief that some legislating was not only legitimate, but absolutely necessary if the convention was to do its job properly.

Insight into this tension can be gained in the debate over inserting a provision in the Bill of Rights prohibiting the creation of lotteries in the state of California. This issue first arose in a provision that combined prohibitions against lotteries and the granting of divorces by the legislature as well as protections for the right of peaceable assembly. One delegate objected to "mixing up" all these issues in a Bill of Rights mainly because it was "improper to insert legislative enactments" in a constitution.[73] Another delegate opposed the prohibition against lotteries on the grounds that they might become an important source of revenue for the future state and he did not wish to restrict future legislatures with respect to the matter. Essentially, the argument against such a prohibition considered the matter an issue for the legislature to decide and that the convention's task was instead to "lay down the broad fundamental principles of a republican form of government, without ... [depriving] the people of the right to pass such laws, not inconsistent with those principles, as they thought proper."[74]

On the other hand, proponents of the lottery prohibition pointed out that if limiting the legislature's power was an objective, the prohibition in question "fixes a very important limit upon those powers."[75] What ultimately carried the day, however, was the argument that the prohibition represented an important moral restriction upon the powers of the legislature that ought to become part of the state's fundamental law. This argument rested on both functional and policy grounds. One delegate rhetorically responded to the assertion that the convention should not make laws by asking:

> [A]re we not here to make a Constitution — the strongest law known under our system of government. That Constitution only requires the sanction of the people to become the fundamental law of the country. Other laws, passed by the Legislature, will be subservient to it.[76]

Furthermore, he urged the state not to "adopt an immoral system of taxation as a source of revenue. The best policy for governments, as well as individuals, is a strict adherence to legitimate and honorable means of support."[77] The convention evidently agreed because the prohibition found its way into the constitution.[78]

The debate over the lottery provisions also illustrated the recognition of the legitimacy of law making in the process of drafting a constitution, because one of the functions of fundamental law was to deal with the most important issues — political, economic or moral — that faced a state. One delegate expressed this in terms of a mandate to the convention:

> The people of California have sent you here to make a Constitution for them. ... In making this Constitution, they expect you to settle many important questions relative to the interests and wants of the people of this country.[79]

This attitude toward constitution making not only suggested that many substantive issues were appropriate concerns for a constitutional convention, but that they might actually require constitutional status in order to settle the issue. Arguments that suggested that potentially legislative matters should be placed in the constitution if they were important enough, surfaced in the debates over community property. This issue, as with the prohibition of lotteries, found its way into the constitution,[80] as a majority of delegates agreed that the matter should not be left to the legislature.

The refrain of legislation versus constitutional provision continued to echo through the debates of nineteenth-century conventions.[81] However, such concerns gradually underwent a change in that justifications for legislating were more clearly articulated and based on a growing suspicion if not distrust of legislatures. Moreover, the growing collective experience of nineteenth-century constitution making provided a more confident expression of the theoretical legitimacy and appropriateness of delving into greater and greater detail in the course of drafting a state's fundamental law.

In the end, this unwillingness to trust legislatures to address important issues in the correct way convinced delegates that conventions should speak with a definitive voice. On some issues a consensus existed which made this approach less susceptible to criticism that it invaded the prerogative of the legislature. Whether delegates agreed on the appropriate resolution of the issue in question or not, ultimately it was the preference, as a delegate to the Nevada convention put it, that the provision be "not written in the sand, but written on parchment" that accounted for the behavior of individual delegates and the conventions collectively.[82]

This trend toward agreeing that some policy needed to be placed in the constitution continued in the 1878 California convention. But in contrast the California delegates, in addition to expressing substantive agreement over certain issues the majority of delegates could agree belonged in the constitution, also asserted an institutional role for the convention in settling political issues by constitutionalizing them. Indicative of this self-consciously political approach to constitution making was the first appearance in any western convention of the phrase "constitutional legislation."[83]

The clearest and most important expression of the role of the convention to act in lieu of the legislature was in the area of restraints on corporations and limitations on state and municipal debt. In the case of controlling corporate power, including the railroad companies, the convention asserted not merely a failure, but an institutional inability of the legislature to act. Moreover, a majority of delegates saw the question of controlling corporations and debt as issues upon which "the people" had given the convention a mandate to act. The debate over corporations and corporate power entailed heated arguments as some characterized corporations as a positive force for the economic development of California while others viewed them as inherently evil and protected by corrupt legislators.[84] What is striking about this debate in terms of the convention's sense of its role was both the distrust of the legislature and the explicit acknowledgement that the delegates were legislating.

The chairman of the corporation committee captured this distrust of the legislature well in characterizing approval of the suggested provisions as a "stamp upon the organic law of California" that regulated railroads "for the protection of the people," by taking "from the halls of legislation the corrupting influence of corporate power."[85] Given the enormity of their powers and economic impact on the state, the chairman stated as a general proposition that "constitutional conventions should provide a means whereby all railroad companies may be controlled."[86] The specific and detailed nature of those controls and regulations did not phase many delegates who frankly admitted that they made the constitution "to a certain extent a code."[87]

In the process of identifying the grounds of agreement over the political issues that the convention wished to settle, delegates described themselves in revealing terms. Some spoke of being "law-makers" and others distinguished between the people "for whom we come here to legislate" and "the home corporations or the foreign corporations."[88] Indeed, many delegates described their participation in the revision of California's constitution in terms of a political and moral mandate to effect specific changes. One delegate expressed this feeling clearly:

> The men who own the banks, the men who run the banks, are not the men who voted for me; ... the men who voted for me are the men who have been swindled, are the men who have felt and do feel the great wrongs of this evil irresponsibility in these corporation managers, and [who] with their votes asked me to come here and do what I could to remedy this evil of irresponsible corporate management, and for one I am here to do it, and right now.[89]

Wyoming's convention offers a clear example of the breakdown of an initial resolve to avoid legislation. Its 1889 constitution provides insight into the dynamics of the process of late nineteenth-century constitution making. By organizing itself into seventeen standing committees the convention practically insured that it would be considering many provisions that went beyond the broad and general principles of the idealized short constitution. Nonetheless, in the early stages of the convention delegates seemed to share the opinion that it was of "great importance" not to interfere "with matters which may be left to the legislature."[90]

Notwithstanding this goal, it soon became evident that individual delegates and the convention as a whole routinely created exceptions when the matter or issue at stake was deemed important. Moreover, the definition of "important" was relatively liberal and did not merely entail the major political issues of the day, as for example questions about the formation of corporations. Indeed, one of the first deviations from the goal of a nonlegislative constitution entailed a provision that voided any contract in which an employee waived any right to recover damage for death or injury. Despite conceding the legislative nature of the provision, one delegate wanted its incorporation into the constitution because "we cannot be too careful in protecting the rights of the great laboring classes."[91]

In relatively short order numerous detailed provisions were accepted by the convention — even in the absence of analogues in other state constitutions — if the provision could be defended on the grounds that it would be helpful or beneficial to the state government. When some delegates objected to a provision that sought to define "appropriation" in the water irrigation context, others, while admitting it smacked of legislation, felt such definitional language might avoid ambiguity later.[92]

Once established, such a pattern of accepting detailed provisions was difficult to break even if an occasional delegate declared: "We are here to make a constitution and not for legislation."[93] Eventually, the Wyoming convention's practice itself came to justify provisions. With respect to a provision limiting work to an eight-hour day a delegate acknowledged "that this is legislation, but we have done considerable legislation, and this covers but one or two lines in the constitution."[94] Toward the close of the convention this rationale became increasingly persuasive. In the discussion over a provision that prohibited corporations from disclaiming liability for injuries to their employees, one delegate was straightforward:

> You may say, is not this pure legislation? What if it is. We have voted for a great many things here that are legislation, and if we are going to have legislation here at all, let us get the best there is.[95]

The idea that conventions should make constitutional legislation, particularly when important issues were at stake, received a boost in the Idaho convention when a delegate rejected a suggestion that an innovation for the jury system ought to be left to the legislature. He suggested that the convention's composition gave it a special mandate to act: "The territory has never been represented as it is represented here today."[96] Another delegate to the Idaho convention expressed a similar unwillingness to let the legislature "pass upon something I consider of such vast importance to the people that it should be engrafted in the organic law of the land."[97]

Thus, from California's first convention in 1849 through to the western conventions of the late 1880s, delegates recognized that one of the principal purposes of the constitutions they were drafting was express limitations on the powers of state legislatures.[98] Nonetheless, some delegates suggested the conventions also had a positive role as well. The efforts to place provisions in the constitution that expressly permitted the legislature to enact laws dealing with a wide range of activities at its discretion generated interesting discussions on the contemporary nature of federalism. Such provisions, which some delegates referred to as directory provisions, were inherently contrary to the concept of state constitutions. If state governments exercised the residual power left after specific limitations imposed by the constitution it was unnecessary and made little theoretical sense to spell out such residual powers.

Those who advocated directory provisions and sometimes succeeded in getting them adopted were not ignorant of the theoretical principles that underlay nineteenth-century constitution making. Rather, they showed a shrewd appreciation for the process of constitutional interpretation and a pragmatic concern that the third branch of government might frustrate their efforts at law making. When the conventions could agree on the necessity of constitutional legislation, they embodied such detailed instructions, principles and political choices into the fundamental law. When such a consensus or requisite support was missing, a directory provision was the best alternative. On one occasion, a California delegate in 1878 provided a glimpse of one reason some delegates supported directory provisions. He argued that while the legislature might be deemed to have certain powers, the state's supreme court would be the body to make that final determination. Therefore, if the convention indicated in the constitution "that the legislature shall have the power to do some certain things, ... no court in the State of California would ever go behind that declaration in the constitution."[99] Thus, far from being slow students of American government, such a justification of directory provisions showed a sensitivity to the process of constitutional government and judicial review.[100]

CONCLUSION

Western constitutional conventions clearly attributed importance to what they were doing and saw their work as part of a larger American tradition. A delegate to Oregon's convention in 1857 noted that "the people of this country attach importance to their fundamental law; importance gathers around it, and it is no children's play to form a good constitution."[101]

Occasionally, the contemporary political disputes that came into the convention tended to overshadow the process of making fundamental law. In the debate and discussion over changes to the Bill of Rights in the 1878 California convention, one delegate complained that the convention was moving too quickly to insert provisions that were going to have major impact and were becoming part of the fundamental law. He compared the care and length of time it had taken John Adams to draft the Preamble and Bill of Rights of the Massachusetts constitution with what he saw as the tendency among his fellow delegates. Unlike the seven months Adams spent composing "in the solitude of his chamber," "we seem to think that we can come upon the floor of this convention and suck a stump of lead pencil for five minutes, take an old scrap of paper and prepare any amendment for the constitution of the state."[102]

As we have seen, the experience of western states in creating state constitutions is revealing in a number of ways. First, it is clear that these states did not fashion their fundamental law in isolation or unaware of constitution making in other states. The myth of "frontier" constitution making must be regarded as such — a myth. Varying levels of sophistication among delegates and the work they produced existed, but in the process of creating constitutions (and on one occasion revising an existing constitution) delegates to western constitutional conventions demonstrated their connection with broader regional and national developments in constitutionalism.

Second, despite considerable attention to local concerns and substantive issues, western state conventions disclose numerous similarities in the process of constitution making and how delegates understood that process. These areas of agreement and their significance emerge when attention is shifted from the "westernness" of these conventions to the generic process of constitution making.[103] That is, it is necessary to look through the "western" issues — not to ignore them — in order to focus on matters and challenges that all constitutional conventions faced and in varying degrees debated. Namely, how did western delegates to conventions perceive their purpose, and the effect of the convention? The answer to these questions — which go to the essence of what I have called notions of constitutionalism — suggests that western delegates and constitutional conventions formed part of a broader, developing understanding of the nature and meaning of constitutions.

The history of constitution making in the western United States, along with state constitution making generally, has traditionally been overshadowed by interest in the formation of the federal Constitution. With recent interest in state constitutions as documents having an independent source of constitutional authority, the ingrained habit of studying American constitutional law from "the top down" may diminish, and scholars may enjoy a less federal perspective on the nature of constitutional law.[104]

NOTES

The author would like to thank Dean Leo Romero for support in the form of a summer research grant, and Marlene Keller, Joseph Franaszek and Stephen Wasby for comments on an earlier draft of this essay.

1. *Official Report of the Proceedings and Debates of the First Constitutional Convention of North Dakota, Assembled in the City of Bismarck, July 4 to August 17, 1889* (R.M. Tuttle, official stenographer) (Bismarck, ND: Tribune, State Printers and Binders, 1889), 45.

2. Ibid.

3. See Clyde E. Jacobs, *Law Writers and the Courts: The Influence of Thomas M. Cooley, Christopher G. Tiedman and John F. Dillon Upon American Constitutional Law* (Berkeley: University of California Press, 1954) and Alan R. Jones, *The Constitutional Conservatism of Thomas McIntyre Cooley: A Study in the History of Ideas* (New York: Garland Publishing, 1987).

4. North Dakota, *Debates* (1889), 66.

5. One of the major reasons for long state constitutions was the Tenth Amendment of the federal constitution. If state governments were to be limited in the powers reserved to them by that amendment, limitations had to be specified and that process alone resulted in longer constitutions, not to mention bills of rights. Nonetheless, the calls for the desirability of short constitutions were heard from the start of constitution making in the nineteenth century.

6. For some exceptions dealing with the nineteenth-century western experience see Harry N. Scheiber, "Race, Radicalism, and Reform: Historical Perspective on the 1879 California Constitution," *Hastings Constitutional Law Quarterly* 17 (1989): 35-80; Gordon Morris Bakken, *Rocky Mountain Constitution Making, 1850-1912* (New York: Greenwood Press, 1987); and Carl B. Swisher, *Motivation and Political Technique in the California Constitutional Convention, 1878-79* (1930; New York: Da Capo Press, 1969).

   Much additional work is in unpublished form. See, for example, David A. Johnson, "Pioneers and Politics: Statemaking in the Far West, 1845-1865" (PhD dissertation, University of Pennsylvania, 1977); Kent D. Richards, "Growth and Development in the Far West: The Oregon Provisional Government, Jefferson Territory, Provisional and Territorial Nevada" (PhD dissertation, University of Wisconsin, 1966); and John W. Smurr, "Territorial Constitutions: A Legal History of the Frontier Governments Erected by Congress in the American West, 1787-1900" (PhD dissertation, Indiana University, 1960).

7. There are relatively few studies that seek to interpret the history of state constitutional development, particularly those that draw on convention debates. See, for example, Walter F. Dodd, *The Revision and Amendment of State Constitutions* (Baltimore: John Hopkins University Press, 1910); James Q. Dealey, *Growth of American State*

Constitutions; From 1776 to the end of the year 1914 (Boston: Ginn and Co., 1915); and Roger Sherman Hoar, *Constitutional Conventions: Their Nature, Powers, and Limitations* (Boston: Little Brown and Co., 1917).

More recent studies include: Bayard Still, "State Constitutional Development in the United States, 1829-1851" (PhD dissertation, University of Wisconsin, 1933); George P. Parkinson, "Antebellum State Constitution Making: Retention, Circumvention, Revision" (PhD dissertation, University of Wisconsin, 1972); and Morton Keller, "The Politics of State Constitutional Revision, 1820-1930," in Kermit L. Hall, Harold M. Hyman, and Leon V. Sigal, eds., *The Constitutional Convention as an Amending Device* (Washington, DC: American Historical Association, 1981).

Some of the best scholarship on state constitutionalism has been somewhat limited by its regional focus. See, for example, Bakken, *Rocky Mountain Constitution Making*; Don E. Fehrenbacher, *Constitutions and Constitutionalism in Slaveholding South* (Athens: University of Georgia Press, 1989); Fletcher M. Greene, *Constitutional Development in the South Atlantic States: A Study in the Evolution of Democracy* (New York: W.W. Norton, 1966); John D. Hicks, *The Constitutions of the Northwest States* (Lincoln: University of Nebraska Press, 1923); and Johnson, "Pioneers and Politics."

8.   For the political theory that underlay the process of early American constitution making, see Daniel J. Elazar, *The American Constitutional Tradition* (Lincoln: University of Nebraska Press, 1988) and Elazar, *Republicanism, Representation and Consent: Views of the Founding Era* (New Brunswick, NJ: Transaction Books, 1979).

9.   The seven states are California (both the 1849 and the 1878 conventions), Oregon (1857), Nevada (1864), South Dakota (both the 1885 and 1889 conventions), Wyoming (1889), Idaho (1889), and North Dakota (1889). The debates for Colorado, Washington, and New Mexico were not preserved and the conventions (with debates) in Utah and Arizona were too late for my purposes. For this essay, I have not attempted to integrate the existing literature that discusses the conventions I have examined. Instead, I chose to focus on contemporaneous discussions of constitutions by the delegates themselves.

10. One obvious distinction in the context of constitution making not dealt with in this essay is the difference between the initial formation of a constitution and subsequent revisions of an existing document. Territories seeking statehood operated within the constraints of a congressional enabling act and delegates to such conventions were acutely aware that their finished product would have to meet congressional approval.

11. *Report of the Debates in the Convention of California on the Formation of the State Constitution in September and October, 1849* (J. Ross Browne, reporter) (Washington, DC: n.p., 1850), 33.

12. *Debates and Proceedings of the Constitutional Convention of the State of California, convened at the city of Sacramento, Saturday, September 28, 1878*, 3 vols. (E.B. Willis and P.K. Stockton, official stenographers) (Sacramento, CA: State of California, 1880-1881), vol. 2, 1059.

13. See Bakken, *Rocky Mountain Constitution Making*, 101-03. Bakken, for example, sees Rocky Mountain constitution makers (defined as those in Arizona, Colorado, Idaho, Montana, Nevada, New Mexico, Utah, and Wyoming) as essentially responding to their environment — aridity and territorial status and experience. To the extent that he posits any shared constitutionalism he describes it in terms of an inherited tradition dating back to the federal Founding Fathers. Largely because Bakken has focused on the substantive issues within conventions and especially on the broader political context of state making, he overlooks the process of constitutionalism I have described. In fairness, his work does not explicitly seek to understand how the ideas about constitution making changed and evolved over time.

14. The full title of the first edition was *The American's Guide. The Constitutions of the United States of America; with the latest amendments; also the Declaration of Independence, Articles of Confederation, with the federal Constitution, acts for the government of the territories, Washington's farewell address, and the inaugural speeches of the several presidents* (Philadelphia: Joshua Fletcher, 1810). Other editions appeared in 1828, 1830, 1832, 1833, 1834, 1840, 1841, 1849, and 1864.

15. California, *Debates* (1849), 221.

16. Andrew J. Marsh, *Official Report of the Debates and Proceedings in the Constitutional Convention of the State of Nevada, Assembled at Carson City, July 4, 1864, To form a Constitution and State Government* (San Francisco: Frank Eastman, 1866), 100.

17. Nevada, *Debates* (1864), 691.

18. *Dakota Constitutional Convention, Held at Sioux Falls, September, 1885*, 2 vols. (Huron, SD: Huronite Printing Company, 1907), 349-60.

19. See California, *Debates* (1878), vol. 2, 1022 and vol. 3, 1452. See also, ibid., vol. 1, 18-31.

20. Ibid., vol. 2, 729-31.

21. Ibid., vol. 1, 256.

22. I.W. Hart, ed., *Proceedings and Debates of the Constitutional Convention of Idaho, 1889*, 2 vols. (Caldwell, ID: Caxton Printers, 1912); Idaho, *Debates*, vol. 2, 1597-98. See Thomas M. Cooley, *A Treatise on the Constitutional Limitations Which Rest upon the Legislative Power of the States of the American Union* (Boston: Little, Brown, 1868). The work went through six editions with the sixth edition appearing in 1890.

23. California, *Debates* (1849), 26-27 (re New York) and 310 (re Michigan).

24. Charles H. Carey, ed., *The Oregon Constitution and Proceedings and Debates of the Constitutional Convention of 1857* (Salem, OR: n.p., 1926), 59, 68-69.

25. California, *Debates* (1878), vols. 1-3.

26. Nevada, *Debates* (1864), 16. See also, ibid., 199 and 551-52, for references to other conventions that had met in the past fifteen years such as Massachusetts, Pennsylvania, Ohio, Indiana, and Illinois.

27. Idaho, *Debates* (1889), vol. 1, 853-54 and vol. 2, 1120.

28. Ibid., vol. 2, 2039.

29. See Christian G. Fritz, "More Than 'Shreds and Patches': California's First Bill of Rights," *Hastings Constitutional Law Quarterly* 17 (Fall 1989): 13-34.

30. California, *Debates* (1849), 51.

31. Ibid., 379.

32. In addition to the conventions discussed in the text, see also, Idaho, *Debates* (1889), vol. 1, 520, 638, 793 and vol. 2, 1622-23; Wyoming, *Debates* (1889), 448 and 721; and South Dakota, *Debates* (1885), 180-96 and 340.

33. Oregon, *Debates* (1857), 108-09.

34. To the extent that such an approach suggests a "constitutional Darwinism" it should be noted that the process was not characterized by a survival of only the "fittest" constitutional provisions. While some provisions were indeed deleted because they no longer accorded with the present political or constitutional understandings, the stress was on the growing elaboration of provisions and constitutional mechanisms rather than an aggressive paring down of the ever-growing nineteenth-century state constitutions.

35. California, *Debates* (1878), vol. 1, 74.

36. Ibid. See also, vol. 1, 99. By the time of California's second constitutional convention, delegates routinely organized by creating anywhere from one to two dozen separate committees, whose subject matter of concern often followed topics traditionally dealt with in separate articles in earlier constitutions.

37. Ibid., vol. 1, 185.

38. Ibid.

39. Nevada, *Debates* (1864), 15-16.

40. California, *Debates* (1878), vol. 1, 489.

41. Ibid.

42. See, for example, California, *Debates* (1849), 113 and 116; Oregon, *Debates* (1857), 141; Nevada, *Debates* (1864), 18; Idaho, *Debates* (1889), vol. 1, 55, 290, vol. 2, 1120 and 1623; and North Dakota, *Debates* (1889), 19-20 and 103. See also, *Journal and Debates of the Constitutional Convention of the State of Wyoming begun at the city of Cheyenne on September 2, 1889, and concluded September 30, 1889* (Cheyenne, WY: The Daily Sun, Book and Job Printing, 1893), 605.

43. Oregon, *Debates* (1857), 101.

44. Ibid., 101.

45. Ibid., 102.

46. Nevada, *Debates* (1864), 564. See also, Wyoming, *Debates* (1889), 422.

47. Nevada, *Debates* (1864), 564.

48. California, *Debates* (1878), vol. 1, 203.

49. Ibid.

50. Oregon, *Debates* (1857), 302. The "more distinct separation of church and state" was attributed to the western states and in particular the Indiana constitution, according to a delegate of Oregon's 1857 constitutional convention. See ibid., 302.

51. Ibid., 397.

52. Ibid., 388.

53. Ibid., 390.

54. 1849 California Constitution, art. 6, sec. 16.

55. As noted, the issue was capable of being decided on narrower grounds. Some delegates simply concluded that the pre-existing provision of the 1849 constitution did not apply and that no reason existed, therefore, to exclude the delegate.

56. California, *Debates* (1878), vol. 1, 172.

57. Ibid.

58. Ibid.

59. Ibid.

60. Ibid.

61. Ibid.

62. Ibid., vol. 1, 173.

63. Ibid., vol. 1, 175.

64. Ibid.

65. Ibid., vol. 1, 194.

66. Ibid., vol. 1, 199.

67. Ibid., vol. 3, 1167.

68. Ibid., and 1168.

69. California, *Debates* (1849), 52.

70. See, for example, California, *Debates* (1878), vol. 1, 209.

71. Idaho, *Debates* (1889), vol. 1, 343. Delegates to western conventions, particularly after the Civil War, expressly understood that the federal constitution also stood as a limitation to state power.

72. California, *Debates* (1878), vol. 2, 826.

73. California, *Debates* (1849), 42.

74. Ibid., 91.

75. Ibid., 92.

76. Ibid., 93.

77. Ibid.

78. Art. 4, sec. 27 of the 1849 California constitution read: "No lottery shall be authorized by this State, nor shall the sale of lottery tickets be allowed."

79. California, *Debates* (1849), 183.

80. Art. 11, sec. 14 of the 1849 California constitution.

81. See, for example, Nevada, *Debates* (1864), 44, 245, and 367; California, *Debates* (1878), vol. 1, 295, 398, 403, and 488; South Dakota, *Debates* (1885), vol. 1, 165; Wyoming, *Debates* (1889), 445; and Idaho, *Debates* (1889), vol. 1, 226.

82. Nevada, *Debates* (1864), 264.

83. California, *Debates* (1878), vol. 1, 473.

84. For the debate over corporations and corporate power, see ibid., vol. 1, 376-626.

85. Ibid., vol. 1, 377.

86. Ibid., vol. 1, 380. See also, Idaho, *Debates* (1889), vol. 1, 520, 676, 884, vol. 2, 1515; South Dakota, *Debates* (1885), vol. 1, 179, 332-37; and Wyoming, *Debates* (1889), 417 and 668.

87. Ibid., vol. 1, 440.

88. California, *Debates* (1878), vol. 1, 384.

89. Ibid., vol. 1, 397.

90. Wyoming, *Debates* (1889), 445. See also ibid., 498-501.

91. Ibid., 445.

92. Ibid., 501-02.

93. Ibid., 581.

94. Ibid., 608. See also ibid., 668.

95. Ibid., 797.

96. Idaho, *Debates* (1889), vol. 1, 218.

97. Ibid., vol. 1, 228.

98. See California, *Debates* (1849), 52-53 and 201; California, *Debates* (1878), vol. 1, 242 and 440, vol. 2, 810, 837, and 917; Wyoming, *Debates* (1889), 668; South Dakota, *Debates* (1885), vol. 1, 555-57; North Dakota, *Debates* (1889), 91; Nevada, *Debates* (1864), 367; and Idaho, *Debates* (1889), vol. 1, 343.

99. California, *Debates* (1878), vol. 2, 815.

100. The strategic advantages behind directory provisions were sometimes not understood or occasionally dismissed out of hand on theoretical reasons even by otherwise politically adept delegates in conventions. See, for example, ibid., vol. 2, 946.

101. Oregon, *Debates* (1857), 80.

102. California, *Debates* (1878), vol. 1, 441.

103. Many of the regional studies of state constitutionalism cited in note 6 suffer from an overemphasis on the peculiarities or local issues of the region under study.

104. Much of the current interest in the role of state constitutions has been stimulated by the legal argument that state constitutions provide independent grounds for often broader protection of individual rights and liberties than those provided by the federal constitution. See, for example, William Brennan, "State Constitutions and the Protection of Individual Rights," *Harvard Law Review* 90 (1977): 489; and Hans Linde, "First Things First: Rediscovering the States' Bills of Rights," *University of Baltimore Law Review* 9 (1980): 379.

   For other studies that have examined the state/federal relationship closely, see, Daniel J. Elazar, *Exploring Federalism* (Tuscaloosa: University of Alabama Press, 1987); G. Alan Tarr and Mary Cornelia Aldis Porter, *State Supreme Courts in State and Nation* (New Haven: Yale University Press, 1988); and Robert F. Williams, *State Constitutional Law: Cases and Materials* (Washington, DC: United States Advisory Commission on Intergovernmental Relations, 1988).

Contributors

RICHARD MAXWELL BROWN is Beekman Professor of Northwest and Pacific History at the University of Oregon. He has written a number of books on the history of violence and vigilantism in the United States, and is currently Vice-President of the Western History Association. Dr. Brown's most recent book is *No Duty to Retreat: An American Theme*, published by the Oxford University Press in 1991.

KEN COATES is Vice-President, Academic, of the University of Northern British Columbia. He has authored, co-authored and edited a number of books on northern and native history, the most recent of which is *Best Left as Indians: Native-White Relations in the Yukon Territory*, published in 1991 by McGill-Queen's University Press.

HAMAR FOSTER is an Associate Professor of Law at the University of Victoria. He has published a number of articles on the legal history of the fur trade, comparative criminal law, and the historical foundations of Indian title and sovereignty.

CHRISTIAN G. FRITZ is an Associate Professor of Law at the University of New Mexico. He served for three years as Historical Law Clerk to Judge Robert F. Peckham of the Northern District of California. One product of that experience was his book, *Federal Justice in California: The Court of Ogden Hoffman, 1851-1891*, published in 1991 by the University of Nebraska Press.

STEPHEN HAYCOX is a Professor of History at the University of Alaska in Anchorage. He has published both a collection and an anthology of essays on Alaska history, and is currently completing a book on the Alaska Native Brotherhood and the career of Tlingit leader William L. Paul.

RODERICK C. MACLEOD is a Professor of History at the University of Alberta in Edmonton. In addition to his *The North West Mounted Police and Law Enforcement 1873-1905*, published by the University of Toronto Press in 1975, he has written and edited a number of books on policing and the prairie west.

JOHN P.S. MCLAREN is Lansdowne Professor of Law at the University of Victoria. His research interests have lain primarily in the social and intellectual history of the law, focusing on morals law (prostitution and obscenity) and the law as both an instrument of, and curb on, racial and ethnic discrimination.

WILLIAM R. MORRISON is Dean of Arts at the University of Northern British Columbia, Prince George. He has authored, co-authored and edited books on the history of the Mounted Police and northern history generally. His most recent book, co-authored with Dr. Coates, is *The Army of Occupation: Americans in the Canadian Northwest During World War II*, to be published in 1992 by the University of Oklahoma Press.

CHET ORLOFF is currently Executive Director of the Oregon Historical Society. He was previously founding Director of the Ninth Judicial Circuit Historical Society and the first editor of its journal, *Western Legal History*. He participates actively in the preservation of the historical heritage of his home city of Portland.

DAVID R. PERCY is Professor of Law at the University of Alberta. Resources and environmental law are his teaching and research interests. He is the author of *The Framework of Water Rights Legislation in Canada and Water Rights in Alberta*, published by the Canadian Institute of Resources Law in 1987.

JOHN P. REID is Professor of Law and Legal History at New York University. He has written widely on American legal history, with books on the American Revolution, U.S. constitutional history and the legal history of the American West. His *Law for the Elephant: Property and Social Behavior on the Overland Trial*, published by the Huntington Library in 1980, is the classic work on the spread of Anglo-American conceptions of law to western North America.

PAUL TENNANT is Professor of Political Science at the University of British Columbia. He specializes in aboriginal issues as well as national and provincial politics. He is author of *Aboriginal Peoples and Politics: The Indian Land Question in British Columbia, 1849-1989*, published in 1990 by the University of British Columbia Press.

JOHN R. WUNDER is Professor of History and Director of the Center for Great Plains Studies, University of Nebraska-Lincoln. His most recent book is *The Kiowa*, published by Chelsea House Press in 1989. Dr. Wunder is currently working on two legal history book-length projects concerning North Americans and the Bill of Rights, and Chinese and American law on the Trans-Mississippi West frontier.